# Cities and Regions in Crisis

# Cities and Regions in Crisis

## The Political Economy of Sub-National Economic Development


Martin Jones

*Professor of Human Geography and Deputy Vice-Chancellor, Staffordshire University, UK*

Cheltenham, UK • Northampton, MA, USA

Published by
Edward Elgar Publishing Limited
The Lypiatts
15 Lansdown Road
Cheltenham
Glos GL50 2JA
UK

Edward Elgar Publishing, Inc.
William Pratt House
9 Dewey Court
Northampton
Massachusetts 01060
USA

Paperback edition 2021

A catalogue record for this book
is available from the British Library

Library of Congress Control Number: 2018960949

This book is available electronically in the **Elgar**online
Social and Political Science subject collection
DOI 10.4337/9781788117456

ISBN 978 1 84376 876 0 (cased)
ISBN 978 1 78811 745 6 (eBook)
ISBN 978 1 80088 241 6 (paperback)

Printed and bound by CPI Group (UK) Ltd, Croydon, CR0 4YY

# Contents

# Preface and acknowledgements

> Geography deals with complex open systems in which today's activities take place in contexts not of current agents' making, but nevertheless constrained and enabled by them. In such systems there are at best temporary and local regularities. Yet one could still explain what happens in them by tracing connections and looking for causal mechanisms.
>
> (Sayer 2018: 105)

*Cities and Regions in Crisis* captures my 20-year intellectual research journey with sub-national geographies of economic governance in England's cities and regions. It offers detailed theoretical and empirical insights into putting local and regional economic development in its place by questioning the what, where, how and why of state intervention. This facet of public policy has seen so much policy-churn since the 1980s that those working inside it struggle to comprehend ongoing events. Rarely a week goes by without a new government department being (re)-created, a 'new' economic development policy initiative being announced, often followed by the deep cynical sighs of those on the receiving end of it—seen this before, albeit always called and packaged as something different. Appearances of activity and policy failures run deep. Often the same people are involved in its delivery, with civil servants and policy communities sceptical about any success likely to happen, keen to predict failure and critique the next economic development policy downfall. By going backwards to go forwards, *Cities and Regions in Crisis* offers an in-perspective political economy analysis of the mechanisms, sites, and geographies of sub-national economic development, probing on how policy-makers frame problems and articulate their solutions by deploying crisis spaces.

This multi-causal and inter-disciplinary boundary spanning research on the broad area of economy, society, and space, and specifically on the interfaces between economic and political geography, started with my collaborations with Jamie Peck, extended to Graham Haughton, Gordon MacLeod, Adam Tickell, Kevin Ward, and David Etherington. The 2000s saw these links continue and extend further to collaborations with Neil Brenner, Bob Jessop, Mark Goodwin, Rhys Jones, Mike Woods, Sally Hardy, Jesse Heley, Anssi Paasi, John Harrison, David Beel, and Ian Rees Jones. I would also like to acknowledge additional Aberystwyth University colleagues—Deborah Dixon, Matthew Hannah, Peter Merriman, and Mark Whitehead—involved in our space, place, and politics book and other projects. The influences of these peopled experiences are heartfelt through the chapters, with some of the arguments and evidence drawing on our jointly authored research. I would also like to acknowledge Huw Beynon, Allan Cochrane, Gill Valentine, Bob Jessop (again), and Steve Rogers for inspiration and support over the years. Thanks also goes to four Vice Chancellors—Noel Lloyd, April McMahon, Keith Burnett, and Liz Barnes—who have recognised and supported the strategic coupling of my research with my leadership and management career. At Staffordshire University, credit goes to Rosemary Duncan for technical instance with Figure 1.7. At Edward Elgar, this book could not have happened without the endeavours of Matthew Pitman, Katy Crossan, Stephanie Hartley, Barbara Pretty, and Sarah Price. Lastly, closer to home, I am not sure that Victoria and Harley agree with all my (sometimes crackers) arguments in *Cities and Regions in Crisis*, but we can all agree on 'cheese as productive fuel' for tackling the crisis of crisis-management.

These collaborations have been always been concerned with: first, capturing the real-time restructuring dynamics of an increasingly neoliberalising local and regional economic development world; second, deploying this empirical material to build an inter-disciplinary geographical political economy, with crisis and contradiction-analytic perspectives of state intervention at its core; and, third, combining all this to formulate and deliver an impactful research agenda. Place and region matters: I have always seen the (privileged) importance of the institutions of higher education to connect with and inform praxis in political and civil society. *Cities and Regions in Crisis* draws on empirical work conducted in and around my university places—Manchester, Aberystwyth, Sheffield, and Stoke-on-Trent—working with local community groups and public policy officials (civil society) to seek to improve economic and social conditions and the life chances of disadvantaged people in forgotten places. I have had the pleasure of giving evidence to UK Government Select Committees on skills, business support, and regional development and have worked alongside various government departments, the European Commission, think-tanks, and pressure groups. This is geographical knowledge to inform and empower others, and in doing so, make a better world—albeit from the field of local and regional economic development. In this context, as Orwell (1946) would have it, this book has a 'political purpose and attitude'.

The chapters draw on aspects of previously published work, edited to provide a narrative. Figures, tables, and footnotes have been mostly removed from their original versions and I would recommend reading these for further insights.

In line with Harvey (2001: 9), I have endeavoured to 'rub together' different conceptual and empirical 'blocks together to make an intellectual fire'. The selection and inter-weaving of them to develop the *political economy of sub-national economic development*, I hope, is my distinctive 'fire' contribution to geographical knowledge. The authored and co-authored sources are listed below and I wish to thank those listed, who have kindly given permission for the use of copyright material. I am also grateful to the editors and reviewers of those journals and book chapters for helping me develop this work and building my confidence in it. No one, however, is to blame for what follows: the responsibility for the text and all its faults is fully mine.

The 'Introduction' (Chapter 1) derives in part from: Martin Jones (2013) 'It's like déjà vu, all over again' in M. Ward and S. Hardy (eds) *Where Next for Local Enterprise Partnerships*, London: Smith Institute, 86–94; Martin Jones (2019) 'The march of governance and the actualities of failure: the case of economic development twenty years on' *International Social Science Journal* (DOI: epdf/10.1111/issj.12169).

Chapter 2 derives in part from Martin Jones (1998) 'Partnerships as modes of economic governance: A regulationist perspective', in N. Walzer and B. Jacobs (eds) *Public–Private Partnerships for Local Economic Development*, Westport: Praeger, 205–226.

Chapter 3 derives in part from: Martin Jones and Kevin Ward (2002) 'Urban policy under capitalism: Towards a "fourth-cut" theory of crisis', Spatial Policy Analysis Working Paper 50, Manchester: University of Manchester, School of Geography.

Chapter 4 derives in part from: Graham Haughton, Martin Jones, Jamie Peck, Adam Tickell and Aidan While (2000) 'Labour market policy as flexible welfare: Prototype Employment Zones and the new workfarism', *Regional Studies*, 34, 669–680.

Chapter 5 derives in part from Martin Jones (2001) 'The rise of the regional state in economic governance: "Partnerships for prosperity" or new scales of state power?' *Environment and Planning A*, 33, 1185–1211.

Chapter 6 derives in part from Martin Jones (2004) 'Social justice and the region: Functional regionalization and civil society regionalism in England', *Space and Polity*, 8, 157–189.

Chapter 7 derives in part from: Martin Jones and David Etherington (2009) 'Governing the skills agenda: insights from the Sheffield city-region', *Local Economy*, 24, 68–79.

Chapter 8 derives in part from: Martin Jones (2017) 'New localism, new localities …', in Ian Deas and Stephen Hincks (eds) *Territorial Policy and Governance: Alternative Paths*, London: Routledge, 17–35.

Chapter 9 derives in part from: David Beel, Martin Jones and Ian Rees Jones (2018) 'Regionalisation and civil society in a time of austerity: The cases of Manchester and Sheffield', in Craig Berry and Arianna Giovannini (eds) *Developing England's North: The Northern Powerhouse, Devolution and the Political Economy of Place*, London: Palgrave, 241–260.

Chapter 10 derives in part from: David Etherington and Martin Jones (2018) 'Re-stating the post-political: Depoliticization, social inequalities, and city-region growth', *Environment Planning A*, 50, 51–72.

Chapter 11 derives in part from: David Beel, Martin Jones, Ian Rees Jones and Warren Escadale (2017) 'Connected growth: Developing a framework to drive inclusive growth across a city-region', *Local Economy*, 32, 565–575.

Chapter 12 derives in part from David Etherington and Martin Jones (2004) 'Whatever happened to local government? Local labour market policy in the UK and Denmark', *Policy and Politics*, 32, 137–150.

The approach adopted in *Cities and Regions in Crisis*, then, draws attention to more than specifics of economic development. It encourages scholars and practitioners to think about the historically contingent and politically charged context-specific processes and practices of economic governance. The book seeks to provide a window into the dynamics of economic development where the state is a 'political process in motion' (Goodwin et al. 2012, 2017). This has required a multi-methods research design deployed over a period of 20 years to capture the real-time restructuring of local and regional economic development across England's cities and regions. The individual research projects that have produced the various chapters, funded by a number of research entities—and I would particularly like to acknowledge the financial support of the Economic and Social Research Council (ESRC) for funding WISERD Civil Society (Grant ES/L0090991/1), work package Spaces of New Localism and Impact Accelerator funding (Making City-Regions Work: Inclusive Governance, Skills, and Labour Market Disadvantage)—have all involved a number of phases.

Phase 1 has involved the analysis of economic development strategies, construed, first, in national-level government documentation (bills, acts, white and green papers) and, second, how this is translated through the various sub-national institutions and projects of the state. Phase 2 then turns to examine the experiences of economic development through a series of contemporary case studies, where the state-making practices and struggles become evident. Each of the case studies featured in this book were designed to explore how effectively the institutions of economic governance have been able, or not, to meet the challenges of economic development within their various localities. This was explored by looking at the nature of intergovernmental relationships vertically and horizontally to get a handle on levels of institutional cooperation and collaboration and the alignment of policy responsibilities and working practices.

Taken together, the *Cities and Regions in Crisis* approach foregrounds the 'capacity to act' (Goodwin et al. 2012, 2017) of the institutions of economic development through a 'close dialogue' (Clark 2010) with policy-making, in the process contributing to a theory-building of geographical political economy. Each case study was undertaken using a combination of documentary analysis and semi-structured interviews. Over 250 interviews have been undertaken between 1993 and 2018 with a wide variety of people working in, and connected to, the field of economic development, ranging from ministerial and chief executive levels, to those engaged in policy formulation and delivery on the ground. Several individuals were interviewed several times, often over a period of several years, where the roles undertaken remained broadly the same but the name of their institution and its geographical reach had changed. For reasons of confidentiality, the individuals are not named; anonymous quotations feature in some chapters and in others, the 'voices' feature in the analysis of policy.

These interviews were supported and triangulated by the analysis of policy documents, and vice versa, including institutional minutes, policy briefings, strategy papers, and media analysis. *Cities and Regions in Crisis* offers a reflexive institutional historical take on local and regional economic development, conscious of not falling into the Eighteenth Brumaire—'tragedy' then 'farce'—(policy) history repeating itself trap, flagged by Marx (see Jessop 2002a). My various crisis and contradiction theory-building endeavours in subsequent chapters require this immersed 'mode of retroduction' (Sayer 1992)—not just interviewing, but where possible experiencing, following, and living the economic development complexities that I am seeking to understand in order to pin down the causes and conditions of failure.

On this last note, the book is dedicated to my parents for giving me social capital and always being supportive of my academic ambitions and career over the past 25 years: successes, failures, and some crises.

# Preface to paperback edition

It is two years since the hardback of *Cities and Regions in Crisis* appeared and so much has happened in the sphere of local and regional economic development to support my blend of critical governance studies, crisis and contradiction theory, and case studies drawn from 25 years of research. The pertinence of my argument has been neatly summarised by Steven Griggs in *Local Government Studies*. For Griggs, I told a story of the crisis of British crisis-management, positing that policy failure has become the norm in advanced capitalism, with government interventions doing little more than moving the 'problem around' in an effort to displace and defer political opposition. As the state has absorbed market failures, I concluded that it has effectively morphed into an 'impedimenta state', or a capitalist state weighed down by the disorienting legacies of earlier interventions in local and regional economic development. Indeed, the best we, and policymakers, could hope for, is to generate a series of temporary and temporal crisis spaces, which can only stall crises for limited moments, as the accumulation of unsolved contradictions mounts up to impedimenta proportions. Drawing on case studies of cities in the North and East Midlands, I identified a litany of strategies of displacement and deferral, which have punctuated the restructuring of the local British state, from devolving problems down to communities, to strategies of depoliticisation, agentification and local privatism, and on to competition between authorities and fragmented scales of governance. More importantly, feeding back into conceptual debates on neoliberalism and state spatial restructuring, I sought to demonstrate that these are not disconnected processes of state restructuring and policy formation. Rather, they are differentiated outcomes of ideologically infused political decision-making that cannot be separated from the inherent crisis tendencies of capital accumulation, state formation, and state intervention.

As noted by Griggs, in presenting the reader with an ambitious critique of the messy continuities, twists and turns, and persistent unevenness of sub-national economic development in England since the 1980s, my narrative merits a further hearing in this paperback edition, as we arguably move towards post-Brexit and post-COVID futures – a world in which my arguments hold an increasing amount of water and increasingly vocal calls are being made for a new economic, political and social settlement that goes beyond the critical failures of business as usual state intervention. Brexit featured in the hardback edition, of course, drawing on the example of Stoke-on-Trent.

COVID is a new and serious phenomenon affecting contemporary capitalism, deeply geographical in its emergence and ongoing development.

At the time of writing, there is a coronavirus global pandemic (COVID-19, Coronavirus) outbreak. As of 1st December 2020, there have been over 1.4 million confirmed worldwide deaths and over 60 million confirmed cases. The pandemic has resulted in mobility restrictions and nationwide and local 'lockdowns' to slow down the rates of infection and ease the pressure on national health and other services. The lockdown has created the conditions for a world-wide recession by exposing the fragility of the neoliberal economic social contract and the many imbalances in contemporary society and space. With productivity slowing and large groups of individuals on either short-term contracts and/or unable to work from home, millions have been forced out of work and onto a series of welfare benefits such as (in the UK) Universal Credit. In the early months of lockdown, for instance, the UK unemployment count has rapidly increased with over 2.5 million new benefit claims and predictions of 8 million (25+ per cent of the workforce) jobs being at risk. This has impacted disproportionately on civil society, heavily reinforcing existing patterns of labour market inequality and precarity. Weak labour markets dependent on low-skills and localities of poverty within the areas of multiple deprivation have taken the brunt of intense economic restructuring. In the West Midlands, for instance, for the private sector, this would equate to 26,000 firms and 375,000 jobs. Moreover, COVID related death rates in the most deprived areas are more than double those of the less deprived and the socioeconomic gap in COVID mortality is bigger than the general mortality gap.

The political economic geography of crisis metamorphosis and recovery is critical to the subject matter of this book, with predictions of economic contraction being at least 20 per cent for the UK economy, compared to an OECD average of nearly 10 per cent, with time-periods being modelled and supply-chain critical sectors (such as advanced manufacturing) being hit hardest. The UK Government stepped in to rescue the economy with an unprecedented intervention financial package to support jobs, incomes, and businesses, acting in nothing short of a wartime 'do whatever it takes' measure by the Conservatives. The stimulus package, which included a Job Retention Scheme for 'furloughing' 8 million jobs (covering one-third for all private sector employees) and a massive 'bounce back' loan guarantee scheme for businesses, collectively costing over £250bn (20 per cent of GDP) far exceeding the scale of the rescue measures taken in the wake of the 2008 financial crash. There is limited provision for contingent workers identified by zero-hour or seasonal work.

Local authorities have been asked by the government to 'make things happen' to prevent societal collapse, particularly for older and disabled people at risk. The Local Resilience Forums (LRFs), created under civil contingency planning legislation, were activated and deployed at local authority spatial scales in England and the city-region scale in Wales alongside regional Corporate Joint Committees (CJCs) to provide the conditions for multi-agency strategic and operational responses. Gaps immediately emerged between the metagovernance rhetoric of planning and the continued march of austerity and its impact on the local state. A study undertaken by the Special Interest Group of Municipal Authorities (SIGOMA) for instance estimated, for England's 343 local authorities, a financial shortfall of £8bn for 2020 – caused by increased emergency expenditure (food packages, social care etc.) not covered by central government and lost revenues from business rates, council tax, and commercial activity.

In the case of Greater Manchester, government intervention initially covered only 12 per cent of the forecast financial impact of COVID. This produced a shortfall of £541m, putting Manchester City Council on the brink of ruin. With civil society actors claiming locality experiences of nothing like this since the 1930s, wider claims of the fracturing and even collapse of central-local relations in the wake of this crisis have been made. This reached a head in October 2020 with a stand-off between Andy Burnham (Labour Metro Mayor of the Greater Manchester Combined Authority) and central government over the levels of support package for their local tiered lockdowns. This has turned a broader searchlight on the hidden cracks in the UK's over-centralised, piecemeal, and increasingly polycentric devolution settlement revealed in *City and Regions in Crisis*. Fifty-four backbench MPs subsequently formed a Northern Research Group (NRG) to demand a clear exit strategy from COVID restrictions, as well as a clear economic recovery framework for the northern region. This, in turn, led to 'devolution disaster' comments made in a meeting with them by PM Boris Johnson, with further central-local 'muscular devolution' tensions occurring around the Internal Market Bill in November.

The COVID crisis exemplifies the need to seriously engage with the shortcomings of the UK's current growth model and broader conceptions of social reproduction and social regulation enabled through economic development. The book notes that the state is forced to reconcile an ongoing tension between the neoliberal necessity to maintain the expansion of surplus value, the accumulation strategy of the economy at large, with the need to sustain social harmony and its own legitimation during the crisis. In the context of COVID, this is most prescient in the context of care, healthcare being obvious, but also broader notions of social care (including childcare, disability care, care for the elderly and so on). Many currently working from home have discovered this for themselves; without the support of nurseries, schools and home caring services, their ability to complete a day's labour has become increasingly difficult. Added to this has been an awareness of which industries really matter in a crisis by what is comprehended as 'key work/worker'; those who have had to keep going despite obvious risk, represent the parts of economy and society that cannot be allowed to stop in order to not only maintain the current economy, but the fabric of society itself. There are also parts of the economy and society that simply cannot afford to stop or cannot work remotely from home. This is either due to the nature of their employment, particularly those self-employed, or the nature of the work they do, which has meant COVID has increased their precarity.

The need for and belief in solutions to the antecedents of the contemporary crisis, however, has not been reflected in the policy choices of the last decade. Whereby, the focus shifted towards the maintenance and recovery of the neoliberal accumulation strategy, for the UK state, following the 2008 Global Financial Crisis. This coincided with an ideological attack upon the functioning of the state (especially the local state) via austerity, as outlined in the book. 'Austerity localism', which I identify throughout this book, plus the devolution of risk and responsibility away from the state to protect both state and market from undue demands on their resources, defines this retrenchment of the local state and has greatly undermined the capacity of institutions and actors therein. This means austerity, combined with multiple waves of market-making privatisation, in the years prior to the COVID crisis has routinely stripped sectors (particularly those around health, social care, worker support, police and local authorities themselves) of their capacity to act with, or without, the current crisis, whilst focusing spending on other sectors of the economy. Yet, it is these underfunded parts of the economy, the state and more broadly civil society that are now most crucial to dealing with the crisis.

Summarising these manifold economic and social concerns across the UK, the COVID pandemic has caught the United Kingdom woefully underprepared and exposed vividly its (often devolved) crises and contradictions. The present crisis has revealed the distressed state of our local economies, particularly in 'left behind places', and the brittle condition of the local public sector following decades of underinvestment and disrespect. At the same time, this dual public health and economic emergency has underscored the centrality of locality and community to our everyday lives. As we ready ourselves to rebuild and reconstruct within the shattered post-COVID landscape, we must strive to make the economic recovery the starting point for economic reform and a new birth of community in this country. The redistributive switching of the UK state under austerity has also, although in a deeply contradictory sense, sought to empower the 'local' via devolution to city-regions. This has been a very specific form of 'empowerment', which the book argues should be viewed as a broader metagovernance state strategy, which is spatially selective and seeks to only give agency to certain strategically significant actors. As I have demonstrated in this book, this economy-first narrative with an emphasis on agglomerative growth (often measured in terms of GVA uplift) has been written through the process of building city-regions. This agenda has focused upon high-end growth, whilst simultaneously ignoring the foundational aspects of the economy on which it is built. Moreover, non-economic agency is distanced through the creation of institutions such as LEPs, alongside devolution, city, and growth deals. Civil society is increasingly placed on the outside, whereby actors have to repeatably contest (with some albeit limited success) the prevailing direction of city-region building.

The cumulative consequences of the above have, of course, resulted in an unbalanced form of economy being developed. Indeed, government policy since 2019 has acknowledged this and suggestions have been made for 'levelling up' – a shorthand for the squashing of regional inequalities through moving around government investment, although nobody knows what levelling up actually means. To close the regional productivity gap, the government's current solution is based on creating functional economic areas led by 'metro-mayors' and connecting these together through infrastructure projects. Early indications from recent Budgets are that levelling up is focusing on physical infrastructure projects, free ports, transport initiatives, and devolution deals etc., based on stimulating the growth of large cities, on the understanding that trickle-down occurs to surrounding areas.

*Cities and Regions in Crisis* argues that tackling the problems of left behind places requires the energy and passion of the people who live there, and that is going to work much better if the project is led by the city-region, town and its people, rather than by central government diktat and political fiat. In short, the paralleled or entwined processes of austerity and city-region devolution have disempowered, depoliticised and weakened the structures of social reproduction in favour of a neoliberal growth model. This means that during the COVID crisis itself, the state is and has been less well equipped to deal with the strains that are being placed upon it. This could have catastrophic effects in the short- to medium-term, with regards to how the crisis will develop, but it also grants an opportunity to think through what next and what sort of economy should be built post-the-crisis.

There is much to learn from infrastructural growth models predicated on the 'foundational economy' and the socially responsible supply of basic goods and services for citizens. This reconsiders the socioeconomic foundation of the city-regional economy and offers a more constitutional model of economic development based on promoting place-based social innovation. This in turn reformulates the local state's everyday (goods and services consumed by all) and future assets (such as 5G-era digital infrastructures) into circuits to capture community wealth and build local strategic capacity. This is not about 'levelling up' but rethinking how we approach the wellbeing of our citizens and our cities and shift to patterns of sustainable consumption, while refashioning centre-local relations and reversing the direction of travel of some 40 years of failed regional economic development. An English Devolution and Local Recovery White Paper is promised during 2021 to reconcile these tensions. We live in hope.

# 1. Introduction: geographical political economy, neoliberalism, and the crisis space impedimenta state

*Capital never solves its crisis tendencies; it merely moves them around.* This is what theory tells us, and this is what the history of the past 40 years has been about.
(Harvey 2011: 11, emphasis original)

[N]ot only do crises get moved around, but crises are embedded in the very structures of what capital accumulation is about.
(Harvey 2016: 55)

The ability to define a situation as a crisis and to prescribe the appropriate response to it is one of the most important expressions of political power.
(Gamble 2014: 32)

Government has a tendency to recreate policies and organisations on an alarmingly regular basis. New organisations replace old ones; one policy is ended while a remarkably similar one is launched ... no organisation has survived longer than a decade.
(Norris and Adam 2017: 3)

We need to be clear what the problems are that we are trying to solve. What continues to disappoint me is that we rarely try to define the skills problem, we just endlessly repeat the mantra of having a skills problem, having a skills problem ... What continues to define the agenda is the endless range of initiatives that the skills agenda spawns. So in my time ... we have had Area Manpower Boards, Industrial Training Boards, the MSC, the Training Commission, the Training Agency, Local Employer Networks, TECs, CCTEs, LSCs, Employment and Skills Boards, and now just announced, Skills Advisory Panels. All these with the professed same aim of bringing to balance the needs of employers with the needs of the local labour market. The very fact that we are still discussing the same issues as we were 40 years ago shows that collectively we are as far as ever from solving the skills problem. And added to that, we have the ongoing programme of new initiatives that are relentlessly launched. So in the last 3 weeks alone, we have seen Ministers make the following statements. £170M for Institutes for Technology, £10M for Career Learning Pilots, T Levels ...
(Frost 2017: 1)

## INTRODUCTION: IT'S LIKE DÉJÀ VU, ALL OVER AGAIN

*Cities and Regions in Crisis* is situated at the heart of debates about public policy: the specific concern is with economic governance—the body of literature associated with the nature and practice of economic management, economic regulation, and, specifically in this book, local and regional economic development as the state project manifestation of this. Economic governance is necessarily broad and covers the ongoing interactions between markets, policies, institutions, and networks, with empirical attention focused on the frameworks and mechanisms underpinning economic development. Over the past century, there have been no states in the West that have fully aimed at allowing free rein to markets; they have always, and in a variety of ways, aimed to organise them. The lessons from Polanyi (1944) and the regulation approach (Chapters 2 and 3) is that there have been, and there can be, no markets that do not rely on some rules they cannot themselves set. There is always both a plurality of modes of economic governance and a variety of forms of state intervention to make and regulate markets. Instruments of economic development come into play here and cover the field of: urban and regional policy; training and skills policies; enterprise and business support; infrastructure and services; and the wider realm of fiscal and monetary policies impacting on the local state.

The question of economic governance, then, refers to the mobilisation of available institutional and productive resources to develop a coherent sense of economic identity. In more blunt terms, Farnsworth (2015) posits this a 'corporate welfare' machine of wage subsidies and grants to privately owned companies that both socialise business risks and help to maintain a level of surplus value—in the context of searching for 'frictionless market rule' (Peck 2010: 16). In this context, economic governance, moreover, is a distinctly geographical and seemingly always spatially shifting project: it is constituted in space and remakes the space of such constitutions in the process of performing economic development (Goodwin et al. 2012, 2017). The sub-national territorial space, then, is critical to where economic development has been happening and *Cities and Regions in Crisis* engages with this changing 'arena of capital' in and through which economic interrelations are being forged (Dunford and Perrons 1983). This introduction lays the foundation for this argument.

The title of this section comes from Yoggi Berra—not the family cartoon character, but the baseball manager and long-time player for the New York Yankees. Berra is well known for his pithy comments and witticisms, known as 'Yogiisms', which often take the form of either an apparently obvious tautology, or a paradoxical contradiction. Local and regional economic development in England certainly fits this. The title, *Cities and Regions in Crisis*, has been deployed to suggest that some of the emerging problems of England's devolution by 2018 uncannily resemble the problems with the new localism of the late 1980s and early 1990s. 'Déjà vu, all over again' … That was the 'new localism' last time, under the Thatcher and then Major Conservative Party regimes in Britain; now is the 'new new localism' of the Conservative Party government, again. Both moments, 1989 and 2018, though nearly 30 years apart, are very similar in policy architecture, outlook, policy limits, and flaws. Both are business-led and locally based (in rhetoric), involve drawing new boundaries across the local state, have been fired with an all-singing and all-dancing can-do bravado of the enterprise revolution and business-knows-best. But then both experience—strangely enough—a reality of political fiat and central government diktat, experienced on the ground as limited government funding, create a national coordinating body to talk to central government, have limited powers to influence and raise income from the private sector, and exhibit blurred accountability with issues of stakeholder involvement and community input. More importantly, both are private sector ideological solutions to the private sector caused problem of market failure in the skills and employment industry (Jones 2013).

The two state projects in question are the contemporary 'Growth Agenda' Local Enterprise Partnerships (LEPs) and their 'devolved' deal-funding regime, and the 'decentralisation' Training and Enterprise Councils (TECs)—trail-blazers of radical Thatcherism and the 1980s enterprise culture revolution. Both suffered whimper noises after big-bang launches. New localist TECs were trumpeted as 'serious business' and 'big business', 'not a quick fix' but 'a network that must stand the test of time' (Training Agency 1989). TECs failed. LEPs, described by Lord Heseltine (2013) as 'the Government's chosen engine of local growth' and by the Department for Business, Innovation & Skills as 'a real power shift away from central Government and quangos and towards local communities and local businesses who really understand the barriers to growth in their areas' (Business, Innovation and Skills Committee 2013) are also failing to deliver: a symptomatic project of 'compulsive re-organisation'—whereby economic development is a battlefield of the 'wholesale sweeping away and re-creation of organisations and an endless tinkering and meddling with what currently exists' (A. Jones 2010: 374). Both state projects have complete geographical coverage of England, 'make decisions that transcend local administrative boundaries' (HCLG 2018: 22), and are associated with enacting a raft of market-making and economic competitiveness measures, triggering in turn, social cohesion and inequality concerns.

Why are LEPs, and the wider devolution agenda in England, under constant review and failing? As part of a 'local growth' agenda, in 2010 the Coalition government announced that Regional Development Agencies (which superseded some of the functions of TECs) would be abolished and regional economic development would be delivered through the new LEPs, established as locally derived business-led partnerships between the private and public sector that would drive local economic growth. There are now 38 LEPs and their role has developed considerably since 2010. Under the Conservative administration (from 2015–) LEPs now have responsibility for around £12 billion of public funding and are the mechanism for channelling the Local Growth Fund to localities. In contrast to what had come before—'a century of centralisation' with 'anti-localist measures', expense, bureaucracy and the erosion of local voice—for Government, initiatives such as LEPs instead represented 'control shifts' in the devolution of power and responsibility from the central state to local communities (Conservative Party 2009). LEPs accordingly would offer a clear vision and strategic leadership to drive sustainable private sector-led growth and job creation in their area. Eight years on, a major review is underway to produce a 'revised national assurance framework' (HCLG 2018), as strategy, funding and resource, and geographical issues run deep. The government has provided limited core funding, which pump-primes business engagement activities and allows for the employment of core staff. Outside this, LEPs are expected to use their powers of business influence and coercion to raise funds from the private and public sectors to make things happen. This is proving to be problematic. LEPs have responsibility over local business and communities but are without powers. Some critics are arguing for revenue-raising powers, with the government response being that this could potentially damage their reputation and standing within the business community (Jones 2013).

Critiques also point to the lack of legal and statutory foundations, the inability to procure contracts, and an ability to manage programmes properly due to limited running costs (see Etherington and Jones 2016a; Pike et al. 2015, 2018). Like multiple economic and social development state projects before them, LEPs are bound up in a multi-scalar game of relationship jockeying, which is bringing with it concerns of responsibilities and representation. On one upward level this relates to relationships with Whitehall government departments. On a downward level, it touches on issues of board membership and accountability. Lobbying is prevalent for increased local flexibility, given the need to hit government targets for the funding streams, and also to be seen to be doing interesting things locally. The 'blancmange' of government and lack of coordination in Whitehall makes attaining and maintaining sustainable business leadership a real challenge for LEPs (Jones 2013). A cyclical isomorphic dysfunctionalism, stemming from the 'short termism of programmes, policies, and institutions [reproduces] the uncertainty and unwillingness of business and other stakeholders to invest in relationships [and] leads to a loss of institutional memory and tactic knowledge in the region' (Fairburn and

Pugh 2010: 1). 'Politically conditioned institutional instability', as Fairburn and Pugh add (ibid:1), runs deep.

Rewind 30 years and hear the same concerns … TECs were proposed in the *Employment for the 1990s* White Paper, December 1988. Like the LEPs, TECs had deep inherited institutional legacies and were always going to be better than previous moments of institutional change. Similar to LEPs, the narrative suggested that public sector conceived agencies have sought to tackle the issues of economic change. The outcome, in many respects, was unsatisfactory. They failed (see Peck and Jones 1995; Jones 1999; cf. Bennett et al. 1994). Like LEPs, they were an example of a new institutional form of governance being forced to fill two roles. TECs were first a customer of government and, second, saw their communities as clients. TECs, then, like LEPs, were unaccountable by design. Board directors were appointed as individuals and were not representative of any organisation that could remove or replace them. TEC boundaries, as for LEPs, were not centrally prescribed. This did not, however, hide the fact that TECs were, like LEPs, explicitly central government creations. TECs talked about the training market, but this was based, like LEP initiatives, on central government funds, public funds, in which the parameters and the incentives for action were determined by central government. South Thames TEC went bankrupt for trying to operate outside this (Jones 1997a) and Greater Cambridge/Greater Peterborough LEP was investigated for trying to abuse this, with conflicts of interests and financial irregularities being reported (National Audit Office, 2017).

In short, a 'British vice of perpetual restructuring' is eating away at local economic development in England, where 'the whole system is paralysed by uncertainty about who will be left standing when the game of musical chairs comes to an end' (Mulgan 2010: 1). More fundamentally, for Pike and colleagues, these neoliberal models of economic development are at a critical crossroads: we have lost sight of what local and regional economic growth and development is for; who is involved, why, who benefits; there is a consensus things aren't working through decentralisation, but there are also limited offerings on where to go next (Pike et al. 2015, 2016a, 2018). As noted by Frost (2017) above, those deeply involved in economic development do not disagree with this history and its critique. The challenge is contextualising and explaining all this: how we ended up here, what it means, and why this matters.

## EXPLAINING SHIFTS WITHIN LOCAL AND REGIONAL ECONOMIC DEVELOPMENT

*Cities and Regions in Crisis* maintains that these opening remarks are not cursory or speculative glances through the rear-view mirror of state intervention in economic governance taking the form of local and regional economic development. These public policy histories and legacies have been subject to much scrutiny. In recent years, further reports have highlighted the 'endless tinkering' of government policy with respect to local and regional economic development in England. A particularly hard-hitting and historical significant report published in 2017 by the Institute for Government (IfG), aptly titled *All Change: Why Britain is so Prone to Policy Reinvention, and What Can Be Done about It*, claims that considerable damage is being done to economic governance and public policy generally by such perpetual tinkering, the rationale of which is startlingly unclear. With 28 changes to legislation and 48 Secretaries of State in 30 years, the IfG review looked into the now extreme rapid rate of change to government policies and how this had affected many sectors, including regional government, as well as industrial strategy and further education.

The reason for the changes, or an 'appalling churn' as the IfG called it, could be put down to a number of factors, including disagreement about the purpose of regional governments, or the appropriate spatial level at which to devolve powers and Whitehall's unwillingness to trust existing local institutions, but opinions from documentary research were uneven and inconclusive. In short, the 'constant reinvention' in these three policy areas and more widely in government, noted as one of 'redisorganisation' and 'accordianisation'—the need to keep everyone confused by instituting continuous centralisation and decentralisation—could not be adequately explained. 'In the space of just over 20 years, the main vehicles for regional governance have included government offices, regional assemblies, regional development agencies and, currently, local enterprise partnerships', the report stated, with the annual cost of continual reorganisation for a single government department alone costing around £15 million a year (Norris and Adam 2017: 3).

Put simply, IfG researchers, and a launch panel (held on 14 March 2017) consisting of former permanent secretaries and other senior policy-makers, did not know whether these perpetual and cyclical changes have been taking place due to the new policy challenges facing local and regional economic development in the midst of globalisation, or whether policy change is a response to repeated policy failures and, linked to this, ad hoc political interference vis-à-vis ideological change without an evidence-base. Skills policy, for instance, is deemed 'vulnerable to churn' due to it being the domain of junior ministers, rather than this being interpreted as the obvious place where market failures are prevalent and increasingly endemic under neoliberalism (see Offe 1985; Peck 2010). As Dunford and Perrons (1992: 398) summarise: '[s]kills and training make up another area in which unregulated market mechanisms are, in fact, self-destroying'. The IfG's detailed policy reflections are captured in Figures 1.1, 1.2, and 1.3, which clearly show the churns in skills strategy, regional government, and industrial policy accelerating rapidly over time with respect to policy, structural and personnel changes.

The IfG 'patterns of churn' analysis is not isolated; it builds on a key intervention offered by the National Audit Office on the *Funding and Structures for Local Economic Growth*. This landmark report acknowledges that addressing uneven economic growth between and within regions has been a focus of government policy for a number of years and thus a legitimate object of state intervention. Local 'growth policy', though, has seen a sequence of initiatives over a number of decades where structures and funding regimes are often replaced by new schemes (see Figure 1.4). With some 38 changes to the landscape of economic development since the inception of urban policy in the early 1970s, again staggering in itself and not explained by the authors (other than it represents 'poor value for money'), the phase of change in place since 2010 is deemed to be 'distinctive' because:

> it has entailed the almost complete removal of existing structures and funding for local growth, both locally and regionally, and their replacement with new structures and funding, local freedoms and responsibilities. In contrast, previous phases of change have tended to be incremental and overlapping. As we have reported previously, reorganisations can be poor value for money due to poorly specified objectives, limited cost and benefit monitoring, and poor implementation planning. (National Audit Office 2013: 16)

Asking the central question of what indeed is happening in Britain (and England specifically), *Cities and Regions in Crisis* shines a light on, and begins to explain, these geographical peculiarities of state intervention. In stark contrast to many of the academic offerings on local and regional economic development over the past 20 years (see journals such as *Local Economy*, *Policy and Politics*, *Journal of Urban Regeneration and Renewal*, etc. and the many conference presentations that I have witnessed between 1993 to 2018), which frequently fetishise and evaluate policy on self-referential terms, and are always surprised that 'top-down' state intervention seems to somehow fail 'bottom-up' localities, *Cities and Regions in Crisis* considers why, and in what ways, particular policy problems are constructed and reveals the economic, political, and social processes through which spatial scales and regulatory governance mechanisms become codified as the solution to such problems. It considers this to be important not only to *explain* the inability of state intervention to make a difference, given that academic and popular analysis has highlighted the widening and deepening of uneven development across the UK and the extension of the North–South divide (McCann 2016). *Cities and Regions in Crisis* offers a political economy 'explanatory power'—that which highlights the mechanisms that best explain the events observed (Sayer 1992)—and argues that it is academically and politically essential to draw

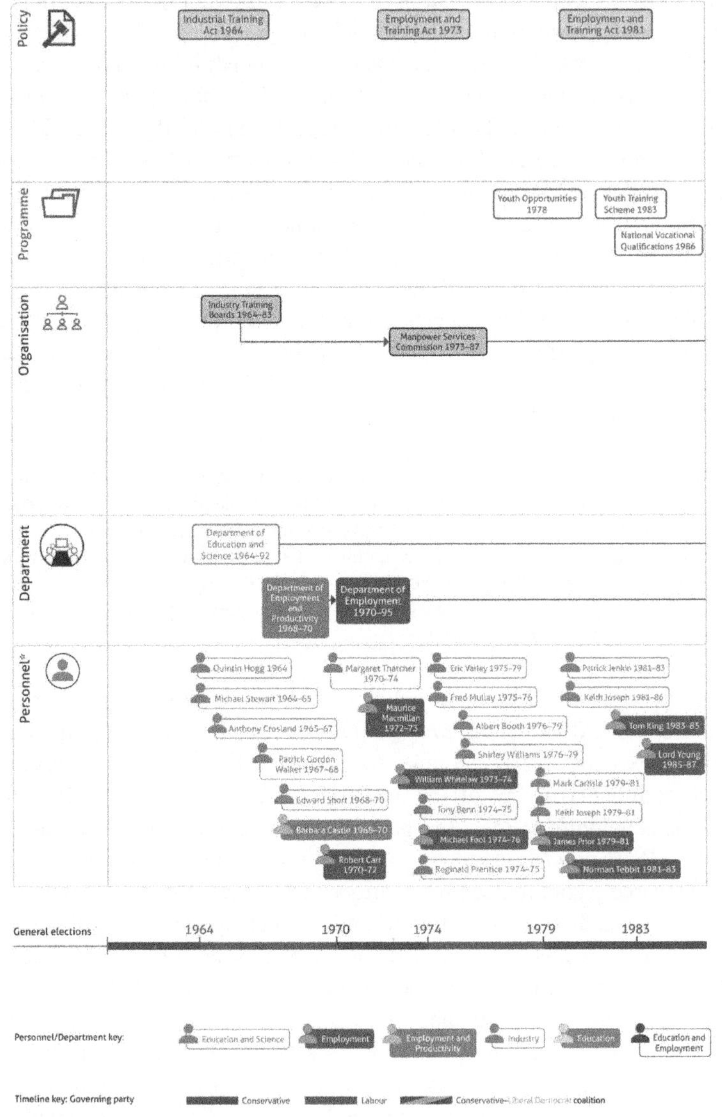


*Source:* For a colour version, see Norris and Adam (2017: 6–7; https://www.institutefor government.org.uk/sites/default/files/publications/IfG_All_change_report_FINAL.pdf), design by Sarah Henley. Information correct as of March 2017.

*Figure 1.1* *Churn in the further education sector: a timeline of policy, structural and personnel changes*

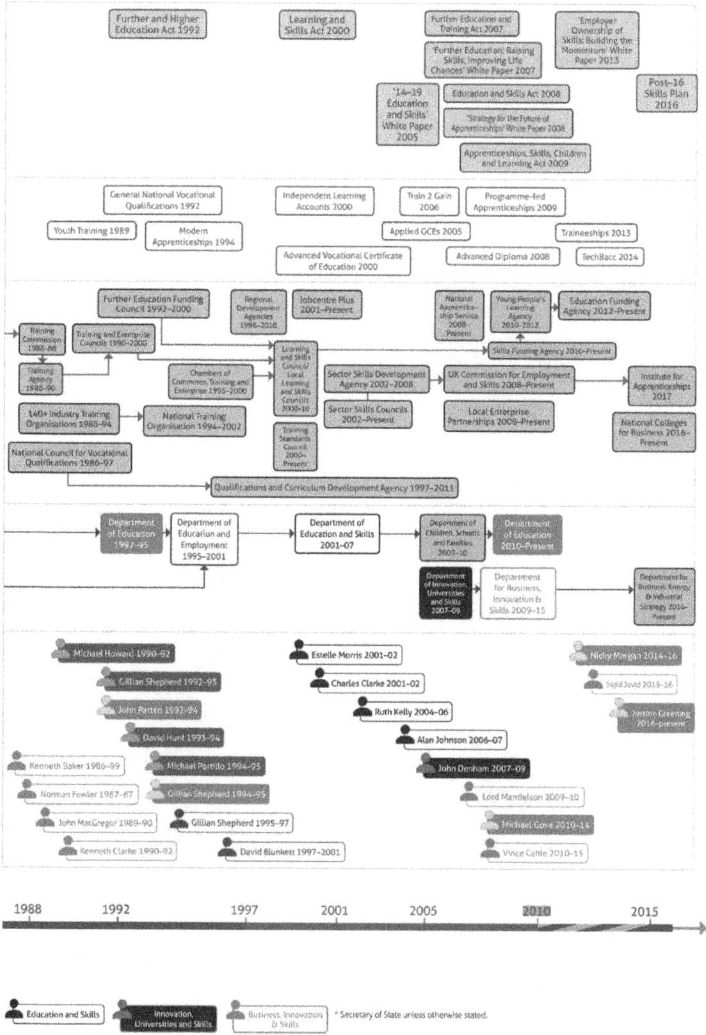


*Figure 1.1* *Continued*

attention to how seemingly unconnected processes of state restructuring and policy formation are in fact differentiated outcomes of ideologically infused political decision-making that cannot be separated from the inherent crisis tendencies and contradictions of capital accumulation, state formation, and state intervention. Put simply, policy failure is not a random and surprising

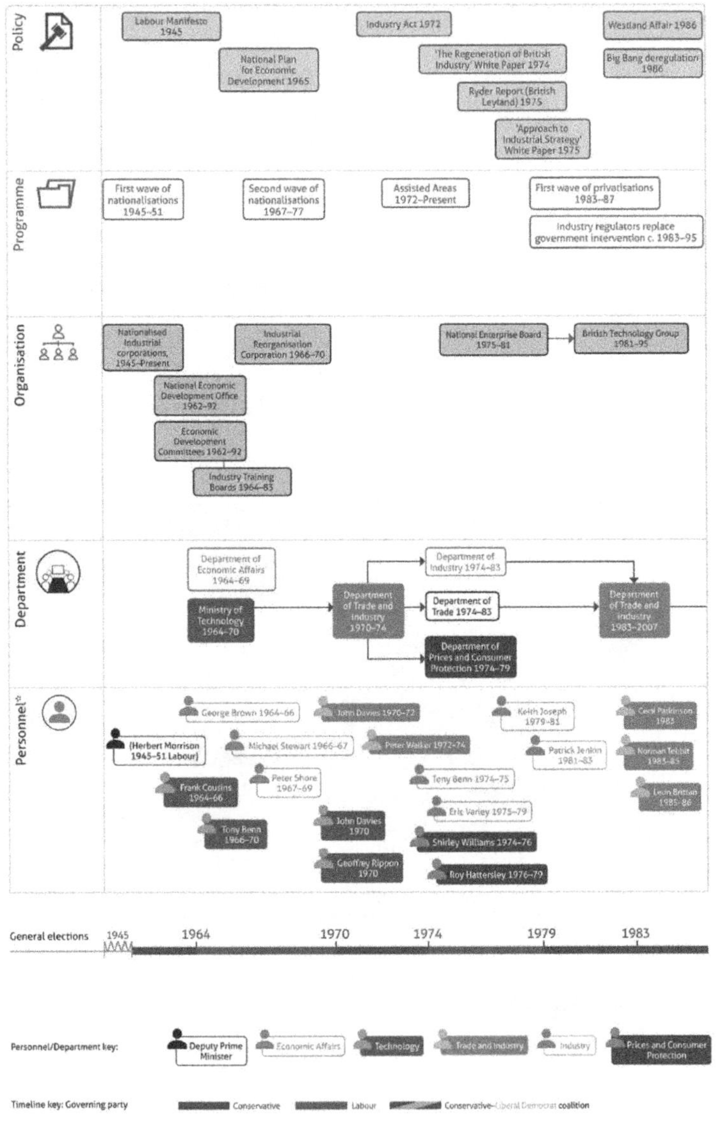


*Source:* For a colour version, see Norris and Adam (2017: 12–13; https://www.institutefor government.org.uk/sites/default/files/publications/IfG_All_change_report_FINAL.pdf), design by Sarah Henley. Information correct as of March 2017.

*Figure 1.2* *Churn in regional government: a timeline of policy, structural and personnel changes*

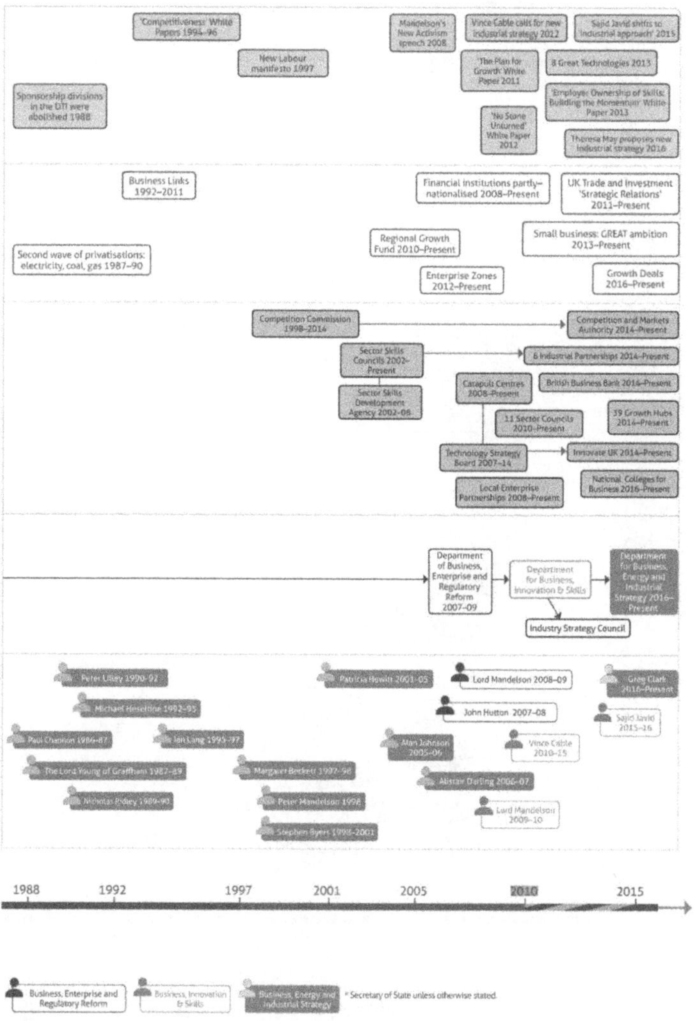


*Figure 1.2* *Continued*

phenomenon; it is the norm and increasingly endemic to advanced capitalism and its late neoliberalism spatial forms.

Following the entry quotes from Harvey (2011, 2016), *Cities and Regions in Crisis* suggests that the problem of economic development has indeed been continually *moved around*. Contradictions necessitate displacement and

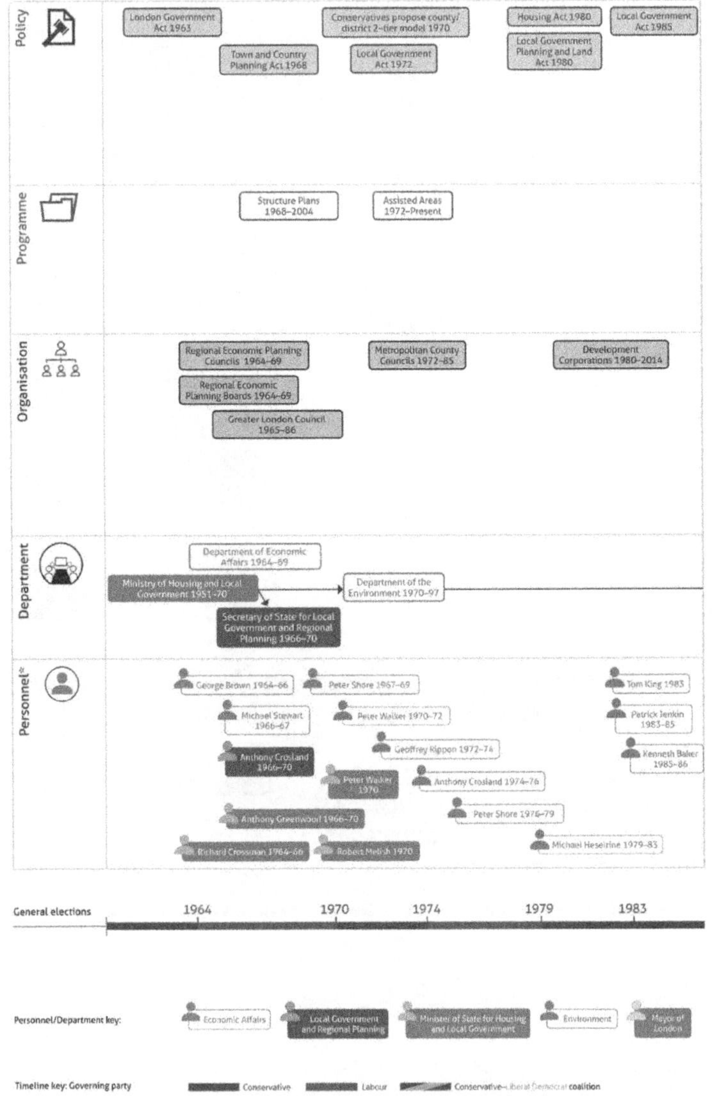


*Source:* For a colour version, see Norris and Adam (2017: 18–19; https://www.institutefor government.org.uk/sites/default/files/publications/IfG_All_change_report_FINAL.pdf), design by Sarah Henley. Information correct as of March 2017.

*Figure 1.3* *Churn in industrial strategy: a timeline of policy, structural and personnel changes*

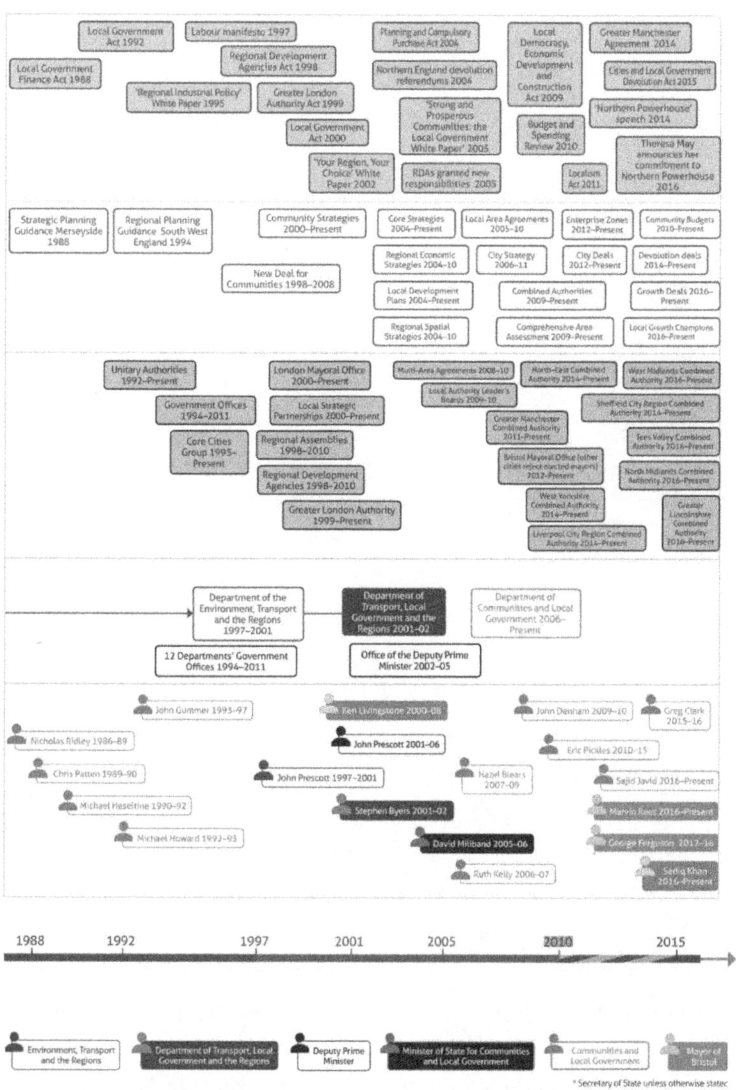


*Figure 1.3* *Continued*

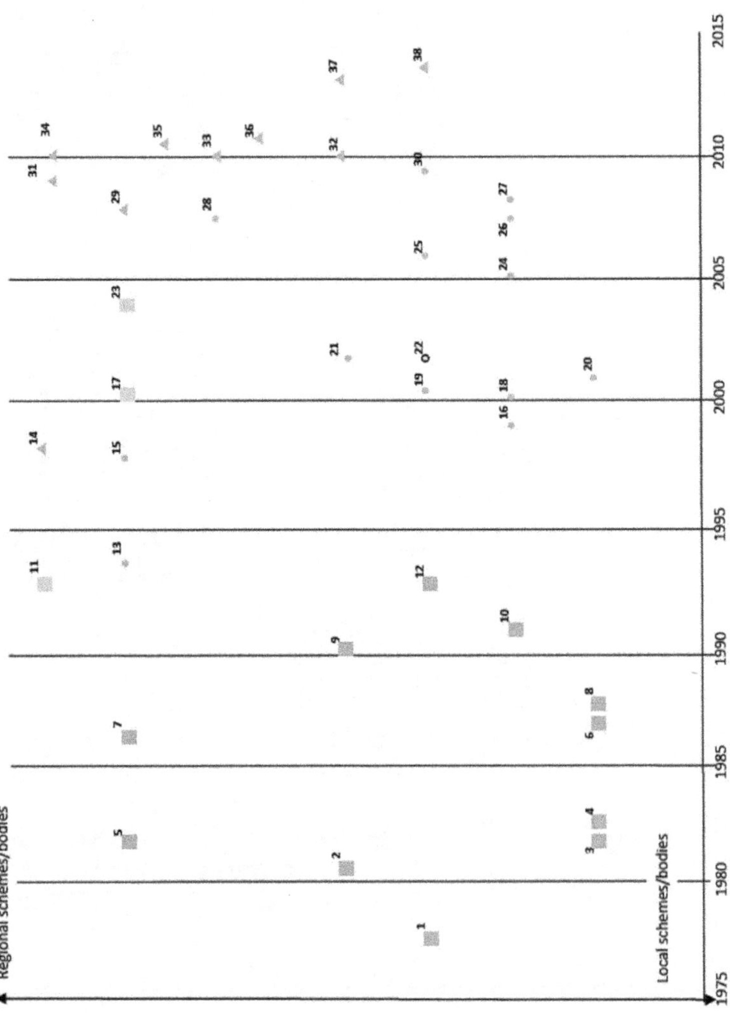


*Source:* Pike et al. (2018: 137) based on National Audit Office (2013: 17).

*Figure 1.4 Evolution of initiatives for local growth in England, 1975–2015*

1 Urban Programme (expansion)
2 Urban Development Corporations
3 Urban Development Grant
4 Derelict Land Grant
5 Regional Development Grant (revision)
6 Urban Regeneration Grant
7 Regional Enterprise Grant
8 City Grant
9 Training and Enterprise Councils
10 City Challenge
11 English Partnerships
12 Single Regeneration Budget
13 Government Offices for the Regions
14 National Coalfields Programme
15 Regional Development Agencies
16 New Deal for Communities
17 Enterprise Grant Scheme
18 Urban Regeneration Companies
19 Local Strategic Partnerships
20 Neighbourhood Renewal Fund
21 Housing Market Renewal Pathfinders
22 Local Authority Business Growth incentive
23 Selective Finance for Investment
24 Working Neighbourhoods Fund
25 Local Area Agreements
26 Local Enterprise Growth Initiative
27 City/Economic Development Companies
28 Multi Area Agreements/City Region Pict
29 Grants for Business Investment
30 Future Jobs Fund
31 Homes and Communities Agency
32 Enterprise Zones (new phase)
33 Local Enterprise Partnerships
34 Regional Growth Fund
35 City Deals
36 Growing Places Fund
37 Tax Increment Finance
38 Business Rates Retention

▲ Currently operational
● Closed since 2010
■ Closed prior to 2010

*Figure 1.4 Continued*

transformation, but the crisis-management strategies of the state *themselves* are always subject to new forms of crisis tendency, which points to the always unstable nature of economic governance and economic development. The evidence in Figures 1.1, 1.2, 1.3, and 1.4 does not point to a coherent institutional-fix that supports this neoliberal growth project, but is instead best regarded as heterogeneous, mutable, and involving variegated responses and producing unstable uneven geographical outcomes (Allmendinger and Haughton 2015). Peck denotes this as public policy 'failing forward' in that 'manifest inadequacies have—so far anyway—repeatedly animated further rounds of neoliberal invention. Devolved governance, public–private partnerships, management by audit, neopaternalism … all can be seen as examples of institutional reinvention spawned as much by the limits of earlier forms of neoliberalization as by some advancing "logic"' (Peck 2010: 6–7). A geographical political economy framework for grappling with this is desperately needed and delivering on this behoves: first, a consideration of the relationship between geography, public policy, the state, and space; second, a long-run analysis of the historical specificities, trends, and counter-trends of state intervention within capitalism; and, third, the interconnecting of analyses of economic development with changes in social policy, given the wage-relation and value-relation aspects of capitalism within which state intervention occurs (see Chapter 3; also Offe 1984: 92). The unpacking of this argument and signposting of the chapters and moments contained within *Cities and Regions in Crisis* to demonstrate this is outlined below.

## GEOGRAPHY, SHALLOW, AND DEEP POLICY ANALYSIS

The relationship between geography and public policy—defined as 'any form of deliberate intervention, regulation, governance, or prescriptive or alleviative action, by state or nonstate bodies, intended to shape social, economic or environmental conditions' (Martin 2001: 206)—has been subject to debate in the past two decades, with geographers working 'themselves up into quite a lather' (Massey 2002: 645). Peck (1999a) has made a critical distinction between 'shallow' and 'deep' public policy analysis. 'Shallow policy analysis' is research confined to addressing the 'stated aims and objectives' of policies from within an orthodox theoretical position. This often serves the needs of the policy-making system, which it takes for granted, by licensing quick-fix solutions. By contrast, 'deep policy analysis' takes a theoretically unorthodox position and questions the embedded and path-dependent nature of public policy. Deep policy analysis, therefore, delimits research that engages 'critically and actively with the policy process itself' (Peck 2000: 255). Key here is teasing out relationships *between* different levels of public policy 'to connect together the smaller pictures with the bigger pictures of the policy process, to connect the specific with the general, without undermining the integrity of our particular take on the policy process' (Peck 2000: 257). As the IfG report above highlights, some 20 years later, the political economy of the policy process—linked to how we conceptualise the capitalist state, its organisation, and its modes of intervention—remains a gap in our understanding.

Put simply, successful policy-making depends on an understanding of the policy process *itself*, which, in turn, depends on some appreciation of the structure of power in society, which, in turn, requires a critical appreciation of the state. We need to focus on how government responds to and represents its 'wider social environment' (Jessop 1990a). State intervention constitutes a 'moral geography': by understanding the social situations and politics that go hand in hand with forms of state intervention, we can go some way to understanding what makes public policy tick, and why these churn-changes within economic development have been taking place. To understand local and regional economic development, we need to understand the multiple geographical terrains of the capitalist state and state-making processes—the main arena in and through which public policy is made and coordinated—and how this relates to the regulation and governance of capitalism, its contradictions, and crisis tendencies.

## STATES, ECONOMIC DEVELOPMENT AND GEO-PERIODISATION

> Capitalist development is inherently and unavoidably uneven, contradictory, and anarchic. Attempts to manage it more smoothly via state activity do not abolish these contradictions but instead internalise them within the state itself. There may be periods when it may seem as if the contradictions have disappeared and that the interests of capital and labour are, after all, compatible; that capitalist development can, in a sense, be successfully managed by the state. But such periods reflect combinations of contingent circumstances, which disguise but do not abolish the deeper contradictions. In due course these re-emerge. (Hudson 1989: 386)

The most general feature of the state (pre-modern as well as modern and pre-capitalist as well as capitalist) is that it comprises a set of institutions concerned with the territorialisation of political power. This involves the intersection of politically organised, coercive, and symbolic power, a clearly demarcated core territory, and a fixable population on which political decisions may be made collectively binding. Thus, the key feature of the state is the historically variable ensemble of technologies and practices that produce, naturalise, and manage territorial space as a relatively bounded container within which political power is exercised to achieve various, more or less well-integrated, and changing policy objectives. The state, then, is distinct and different from say a multinational corporation, by virtue of its territorial integrity and its political legitimacy. The state is also different in the various roles that it can play. As Hudson (1989, 2001) above reminds us, states can respond to the contradictions, dilemmas, and problems of capitalism by creating the general conditions for the production and social reproduction of the capital relation, that is, the environment for economic growth and development. The state does this in part by seeking to promote growth and development and/or by responding to the effects of this, that is, uneven growth, change, and restructuring. The state though is omnipresent: due to its development and penetration into most spheres of life, it appears to be everywhere and nowhere at the same time.

Following Gramsci (1971), the state is a complex and broad set of institutions and networks that span both political society and civil society in their 'inclusive' sense. Building on this insight, states can be viewed as strategic terrains, with emphasis being placed on strategic considerations and strategic actions. Offe (1975, 1984, 1985) discusses this arrangement by drawing attention to the state and its circuits of power and policy implementation, which provides a window on the patterning of state intervention and the everyday nature of policy-making under capitalism. Building on Offe and Gramsci, Jessop's approach to the state, which is peppered throughout *Cities and Regions in Crisis* and further developed in Chapter 10, has significantly moved forward these arguments. For Jessop, the state needs to be thought of as 'medium and outcome' of policy processes that constitute its many interventions. The state is both a social relation and a producer of strategy and, as such, it does not have any power of its own. State power in relation to the policy process relates to the forces that 'act in and through' its apparatus. According to this view, attempts to analyse the policy process need to uncover the strategic contexts, calculations, and practices of actors involved in strategically selective, or privileged, sites (Jessop 1990a, 2016a). This can be summarised as a framework that demonstrates 'systems analyses' for the undertaking of 'systematic' forms of public policy analysis—drawing attention to the intricate links between actors and forms of representation, institutions and their interventions and practices, and the range of policy outcomes available. The state, then, is both a strategic and relational concern, forged through the *ongoing* engagements between agents, institutions and concrete policy circumstances. This seeks to get to the heart of the 'policy process itself' and the why, where, and when of local and regional economic development.

Rhodes (2007: 1254, emphasis added) reminds us that 'patterns of rule arise as the contingent products of diverse actions and political struggles informed by the *beliefs of agents* as they confront dilemmas that are understood differently in contending traditions'. Heeding this call for causal explanations of state intervention, where the uncovering of apparent purpose matters, two crucial elements of statehood and policy-making, which run through *Cities and Regions in Crisis*, need to be considered. The first is the notion of 'discursive geographies' (Jones 2008). This encourages us to think of the state as not 'always-already there': the relationship between states, ideology and discourse matters in and through the production, dissemination and consumption of ideas and concepts to understand the whereabouts of state intervention and public policy. As the empirical evidence above (Figures 1.1–1.4) and below in the chapters of *Cities and Regions in Crisis* documents, new institutions are continually being built by the state and cadres of 'experts' strategically assembled that can be proposed as the appropriate caretakers, teachers, and practitioners of knowledge. As knowledge is transferred, though, 'from one scale to another, the particular social, political, and economic context within which it was produced is stripped away, allowing the presentation of abstract programmatic statements that are valorised as universally applicable' (Dixon and Hapke 2003: 143).

Second, the 'geography of discourse' (Jones 2008) itself matters, i.e. the way objects of regulation and governance are constituted in relation to each other. The construct of policy does not stand independently from the ideas and beliefs of politicians and policy-makers, but has to be always contextualised in relation to concepts and ideas that are unstated. For Dixon and Hapke (2003: 143), the state is able to establish this line 'via the play of binaries for example, free/fettered, family/corporate, rural/urban, welfare/investment, safety/risk, individual/ social, us/them—one side of each of which becomes prioritized to the detriment of its opposite' (Dixon and Hapke 2003: 143). Sum and Jessop (2013) deploy the notions of 'semiosis' and 'construal' to combine these twin insights. Semiosis refers to sense-making and meaning-making, whereby policy-makers can give appreciation and meaning to their actions world', which is in turn predicted on 'construal'—how a particular policy problem is perceived and the solution constructed in response to this. Put very simply: 'Policy makers are not faced with a given problem. Instead they have to identify and formulate their problem' (Lindblom 1968: 13) and 'the definition and construction of a "problem" *contains within it* the "solution" to that problem' (Atkinson 2000: 211, emphasis added). Hadjimachalis usefully adds:

> When failures turn to crises, those actors who are capable of making decisive interventions, apart from acting to 'solve' the problem, promote a particular discursive construction of the crisis, suitable to their interests. In this mediation, powerful actors [play] key roles, such as the mainstream media, politicians, bureaucrats and European, national and international institutions, bankers and think tanks. In doing this, old and new imaginations, prejudices and 'scientific' analyses [are] mobilised, targeting mass public moral sentiments and beliefs. (Hadjimachalis 2018: 79)

Economic development is no exception here and the nature of the problem and the solutions to this have changed considerably over time and across space—perpetually in a state of flux, as noted above.

These concerns can be further rolled together through the idea of 'spatial fixes' (see Chapter 3) and 'spatio-temporal fixes' (see Chapter 10), both concepts deployed to comprehend the dynamics of state spatiality, state spatial restructuring, and the geographies of state intervention specifically. The state performs the role of securing the relative stabilisation of society by endeavouring to manage the various economic and political contradictions within the state system (Hudson 1989). This is inherently spatial, as state intervention is articulated through the constructions of spaces (scales, levels, horizons, etc.) of intervention, the fixing of borders, the stabilisation of places, and, in short, attempts are being continually made to produce and reproduce a territorially coherent and functioning socioeconomic landscape.

This has been referred to elsewhere as state 'spatial selectivity'—the processes of spatial privileging and articulation in and through which state policies are differentiated across territorial space in order to target particular geographical zones, scales, and (organised and disorganised) interest groups (Jones 1997b, 1999; see also Omstedt 2016). The latter dimension forms an integral element of how political structuration occurs within the state apparatus via the creation of territorial coalitions, or what Cox (1998) calls 'spaces of engagement', to mobilise strategically significant actors and exclude others where 'spaces of dependency' (interests and attachments) rule out their possibility for incorporation. The tension between engagement and dependency, of course, creates a politics of scale and a scaling of politics, where some localities are either more or less engaged in networks of association beyond their immediate territories than are others (see Jonas and Wood 2012).

As noted previously (Jones 2009), Brenner's (1998: 474–477) work on state spatiality offers a useful geo-periodisation bridge to frame this, alongside which the arguments within *Cities and Regions in Crisis* on the spatial selectivity of local and regional economic and social development can be discussed. Brenner draws attention to three periods: 'encagement' (1890s–1930s), 'entrenchment' (1950s–early 1970s), and 'de-nationalisation' (post-1970s onwards), which are unpacked in turn.

## Space of Localism: Municipal Local States

Taking these in turn, until the late nineteenth century, there was a distinct polarisation between industrialising city-regions and predominately rural agricultural peripheries, which was reinforced at a global scale through colonialism and imperialist expansion. The global depression of the late 1890s and after, however, drove a search for a state-managed and organised capitalism. With the development of market societies, 'states were forced to adopt measures to prevent the self-destruction to which self-adjusting markets were inclined' (Dunford and Perrons 1992: 391). An emerging 'encagement' of socioeconomic relations was taking place due to the increasing spatial convergence between the interests of capital and the state, which fuelled the development of global urban hierarchies and increasingly territorial states (Brenner 1998: 473). Geoeconomic interests began to dominate here and the continued expansion of capital growth and development drove the search for a spatial symmetry between a national economy, state bureaucracy, civil society, and national culture, all feeding each other. This was secured through mainly public infrastructure development across territorial space, industrial infrastructures, national economic planning, and an expanding state apparatus.

Over a 40-year period, the state thus acquired a major role in the construction of numerous interlocking territorial infrastructures—public transportation, education and housing facilities, communication networks, utility supplies, and other aspects of the expanding urban and regional fabric—as market mechanisms of distribution had failed as mechanisms of production and modernisation. Economic development trajectories in England broadly align to this. Victorian 'localist' public health legislation, for instance, made possible the expansion of the (local) state's roles in responsibility for water and sanitation through a combination of local taxation and municipal trading. The context for these local rounds of state intervention was 'countering localized market failure' (Hall 2016: 313) and as the nineteenth century progressed, other services were developed in a similar way, including gas, electricity and public transport (Ward 1988).

## Spatial Keynesianism: National Welfare States

Following the Great Depression of the 1930s, and certainly after the Second World War, this model of statehood was consolidated through modernisation, nationalisation, and rationalisation to make space for a new wave of capitalist expansion, despite the onset of serious and lasting economic crises. Britain, for instance, faced growing international competition and local authorities experienced economic problems that precipitated engagements with industrial promotion activity, which accelerated in the inter-war years. As Mawson points out:

> The fact that the burden of addressing the social consequences of mass unemployment was borne at the local level through poor relief further encouraged local municipal leadership to promote the local economy and associated tax base. In some areas this development took places as an adjunct to central government's emerging regional policies as heralded in the 1934 Special Area Act. (Mawson 2009: 40)

These emerging regional policies were seeking to deal with the problems of uneven development and rising spatial inequality between a growing south and declining north. Consequently, throughout the Fordist–Keynesian period, roughly from the 1950s to the early 1970s, the role of the territorial state as a geographical container of capital accumulation and social development intensified and solidified (Brenner 1998: 474). From the 1930s, states had begun to engage directly in attempts to devalue and revalue capital through subsidies, grants, loans, tax advantages, public investments, and state ownership of production facilities. In Britain, for instance, the Barlow Commission of 1937–1940 was a landmark event, which placed a national duty on government to control capital to prevent the overheating of London and the South East and argued for national control of industry through planning. The spatial distribution of capital via the levers of industrial and regional policy followed (see Hall 1989) in the increasing context of also attempting to deal with, and counteract the problems with, a 'Britain in decline' (see English and Kenny 2000; Gough and Eisenschitz 1996a, 1996b) growth model, where:

> British capitalism does not work, because it is a competitive system in which private profit is and must be the main objective. It is a system in which all the prevailing forces are pulling in opposite directions and the interests of the individual are as often as not opposed to those of the state. (Orwell 1940: 50)

This practice of capital regulation and spatially targeted investment progressed through rounds of regional policy, such as the Local Authorities (Land) Act 1963 and The National Plan, with regional and local state institutions becoming 'transmission' for interventionist central state policies concerned with addressing 'the balance of payments [via] an intensive effort by all concerned' (HMSO 1965: A3). Their goal was simultaneously to maximise growth by 'overcoming the obstacles to growth' (HMSO 1965: A3) and to redistribute its effects as evenly as possible on a national scale. Between the 1950s and the 1970s, further rounds of regional (industrial) policies, such as the Hunt Report on Intermediate Areas, were introduced to promote industrialisation within each state's under-developed peripheries. The spaces mostly outside declining cities became hosts to industrial estates, employment parks, and other exhibits of fixed-capital investment to attract jobs through inward investment, as well as growing (often failing) local/regional economic talent. This was supported by the expansion of the welfare state, increasing universal rights and social citizenship, and politics predominately related to achieving and raising social benefits. The state's role in territorialising capital and in securing a spatio-temporal fix for social relations, therefore, converged around the nation state. In this manner, the 'national scale operated as the critical geographical framework for capitalist production and exchange, as the dominant institutional site of sociospatial polarisation, and as the most central arena for addressing sociopolitical contestation' (Brenner 1998: 475).

The crises and contradictions of capitalism were in effect delicately balanced, or what Dunsire (1993: 11-12) calls 'collibrated', into a durable spatio-temporal fix. As Lefebvre (1976: 111) puts it: 'the ship of capitalism and its leaders found itself with a motor, a rudder and a fixed course'. The limits to this became apparent during the mid-1970s with the collapse of Atlantic-Fordism (see Chapters 2 and 3). Key for Britain was social and political unrest, with the government responding with the raft of state interventions on urban policy ignited by the 1977 Urban White Paper and 1978 Inner Urban Areas Act (Chapter 3), where 'local economic development was encouraged by the policy vacuum created by the retreat of national regional policy in areas of increasing unemployment and by the introduction of locally delivered national schemes such as the Urban Programme' (Mawson 2009: 41).

## De-Nationalisation Scalar Relativisation: New Localism and New Regionalism

Consequently, 'de-nationalisation' (Brenner 1998: 475) has had more profound implications on geography of world capitalism and the political-economic geography of the state than the two preceding waves of spatio-temporal fixing. Shifts within the international division of labour, aided by technical change, brought about intense economic restructuring, which transformed some industrial heartlands into wastelands and provided new post-industrial opportunities for others. Accordingly, on sub-state levels, 'interspatial competition' has intensified among cities and regions competing with one another to attract capital investment and secure state subsidies (Brenner 1998: 475). In addition to these globally induced reconfigurations of the national scale, there has been a series of highly contested forms of reterritorialisation involving the state and its interventions, restructuring impacts, and responses to this. Two overarching broad trends are worth mentioning and these have been defining research agendas in political geography and human geography more broadly in recent years.

First, scholars have highlighted a 'relativization of statehood' (Collinge 1999). In contrast to the era of Fordism–Keynesianism, described above, there is no privileged level around which the state can influence the unfolding of capitalism. The relativisation of statehood thus implies: (1) an increasingly tangled hierarchy of overlapping, continually changing arrangements associated with multilevel interventions; and (2) the systematic lack of any dominant scale, or system of governance, that encompasses or subsumes competing scales of political-economic organisation. To understand this, the crisis of Fordist capitalism and the subsequent burst of globalisation should be understood as a de-centring of nationally scaled regulatory arrangements, as sub-national and supra-national scales of political-economic life have acquired a renewed, and in some cases unprecedented, significance through a variety of trial-and-error, often ad hoc, political initiatives, in especially economic development. This often involves the shift from government to governance, as new arrangements for state management now involve an array of different socioeconomic partners and not just those in formalised state structures (Chapter 2).

Figure 1.4 captures some of this, with an increasingly relativisation of scale and an almost 'filling-in' (Goodwin et al. 2012, 2017) of all horizons (national, regional, local) of state intervention. While the Keynesian welfare national states of the post-war era were intent on harmonising the equalisation of wealth, population, and infrastructure across national territories, contemporary neoliberal state projects are promoting territorial competitiveness within certain strategic sub-national sites such as cities, city-regions, and industrial districts, which in turn are to be positioned within supra-national and global circuits of economic development. While certain aspects of this entrepreneurial reorientation of local and regional policy has occurred from below, as fiscally stressed localities and regional states have attempted proactively to attract new sources of investment through the actions of development agencies and other institutions, sub-national economic development must also be construed, to a significant degree, as national state projects concerned with providing 'new avenues for capital accumulation' (Hadjimachalis 2018: xii) by increasing the reach and depth of state-space.

Second, accordingly provoked by hegemonic discourses of globalisation and business civilisation alongside a political rhetoric of fiscal prudence, national states have actively sought to reduce commitments to integrated welfare entitlements and redistributive urban and regional policies in favour of supply-side neoliberal initiatives intended to promote technological innovation, labour market flexibility, lean management, and endogenous growth. This is discussed further below.

As outlined in Chapters 2 and 3, Metropolitan County Councils were abolished in Britain, reflecting central government's hostility to their deemed to be socialist interventionist range of economic development policies, and 'new localist' state-sponsored institutions, such as Urban Development Corporations (UDCs) and TECs (noted above), put in their place. The 'patchwork quilt' (Audit Commission 1989) of local complexities was replaced by a 'new regionalist' 'bowl of spaghetti' (Johnstone and Whitehead 2004) of responding to new market opportunities through new forms of organisational capacity and business leadership through Regional Development Agencies (RDAs), working in tandem with, but also getting tangled-up with, Local Learning and Skills Councils (Chapters 5, 6 and 7). In the words of the Lord

*Source:* Original commissioned artwork, drawn by Adrian Teal.

*Figure 1.5* *Crisis-analytic depictions of the sub-national review*

Peyton of Yeovil, criticising the government's neighbourhood renewal unit at that time:

> The organization has no fewer than seven divisions and 14 subdivisions. Its habit of breeding, which is endemic in the Office of the Deputy Prime Minister, has spread to boroughs. The government has produced an indissoluble union between gobbledy and gook. (quoted in Weaver 2003: 17)

Throughout this period, as Deas and Ward (1999: 130) highlight, the new localist 'song' had mostly ended, but the complexity 'melody lingered'. In other words, this new regionalism is 'just one element in a wider complex of overlapping agencies, structures and policies, the logic and coherence of which remains to be proven'. Local Strategic Partnerships (LSCs) and later a series of Area Agreements (Local then Multiple AAs) were deployed so that local stakeholders could work together to agree and deliver local policy priorities within this quagmire, but, with limited statutory powers and minuscule budgets, the government's increasingly performance management regime for government programmes largely bypassed the new structures and added to the existing complexity (Chapter 7). This is evident by the rapidity of institutional developments in Figures 1.1–1.4, culminating ultimately in what Sullivan and Skelcher (2002) refer to as a 'congested state', in which a 'considerable amount of time and resources are chewed up in getting new organisations off the ground and in constructing partnership relations so that *something might get done*' (Corry and Stoker, 2003: 10, emphasis added). Figure 1.5, sketched during the period of the 2009 sub-national review, seeks to capture this.

## New New Localism: Devolution Deals and Beyond

The resulting spatio-temporal fix to deal with this dysfunctional multi-scalar complexity increasingly became a 'new new localism' of city-regions, given the desire to create institutional projects able to hold-down the global through functional economic areas (Chapter 8). The HM Treasury (2007) sub-national review (SNR) had proposed Urban Regeneration Companies (URCs) and subregions became key spatial units in increasingly devolved contexts (see Ayers and Stafford 2009). Post 2010, a Devolution and Local Government Act and Local Growth agenda pushed 'functional economic areas' further through LEPs, City Deals and Devolution Deals (Chapters 9 and 10). The Royal Society of Arts' (RSA's) City Growth Commission represented a key moment, leashing metro-growth, through a series of city-regions, or 'metros'—defined as the 'larger constellation of cities and towns that constitute a functional economy within built up areas' (RSA 2014: 11)—with critics noting this fuzzy-space city-region building as adding further to the tangled problem of governance complexity; nothing short of an imbroglio of institutional crises that reproduces the labour market deep inequalities by focusing only on the most profitable and high-tech sectors of the local and regional economy (Etherington and Jones 2016a). Moreover, there is little new money, more a 'menu of specials', where:

> A number of items have been made available to most areas, but each deal also contains a few unique elements or 'specials' (typically consisting of commitments to explore future policy options). (Sandford 2018: 9)

While the principal historical function of local authorities was the concern with delivering public services in the context of addressing the fallout of uneven development (Duncan and Goodwin 1988), merging LEPs with local government functions through the various Combined Authorities (CAs) and Mayoral CAs (see HCLG 2018) twisted and turned the function of the local state towards the ideological purpose of economic growth 'by negotiation' with central government (see Hatcher 2017; O'Brien and Pike 2018). The deployment of depoliticising processes are crucial here to limit opposition and resistance (see Chapters 10 and 11), alongside the ongoing process of joining up economic development with the market-making and welfare reform agenda (see Hackett and Hunter, 2017), given policy desire to have locally sensitive and coordinated approaches (Mawson 2009), drawing on the lessons of the Prototype Employment Zones (Chapter 4) and City Strategy Pathfinders (Chapter 7). Back to where I started on LEPs, for Toynee and Walker, making the link between state 'dismembering' and waves of privatised localism:

> [LEPs] are wonderful specimens of the administrative exotica created by ministers who would rather do nothing but can't get away with it. In 2010 they summarily abolished the regional economic development agencies: *clearing the ground for a market solution*. But business in the regions demanded a replacement, hence LEPs, which are committees of local businesspeople who give grants to ... local businesspeople. (Toynbee and Walker 2017: 78, emphasis added)

Consequently, noting what Peck (2010: 16) calls 'state/market configurations' these activities have been bringing with them 'authoritarian politics' with deep consequences across cities and regions, as inherited and hard-won forms of popular control over welfare state institutions are being gradually eroded. Insofar as they have entailed a 'productivist' reordering of social policy and the increasing privileging of economic competitiveness (Brenner 2004), shifts to entrepreneurial governance have also contributed to a reduced commitment to the concerns of collective consumption for poorer sections of society. For Harvey (2005: 76) 'a way has been found to integrate state decision-making into the dynamics of capital accumulation and the networks of class power'. Accordingly, the move from RDAs to LEPs effectively removed two-thirds of core regeneration and ended the 40-year history of area-based regeneration initiatives 'targeted at the most deprived parts of England' (Crowley et al. 2012; Hetherington 2013). As Hall summarises:

> the Conservatives and Liberal Democrats have pre-sided over the effective cessation of urban regeneration as a form of public policy. Legacy programmes have been allowed to expire without replacement or, in the case of Housing Market Renewal, simply terminated. Total government expenditure on regeneration was reduced by some two-thirds within the financial year 2011/2012. For the first time since the 1960s, *there is no national framework of area based regeneration initiatives and supporting financial and institutional resources in the cities of England* ... Indeed, it can be argued that the Coalition government has rejected a role for itself in respect of the monitoring and elimination of poverty and social exclusion. (Hall 2016: 324, emphasis added)

New landscapes of power have indeed been created in this gap, in which new forms of exclusion, subordination, and also resistance are inscribed into urban and regional space (Ellis and Henderson 2013). One notable ingredient in this political endeavour has been escalating welfare-to-work or 'workfare' interventions (see Chapters 4, 7, 10), which aim to secure a new relationship between the state and its subjects by requiring work or active labour market activities in return for unemployment benefit and welfare assistance. The discussion on the rollout of Universal Credit, which involves replacing six means-tested benefits for working-age households (see Chapter 10), is the culmination of this regime, with the National Audit Office (2018) raising serious questions on the operability of a system that is causing hardship and misery for thousands.

## Neoliberalism and its Spatial Conditions

This neoliberal growth strategy should neither be seen as an all-encompassing, universal and settled project, nor a binary process of switching one spatial scale with another (local-regional and regional-local). In the words of Brenner et al.:

> To speak of neoliberalism 'in crisis' needless to say, presupposes an understanding of the character of this elusively dispersed yet deeply embedded form of social rule. A singular, monolithic and unified neoliberalism might indeed be prone to a correspondingly 'total' crisis. But neoliberalism has never displayed such a singular, monolithic character. It may be deeply integrated, but it has always been unevenly developed—most notable across nations, cities and regions … [N]eoliberalism's proven capacities in the (downward and outward) displacement and (forward) resheduling of risks and crisis tendencies mean that its associated regulatory landscapes are especially dynamic. (2012: 17–18)

It is important, then, to highlight the contingent 'mechanisms' or 'processes' in and through which this project is being politically made and contested with 'some forms of agency' to avoid 'over generalizations' (Le Galès 2016: 168). Following Offe (1984: 37), *Cities and Regions in Crisis* favours a 'processual' approach, which seeks out the mechanisms ('cross-scalar *relations*' as Brenner et al. (2012: 60, emphasis original) put it) that generate events and can highlight developmental tendencies and tease out important counteracting tendencies and opportunities for progressive localisms. All this raises some searching questions, which *Cities and Regions in Crisis* seeks to address. How is the 'relativisation of statehood' (Collinge 1999) unravelling in different geographical contexts and is there an emerging spatio-temporal fix to replace the primacy of national territory, national economic space, national social formation, and national networks? Are new forms of state configuration emerging that seem to be consolidating and ossifying to create a relatively stabilised landscape of regulation, or are multispatial arrangements set to continue with an ongoing search for different possibilities? Figure 1.4 indicates an increasingly multispatial economic statehood, where no single scale is dominant, but where nodes of activity appear to be settling then shifting periodically. Are multiple rounds of 'filling-in' occurring, which challenges assumptions that with globalisation the state is 'hollowing out', declining, and being eroded away (Goodwin et al. 2012, 2017)? Who has access to the state apparatus; who participates when and how? What is the relationship between different types of state and non-state actors and between different levels? How are issues of democracy and legitimacy dealt with? And how are the conflicting demands of competitiveness, cohesion, and sustainability dealt with?

*Cities and Regions in Crisis* tackles these and thus gives an insight into the ways in which state actors walk a difficult line between ensuring the right environment for economic growth and development but at the same time guarding against a crisis of electoral support (issues of legitimation crisis). Instances of regulatory failure across cities and regions are becoming apparent, as state policy-making constantly switches economic problems in concerns of state rationality that can be more easily addressed through public policy. State actors appear to be continually reinventing policy initiatives, often in response to the problems and contradictions caused by previous rounds of state intervention, in a search to get things right. As Brenner et al. put it:

> the *practice* of neoliberal statecraft is inescapably, and profoundly, marked by compromise, calculation and contradiction. There is no blueprint. There is not even a map. Crises themselves need not be fatal for this mutable, mongrel model of governance, for to some degree or another neoliberalism has always been a creature of crisis. But selectively exploiting the crisis of Keynesian-welfarist, developmental or state-socialist systems is one thing, responding to crises of neoliberalism's *own* making is quite another. (2012: 45)

How are state actors dealing with these challenges, that is, how is failure being presented and interpreted, addressed, new solutions proposed, and are these becoming successful? Provisional answers to these big questions are below.

## SPATIAL DIVISONS OF THE STATE: MULTISPATIAL METAGOVERNANCE AND THE NEW GEOGRAPHIES OF ECONOMIC DEVELOPMENT

*Cities and Regions in Crisis* demonstrates the unravelling of the Keynesian welfare national state institutional compromise and the making of a crisis space impedimenta neoliberal state. Figure 1.6 depicts how this has been playing out in the field of local and regional economic and social development over the past 40 years. A pendulum swing effect has been experienced, whereby UK state strategy, in turn linked to how the policy problem is constructed and its solution articulated, has *moved* and oscillated between national, regional, and local patterns of state projects and modes of state interventions. The previous round of state spatial restructuring has been used as the explanation for state

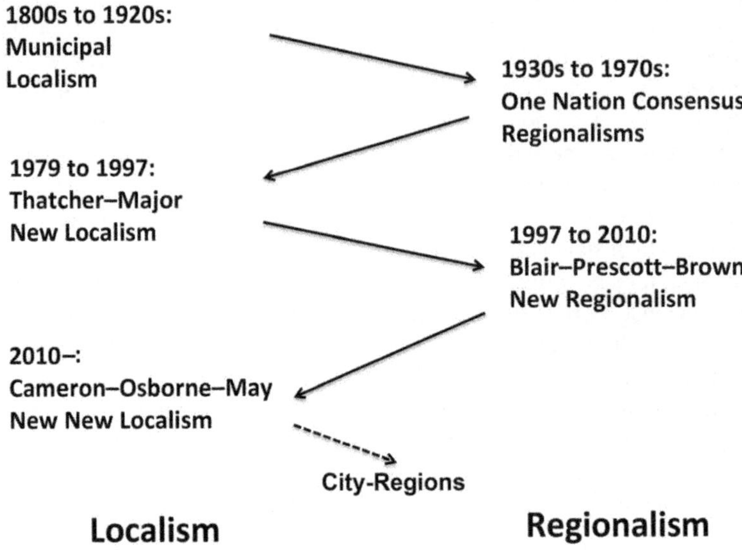


*Source:* Adapted and updated from Pike et al. (2016b: 10).

*Figure 1.6 Pendulum swings in governing economic development*

intervention failure, with the next round seeking to address this through developing new spatial horizons, also failing in turn (Jones and Ward 2004). Part I (Chapters 2, 3, and 4) examines the 'new localism' of the Conservative Party administration (1979 to 1997). Part II (Chapters 5, 6, and 7) turns to look at the 'new regionalism' of the Labour Party administration (1997 to 2010). Part III (Chapters 8, 9, 10) unpacks the 'new new localism' of both the Coalition administration (2010 to 2015) and the return of the Conservative Party (2015–).

What becomes apparent from these local and regional economic development journeys is the appropriateness of not talking of a single crisis and in mono-causal terms (MacLeod and Jones 2018). *Cities and Regions in Crisis* is embedded in a political economy tradition where the interrelationships between economic, social, and political processes, which are forged through power relations as 'moving parts', matter. The book offers a multi-causal approach to crises and thereby expands the definition of crisis by initiating a movement from the primacy of the economy, to the primacy of the state, and then to the primacy of the political. Combining these approaches and 'doing political economy' facilitates the study of how the inherent contradictions and crisis tendencies of capitalism are governed within economic development and through a historically variable set of institutional, spatio-temporal, and semantic fixes—all partial, provisional, and temporary. Subsequent chapters accordingly offer a neo-Marxist syncretism by building on Marxism and Frankfurt School Critical Theory (Chapter 3), regulation approaches and strategic-relational state theory (Chapters 2, 3, 4, and 10), associative institutional theories (Chapters 5 and 6), relational approaches to space and place (Chapters 7 and 8), and cultural political economy framings of politics and depoliticisation (Chapters 9 and 10) to collectively argue that policy actors, politicians, and business leaders are locked into the market model of delivery, neoliberalising modes of representation, and subsequent failures in economic regulation and governance. The book illustrates how local and regional economic development has a 'deficit in local regulatory capacity' and some state forms and functions have clearly become 'counter-regulatory' (Painter and Goodwin 2000). Governance failure (a response to both state failure and market failure), i.e. the 'failure to redefine objectives in the face of continuing disagreement about whether they are still valid for the various partners' (Jessop 2000: 18), is occurring.

There are a number of dimensions to governance failure, which are embedded in economic development (see Etherington and Jones 2016a, 2018). First, is the apparent tension between devolving responsibilities in relation to policy formation and implementation and the tendency towards centralisation in decision making, whereby local actors are charged with implementing nationally determined targets and programmes. The challenge here is the adaptation of national programmes to local conditions.

Second is the increasing tendency towards institutional and policy fragmentation at the sub-regional level, with issues of accountability being raised. Governance becomes a new site for conflicts and political mobilisation, as the nature and complexity of partnerships means more and more 'actors' and 'stakeholders' involved in the design and delivery of labour market programmes. Outcomes at one scale may be dependent upon performance at another scale of governance, therefore coordination dilemmas can occur. Furthermore, these coordination mechanisms may have different 'temporal horizons' and there may be continuous tensions between short-term and long-term planning goals in policy planning.

Third, and related, is the failure of current policies to address deep-rooted problems of labour market inequalities that are integral to market failure. This is exemplified in many localities by the employment gap and lack of sufficient sustainable employment growth to 'revitalise' city-region economies. Finally, governance in the form of economic partnerships, dominated by private sector interests, is continuing to replace elected and representative government in terms of local economic development, which in itself poses a number of problems between government and its elected representation model of democracy and partnerships, and which tend to be elite-forming with blurred lines of accountability, often far removed from those who are disadvantaged and disenfranchised. Depoliticisation is also occurring and increasing (Fawcett et al. 2017), as opaque representational structure and lines of accountability close down and restrict possibilities of negotiation and contestation (see Chapter 10).

As noted by Bakker (2010), these processes have been neither 'tidy in practice' nor 'linear in fashion': market failures, state failures and governance failures *coexist*, 'exhibit a range of failures', and are used to justify the 'problem' requiring ongoing state intervention. It is, therefore, important to consider notions of 'crisis metamorphosis'. Thompson distinguishes this from the approaches of Harvey (above) and Habermas (see Chapter 3) by insisting that:

> Metamorphosis implies a *change in form*; it does not imply, as displacement does, that the crisis has moved from one sphere of social life to another. A financial crisis that metamorphoses into a political crisis or a social crisis does not necessarily cease to be a financial crisis: it simply becomes something else. It changes form and, in doing so, it becomes something *more* than a financial crisis per se, taking on new characteristics in the process. (Thompson 2012: 64–65, emphasis original)

Moreover, as forms of governance become more widespread and constantly change their form (metamorphosis) 'the question of governance failure becomes more acute' (Bakker 2010: 45). The state's answer to governance failure is to develop forms of metagovernance, which involves attempts to manage the ongoing complexity, plurality, and tangled hierarchies characteristic of prevailing modes of coordination (see Jessop 2000, 2008, 2016a). It involves, then, continually defining and redefining boundary-spanning roles and functions, creating and recreating networking and linkage devices, sponsoring and redesigning new institutions, identifying appropriate lead strategic institutions to coordinate other partners, and continually generating discourses and narratives on the economy (the 'shaping of context', according to Jessop 2011) to facilitate relative geographical coherence through repetition of the 'problems' to be addressed and the solutions to these—metamorphosis played out.

Government plays an increasing role in metagovernance: providing the ground rules for governance and regulatory order in and through which governance partners can pursue their aims and seek to ensure the compatibility or coherence of different governance mechanisms and regimes; seeking to balance and rebalance power differentials by strengthening weaker forces or systems in the interest of social cohesion or integration; and providing political responsibility in the event of governance failure (Etherington and Jones 2016a; Whitehead 2003a). These emerging roles mean that networking, negotiation, noise reduction, and negative as well as positive coordination occur 'in the shadow of hierarchy'. It also means that, as Jessop reminds us, there is 'the need for almost permanent institutional and organizational innovation to maintain the very possibility (however remote) of sustained economic growth' (Jessop 2000: 24). Economic development initiatives are thus frequently produced through a combination of political fiat, central government diktat, and local state opportunism. The research agenda put down by Jessop for doing metagovernance, which *Cities and Regions in Crisis* addresses is the:

> extent to which the multiplying levels, arenas, and regimes of politics, policy-making, and policy implementation can be endowed with a certain apparatus and operational unity horizontally and vertically; and how this affects the overall operation of politics and legitimacy of the new political arrangements. (Jessop 2008: 222)

Effective governance and metagovernance, in turn, depend on displacing (via the metamorphosis of the problem and its solution) certain governance problems elsewhere and/or on deferring them into a more or less remote future. This is possible because the state can transform its own internal structures and patterns of intervention spatially in an attempt to temporarily reconcile the contradictions inherent in its involvement in economy and society (Hudson 2001). Whereas the positively charged policy-context of many of the chapters below point to a can-do 'steering optimism', where there is deemed to be a capacity to engage fruitfully and with purpose to produce temporary spatio-temporal fixes, *Cities and Regions in Crisis* points to 'steering pessimism' and a 'crisis of crisis-management' (Offe 1984). In short, state intervention has come to operate not only as a political strategy for promoting local economic development, but also as a form of crisis-management designed to manage the regulatory deficits, actor dislocations, and geographical conflicts induced through earlier rounds of state spatial restructuring (Jones and Ward 2004). As the various chapters seek to demonstrate:

> a crisis-induced recalibration has been unfolding since the mid-1990s [whereby] a rescaled layer of state spatial projects and state spatial strategies has been forged whose purpose is to confront some of the major regulatory failures generated through state intervention. (Brenner 2004: 266)

In turn, there are structural economic obstacles to effective governance and metagovernance, that, 'by virtue of the simplification of the conditions of action, so often lead to the "revenge" of problems that get ignored, marginalized, displaced, or deferred' (Jessop 2011: 117). Figure 1.7 summarises the key dimensions of this geographical political economy conceptualisation of crisis and contradiction theory and points to the importance of the accumulation, and inescapable intensification, of the unresolved contradictions of doing local and regional economic development. Brenner (2004: 263–265) neatly summarises these as the outstanding problems of: inefficiency and waste; chronic short-termism; regulatory undercutting; increasing uneven spatial develop-

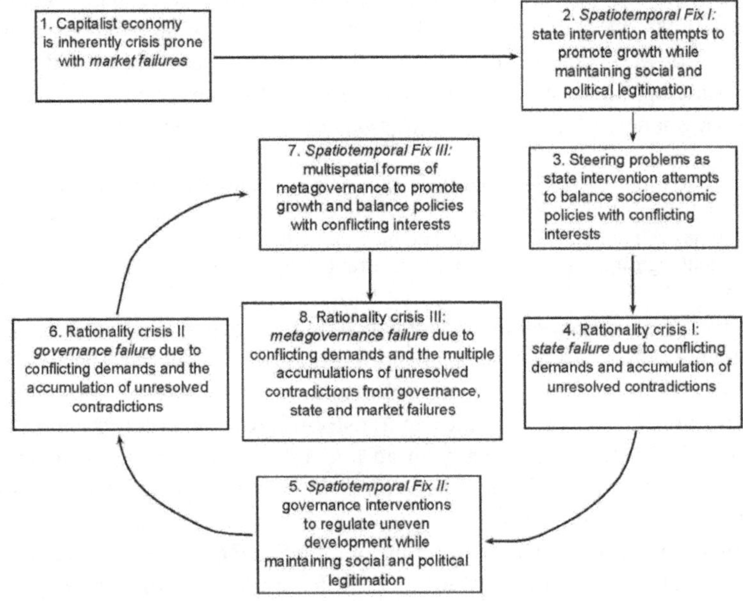


*Source:* Author's analysis.

*Figure 1.7 The geographical political economy of crisis spaces*

ment and territorial conflicts; problems of interscalar and inter-territorial coordination; democratic accountability and legitimation problems. For Fuller and Geddes, this gambit of regulatory problems and crisis-tendencies likewise revolves around:

> tensions between nation-state control of urban regulatory spaces and local autonomy and discretion; the challenges created by the focus on 'joining up' agents in urban spaces for purposes of addressing deprivation; and issues around the extent to which communities and citizens have the capacity to lead and influence governance arrangements within the context of devolved responsibility. (Fuller and Geddes 2008: 266)

The various chapters of *Cities and Regions in Crisis* provide empirical reflections on this 'crisis space' (Hadjimichalis 2018) in action. The solution to metagovernance failure is the state's ability to undertake, through further acts of spatial movement and geographical displacement, multispatial metagovernance (MSMG). According to Jessop (2016b), this recognises the complex, reciprocal, and interdependence of several spatio-temporal social fields that the state can draw on to frame its modes of intervention and policy-making capacities. The basis of this rests on earlier work with colleagues on the 'TPSN schema' (denoting the concepts of **t**erritory, **p**lace, **s**cale, and **n**etwork), which explored the interaction between these four spatial moments of social relations considered both as structuring principles and as fields of socio-spatial organisation (see Jessop et al. 2008). These moments of socio-spatiality, which seek to go beyond analysis of the state in one-dimension, can be combined to produce more concrete–complex analyses of particular socio-spatial configurations, tied to specific substantive relations and processes, and articulated in different kinds of state spatial strategy to intervene in the economy. Each socio-spatial organising principle, then, has its own forms of inclusion–exclusion and entails differential capacities to exercise state powers. This opens a strategic field in which social forces seek to privilege different modes of socio-spatial organisation to privilege their ideal and material interests. Moreover, strategies of crisis resolution involve attempts to reorder the relative importance of the four dimensions and their associated institutional expressions and, hence, to modify the weight of their role in displacing crisis tendencies and contradictions—*moving them around* as Harvey (2011) put it.

Table 1.1 accordingly summarises how *all* the spatial combinations have been used as sites for doing local and regional economic and social development over the past 40 years. A discernible shift can be noted, whereby: **p**lace–**p**lace state spatial strategies of the Victorian's localist era existed; **t**erritory–**p**lace strategies of the spatial Keyensian welfarist era replaced this regulatory fix; **p**lace–**n**etwork and **s**cale–**n**etwork forms of neoliberal state intervention were dominant the new localism and new regionalism; and **n**etwork–**p**lace state spatial strategies are the game face of the new new localism. This generalisation, though similar to other European experiences (see Piattoni and Polverari 2016; Bachtler et al. 2016), conceals some of the relativisation tendencies at work (see above). In terms of metagovernance, as the chapters of *Cities and Regions in Crisis* reveal, competing and rivalled socio-spatial strategies have existed and coexist. Attempts to collibrate the relative weight of the socio-spatial configurations, illustrated by the state project descriptions in these cells, have indeed failed to create a stable economic and social compromise—instead 'intensify[ing] uneven development, especially when declining regions are blamed for their own decline, required to make themselves attractive to capital based on mobilizing their own resources, or left to rot' (Jessop 2018: 7).

A lack of symmetry accordingly now exists between the 'spatial division of labour' (Massey 1984)—put simply, the geographical organisation of relationships on production and accumulation—and the 'spatial division of the state'—put simply, the relationships horizontally and vertically within and between forms of regulation and governance. Moreover, these two spatial

*Table 1.1 The multispatial metagovernance of economic development*

| | Structuring principles | | | |
|---|---|---|---|---|
| **Structuring fields** | **Territory** | **Place** | **Scale** | **Network** |
| **Territory** | Territorialisation of local authorities, creation of local state institutions (e.g. TECs, LEPs) | Management of uneven development, integrating places into a territory (e.g. Urban Programme) | Spatial Keynesianism, coordinating different scales (e.g. Regional/ Urban Development Policy) | Multi-area government and governance (e.g. Government Offices for the Regions, CAs) |
| **Place** | Land-based agencies with zonal-extent (e.g. UDCs, EZs, English Partnerships, URCs) | Designating towns and cities, contiguous regions and city-regions | Glocalisation, glurbanisation, urban–global interrelationships | Local, urban, regional governance partnerships (e.g. Single Regeneration Budget, City Challenge, LSPs, LAAs, MAAs) |
| **Scale** | Filling-in of administrative functions: Unitary, District, Borough institutions | Twinning arrangements, local–global linkages | Soft or fuzzy spaces, non-contiguous city-regions (Core City and Key City networks) | Nested or tangled scalar projects (e.g. RDAs, Regional Assemblies) |
| **Network** | Spatial Imaginaries, virtual, relational, and cross-border regions (e.g. Northern Powerhouse, Midlands Engine) | Polycentric cities and multi-city regionalism, deal-making policy (e.g. City Deals, Devolution Deals, Sector Deals) | Private international regimes, providers of state services (e.g. Work and Health Programme, Transport Infrastructures) | Fast-policy transfers, networks of networks (e.g. Business Improvement Districts) |

*Note:* TECs: Training and Enterprise Councils, LEPs: Local Enterprise Partnerships; CAs: Combined Authorities; EZs: Enterprise Zones; UDCs: Urban Development Corporations; LSPs: Local Strategic Partnerships; LAA: Local Area Agreements; MAA: Multi-Area Agreements; RDAs: Regional Development Agencies.
*Source:* Adaptation and application of Jessop et al. (2008: Table 2).

divisions are interrelated, as '[v]ariations in the role of the state are a result of a number of factors, including the structure of industry, administrative organization, and the character of the ruling political coalition' (Dunford and Perrons 1992: 391). Building on the notion of 'regulatory capacity', the state, then, is part and parcel of the coordination deficit dilemma of economic development as a result of a problem of 'territorial non-correspondence', as Cox (2008: 342) puts it—i.e. the desire and need to have competence, influence, and where control is out of reach and exceeded by capacities occurring at other territorial scales. The answer is not to seek a resolution through coterminous boundary drawing (cf. Ney 2017; HCLG 2018), but to challenge the fundamental spatial and geographical logic of the British growth model and the ways in which the forces of capital actively help to produce and reproduce combined and uneven development. The challenge to this has frequently come from those advocating new spaces of citizenship and belonging through the windows of state spatial restructuring. Chapters 6, 9, and 10 flesh out some of the opportunities for, and limits to, civil society place-attachments in the 'new regionalism' and 'new new localism' strategies, noting practices in the field of 'contentious politics' (Nicholls et al. 2013) within local and regional economic development.

## Brexit Impedimenta: Revenges of Uneven Development and Inequality

In summary, *Cities and Regions in Crisis* argues that the growth of neoliberal modes of intervention, driven by absorbing market failures into the state apparatus, which in turn leads to state and governance failures in new, and old, institutional and spatial forms (Figure 1.7) has led to an 'impedimenta state' (Jones 2010)—the capitalist state with accumulated ambivalence and disorientation, increasingly weighed down by policy journeys travelled in local and regional economic development. In situations of crisis-management, the best that policy-makers can hope for is a series of temporary and temporal 'crisis spaces' (Hadjimichalis 2018) of conflict solution, which can only stall crises for limited moments, as the accumulation of unsolved contradictions mounts up to impedimenta proportions. The state has baggage and is increasingly bag-like in its appearance, accumulated actions, and reactions. The trouble with bags, though, is that they demand to be filled, and impedimenta, like some parasitic virus, seem to rapidly replicate geographically. The evidence provided here points to the state carrying a rucksack or trailer of crisis legacies over time, which is getting heavier into coming years of policy-making. This is being derived from the state responding to problems caused by its own interventions, attempting to leave behind accumulated policy legacies, such that the state has become irrational and a site of, and for, bureaucratic ponderousness in and through administrative inertia and modes of negative coordination. As predicted 50 years ago, not dealing with this would result in problems of both 'state rationality' and a 'legitimation crisis' (see Chapter 3).

> The cohesion of societies … can be maintained only by an incoherent mixture of ideology, violence, pressure and repression. The authoritarian actions of the state cannot resolve either old or new contradictions; they try to evade their impact by reducing problems and possibilities. By utilizing for this irrational and

> specialized—i.e. reduced and reductive—activities, political action pretending to totality becomes itself reduced and reductive. This gives rise to new contradictions. (Lefebvre 1969: 136, emphasis removed)

The 23 June 2016 vote in Britain to 'Brexit' the European Union was in large part driven by those in distressed rust-belt post-industrial areas, disenfranchised within an impedimenta state 'geography of discontent' (Los et al. 2017) and lacking confidence in politicians and policy-makers to manage economy and society through the various rounds of industrial restructuring-induced economic development over the past 40 years. In Elliott's eyes:

> old industrial Britain is still suffering from the consequences of the closure of factories and pits three or four decades ago. These communities have higher levels of unemployment and higher concentrations of people on disability benefit, and have suffered much more grievously from government welfare cuts. Unsurprisingly, they were also strongly in favour of leave. North of the line that runs from the Severn estuary to the Wash, Brexit was the culmination of a 40-year process of de-industrialisation and casualisation of work. It was a protest about dead-end jobs, and about run-down communities being lorded over by London, talked down and bossed around. (Elliott 2017: 12)

This is the 'revenge of the places that don't matter' as Rodríguez-Pose (2018: 189) puts it, and this book's 'Postscript' discusses how this has been playing out in the Stoke-on-Trent city-region, which lends itself to a multi-causal analysis of crises (see also MacLeod and Jones 2018). British economic development does not have to be this way. Part IV discusses some alternative pathways to this crisis end-point by, first, engaging with contemporary analyses of inclusive growth and the place of civil society in Britain (Chapter 11). Chapter 12 discusses a 'negotiated' model of economic governance in Denmark, recalled from a period of silence with this kind of thinking in Britain (Etherington and Jones 2004a, 2004b), which I argue remains increasingly valid for addressing the contradictions of neoliberalism and the crises facing our cities and regions. Chapter 12 highlights how institutional, spatio-temporal, and semantic fixes work best when they connect different spheres, scales, and institutional sites of social action and have in-built sources of redundancy and flexibility that can be mobilised in the face of instability or crisis.

# PART I

# The new localism

# 2. Government and governance

## INTRODUCTION

This chapter undertakes four tasks. First, it offers an introduction to the regulation approach (RA). The RA, a distinctive form of evolutionary and institutional economics, is a continually developing heuristic framework that is being widely discussed in European social and political sciences. The RA places an emphasis on the role of institutions and networks in the governance of capitalism. In particular, it focuses more on the extra-economic dimensions to economic development, for example, the role of institutions and partnerships as coordination strategies or the role of urban entrepreneurialism in creating competitive advantages.

Second, the RA is used to provide an overview of the contemporary trends in local and regional economic development. To do this, the RA is extended through Jessop's (1993, 1994a, 1994b) idea of the Schumpeterian Workfare State (SWS). Under the SWS, economic development is associated with governance, in contrast to a Keynesian Welfare State (KWS) government. Governance is a way of conceptualising the growth of unelected local agencies and public–private partnerships that are being established alongside traditional forms of management undertaken by local government. This chapter argues that the contemporary period is one of economic govern*ance*, as opposed to economic govern*ment*. Third, the emergence of neoliberal *economic* governance in the United Kingdom is discussed. Fourth, two contrasting forms of UK economic governance are evaluated: a centrally imposed 'top-down' enterprise partnership, illustrated through Business Link in England, is contrasted with a nascent 'bottom-up' social economy-based partnership model popularised in Glasgow, Scotland. In conclusion, the RA is used to throw light on why these experiences differ.

## BASIC TENETS OF THE REGULATION APPROACH

The RA emerged from a particular strand of thinking in France during the early 1970s. Researchers at the Centre for Mathematical Economic Forecasting Studies Applied to Planning (Centre pour la recherche économique et ses applications—CEPREMAP) were faced with an especially interesting set of problems that could neither be resolved through conventional economic planning nor explained using existing theories of political economy. Between the late 1960s and early 1970s, the post-war economic consensus, based on Keynesian planning, structured international financial systems, and full employment, began to disintegrate. A new international division of labour was emerging (Dicken 1992), based on the rise of newly industrialising countries (NICs). Faced with the penetration of European and North American markets by NICs and with the collapse of the Bretton Woods regulated financial system, France, like many nations, experienced stagflation (the coexistence of unemployment and inflation) and internal problems in the mass production-based labour process. Despite attempts to resolve stagflation, Keynesian governmental intervention merely added to national economic instability.

Analysing this situation from a theoretical perspective, French regulationists faced two challenges. First, general equilibrium theory (more formally referred to as neo-classical economics) could not account for these changes. If neo-classical economics holds, Pareto-optimality occurs and markets achieve self-regulation. In theory, unemployment and inflation should not exist at the same time. This was obviously not the case (Boyer 1979).

Second, it was claimed that Marxism could not explain complex processes of change. The basic assumption of structural Marxism was that capitalist structures of exploitation and domination reproduced themselves automatically through the interlocking of different structural forms and their resulting restriction of capacity to challenge or change them. From this perspective, not only was the collapse of post-war full employment capitalism inexplicable but also economic policy-makers were bereft of power to change things. According to regulationists, the breakdown of stability could not be explained within this crude framework (Lipietz 1989). Faced with these dilemmas, the regulationists turned their attention to the roles played by economic institutions and societal networks at different spatial scales: local, regional, national, and supranational.

The RA offered an alternative analysis of economic change. Its starting point was simple: 'What forces transform the social system and guarantee its long-run cohesion?' (Aglietta 1979: 16). Addressing this question, Aglietta, the first regulationist, argued that socially embedded institutions and their networks were reconceptualised as a series of 'structural forms' (1979: 19), referring above all to the state, trade unions, and financial institutions. These dimensions were linked, in later regulationist work, to modes of regulation (Lipietz 1989). Using historical analysis, Aglietta (1979) claimed that periods of economic (and political) stability existed and were assisted by a matrix of different structural forms. More importantly, in certain historical periods, structural forms linked with complementary state economic policies and firm strategies to reproduce periods of economic growth. Regulationists call these phases 'regimes of accumulation' (Aglietta 1979: 68). This does not mean, however, that the RA is a reworking of functionalism. Regulationists, instead, are at pains to emphasise that institutions, networks, and partnerships are coupled with different economic policies through state intervention and policy experimentation. This process of 'structural coupling' (Jessop 1990a: 328) insists that regimes of accumulation are in fact 'chance discoveries' (Lipietz 1987: 15). Focusing historically on the US national economy, Aglietta (1979) identified five regimes of accumulation, each associated with structural forms and complementary economic systems. The most important and much documented of these, Fordism, occupied the post-war boom (1945–73) and was associated with mass production, mass consumption, and the urbanisation of North America and Western Europe (Scott 1988).

Various RAs have emerged (Jessop 1990b). Jones (1997b) discusses the emergence of three generations within regulation theory. The first generation focuses on the production process and its links with national economic development (Aglietta 1979). Second-generation regulation theory analyses international regulation and the relationships between nation-states. Boyer (1988: 74) deploys the concept 'mode of adhesion to the international regime' to describe this relationship. Links are apparent here with international regime theory and the international political economy.

Third-generation regulationism, used mainly by British and North American geographers (and sociologists), examines the uneven transitions of national (and more recently) local economies away from Fordism. Viewed theoretically, this transitory phase has led to different versions of the post-Fordist thesis: neo-Fordism, *after*-Fordism, flexible specialisation, flexible accumulation, and disorganised capitalism. These differing (and frequently conflicting) scenarios are not discussed here, as they have been debated at length by others (Amin 1994; Tickell and Peck 1992). Third-generation advocates prefer to move away from the focus of post-Fordism and, by using the term regulation approach (RA), they argue that the present period is one of experimentation—a search for a series of 'institutional fixes' at the local and national levels (Peck and Tickell 1994: 292). It is, therefore, more important to see the RA not as a theory systematic, but as a heuristic framework for analysing 'the institutional infrastructure around and through which capitalist development proceeds' (Peck and Miyamachi 1994: 643). This theme is developed further in the next section.

## APPLYING THE REGULATION APPROACH: SCHUMPETERIAN WORKFARE STATES

The explanatory power of the RA in the field of local economic development can be extended by linking it to neo-Marxist state theory (Jessop 1982). For example, Jessop (1994a: 252) suggests that the state and its intervention networks have a key role in the social mode of economic regulation through their involvement in helping secure conditions for capitalist economic growth and the reproduction of labour power. More importantly, in this context, Jessop (1993, 1994b) claims that there is a major transition underway from a KWS to a SWS and, more recently, to a Schumpeterian Workfare Regime (SWR). Combing RA and state-theoretical arguments, Jessop's notion of the SWS can be used to contextualise and explore how economic networks and partnerships work in various national settings.

Jessop's analysis stems from his reading of the KWS and its place within the Fordist regime of accumulation. The KWS underwrote the social reproduction of Fordism in four ways: (1) it managed aggregate demand and economic stability; (2) it underwrote competition policy, infrastructure development, transport, and housing; (3) it promoted full employment and big business; and (4) it managed social problems and generalised the norms of mass consumption through universal welfare rights and rising social expenditures (Jessop 1994a). Contrasting with KWS arrangements, the SWS is concerned with the promotion of 'innovation-driven structural competitiveness' in the field of economic policy (hence, Schumpeter) and the enhancement of flexibility and competitiveness in the field of social policy 'away from redistributive concerns based on expanding welfare rights in a nation-state towards more productivist and cost-saving concerns in an open economy' (hence workfare) (Jessop 1993: 18). It is too soon to suggest that the SWS will be equally as functional for post-Fordism as the KWS was for Fordism. Indeed, the two contrasting case studies will demonstrate some of the problems involved in making such a claim.

In the context of economic governance, the most important dimension to SWS is that shifts from the KWS are being accompanied by a fundamental spatial reordering, as the nation-state is progressively denationalised ('hollowed-out'). Drawing a parallel with the 'hollow corporation', hollowing out is associated with the displacement of power in three directions: (1) upwards to supranational states (for instance, the European Union); (2) outwards to international networks of local and regional states (in the example of the US–Mexico border trading arrangement); and (3) downwards to local states to facilitate a greater emphasis on economic regeneration and competitiveness (Jessop 1993: 28). Jessop cites 'new forms of local partnership' with their interests in enterprise policy, labour-market policy, venture capital, and technology transfer. Jessop (1994a: 272) adds that in 'this sense we can talk of a shift from local government to local governance'. Whereas the KWS scripted a role for local government as part of a 'local welfare state' (Cochrane 1994), the SWS encourages local competition via place-based partnerships between 'local unions, local chambers of commerce, local venture capital, local education bodies, local research centres and local states [who] enter into arrangements to regenerate the local economy' (Jessop 1994a: 272). In sum, downward shifts within the SWS give rise to a proliferation of local and regional economic initiatives involving a multitude of different governance arrangements.

To enable comparisons to be made in different local and national contexts, Jessop (1993: 32) identifies ideal-types of the SWS: The neoliberal, the neocorporatist, and the neostatist. These are pitched within different national contexts as ideal-type strategies, and Jessop stresses that it is unlikely that they will be found in their pure form, either locally or nationally. Indeed, 'elements of these strategies can certainly be combined. This can be at all levels of political intervention.' Briefly, the different SWS strategies are distinguished by the following (general) characteristics (from Jessop 1993, 1994a, 1994b).

The neoliberal SWS, which can be seen as a dominant trend in the United Kingdom and United States, is based on seeking flexibility through the liberalisation of market forces and, at the local level, the instigation of institutional competition. Neoliberalism rejects corporatist (social partnership) models; instead, it favours the incorporation of the private sector into governing coalitions and the support for organisations and associations drawing a majority representation from business sectors. This policy is frequently achieved through the commercialisation of welfare, the privatisation of state enterprises, and the empowering of employer-based organisations. This project is reinforced by ideological support for wealth creation through enterprise promotion. With respect to economic governance, the neoliberal SWS is best described as one of 'institutional Darwinism' (Jessop 1991: 155)—vigorous policy experimentation aimed at fostering innovation through inter-institutional competition.

The neocorporatist SWS, found in Denmark (Chapter 12), leans more towards the search for flexibility through the virtuous balancing of competition and cooperation. Neocorporatism favours selective social partnerships by delegating governance functions to intermediary organisations and ensuring links between private economic interests and arrangements to maintain a socially embedded, socially regulated economy. A process of monitoring to ensure regulated self-regulation, as well as decentralising power achieves this. Ideologically, neocorporatism rests on innovation through cooperation. With regards to economic governance, the neocorporatist SWS is best described as a 'negotiated' (Amin and Thomas 1996: 257) strategic development based on institutional pluralism and social solidarity.

The neostatist SWS, found in France, seeks flexibility through active structural policies and market guidance. Operating weak and very selective forms of corporatism, social partnerships are frequently subsumed by state-sponsored approaches to economic reorganisation. Neostatist practices, therefore, involve state-dictated targets relating to innovation systems, infrastructure development, technology transfer, and other mechanisms to achieve sectoral structural competitiveness. While the central state remains in control, neostatism offers concessions through some local and regional political autonomy. There is also an active role for business organisations such as chambers of commerce. With regards to economic governance, the neostatist SWS can be summarised as being 'dirigiste'—a centrally prescripted development focusing on a coherent and competitive industrial core (Betrand 1986: 99).

## THE NEOLIBERAL SWS: GOVERNANCE UNITED KINGDOM STYLE

It has been argued elsewhere that the United Kingdom is clearly a neoliberal variant of the SWS (Peck and Jones 1995). It exhibits the main features of privatised institutional Darwinism and the search for competitiveness based on the liberalisation of markets. The United Kingdom's transition from the KWS to SWS, like most, is complex and contradictory. The complementarity of accumulation and regulation during the Fordist era was far from stable. Because of failure to realise the virtuous circle of mass production and mass consumption, Jessop has argued that flawed-Fordism is an appropriate term to describe UK economic development during the period 1945 to 1973 (Jessop 1991, 1992). By contrast, during the period 1979 to 1997, it is possible to chart a line from government to governance, within economic development.

Elected in 1979, the Conservative Party, led by Margaret Thatcher, inherited an arrangement wherein local government was the formal (local) partner for central government's KWS (Geddes 1994). Local government was actively involved in the management of social economic development through housing, transport, and education policy. Local government also operated in tandem with (tripartite) central government-sponsored bodies such as the Manpower Services Commission (MSC), the National Economic Development Office (NEDO), and Industrial Training Boards (ITBs). These organisations, drawing their representation from the social partners (trade unions, employers, and local government), intervened on behalf of the central state in the social reproduction of labour power and planned economic growth. Economic regeneration, through (big business) industrial development, was carefully articulated with the redistributive mechanisms of regional policy. As noted in Chapter 1, by using Industrial Development Certificates (IDCs) and designating certain (declining) localities as Development Areas, local economies were prevented from overheating, and spatially targeted growth also meant that unemployment could be managed effectively within and between localities and regions (Gouge 1996).

During the 1980s, previous KWS strategies were gradually replaced by neoliberal policies. Regional Industrial Aid was gradually 'rolled back' (Martin 1986), and legislative attacks were continually launched on local government (King 1995). The Conservatives argued that the economy required 'single-minded organisations' slender and flexible enough to 'cut through red tape and press on with action' to create economic growth and national prosperity (Cabinet Office 1988: 5). Local government was presented as an 'overweight' organisation (Ridley 1988: 26), incapable, by virtue of its institutional forms, of 'firing the enthusiasm of local businesses, local leaders and local people: those who know the cities from the inside and have the will to change them' (Cabinet Office 1988: 5). Social economic, or people-led, regeneration was replaced by enterprise policies and strategies aimed at attracting inward investment.

The emergence of 'single minded organisations' within UK economic governance is a complex affair to describe (Jones 1999). Due to the historical weaknesses of chambers of commerce (Cochrane 1993; Jones 1996a; Peck 1995), central government attempted to bypass local government by creating new 'centrally sponsored local institutions' (Duncan and Goodwin 1988: 127)—phenomena also referred to as 'central government localism' (Martin 1989: 54). In the early days of Thatcherism, the Local Government Planning Act of 1980 empowered the Secretary of State for the Environment to designate Urban Development Corporations (UDCs), governed by private sector dominated boards, whose membership rested with central government appointments. By 1988, 11 UDCs had been created for Liverpool, London Docklands, Cardiff Bay, the Black Country, Teesside, Tyne and Wear, Manchester Trafford Park, Bristol, Sheffield, Leeds, and Central Manchester. UDCs were given the responsibility and funds to develop land in these localities and undertake infrastructure developments to maximise property accessibility (Gouge 1996). UDCs often reinforced commercial developments sponsored within Enterprise Zones (EZs). Under the 1980 Act, 25 EZs were created, mainly in inner-city areas, between 1981 to 1984. As UDCs and EZs had a strong presence in the large metropolitan areas, their closely defined contractual relationships with central government brought them into conflict with local government (Duncan and Goodwin 1988).

Under Thatcherism's 'radical' phase (1986–90), the 'single minded' principle was applied to the governance of training and enterprise policy. Following the abolition of the MSC—one of the last vestiges of the social partnership government era—and the returning of responsibility for manpower planning and skills needs to the Secretary of State for Employment under the 1989 Employment Act, 82 Training and Enterprise Councils (TECs) were created in England and Wales, and 22 Local Enterprise Companies (LECs) were established in Scotland (Training Agency 1989). Their institutional design was modelled after North American Private Industry Councils (PICs), established under the 1982 Job Training Partnership Act.

TECs and LECs were launched with a total budget of £3.0 billion to bring about a 'skills revolution' through the delivery of government-supported training programmes for the unemployed, investment strategies for up-skilling those in employment, and policies aimed at assisting the growth of small and medium-sized enterprises (SMEs). These institutions, like UDCs, mobilised the support of the private sector through boards that were also appointed by the Secretary of State. Reflecting a shift from KWS government to effectively privatised SWS governance, a material goal of TECs and LECs was to produce boards that were 'small, select and powerful. The employer lead is a key government objective: employers are wealth creators' (Main 1990: 87). As with the UDCs, this deliberate privatisation of training and enterprise, in the name of business (Peck and Jones 1995), created turf-battles with local governments (Emmerich and Peck 1992; Haughton et al. 1995; MacLeod 1996).

These two examples are merely an illustration of governance trends underway since the mid-1980s. UDCs and TECs are, more formally, part of a quasi-autonomous non-governmental or quango state, a term used in its broadest sense to capture the forever growing unelected local state. Other examples of quangos involved in UK economic governance include Housing Associations and City Action Teams (CATs). According to research undertaken by Hall and Weir (1996), the entire quango state receives £60 billion of annual state expenditure. Skelcher and Davis (1995), charting the emergence of this local 'privatism' (Barnekov et al. 1989), reveal that there are now some 50,000 internally appointed board positions—three times the number of elected councillors within local government. Davis and Stewart (1993: 8) previously referred to this movement from government to governance as being constituted around a 'new lay elite' and a 'new magistracy'—terms intended to capture the sweeping changes underway in the management of the local state from elected councillor to private sector appointee.

By the late 1980s, such was the bulging-unelected-local institutional scene that calls were made to bring some form of coordination (Robson 1988). The Audit Commission (1989), the body formed to improve public services in England and Wales, claimed that the resulting 'patchwork quilt' arrangement blurred responsibility and diluted proactivity. Accordingly, the 1990s became an era of 'governance by partnership' (Shaw 1993; Stewart 1994). Launching the partnership agenda, the Conservative Party's 1992 Election Manifesto, 'The Best Future for Britain', argued that, by forming local partnerships and subjecting local coalitions to competitive bidding, towns and cities would bring 'forward imaginative proposals for regeneration' (Conservative Party 1992). It is debatable whether partnership strategies were introduced in order to provide much needed local coordination. According to critics, 'top-down' partnerships are used as a mechanism for competitive bidding strategies, whereby public expenditure is gradually reduced by trimming the budgets of individual institutions (Robinson and Shaw 1994). DeGroot's (1992: 209) examination of City Challenge, the 'flagship of the government's new regeneration game', highlighted more local losers than winners. Local government received 'a proper strategic role', but at the same time competitive bidding put 'communities up against each other' (DeGroot's 1992: 208).

Discussing the emergence of the Single Regeneration Budget (SRB)—the recent extension of the City Challenge model to the entire realm of urban policy—Ward (1997: 1498) notes that this 'partnership strategy' is centrally prescribed, inflexible, and has been used to top-slice funds previously designated for targeted needs. Ward argues that for 'real flexibility there needs to be the real devolvement of power'.

The following sections contrast the implementation of Business Link (a 'topdown' forced, enterprise partnership model) in England with a 'bottom-up' more negotiated, social market regeneration model used in Glasgow, Scotland. These examples are then used to draw out two different models of the SWS, existing within the same national neoliberal context.

## CONTRASTING PARTNERSHIPS I: 'TOP-DOWN' BUSINESS LINK

Business Link is an excellent example of what Jessop (1995: 1620) has called 'fast policy'—a situation whereby rapidly constructed and prescriptive policy frameworks are forced into local areas by a central government mandate. The origins of Business Link can be traced to two central concerns in England. First, throughout the 1990s, central government has argued that small firms are the 'seed corn of our future prosperity' (Conservative Party 1992: 15) and are, therefore, the real growth machines behind local economic development. Faced by globalisation and a continually slipping performance in the world order of competitive nations, the agenda for economic governance is one of 'helping [the small firm] business to win' at all costs (HM Government 1994: 67).

Second, the Conservatives have always desired a power base in business-led local institutions through which to mobilise private sector energy to deliver support policies for SMEs (Jones 1999). According to the President of the Board of Trade, Michael Heseltine, 'Once the concept of powerful local chambers is accepted, a new horizon … of wealth creation … opens up' (Heseltine 1990: 123).

Rolling together this policy and institutional concern, Business Link was launched as the one-stop shop initiative in July 1992, with the central aim of creating a single integrated institutional partnership—a chamber of commerce substitute (Jones 1996b) in every local area—through which SMEs can obtain a wide range of business advice, consultancy, and information services. According to the Department of Trade and Industry (DTI) (1992: 7), the pre-existing business and advice services for small firms were associated with market-failure exhibited through 'customer confusion caused by the current profusion of agencies and services'. Claiming to offer a 'new deal', the Business Link partnership concept involves the pooling of resources and mergers to achieve 'organisational co-location'. Those to be involved in the partnerships are the TECs, local government business support units, chambers of commerce, and enterprise agencies. According to the DTI, this coherent framework replaces the '*clutter of the past*' and is thus seen as a coherent new mode of governing (1992: 7, emphasis added).

Helping business to win, at all costs, involved the establishment of 200 local Business Link outlets. At least one 'hub' and a series of five or more 'spoke' offices were required for each county-level local government unit. Failure to establish a Business Link would lead to the termination of DTI funding for SMEs. Local areas were 'invited' to bid for development funding from December 1992, with the expectation that a national network would be established by the end of 1995. The first 15 partnership pilots were launched in early 1993 and further 57 areas were later approved. Progress after this date was slow, marred by complex local political struggles between the various partners, who were proving reluctant to form a single organisation. The Secretary of State, Michael Heseltine, frustrated at not being on track for creating 200 Business Links by late 1995, told delegates at Birmingham Chamber of Commerce's 1994 annual conference: 'You cannot allow yourselves to be seen as watching on sidelines like a pack of vultures waiting to make a hearty meal of the carcass ... Do not let sentiment and parochial feelings prevent you from doing what you know to be right for our business' (quoted in Bassett 1994: 21).

As with any new policy, Heseltine's comments can be interpreted as a reaction to inevitable 'teething problems' (Ernst & Young 1996; Institute of Directors 1996). Events after June 1994, however, confirmed that cracks were developing in the Business Link model, brought on by the duplication of existing enterprise support services and the issue of long-term funding, putting the whole notion of a partnership at threat and raising the deeper issue of policy and governance failure taking place through state intervention.

The Business Link tracking study found that when seeking advice, most SMEs went to 'their accountant, bank manager or solicitor', all agencies excluded from the Business Link network (MORI 1994: 3). The fragmentation of business support is, therefore, perhaps not a problem and could be seen as a locally embedded strength (Jones 1996b). Additionally, when Business Link was launched, pump-priming funding was promised for a limited period, after which partnerships were to be self-financing. The argument was that a substantial level of funding was required to construct and maintain new, purpose built, offices. It was announced in 1994 that the pump-priming period would only last three years. This created tensions within partnerships, with individual partners feeling uneasy about the prospect of relinquishing their identity in favour of a single structure, which would be forced to earn its financial upkeep by charging for services on a commercial basis. Questioning the viability of the Business Link network after the pump-priming period, the DTI's (1995: 7) own internal auditors argued that 'the assurance which we are able to give is accordingly limited'. Based on this report, the press added that Business Link was '*a monster* that will come to haunt its creator' (Wood and Hamilton-Fazey 1995, emphasis added).

The tension of imposing a top-down partnership model, in and through which to deliver a set of prescribed policy responses, has created what can only be described as havoc at the local level (Jones 1996b, 1996c). Less than a year after opening, Business Link Merseyside has been the subject of much controversy. When launched, Business Link Merseyside was one of the more expensive in England, costing £3 million a year to run, employing 61 staff in four offices, and requiring a £1.143 million grant from the DTI to pump-prime the partnership. Due to financial problems resulting from a low-level of SME activity (indicative of an area with unemployment problems and low entrepreneurial demand for support services) and a payment system based on output-related funding (that encourages the scope for the manipulation of targets and fraud), central government clawed back a six-figure over-claim. Fearing insolvency, the Business Link board called in insolvency experts. Merseyside TEC was forced to bail out the Business Link at a cost of £515,174 (Jones 1996b).

The Merseyside case is not an isolated incident. In November 1996, an estimated £600,000 was missing from Wirral Business Link—only three months after the government-approved board accredited it. Again, this locality suffers problems of economic inactivity, resulting from the restructuring of port-related industries, and is predicted to have more problems when its pump-priming funds are withdrawn (Wighton 1996). At the same time, internal issues came to a head in Sheffield, an area renowned for local government proactivity in economic development (Wagstyl 1996). Frustrated at the inability of partners to come together as one, the chief executive resigned, claiming, 'The partnership challenge in Sheffield is that business support organisations finally deliver the partnership which they claimed was in place in 1994 when they set up our Business Link. Why has it taken nearly two-and-a-half years to realise they are to blame for the current confusion?' ('Why I'm quitting', 4 December 1996). Hayman captures these governance tensions:

> The former director of Sheffield City Council's Department of Employment added, Business Links, set up as the one-stop shop brainchild of Michael Heseltine are suffering all the problems of organisations which have been rushed into action with

> unreal expectations of what they can do … It should therefore be no wonder that there is continued lobbying for position by those with power, seeking to meet the interests of their own organisation, even though the marketing rhetoric pretends otherwise. In order to stand any chance of being an economically successful city in the 21st century Sheffield cannot afford such play acting about partnership and working together … It should be the role of the City Council as Sheffield's elected local government, to convene an independent panel to report on how those needs are best met. (Hayman 1997: 6)

A similar cloud of confusion surrounded the future of Business Link Staffordshire. From its inception, Staffordshire TEC invested heavily in Business Link. During 1993–94, £500,000 was allocated for one-stop shop development. This decreased to £290,000 for 1994–95. Business Link Staffordshire accounts for 1995–96 reveal that the County Council (along with the TEC and other partners) spent a further £1.486 million—£990,000 in cash and £496,000 in kind (Business Link Staffordshire 1996). Staffordshire County Council also invested £1.1 million in the infrastructure of a Technology Park and Innovation Centre, which was to house the Business Link headquarters, the county's own business support staff, and a series of university-backed high-tech research outlets, with Staffordshire TEC providing funding for marketing (*The Business* 1994). During 1995–96, the DTI allocated a pump-priming grant of £305,300. In sum, total investment exceeded £3 million. Staffordshire's Business Link network was finally established in July 1995, consisting of a 'central hub' (Stafford) and seven locally based 'spoke' offices (Stafford, Cannock, Burton-upon-Trent, Lichfield, Leek, Stoke, and Tamworth).

In December 1996, in an attempt to reduce Business Link Staffordshire operating costs and shift resources to front-line business advisors, it was announced that four offices were to be closed (Burton, Lichfield, Leek, and Tamworth). The Business Link headquarters was forced to quit the Innovation Centre. Business Link Staffordshire chief executive, Jennifer Carley, stated in the press, 'There is nothing gone wrong. It's just a case of when Business Links were set up, we felt in Staffordshire a very local service was needed … What we have discovered is that we don't need this local service' (Curry 1996: 3).

Although Staffordshire, perhaps, did not need this centrally imposed partnership, the restructuring of support mechanisms had serious implications for the County Council's enterprise creation agency—the Staffordshire Development Association (SDA). Due to DTI self-funding expectations, the partners decided to channel all future funding through Business Link in order to minimise further losses and sustain DTI funding for SME services. Within this framework, the SDA was left without a role. Despite a longstanding and credible relationship with the County Council and the local business community, the SDA was closed in April 1997. Limited by the 20 per cent local authority ownership restrictions imposed by the 1989 Local Government and Housing Act (Hayton 1989), direct local authority involvement in business services was predicted to cease. The new TEC-dominated Business Link partnership model has long-term implications for the local accountability of business support services, which is picked up in subsequent chapters. Under this top-down model, there is limited scope for grassroots participation and local democratic involvement.

## CONTRASTING PARTNERSHIPS II: 'BOTTOM-UP' SOCIAL ECONOMY

Top-down institutional reform to provide a central network for knowledge-dissemination, which supposedly benefited local economies through SME-activated, 'trickle-down' growth to 'give us the higher standard of living we all seek' (HM Government 1995a: 203), is not the only model available. There are alternatives and all is not gloom in UK economic governance. As a pretext to discussion of examples of bottom-up partnerships, it is perhaps worth taking stock of research undertaken in the United Kingdom, which reveals that 'trickle-down' does not secure social and economic cohesion (Robson et al. 1994), and the pursuit of growth strategies solely through small firms (Curran and Blackburn 1994; Hughes 1996) is not a sustainable policy. During the same period that Business Link dealt with over 100,000 inquiries for assistance (DTI 1996), 41,107 SMEs went out of business (Bowley 1996: 4). Learning from these centrally orchestrated mistakes, bottom-up models use these arguments as their starting point for an alternative solution. According to Robinson and Shaw (1991: 71), 'The challenge of the 1990s is to ensure that the distributional questions of "who benefits" (and who should benefit) are placed at the forefront of the debate.'

These words have been put into practice through the 'social economy' partnership model. In stark contrast to the argument that the free-market and private sector dominated partnerships are wealth creators, social economy proponents advocate a role for economic governance rooted in communities (McArthur and McGregor 1991). According to Wilson (1995: 3), the 'social economy' includes more than just the voluntary sector, as it also encompasses cooperatives, mutual and friendly societies, voluntary organisations, and local authority trading companies. These sectors are distinctive because they are independent from the state, have a concern for human development, offer democratic structures, and practice non-profit distribution. In terms of their value-added, social economy proponents claim that this sector can meet the needs for services and products not provided by the private sector and, more importantly, by filling this gap, sustainable jobs can be created (Simmonds and Emmerich 1996: 12–13). Examples of socially useful work include housing improvements, energy and security projects, urban forestry, and local exchange and trading systems (LETs). This does not mean that privatism is bunk, or that the social economy is 'a magic solution' (Grimes 1996: 1) for economic governance. The social economy should be seen as complementary to the market economy, aimed at achieving a negotiated form of economic governance. Community participation goes hand in hand with private sector energy to achieve partnership 'synergy' (Macintosh 1992: 213).

Social market principles are not an idealistic fantasy. The Wise Group in Glasgow, Scotland, has demonstrated that the social market, in practice, can be harnessed to achieve local results. According to Grimes (1996: 3) of the Wise Group, 'Though the Wise Group is an independent company it has always been that rare thing, a genuine partnership between the local authority, other local economic agents, the Scottish Office, European and local communities. This has taken time to build up but has paid dividends.'

The Wise Group started life as the Scottish Neighbourhood Energy Action Project (SNEAP), a voluntary organisation formed in 1983 to tackle the particular problems of damp housing in Glasgow's 40,000 populated (declining) Easterhouse estate. In partnership with Glasgow District Council, SNEAP secured funding to offer tenants free draft-proofing and insulation services. This service grew through further partnerships with the MSC and with a plentiful supply of labour offered by the MSC's Community Programme (a temporary job creation programme).

In 1987, SNEAP became Heatwise. Then Heatwise, in turn gave birth to Landwise, which was established to rejuvenate open spaces into recreational areas. With further financial assistance from the Glasgow Development Agency (GOA), Treewise was established to develop an urban forest. Other Wise subsidiary companies include Wise Recycling (for glass recycling) and Commercially Wise (a consultancy service). In terms of material achievements, working with Glasgow City Council, GOA, and local communities meant that, by 1995, 120,000 homes had been draft-proofed, 30,000 properties had security and smoke detectors, 500,000 trees had been planted, and 10,000 tons of glass had been collected. In 1995, the total Wise Group turnover was £13.7 million, a quarter of which was generated commercially. This success allowed the expansion of the group into other locations: Wellwise (Motherwell), Newham Wise (East London), and a Wise Group franchise—Routes to Work (Derby) (PA Cambridge Economic Consultants 1996).

The Wise Group's material achievements—improving the quality of life in Glasgow through environmental and energy savings projects—have been matched by their record in creating sustainable employment for the long-term unemployed. During the mid-1990s, the Wise Group was acknowledged as the developer of the Intermediate Labour Market (ILM) model. Whereas the majority of job-training programmes in the United Kingdom (since the mid-1980s) have enforced a workfarist behaviour discipline on the unemployed, through 'trainingfare' (the requirement that trainees have to train for their benefit (Jones 1996d)), the Wise Group has combined the social economy with the labour market to produce the ILM.

Defined in its simplest terms, the ILM offers paid jobs to unemployed people, for a limited period of time, on the understanding that their work has a direct social purpose and/or is work that would not normally be undertaken (Commission on Social Justice 1994). The ILM, therefore, is not an artificial 'make work' training scheme, displacing the activities of other organisations in the area, but instead, it networks with the social economy to provide 'quality projects' (Finn 1996: 29). During their participation within the ILM, trainees are paid the rate-for-the job. After an initial eight-week trial period, during which participants are paid their benefit plus £10, a wage of between £115–£120 per week (for up to 44 weeks) is allocated. Using this model within the various Wise Group subsidiaries, over 5,000 people have received not only socially useful training, but also relevant experience leading to long-term jobs (over 50 per cent). The Wise Group estimates that the gross cost per job is around £14,100. This includes wages, staff costs, training costs, and all overheads. However, allowing for savings in unemployment benefits, increased taxation (direct and indirect), national insurance, ongoing energy savings, and the value of environmental works (totalling some £16,035), the ILM is, to quote Grimes (1996: 3), 'a modest proposal'. Grimes adds, 'Creating jobs for local residents without providing the right physical environment simply means that those getting employment will leave the area for a better one and [this] creates the same spiral of decline. The advantage of the Wise Group model is that it does both, and at a scale that can make an impact in an area' (Grimes 1996: 3).

There is substantial interest in transferring the ILM model to unemployment black spots throughout the United Kingdom (Bewick 1996) as an alternative to the Conservatives' appropriation of North American-style (work-first) workfare, masquerading in England as the Jobseekers Allowance (JSA) and Project Work. These schemes, based on a combination of both compulsory temporary community-sector work experience and compulsory job search activities, add little value to the community and, instead, fuel the expansion of contingent service-sector labour markets, exert downward pressures on the local wage level, and prevent the building of constructive community-based partnerships (Peck 1996).

Glasgow Works, a partnership involving some 25 public-and private-sector agencies, has piloted the idea of transferring unemployment benefits to the local level to achieve matched funding for social economy projects. According to evaluations, 56 per cent of participants take up a job, education, or further training (Finn 1996). Enthused by these results, the Labour Party, in opposition since 1979, plans to make the ILM a national programme through their 'Neighbourhood Match' scheme (Labour Party 1996a). There is, of course, the real danger that making a bottom-up model national and then forcing all areas to adopt a prescribed framework, falls into the pitfall and dilemmas experienced by Business Link.

## CODA: REGULATIONIST REFLECTIONS ON ECONOMIC GOVERNANCE

Contrasting two different models of economic governance within the same national SWS context raises some interesting issues for the regulationist perspective. To date, the RA has tended to hang its claims on national-level 'structural couplings'—between policy and institutions—thereby limiting the scope for different local ways of searching for *after*Fordist solutions to the economic growth crisis (Jones 1997b). There may be, of course, political reasons for the claim that national stability is key to economic growth. As CEPREMAP had a privileged position with the French policy-making system throughout the late 1970s and early 1980s, *dirigiste* neostatism necessitated national-level strategic coordination. The 1980s' Mitterrand experiment of state nationalisation, much influenced by CEPREMAP thinking, however, proved unsuccessful in a largely neoliberal European climate (see Costello et al. 1989).

This chapter has suggested that spatial variations in economic governance are important to the search for a sustainable 'institutional-fix'. This is not to deny that national and supranational strategic coordination are important ways to proceed. Stability is, however, a 'chance discovery' involving trial and error (local) experimentation. Geography is, therefore, important as a window through which to view local struggles over different forms of economic governance.

Using Jessop's meso-level approach, Business Link can be seen as an interesting hybrid of neoliberal and weak neostatist forms (in rhetoric) of the SWS. Between 1979 to 1990, under Thatcher, the Conservatives clearly pursued a neoliberal economic policy, letting markets proceed and institutional Darwinism prosper. The Major period, 1990 to 1997, and the re-emergence of Heseltinomics involved the struggle between neoliberalist free-market marketing and elements of a neostatist involvement for government (enterprise) policy with regards to state-directed market information. Little wonder, then, that Heseltine continually clashed with the Conservative right over the changing role of the DTI (Lorenz and Smith 1992: 7).

Business Link, an attempt to reverse the history of UK local business politics, is clearly a search for a chamber of commerce substitute. Where business politics are locally embedded, a modified one-stop shop model could be successful. In the main, however, top-down Business Link falls into the holes on the map of private sector mobilisation in the United Kingdom. More bottom-up governance partnerships, constructed through the social economy, offer an interesting theoretical contrast. The ILM can be seen as an attempt to formulate neocorporatism at the local level. The social economy contains a different set of actors and institutions to the free market, and there are different possibilities for local intervention. The Wise Group has clearly played an important role in the rejuvenation of Glasgow, and it is no wonder that the ILM model has raised local and national hopes. Perhaps future economic governance strategies should be based on a mix of different local approaches?

# 3. Urban crisis and contradiction

The first essential is a specific commitment on the part of central and local government to the regeneration of the inner cities. The publication of this White Paper marks the Government's commitment to play its part ... At the end of the day the test of success *will be the improvement achieved in the conditions of life of the people living in the inner areas.*

(HMSO 1977: 6, emphasis added)

The failure of the many attempts ... to tackle the problem of inner city decline successfully is striking ... [I]t is noticeable that large sums have been spent to *little apparent effect.* The underlying national economic decline is no doubt one important reason ...

(Scarman Report 1981: 101, emphasis added)

There is, of course, *nothing new* in urban change. Throughout our history towns and cities have risen and fallen only to rise again ... All too many have had their *problems intensified* by misguided post-war planning and development which had the best of intentions but the direst results for the people living there ... We are embarked on a great enterprise which will leave its mark on Britain for decades and carry our towns and cities into the 21st Century in *much better shape.*

(Margaret Thatcher, in Cabinet Office 1988: 2, emphasis added)

[I]n the twenty years since the last Urban White Paper, many of our towns and cities have suffered from neglect, poor management, inadequate public services, lack of investment and a *culture of short-termism.* Previous governments *failed* to stem urban decline because they only addressed *part* of the problem, and ignored the *underlying causes* ... In contrast to the past, we are adopting *long-term policies* which address economic, social and environmental need *together* ... Our aim is to ... deliver a *lasting urban renaissance.*

(John Prescott, Deputy Prime Minister, in DETR 2000a: 5, emphasis added)

This instability, I wish to stress, is something that no amount of state interventionism can ensure (indeed, it has the habit of *generating all manner of unintended consequences out of seemingly rational state policies*). Capitalist development must negotiate a knife-edge between preserving the value of past commitments made at a particular place and time, or devaluing them to open up fresh room for accumulation. Capitalism perpetually strives, therefore, to create a social and physical landscape in its own image and requisite to its own needs at a particular point in time, only just as certainly to undermine, disrupt and even destroy that landscape at a later point in time. The inner contradictions of capitalism are expressed through a relentless formation and re-formation of geographical landscapes. This is the tune to which the historical geography of capitalism must dance without cease.

(Harvey 1985a: 150, emphasis added)

## INTRODUCTION

This chapter begins with five quotes that set the scene for an analysis of how successive British governments have conceived of, and set about solving, the 'urban problem'. So I start with the watershed statement made by the UK Labour Government in its 1977 White Paper *Policy for the Inner Cities*—which outlined for the first time a localised and urban-based solution to the problems of Fordist–Keynesian (urbanised) accumulation and its regulation—before moving on Lord Scarman's insightful observations after the 1981 Brixton riots that were tempered by cross-references to the overall state of the economy, Thatcher's 1988 clarion call for rebuilding cities with an enterprise revolution in *Action for Cities*, and, most recently, New Labour's (*Urban Renaissance*) 2000 White Paper pledge to re-energise the cities through an improved urban environment, increased public participation, and an integrated urban policy framework.

In unpacking these quotes, two of which are drawn from 'landmark' White Papers, in Britain at least it appears that the so-called 'urban problem' persists. Indeed, despite 25 years of experimentation, if anything the 'urban problem' is becoming *more* deeply entrenched. Britain's cities remain centres of low economic activity, possess high (but at times hidden) unemployment and welfare dependency, contain large areas of physical dereliction, and are witness to increased crime and social disorder (compare Danziger 1996; Harrison 1983; Pacione 1999; Turok and Edge 1999). Such concerns were evident during 2001, when several of England's Northern cities were the sites of a number of 'race riots', the scale of which had not been seen for two decades. Although racial tension is undoubtedly an influence in Oldham, Bradford and Burnley, significant connections do exist between ethnicity and poverty (Home Office 2001). In each, the numerous 'rounds of regeneration' (Ward 1997, 2000) since the late 1970s have only had a marginal impact on local economies that have been subjected to intense economic restructuring and now face a depressing post-industrial landscape of deepening inequalities and entrenched social polarisation.

This chapter interprets the current British urban dilemma as a contemporary expression of a much longer history of urban crisis-management. It supplements those studies that evaluate urban policy on its own terms (Atkinson and

Moon 1994; Blackman 1995; Lawless 1986; Robson 1988; Robson et al. 1994) and considers why, and in what ways, particular problems are constructed, and the processes through which spatial scales and regulatory mechanisms become codified as the solution to such problems. It considers this to be important not only to *explain* the inability of British urban policy to make a difference. It is imperative that at this particular historical juncture—in light of ongoing neoliberalisation and the qualitative shifts in the role of the nation-state (on which see Brenner and Theodore 2002a)—I understand the *wider* logic at play in designing and implementing programmatic blueprints. The chapter argues that it is academically and politically essential to draw attention to how seemingly unconnected processes of state restructuring and policy formation are in fact differentiated outcomes of ideologically infused political decision-making that *cannot* be separated from the inherent contradictions of capital accumulation.

In this spirit of political economy—'one of the most urgent tasks confronting economic geographers' today (Martin and Sunley 2001: 155)—the chapter attempts to get *inside* the machinery of British urban policy. Situating contemporary urban policy within the wider context of the ongoing *neoliberalisation* of British cities, it argues that British urban policy since the 1970s has been increasingly neoliberalised across a number of spatial scales (for alternative explanations see Eisenschitz and Gough 1993; Gough and Eisenschitz 1996a, 1996b). These issues are explored by arguing that crisis theory provides a lens for explicitly excavating the regulatory logic of neoliberal urban policy. Less concerned with trying to understand the 'new language and concepts of urban and social policy' (Harloe 2001: 896), important as this is, I am more interested here in *interpreting* such discourses and strategies.

In contrast to Marxist and regulation theory readings of crisis, which (to varying degrees) have a tendency to read off institutional and policy development from the economic logic of accumulation (see Chapter 2), this chapter argues that, despite limitations, there remains considerable mileage in notions of political crisis found in the work of Habermas and Offe. As the chapter is concerned with developing a conceptual framework to inform our understandings of the capitalist state, it suggests that re-reading British urban policy through the lens of the Frankfurt school provides the basis for formulating a 'fourth-cut' theory of crisis—extending the unfinished project of David Harvey (especially, 1982, 1985a, 1989, 1999, 2000) on the geographical displacement and reconfigurations (or 'spatial fixes') of capitalist crisis formation and resolution. It is for this reason that the chapter includes the fifth quote, which draws particular attention to the ways in which the state is embroiled in, and contributes to, the crisis of capitalism—thereby connecting with the urban policy statements that precede it. As part of this 'fourth-cut' project, the chapter offers three arguments that extend the regulation approach, discussed in Chapter 2, and capture the timely and important events taking place within Britain's cities (that also have regulatory origins and echoes in North American and Western European Cities):

1. At a general level, under neoliberalism the contradictions and irrationalities of capitalism are being 'intensified' and 'exacerbated' in and through state interventions at a number of different spatial scales (cf. Lojkine 1976; Poulantzas 1978: 215). It is the form and function of the state as 'problem' that I explore in this chapter.
2. Given that urbanisation is an integral feature of late capitalist accumulation (DETR 2000a; Harvey 1985b; Rees and Lambert 1985), under neoliberalism cities are being presented *both* as the sites of, and the solutions to, various forms of crisis (cf. Begg 1999; Clarke and Gaile 1998; Brenner and Theodore 2002b; Jessop 2002b; Peck and Tickell 2002), often simultaneously, as the 'left' and the 'right' hand of the state fail to work together (Bourdieu 1998).
3. In undertaking this crisis-management role under neoliberalism (the site-and-solution relationship), Britain's cities are host to regulatory responses to the contradictions created by *previous* state-led interventions: in other words the state's *own* contradictions, and not the economic contradictions of capitalist accumulation. The British neoliberal urban condition represents an actually existing example of the 'crisis of crisis-management' (Offe 1984). The design and rolling-out of urban policy is frequently associated with discursively constructed and institutionally mediated crises, and these are diffused, albeit *temporarily* but at the same time continuously and serially, through a centrally orchestrated reorganisation of the policy area and/or a reworking of the state apparatus, only to *reappear* at a later date and require 'new' urban policies that in turn create *further* contradictions and crisis.

The chapter's aim is to establish a framework for analysing contemporary variants of urban neoliberalism. This makes it necessary to reconsider the connections that exist between capitalism, crisis, the state and the city, and urban policy formation—topics that have previously been discussed *separately* (see Gottdiener 1986, 1987; Gottdiener and Komninos 1989; Gurr and King 1987; O'Connor 1973). This conceptual agenda is explored by examining the links between neoliberalism, urban policy, and Britain's cyclical and crisis-prone cities through three themes: the regulatory and scalar geographies of the state, marketisation and the institutionalisation of inter-urban competition and rationalisation as the 'crisis of crisis-management'.

## CAPITAL, LIMITS, AND THE LIMITS TO HARVEY

The term 'crisis' appears to capture a moment of disruption and transformation. It is associated with periods of both destruction *and* creation (compare Boyer 1990; Harvey 1982; Hay 1996; O'Connor 1973, 1987; Smith 1990). Because notions of crises are analogous with the existence and 'metamorphosis' of capitalism, orthodox accounts tend to be found within Marxist political economy. This takes both the economic imperatives and resulting contradictions of accumulation as its starting point (Marx 1919). Indeed, for Harvey (1985b: 11, emphasis added) crises '*are* the real manifestation of the *underlying* contradictions within the capitalist process of accumulation'.

Volume 3 of Marx's *Capital* contains the genesis of a Marxist theory of crisis. In it 'mono-causal' (Mandel 1981) accounts are replaced by three explications that have been deployed to explore changes in profitability, economic growth, and the business cycle (compare Clarke 1994; Mattick 1981; Smith 1990; Webber and Rigby 1996; Wright 1978; Yaffe 1973). First, in his epigrammatic and at times scattered writings on accumulation and its crisis, Marx draws attention to a 'theory of the falling rate of profit'. This suggests that if the rate of economic growth exceeds the size of the labour force wages will rise. To counteract this, and the associated strong bargaining position of labour, capitalists invest in machinery (depending on available technology). This invariably leads to an increased composition of capital, a tendency towards over-production, and a shrinking of profits (the crisis) *if* exploitation does not occur at the same time. Second, Marx draws attention to the problem of 'under-consumption', whereby a gap exists between output (as productive capacity) and mass consumption (defined by wages as purchasing power). Here, the capitalist crisis of over-production triggers over-capacity in commodities and a corresponding circle of declining investment. Third, there is the more provocative 'over-accumulation' theory, built on value theory, that suggests crisis is linked to a deficiency in the production of surplus-value as a share of accumulated capital (i.e. a lack of profit) and the resolving of this (and also the law of the tendency of the rate of profit to fall (LTRPF)) involves class-based exploitation of labour, which in turn is predicted to sow the seeds of capitalist self-destruction through the intensification of class struggle.

Familiar ground, perhaps, but required reading because it provides the entry-point for Harvey's critique of Marx's *Capital*, which I now turn briefly to discuss. In *The Limits to Capital* Harvey (1982, 1999) undertakes a Marxist-based geographical extension of political economy. This is latterly deployed to understand urbanisation, urban change, and advanced capitalism in general (see Harvey 1985a, 1985b, 1989, 2000). It is perhaps the most systematic and rigorous attempt to develop a value-theoretic conceptualisation of accumulation, circulation, the built environment, and urban processes therein under late capitalism (compare Brenner 1998; Sheppard and Barnes 1990; Storper and Walker 1989). Here I concentrate on Harvey's proposition that capitalism can temporarily *resolve* (contrary to Marx's predictions) its internal (economic) contradictions and in-built crisis tendencies through processes of 'switching' (Harvey 1982, 1985a) or practices of 'displacement' (Hay 1996; Jones 2001). This is, in turn, necessitated by a simultaneous search for 'structured coherence' (Harvey 1985b)—a term that Harvey uses to capture (beyond Marx's analysis) the roles played by a myriad of socioeconomic, political, and cultural 'infrastructures' in the 'spatial fixing' of crisis (Quilley and Ward 1999). Notions of crisis, therefore, remain central to understanding the ebb and flow of capitalism and the (temporary) stabilisation of its inherent contradictions (Harvey 1999).

The foundational principles of Harvey's crisis theory suggest that capitalism's internal logic can be explored through three different but interrelated windows or 'cuts', which offer different takes on the inner structure and operation of capitalism and only by moving from one window to the next can the *whole* be explained. The three cuts are, therefore, presented as 'distinguishable but simultaneous *co-present* moments within the internal contradictions of capitalism' (Harvey 1999: xxiv, emphasis added). Each cut has its own dynamics and can be analysed in relation to its own inherent *contradictions*.

Because permanent crisis is said not to exist, Harvey begins by interpreting conflicts between labour and capital (captured through Marx's law of falling profits) as his 'first-cut' theory of crisis. This is said to capture 'the underlying source of capitalism's internal contradictions' (Harvey 1982: 425) and presents itself as number of 'partial crises' (1985b: 12). These can be temporarily resolved through exploiting, amongst other things, the reserve army of labour—a process that is much aided by industrialisation going hand-in-hand with urbanisation and the built environment's material infrastructure (Harvey 1985a)—by reorganising production within a given sector, or by reallocating capital across sectors ('sectoral crisis switching') to restore profitability. Harvey builds on this proposition to suggest a 'second-cut' theory of crisis, whereby the contradictions in production, outlined in Marx's writings on over-accumulation and devaluation, can be temporarily 'switched' through financial and monetary arrangements, or credit systems, that help to preserve capital for future, rather than present, use. Credit systems also address the problem of under-consumption by extending purchasing power. Developments in money thus signify systems of *temporal* crisis displacement, which is again assisted by the acceleration of urbanisation at beginning of the twentieth century (Harvey 1985b).

Working within this context, Harvey is perhaps best known for his 'third-cut' theory of crisis. This represents an ambitious attempt to integrate the geography of uneven development into the theory of crisis (1982: 425) and signifies the culmination of years of thinking on the processes of historical-geographical change. Whereas 'first-' and 'second-cut' theories are predicated on interpretations of time (or temporal rhythms) as mechanisms for crisis switching and crisis containment, 'third-cut' theory starts from the notion that (social) *space* represents a key force of, or 'moment within', production, and geographical reorganisation provides a *further* (temporary) mechanism for the resolution of crises (cf. Lefebvre 1976, 1991; Lipietz 1994). For Harvey, then, the inert nature of capitalist production and exchange can be bridged by exploiting uneven geographical development—which itself is an inherent product of the impacts of capitalism in and through time and space (Smith 1990). Within Harvey's 'third-cut', economic crises are 'switched' and the flows of capital and labour 'exported' through actively engaging a space economy that seeks out new spaces (for example nations, regions, locales, or suburban expansions) within a 'spatial rhythm' of accumulation. The production and utilisation of space thereby 'helps convert the crisis tendencies of capitalism into compensating regional configurations of rapid accumulation and devaluation' (Harvey 1982: 428), and in its wake the resolving of 'geographical switching crises' (Harvey 1985b: 13) builds and rebuilds a geography to reflect the time-specific image of capitalism (Harvey 2000: 54). Harvey, of course, stresses that new spatial arrangements can only be seen as *temporary*; if uneven development is not regulated at a number of different spatial scales '[i]nterrregional competition becomes the order of the day' (Harvey 1982: 427) and rather than containing crisis 'spatial configurations are [*more*] likely to contribute to the problem as resolve it' (1982: 429). This leads Harvey to modify Marx and predict a 'global crisis' that (in the case of the 1930s and 1970s) affects 'all sectors, spheres and regions within the capitalist production system' (1985b: 13).

Despite its lasting impact on human geography (and beyond) *Limits* does not offer a complete theory of the state (compare Brenner 1998; Clark and Dear 1984; Sheppard and Barnes 1990; Harvey 1978). This is acknowledged in the introduction to the Verso edition of *Limits*, where 'processes of state (and civil society) formation' remain 'major problems' because they have only been given a 'tangential rather than the *central positioning* they deserve' (Harvey 1999: xxvii, emphasis added). It is, however, inaccurate to say that Harvey ignores the state. His work is peppered with implicit theorisations of the capitalist state and *Limits* specifically contains several passages that present the variegated state as a key 'co-ordinating mechanism' actively involved in processes of mainly temporal, but also spatial, crisis switching (Harvey 1982: 448). And *Limits* also implies that states have the capacity, but not without a 'price', to internalise further through their apparatus and political arena the multiple contradictions of capitalist accumulation through governmental policy interventions in the urban and regional field (1982: 449; also 1985a: 150). Outside this slender analysis, the 'omnipresent' state and 'controversial subject[s]' such as intervention must await a 'full treatment' (1982: 448). *One* way of addressing this lacuna is to assemble a 'fourth-cut' theory of crisis around the state and the internalisation of the contradictions of accumulation through *mediation*. With this in mind, the chapter turns to examine the ways in which the regulation approach has grappled with crisis theory. This allows us to discuss the complex relationship between state intervention, mediation and accumulation.

## BETWEEN 'THIRD-CUT' AND 'FOURTH-CUT' CRISIS THEORY

The regulation approach revolves around a Marxian theory of capitalist development, which focuses specifically on the role of social, political, cultural and institutional structures in the problematic (social) reproduction of capitalism as a system, despite the inherent tendency towards forms of crisis. Starting from the assumption of the underlying (or necessary) contradictory tendencies inherent in the process of accumulation, its unique contribution rests on claims that capitalism does not possess its own 'self-limiting mechanisms' (Aglietta 1998: 49): instead research explores the regularisation or normalisation of economic life in its *broadest sense*. In turn, both Althusserian structuralism, with its notions of over-determination and the quasi-automatic reproduction of capitalism, and neo-classical economics, premised on a general equilibrium theoretic framework where markets can be normalised through self-regulation, are rejected.

Unlike more orthodox forms of institutional economics, regulationists retain the holistic Marxist framework in that 'structural forms' (Aglietta 1979), 'institutional forms' (Boyer 1990), 'modes of regulation' (Lipietz 1989), or 'modes of social regulation' (Tickell and Peck 1992) are seen to be the codification of social relations and derive ultimately from the commodity relation, the capital–capital relation, or the interaction of both in time and space. Regulationists consequently diverge from orthodox Marxism in that iron laws on the profit logic and/or technological progress are not the primary determinant of, or explanation for, (uneven) capitalist development. Because this elucidation is deemed guilty of reductionism, with its inability to move beyond trans-historical accounts to 'explain the specific features of [capitalism *within*] different countries and different periods' (Mazier et al. 1999: xxiv; see also Tickell and Peck 1992), regulationists stress the contingent coupling, which is always a process of fortuitous discovery, of accumulation systems (patterns of production and consumption within a macro-economic structure) *with* 'modes of regulation' (patterns of competition, the capital–labour relationship, money, the state and government intervention, and international economic relations) (MacLeod 1997). In this respect, then, modes of regulation act as 'mediating mechanisms' (Aglietta 1998) and regulation can be interpreted as a geographically specific set of regulatory 'processes' and practices (Painter and Goodwin 1995), revolving around key institutional sites, *such as cities*. And only when a relatively coherent phase of capital accumulation exists (where the inherent contradictions and crisis tendencies are temporarily internalised and stabilised) can modes of development exist, with attention being frequently paid to the post-war period of Atlantic Fordist accumulation that occupied the long-boom period (see Aglietta 1979).

According to Walker, the regulation approach (RA) offers an 'impoverished theory of growth and crisis' (1995: 169). It is worth pondering on this suggestion, which certainly has some validity if strict economic readings of crisis are followed. However, the RA is not restricted to the either economic analysis or accounts of Fordist stability therein. Instead, its power rests with the 'analysis of capitalism and its tranformation' where 'regulation and crises are linked as intimately as two sides of a coin' (Boyer 2001: 1, 2). This dual reading of the analysis and transformation of capitalism is an ongoing challenge for crisis theory.

Regulation theory identifies three initial and primary levels of crisis. Each one connects to the other and each stems from the intrinsic contradictions within capitalist accumulation and *not* its mediation. First, *micro crises* are identified. These affect individual capital units or branches of capital. These are 'partial' and constitute part of an ongoing process of adjustment that occurs within systems of accumulation. Second, *conjunctural* crises reflect a cyclical downturn in the economy, represented by recessions, and can be resolved within an individual regime of accumulation through modifications that affect spatial divisions of labour (such as 'geographical' or 'sectoral switching'). Third, regulationists specify *structural* crises that are terminal for regimes of accumulation and reflect the exhaustion of the prevailing institutional forms *and* accumulation systems. This can evolve into the 'global crisis' identified by Harvey (1985b), which can only be resolved by the fortuitous discovery of a new coupling between accumulation and regulation.

This reading of crisis, which is predominately focused on the accumulation system, needs to be considered alongside RA research that emphasises forms of crises in relation to the mediation of accumulation through the mode of regulation. For Boyer and Saillard (2001: 336), a crisis of the mode of regulation also exists if the mechanisms supporting accumulation 'prove incapable of overcoming unfavourable short-term tendencies, even through the regime of accumulation'. This has three characteristics: institutional forms are often eroded or destabilised by economic activity; the expectations of economic and politics actors are often incorrect or out-dated; and social conflicts can emerge to challenge the practices of regulation and economic management.

The RA has yet to fully engage in this latter reading of crisis. Outside the observation from Goodwin and Painter that 'regulatory process' can become 'an object of regulation in its own right' (Goodwin and Painter 1996: 638), non-economic readings of crisis require future consideration at both a conceptual analysis and empirical level. And because of its mainly economic reading of crisis, the RA is somewhat restricted as the basis for extending Harvey's three 'cuts'. At a general level, the RA has the tendency to insert an ontological divide between the economy, which is bracketed as a black box and simultaneously cast as a key protagonist, and the cultural and political realms. Following from this, although the RA provides an important bridge between Marxism and a nascent 'political economy of institutions' (MacLeod 2001a), because regulationists appear to be preoccupied with mobilising economic readings of crisis, ongoing developments within the extra-economic coordinating or mediating mechanisms of capitalism are frequently 'read off' from changes in the economy. Despite continual emphasis placed on contingency, this can lead to an inherent danger of presenting institutional processes, institutional practices, and institutional effects—all key questions concerning how institutions actually work—as functional to the needs of accumulation (compare Barnes 1996; Bonefeld and Holloway 1991; Cochrane 1993; Florida and Jonas 1991; Hay 1995; Jessop 1997a, 2001; Jones 1997b; Quilley and Ward 1999; Valler et al. 2000).

These well-documented limitations can, in part, be explained by the inability of the RA to adequately consider *transformations* within the regulatory mix or systems of regulation constituting the mode of regulation (cf. Goodwin and Painter 1996). Notwithstanding the emphasis placed on the need to incorporate socio-political struggle into the RA, there remains an inability to integrate theories of the state, which persist as stubborn 'missing-links' (Tickell and Peck 1992; compare Jessop 1997a). According to Boyer (1990: 41), the RA 'has not generally involved theories of the state … it has concentrated on characterizing various forms of the state and the effects that they have on economic dynamics'. This should not render crisis theories based on institutional mediation as somewhat 'redundant' (cf. Painter and Goodwin 1995). Instead, more thinking *is* required. The RA 'is not (and could never be) a total theoretical solution to *any* conceivable problem in political economy. In this sense it needs to be supplemented through concepts and causal *mechanisms* associated with *other* theoretical perspectives. Without this there is every likelihood that the RA will, indeed, appear overly simplistic, economistic, and functionalist' (Jessop 1995: 1623, emphasis added). Taking a lead from Jessop, the next section examines the Frankfurt school's political and policy-based reading of crisis as a possible way of supplementing the insights generated through the RA.

## RE-STATING MEDIATION: TOWARDS A 'FOUR-CUT' CRISIS THEORY

### Three Propositions on Crisis-Management

The starting point for 'fourth-cut' crisis theory begins with three connected propositions. First, there is a need to specify, beyond economistic parameters, types of crisis, *crisis mechanisms*, and types of response associated with the state as an institutional ensemble (compare Jessop 1995). This is critical to both take forward Harvey's work and also to address the analytical short-circuiting that can result from reducing the RA to a form of political economy that just *observes* the 'institutional infrastructure around and through which capitalist development proceeds' (Tickell and Peck 1995: 363). This can have the tendency to produce 'soft institutionalism': a situation where, in mapping the ebb and flow of regulation through key institutional sites and scales as an explanation for capitalist metamorphosis, process is considered the *cause* of crisis (MacLeod 2001a; also Yaffe 1973). This accounts for everything and nothing because the emergence of institutions, institutional practices/*effects* and policy frameworks *themselves* need to be explained (MacLeod and Goodwin 1999; MacLeod and Jones 1999).

Second, the capitalist relations and crisis tendencies to be mediated are always spatial and mediation always has to be with respect to the various contradictions of capitalism, which can be only temporarily internalised through the variegated institutions of the state. Of course, because space per se has no (a priori) properties or powers of its own, attention must be paid to the 'product of actions' located within space (Werlen 1993: 4). Cities address this concern because they are integral features of late capitalist accumulation as the sites of, and solutions to, various forms of crisis.

Third, a fourth-cut explanation can only operate as an abstraction alongside the first three cuts, which are not sequential but simultaneous dynamics of capital accumulation. Associational thinking is required to unpack different forms of crisis because theories of crisis based around economic explanations often negate the significance of social and political crises, the theorists of which, in turn, have a tendency to play down the economy (compare Cochrane 1989; O'Connor 1987; Hay 1995, 1996; Samers 1998). Remaining discussion focuses on exploring the contributions made by Habermas and Offe as the basis for extending Harvey's analysis of capitalist crisis formation and resolution.

## Crisis Tendencies in Advanced Capitalism

In *Legitimation Crisis* Habermas identifies two distinct forms of crisis—'systems' crises and 'identity' crises. Systems crises are those associated with structural features of a system and the internal contradictions related to socioeconomic and political processes. And 'steering problems' are said to exist when 'crisis effects cannot be resolved within the range of possibilities that is circumscribed by the original principles of the society' (Habermas 1976: 7). In contrast, identity crises occur when those in civil society experience the effects of crisis such that identities and systems of meaning are questioned. Habermas (1976) creates two additional sub-divisions of crisis to produce four distinct levels of capitalist crisis.

Using the useful summary provided by Hay (1996), first, systems crises are divided into 'economic crises' (or crises of economic systems) and 'rationality crises' (crises of the state's political-administrative system and its steering mechanisms). Rationality crisis is where the 'administrative system does not succeed in reconciling and fulfilling the imperatives received from the economic system' (Habermas 1976: 46). Second, identity crises are divided into 'legitimation crises' (of the political system) and 'motivational crises' (within the socio-cultural system). For Habermas, motivational crises relate to the breakdown of the socio-cultural system when it becomes 'dysfunctional for the state and the systems of social labour' (1976: 75). Legitimation crises are linked to crises of rationality and the state's operation. They, however, differ in that while rationality crises emerge out of the objective inability of the state to *manage* socioeconomic systems, legitimation crises are an 'input crisis' that result from the perceived failings of the state by the society from which the state obtains its political legitimacy (1976: 46).

Notwithstanding some limitations (see Held 1996), Habermas's original and innovative presentation of crisis theory points to how the forms of crisis and the tendencies in advanced capitalism *correlate* (Hay 1996). This addresses some of the problems inherent in the regulationist and Marxian readings of crisis stressing the primacy of politics *and* economics. This is evident when Habermas (1976) maintains that the interactions taking place between various moments of crisis, through state intervention within the economy, can be interpreted through the *logic of crisis displacement*. This powerful insight suggests that forms of crisis that originate from within the economy (such as market failure and the flight of capital) can be transferred into the political realm of the state. The state, through its multifarious modes of intervention and policy repertoires, has the strategic capacity to transform economic crises into crises of political management or rationality within new modalities of governance. States can, therefore, displace economic problems into *politically mediated institutional projects* and, to facilitate easier decision-making, new *forms of representation* are often sought that support the ideological and material effects of state intervention (compare Jessop 1990a; Jones 2001). And if the economy is not successfully regulated, Habermas argues that crises of state rationality can become legitimation and motivational crises. It is from such circumstances that the destruction of the liberal democratic political system through a disorganised state apparatus is (ambitiously) predicted.

## Towards a Political and Spatial Theory of Crisis

The work of Offe is crucial for taking forward arguments on the logic of crisis displacement and its consequences. For Offe (1984), the *capitalist* state, because it is essentially capitalist, is dependent on, but not reducible to, accumulation. For this reason the state is, by design, continually snared within the multiple contradictions of capitalism. On the one hand, states have to ensure the continued accumulation of capital; on the other, they have to appear neutral arbiters of interests to preserve their legitimacy. As a consequence, the state depends on stability in accumulation for its own functioning, but because it is not an 'instrument of the interest of capital' a selective 'sorting process' is deployed to incorporate certain interest groups into (and exclude others from) the state apparatus and policy-making process to protect accumulation and ensure relatively crisis-free stabilisation (Offe 1984: 51; also Lojkine 1976).

For the sake of my argument, I stress the ways in which multiple contradictions are planned and *managed* by the state as a consequence of its ongoing involvement in accumulation *through urbanisation*. Based on observations on the Keynesian welfare state and its limits, Offe highlights the need to distinguish between two different types of state strategy, which reflect crisis responses through 'modes of political rationality' (Offe 1985: 223–227; also Jessop et al. 1988: 81). 'Conjunctural' strategies are those that look for a resolution to crisis within *pre-existing* state structures, political-administrative systems, and institutional practices. This represents 'minor tinkering' (Hay 1996). In contrast 'structural' modes of political rationality are adopted in response to conditions of economic and political crisis and require a structural *transformation* of the state apparatus and its relationship with the economy.

In Jessop's (1990a, 1997b) neo-Gramscian approach to the state, which explicitly develops some of Offe's claims, modes of political rationality involves different a reworking of the state's 'internal structures' (the scalar architecture of the state and its power networks), 'patterns of intervention' (distinctions between public and private and economic versus social projects), 'representational regimes' (territorial-based forces, interest groups, state managers), and 'state projects' (modes of policy-making) to create *spaces for manoeuvre*. Together, these dimensions suggest that the contradictions of capitalism can be internalised by the state through 'strategic selectivity', such that:

> Particular forms of economic and political systems privilege some strategies over others, access by some forces over others, some interests over others, some spatial scales of action over others, some time horizons over others, some coalition possibilities over others. Structural constraints always operate selectively: they are not absolute and unconditional but always temporally, spatially, agency, and strategy specific. This has implications both for general struggles over the economic and extra-economic regularization of capitalist economies and specific struggles involved in securing the hegemony of a specific accumulation strategy. (Jessop 1997b: 63)

In this latter respect, for Jones (1997b, 1999), the connections between state strategy and the selection, and realisation through political and social struggle, within different spaces, scale, and territories of regulation and governance requires notions of strategic selectivity to be spatially sensitised and recast as 'spatial selectivity'. This revised reading draws explicit attention to the multiple and contested ways in which strategy frequently *privileges* certain interests in particular places and regions to *contain* crisis. State activity, which is realised through strategy, thereby actively internalises conflicts through the appropriation of territories and spatial scales in and through which to implement particular policy agendas.

Building on this, Offe's significant contribution to political theories of crisis revolves around suggestions that in its perpetual political management of crisis, the state under 'late capitalism' (and I would argue neoliberalism) will frequently be a response *not* to structural economic crises, such as the crisis of Fordist/Keynesian accumulation, but to *crises in the rationality and legitimacy of the state and its modes of intervention*. This does not mean that economic crises do not matter; state intervention is frequently a response to the conditions required by the valorisation of capital (see Poulantzas 1979). Extra-economic intervention, however, becomes increasingly important because of the complexity (or 'bureaucratic ponderness' in Poulantzas's 1978 words) of state functions. This is highly evident with the introduction of supply-side institutional strategies and policy mechanisms (as opposed to demand-side interventions) that create further coordination problems within both the administrative and political system. In other words, 'although (arguably) the state aims for crisis-free stabilization and integration in capitalist economies, the *expanded functions* of the state are *themselves* a source of dysfunction and crisis' (Dear and Clark 1978: 179, emphasis added). This leads to a crisis of 'administrative rationality' *if* there is 'an inability of the political-administrative system to achieve a stabilization of its internal disjunctions' (Offe 1984: 58). And because the state generates unintended consequences out of what might appear to be ostensibly rational interventions, which *sharpen* the contradictions of accumulation, it becomes embroiled in a 'crisis of crisis-management' (Offe 1984). This much-quoted phrase describes the way in which state strategies, modes of intervention and policy repertories are 'recycled' (Hay 1996; Hudson 2001), in an ongoing process of political crisis-management best described as 'muddling through' (Offe 1984: 21; cf. Poulantzas 1978: 194). Here, despite encountering a multitude of 'steering problems' the state's interventions are carefully managed by a continued ability to design and redesign the policy field (Offe 1975: 141–142). New mixes are made from old recipes and the success of the policy system is ultimately dependent on the balance between legitimation and motivational crises (in relation to both the political system and civil society).

## Back to Urban and Regional Studies

The conceptual insight has four important implications for the state's current institutional architecture and modes of urban policy-making, not only in Britain but also arguably in Western Europe and North America (see also Brenner and Theodore 2002b; Jonas and Ward 2002; Leitner and Sheppard 2002; Swyngedouw et al. 2002):

1. It suggests that crises are being *further* displaced, through a complex and contradictory process of state rescaling (see Brenner 1998, 2000a, 2000b; MacLeod and Goodwin 1999), from the political sphere of the state and on to civil society's 'vulnerable groups' (such as the unemployed and the homeless), 'vulnerable' or problem regions through devolution, and more generally a complex mix of individuals, household and local states (Held and Krieger 1982; Swyngedouw 2000). Each one is then blamed, in a social pathological sense, for its own economic failings and made to shoulder the responsibility for a *devolved rationality crisis*. The neoliberal state is trapped within a system of ad-hoc tinkering 'with its back to the wall and its front poised before a ditch' (Poulantzas 1978: 191). Chapter 4 expands on this.
2. Related to this, regulatory experiments and crisis-management tactics appear to be bringing with them a number of contradictions, and several ramifications are worth noting: there are problems of accountability and a blurring of policy responsibility (Jones and Ward 1997); difficulties of coordination exist due to administrative inertia, *both* within and across different spatial scales, due to an emerging system of intergovernmental relations associated with 'multilevel governance' (Scharpf 1997) or 'multi-level bargaining' (Poulantzas 1978) and the bleeding of boundaries between market and state; conflicting time horizons are present between

those formulating and those implementing policy initiatives (Jessop 2000); and policy failure is frequently blamed on devolved institutional structures and their state managers and *not* central government (Cohn 1997; Jones 1999).

3. Building on the above, there is an exhaustion of policy repertories. Old policies are recycled and 'new' ones are borrowed from elsewhere through hyper-policy-transfer. Here, Offe (1996: 52) makes an important distinction between 'institutional gardening' and 'institutional engineering' with the latter term capturing an institutional design open to policy influences from *external* forces. By contrast, 'gardening' implies working with the grain of path-dependency through home grown regulatory mechanisms. In the latter case, policy-making is not driven by the business cycle and/or the need to address sector-based crises: rather it is pushed along by the electoral cycle and the primacy of politics (compare Hoogerwerf 1990; Jessop and Peck 2001; Peck and Theodore 2001).
4. Many of these regulatory strategies and their emerging urban contradictions are being presented as necessary requirements for securing a competitive advantage under globalisation (Brenner and Theodore 2002b; Jessop 2002b). An alternative interpretation, though, of the entrepreneurial direction of contemporary urban policy suggests that the (il)logics and discourses of globalisation represent a *further* scalar crisis displacement political strategy in and through which to legitimise the 'reshuffling of the hierarchy of spaces' (Lipietz 1994: 36).

These claims require 'empirical evidence to be plausible' (Offe 1984: 61) and the chapter now turns to the restructuring of UK urban policy over the last 25 years, engaging with the concern that 'the acid test of any set of theoretical propositions comes when we seek to relate them to the experience of history and to the practices of politics' (Harvey 1985b: 15).

## THE GEOPOLITICS OF BRITISH URBAN POLICY

This section explores these crisis-theoretic propositions through three tendencies that seek to capture the ongoing restructuring of British urban policy and going some way to addressing Offe's concern that crisis must be conceived of 'not at the level of events but rather at the superordinate level of mechanisms that generate events' (Offe 1984: 37). First, it draws on recent urban policy developments to analyse the changing geographies of state regulation (or sites for crisis containment), paying attention to how scale is manipulated in and through different policy frameworks (also Jonas 1994). Second, it explains the ascendance of the competitive mode of policy intervention, as the state distributes resources through the introduction of the market (or 'market proxies') into the distribution of state finances in the form of institutionalised inter-urban competitions. Third, it argues that the contemporary scalar emphasis on coordination and management (witness the growing usage of terms such as 'governance' and 'partnership') in urban policy reveals much about the state's construction of the problem as one not just of economic decline but also as one of failed management, through which the state appears to be engaged in the 'crisis of crisis-management' (Offe 1984).

## The Changing Scalar Geographies of the British State

The Conservative effort to restructure urban policy must be seen in a larger context, an attempt to change the ideological climate of Britain by creating an enterprise culture and replacing state action with market forces (Judd and Parkinson 1990: 20).

But let us go back a little to unpack this statement. Triggered by concern at the time over 'high levels of social need, urban deprivation and racial tension' (Blackman 1995: 43), the 1968 Urban Programme and 1969 Community Development Projects marked the first attempt by the British state to address geographically the wider (flawed) Fordist–Keynesian crisis. By the late-1960s it was generally accepted amongst policy-makers that state modernisation based on regional planning was not working. Faced by disadvantaged communities and a serious deterioration of urban life, policy interventions became structured around the doctrine of 'social pathology'; individualised, localised, and joined-up community-based action was prescribed, in the face of wider economic forces that were leading to regional imbalance and urban decline (see Atkinson and Moon 1994). In effect, at this early stage in the evolution of the crisis tendencies of the British Keynesian welfare state, a 'rationality crisis' (Habermas 1976) of the central state was being displaced onto strategically selected localities. Since that time the 'urban' in policy formations has been in-and-out of political favour, as governments have emphasised different geographical scales through different periods of state involvement (Jonas and Ward 2002).

The 1980s, and the period of 'consolidated' and 'radical' Thatcherism, marked something of a turning point in British urban policy. Of course, the 1968 and the 1977 interventions marked significant 'moments' in the evolution of policy (Atkinson and Moon 1994; CDP 1977), even constituting to some 'a major reformulation of the urban … issue so far as the state was concerned' (Rees and Lambert 1985: 139). For sure the period up to the election of the Conservative government in 1979 was one of significant shifts in urban policy formation. During this time the logic underpinning the state's involvement in what it defined as the 'inner city' changed, reflecting the combination of internal political dynamics and the external forces brought to bear by social groups.

Despite minor shifts in the modes of intervention, though, state strategies to address the effects of widespread and systemic urban economic restructuring remained premised on the Keynesian welfare principle of redistribution. Set in this political economic context, urban policy rested on a 'substantial redirection of resources into the inner cities' (Rees and Lambert 1985: 139).

Despite a period of policy shifts, it was only when the New Right's critique of the welfare state crystallised at the beginning of the 1980s did it become clear that cities would become important sites through which the response to the Fordist–Keynesian crisis of accumulation would be assembled (Deakin and Edwards 1993; Wilks-Heeg 1996; Peck and Tickell 2002). Initially the critique was one of existing state involvement. As part of the Conservatives' wider efforts to reduce public expenditure, urban policy was constructed as failing precisely because of the state's involvement in local economies. New Right thinking had the role for the state in the economy confined to one of maintaining the conditions for markets to function. As Rees and Lambert (1985: 153, original emphasis) argue forcefully:

> [W]hat was involved *at the ideological level* was the radical rejection of the principles which had underpinned the social democratic consensus of Keynesian welfare state. By the massive re-direction of the state's activities, the British economy could be turned around, on terms which necessarily implied the regeneration of capitalism.

Having de-stabilised the existing modes and rationalities of state involvement, the state began to roll out a number of 'nested hierarchical structures' (Harvey 1999: 428–429) to manage the crisis. Each one represented a site for internalising the contradictions of capital accumulation. As noted in Chapter 2, institutional creations such as Urban Development Corporations (UDCs) and Training and Enterprise Councils (TECs) were introduced to regulate urban property markets and urban labour markets (compare Cochrane 1999; Jones 1999). The particular institutional blueprint and policy form of each was not an unmediated response to economic restructuring: rather, it was a politically informed reading of the then 'urban crisis'. And through a process of centrally orchestrated localism certain functions were devolved from the nation-state downwards and delivered through an increasingly complex suite of flanking territorial alliances. New institutions were created to bypass the perceived bureaucratic modes of intervention associated with locally embedded and scale-dependent structures of local government. Through this strategy, the assumptions of how and for whom urban policy should be delivered were challenged, as the rationality for state involvement was systematically remade.

The growth in new urban-based institutions to deliver economic redevelopment marked a break from the Keynesian welfare settlement, where, although local government acted as the dominant regulatory mechanism (Goodwin and

Painter 1996), its role was structured by the actions of the nation-state. Viewed more broadly, this apparent restructuring of the 'representational regime' (Jessop 1990a) was symptomatic of an altogether more complex series of shifts in the ways in which a 'rationality crisis' was being managed through the rescaling of the state apparatus and the containment of conflict through instituting forms of representation. Across a range of policy areas the scale of intervention shifted, as the taken-for-granted primacy of the nation-state was challenged and flanking mechanisms at the local level were introduced.

Set within the context of responding to the so-called needs of globalisation the local was, therefore, constructed alongside the national as a primary scale for the delivery of economic and social policies. More critically, accompanying this reorganisation of the 'internal structures of the state' (Jessop 1990a) went a critical reframing of the mode and the methods of state intervention. As Oatley (1998: 3) argues:

> [T]he government tried to establish locally based business-driven regeneration agencies during the 1980s as a way of constructing an organisational basis for local neo-liberalism; in the 1990s neo-liberal objectives have been pursued through new institutional forms at the local level.

With the discursively mediated 'failure' of these local innovations—in the sense that cities continued to suffer economically and socially—so the state again set about reorganising the scale at which it regulated economic development, while maintaining the neoliberal emphasis in the design of policy. Mirroring the logic underpinning the first wave of *after*-national changes in the contours of state activity, and with the progression of devolution across Western Europe in the 1990s, 'the region' emerged (perhaps more through a political practice of rescaling rationality crisis, than an underpinning territorial economic necessity) as *the* strategically important scale for the state to embed competitiveness within an increasingly global economy (Jones 2001; Lovering 1999; MacLeod and Jones 2001). Hay's (1995) claims on crisis-management as a 'discursively mediated process' are important here; this round of rescaling involved the creation of regional 'myths' and the celebration of (somewhat isolated) success stories.

Accordingly, the creation of Regional Development Agencies in 1999 (see Chapters 5 and 6) marked a substantial centrally prescribed *re-inscription* of the state's regional regulatory capacity. While the nation-state retained its orchestrating capabilities, the region (following on from the local) became constructed as the site at which to mediate successful economic restructuring. Mirroring the deregulatory and the pro-capital logic that was present in the genes of UDCs, Regional Development Agencies were charged with instituting and regulating a 'pro-business' approach to regional development (Deas and Ward 2000; Jones 2001).

In both waves of state scalar restructuring, then, the creation of new institutions was performed as part of the 'rolling back' of the welfare state and the 'rolling forward' of neoliberal state forms and rule systems (compare Peck and Tickell 2002). As part of this emergence of a neoliberal urban policy, I suggest that the logic upon which the state had traditionally intervened—the addressing of uneven economic development and of social inequalities—has been irrevocably altered. Instead, the state has rolled-forward a new programme, codifying and institutionalising its two defining principles: competition and the market.

## Neoliberalisation in Action: Spacing Markets and Institutionalising Inter-urban Competition

A cornerstone of neoliberalism has been the state's internalising and subsequent creation in institutional form of inter-urban competition. This has been achieved by removing the (national) regulatory management of uneven development and also by encouraging more speculative forms of accumulation through the 'promotion of place' rather than the meeting of the needs of discrete territories (Harvey 1989). This has often been enhanced by the marketisation of the state apparatus, which has been made possible through the fragmentation of large units into so-called arms-length (or private) agencies (Clarke and Newman 1997; Harden 1992). As part of this filling in of the 'hollowed out' nation-state (Jessop 1999a, 1999b) the state set the parameters and established the rules to allow the formation en masse of 'territorial alliances' and 'local coalitions'. Places have been pitted against each other, forcing local coalitions to form and to mobilise around making bids for state funding for redevelopment.

In 1991 the British government announced a 'revolution in urban policy' (DoE 1991). Performed amongst much razzamatazz, the first example of the new competitive logic underpinning the state's involvement in urban redevelopment was City Challenge. Initially only those cities and towns that had been eligible for state grants under the old Urban Programme were eligible to bid for City Challenge status. In the first instance, then, the introduction of new policy logic was about changing the political behaviour amongst existing 'competitors'. The competition was tightly parameterised. More than simply a change in policy, the introduction of what became known as the Challenge Fund model marked the rolling-out of a whole new way of performing, of evaluating and even of talking about urban development. As Oatley (1998: 14) explains '[c]hallenge initiatives have focused on opportunities rather than problems'. Illustrating the adoption of neoliberal pro-market language by the state, this model has since evolved to become the defining mechanism through which the state distributes redevelopment money. Whether in terms of training—through TEC Challenge (where TECs compete against each other for extra revenues) or Sector Challenge (where some sectors were privileged over others for state monies)—the process through which issues/places are identified as needing state funds and how this expenditure is then evaluated has been realigned through *neoliberalisation*. Allocation has been marketised. This change in how resources are allocated is illustrative of the new logic that underscores the state's financing of urban redevelopment. Neoliberal urban policy, then, inhabits 'not only institutions and places but also *the spaces in between*' (Peck and Tickell 2002: 387, emphasis original). Rules and mechanisms of inter-local competition rest on four principles, which together help to reproduce the neoliberalisation process:

- The introduction of the market (and the creation of a 'market proxy' if no market exists) into the funding and the delivery of local state services.
- The incorporation into the state apparatus of members of local business communities in the regulation of redevelopment projects.
- The redesigning of the internal structure of the state through the formation of public–private partnerships to decide programme goals, the best means of achieving them, the institutional configuration most suited to meet them and how their successes/failures should be evaluated;
- The creation of new institutions, combining business representatives with state officials to oversee and to deliver all forms of economic and social policy.

What underscores these different areas of programme redesign is the concern to introduce some notion of 'the market' into the state system, through both the formal resource allocation model in the case of Compulsory Competitive Tendering (CCT) and the co-opting of business leaders, such as in the example of TECs and their institutional successors. In their wake, however, the changing geographies of state regulation and the institutionalisation of inter-urban competition has left a series of *unsolved* political and economic contradictions. In response the state introduced a number of new institutions to coordinate the inter-urban competitions/scalar reconfigurations, while at the same time not choosing to address the somewhat negative impacts of inter-urban competition. According to the 'Cantle Report' on the Northern disturbances:

> The most consistent and vocal concern was expressed about the damaging *impact of different communities bidding against each other* and the difficulty of being able to convince them about the fairness of the present approach. Indeed many community leaders were themselves far from convinced about the coherence of the many centrally driven initiatives, often with different timescales, boundaries and objectives. Reference was constantly made to the fact that new initiatives are constantly being

> introduced, even before old ones have been completed; that national schemes, with national targets and priorities, disempower communities; and that the complexity of bidding and funding arrangements take up disproportionate amounts of time. (Home Office 2001: 25–26, emphasis added)

## In What Sense a 'Crisis of Crisis-Management'?

Building upon the above analysis, it is clear that the two tendencies in British urban policy constitute a significant effort by the state to, first, construct and, second, regulate crisis at the urban scale, as opposed to an 'urban crisis'. The construction of a 'new' scale of regulation, whether it be the 'local' or the 'regional', on which to begin to assemble neoliberal regulatory mechanisms and the codification of inter-urban institutional competition, illustrates how the nation-state apparatus continues to set the parameters for 'doing' urban redevelopment (Ward 2000). And I would suggest that these endeavours are indicative of the ways in which a 'rationality crisis' has been created, by displacing economic crises of accumulation into problems for political and policy management, which, in turn, have to govern and reconcile their *own* internal contradictions. Repeatedly, then, the recent history of British urban policy can be read as being one in which the institutions and the programmes *themselves*, and not the economy, become objects of regulation (cf. Goodwin and Painter 1996). And in order to understand and explain the demands on current urban policy, it is necessary to examine how the political/policy sphere has been used as a means of managing (and mismanaging) ongoing urban economic difficulties.

In 1985 City Action Teams (CATs) were formed to manage national programmes locally. This, though, was not just a technocratic process: it was also a political one, ensuring the *melding* of local deliverables with the parameters set through national political strategies, which at the time revolved around the dismantling of a number of the central pillars of the Fordist–Keynesian settlement. It is not altogether surprising that these attempts to mobilise private sector expertise through the urban state apparatus were created in Birmingham, Liverpool, London, Manchester, and Newcastle. These were (for the most part) large (Labour-led) urban city-regions and were those suffering most acutely the effects of economic restructuring. They were also where political resistance to Thatcherism was strongest. With the exception of the Community Development Projects, which were wound down in the late 1970s, this initiative constituted perhaps the first effort to regulate the *previous* years of state intervention and, in particular, to ensure that all programmes designed and introduced prior to the election of Thatcher in 1979 could be realigned, rationalised, or simply abolished. Rather than set about reorganising the national level of policy design and implementation, the creation of city-based institutions had the advantage of effectively devolving the management of crisis *downwards*, not to local government, who were effectively bypassed, but instead to a group of state and business representatives.

The remit of CATs was to minimise the overlap between different programmes. Organised along the lines of the fast-action response teams favoured by contemporary businesses, the CATs were, by design, presented as the 'flexible' alternative to local government. Operating outside the formal local state machinery, CATs could ring out so-called efficiency gains from existing programmes and, more systemically, influence the nature of urban development politics. A year later and eight Task Forces were rolled out across the English localities. This time around London acquired two Task Forces, with the other six being created in Birmingham, Bristol, Leeds, Leicester, Manchester, and Middlesbrough. Again the emphasis was on the local coordination of national institutions and national state grants. Both CATs and associated programmes, such as Enterprise Zones, which were local experiments in creating a de-regulation/anti-taxation space in which inward investment would relocate, came under the auspices of Task Forces.

After this period of experimentation in designing urban institutions to manage crisis, more recent state strategies have involved the creation of national institutions (such as Action for Cities) and national expenditure programmes (such as the Single Regeneration Budget) to manage the effects, and contradictions, of *previous* periods of state intervention. In the first of these the state, to reaffirm the dominant ideology, called for a more coordinated approach (where the scope for local resistance may be less). As noted in Chapter 2, this concern was, in part, driven by concerns that neoliberal urban policy had created a 'patchwork quilt of complexity and idiosyncrasy' (Audit Commission 1989: 4). Instead of addressing this problem, late-Thatcherite state interventions were far from coordinated. For some critics, Action for Cities, and to an extent the Single Regeneration Budget (SRB), presented a 'rag-bag of policies with ill defined objectives' (Imrie and Thomas 1999: 39).

The national election of Labour in 1997 did not disrupt the neoliberalisation project underway in Britain's cities. During the first few formative months of the new Labour administration there were some signs of change: the SRB was discredited as a strategy for 'ensuring coordination' (DETR 1997a). It was, though, retained and modified to respond to contradictions created by a previous lack of community involvement in redevelopment. And even the recent programmatic changes in city-region redevelopment governance, the creation of Regional Development Agencies (RDAs), have in their policy genes the 'effective and proper ... co-ordinat[ion] of regional economic development'

(DETR 1997b: 1). This was also clearly expressed by John Prescott when launching the Government's RDA White Paper:

> For far too long, the English regions have been disadvantaged by the denial of development agencies which helps to explain why English regions have lagged behind other regions in Europe ... Since 1945, successive Governments have introduced many programmes aimed at achieving economic and social objectives, but these have often lacked coherence, particularly at the English regional level. Now, more than ever, the English regions are demanding a strategic lead—for greater focus on wealth and jobs, for effective policy integration, and for co-ordination and local effort. (Hansard Debates, 3 December 1997, col. 357)

However, to rationalise the policy messes and tangled hierarchies created by the RDAs, Labour created a Regional Co-ordination Unit after a hard-hitting report concluded that 'better Ministerial and Whitehall *co-ordination* of policy initiatives and communication' was needed (Performance and Innovation Unit 2000: 5, emphasis added). Such endeavours have been somewhat complicated by the national reorganisation of the state apparatus, involving the abolition of the Department for Environment, Transport and the Regions (DETR) and its replacement with the Department for Transport, Local Government and the Regions (DTLR), which was subsequently replaced by a Department of Transport and the Office of the Deputy Prime Minister. As a consequence, city-region redevelopment is the responsibility of several branches of the state, which only fuels a crisis of crisis-management through further problems of coordination.

In turn, the chapter suggests that attempts by the state to regulate the problems invoked through its own contradictions, bound up within the crisis of crisis-management, are creating a landscape where policy-makers appear to be running out of 'new' repertoires and a 'circularity of policy responses' is emerging (Wilks-Heeg 1996). This trend is illustrative of 'identity crises' under advanced capitalism—a situation within the crisis of crisis-management where state personnel are unable to secure the necessary policy innovation to produce visionary and meaningful frameworks and political legitimacy is questioned (cf. Habermas 1976).

This argument can be briefly applied to the recent urban White Paper, the first for 25 years—*Our Towns and Cities: The Future*—launched in November 2000 (see DETR 2000a; also Urban Task Force 1999). Emphasis is placed here on a 'new vision for urban living' and the need to make towns and cities 'places for people'. The White Paper predicts an emerging 'urban renaissance' that will 'benefit everyone', making towns and cities 'vibrant and successful' and offering a 'high quality life' and 'opportunity for all, not just a few' (DETR 2000a). Celebrating 'successful' developments in Western Europe, the White Paper focuses on the relationships between people and partnerships through new forms of urban leadership. And in doing so, 'the urban' is generally presented as an individualistic and all-round exciting place to be. In stark contrast to the 1977 White Paper, gone are references to poverty; instead the (postmodernist) urban idyll is presented, with curiously no references to the inner city as a 'problem'.

Huge gaps, however, exist between the rhetoric of the policy-spin contained with the pages of *Our Towns and Cities*, and the concrete reality facing Britain's cities. I would suggest that the British state is effectively embracing 'third way' politics as the friendly face of neoliberalism, but in the process exacerbates the contradictions of capitalism and intensifies the crisis of crisis-management through its own interventions (compare Fainstein 2001). Several immediate weaknesses are evident in 'urban renaissance' vision.

This White Paper is not 'revolutionary' at all; its policy gene is a document (with a similar title and content) published some 20 years ago (DoE 1980) and key elements of the 'urban renaissance' are heavily reminiscent of the last urban White Paper, *Policy for the Inner Cities* (HMSO 1977). For Smith, '[t]his language of urban renaissance is not new ... but it takes on far greater significance here' (2002: 438). I agree, and also suggest that there appears to be a 'motivational crisis' within the political/policy system (Habermas 1976). The future is, however, the past with fewer options. And despite continual emphasis placed on further *coordination* within this cultural mode of urban interventionism, no attempt is being made to rationalise the institutional and policy matrix of the city. Although Local Strategic Partnerships (LSPs) are being introduced as a form of 'meta-governance' to address the partnership overload created by 20 years of localised public policy developments, supposedly joining-up the 'different parts of the public sector as well as the private, business, community and voluntary sectors so that different initiatives and services support each other and work together' (DETR 2001: 10), there is no mention of LSPs *replacing* the myriad of partnerships currently in place for education, employment, crime, health and housing. Instead, each LSP 'should work with and *not replace* neighbourhood-level partnerships' (DETR 2001: 11, emphasis added). This strategy appears to be less about cutting out local duplication and bureaucracy and *more* concerned with a recreating and reasserting the identity of (Central) Government Offices for the Regions (GORs); LSPs are answerable to the GORs.

This latter concern with metagovernance within the crisis of crisis-management, which Jessop describes as 'a containing process of muddling through' (2002c: 242), is also indicative of the inability of the White Paper to address market failure and the deep-seated nature of inter-urban competition—key issues that have contributed to the current dilemma (see above). The potential for market failure is being increased through the formation of 'Urban Regeneration Companies' that are concerned with inserting the private sector into the city—a move driven by the contradictions caused by community-led initiatives (see DETR 1998a). At the same time, however, state intervention has been involving the community through a proactive and entrepreneurial attitude towards local strategic action. This response by the state to 'failure' consists of two strands, which demonstrate the ways in which the crisis of crisis-management is connected to 'identity crisis', through the re-working of the sites and scales of urban identity. First, in turning to civil society the state has invoked notions of 'community' and 'neighbourhood' through the creation of a Neighbourhood Renewal Fund (see DETR 1997a, 2000a). These terms are invoked as part of an attempt to shift (through scale) the onus for addressing deepening social inequalities. The second theme is the recent individualisation or atomisation of policies, marking in part a return to the 'social pathology' approach that dominated British urban policy in the late 1960s (CDP 1977) and also demonstrating the influences of 'fast policy transfer' (Jessop and Peck 2001) or 'worldwide ideological marketing' (Wacquant 1999: 321–323). Through the construction of 'the individual' as the problem, the individual also becomes constructed as the solution. This is evident when economic and financial risk is being shifted from the state and to the individual, through welfare-to-work policies such the various 'New Deal' initiatives (Peck and Theodore 2001). It is also evident in the recent (post-Cantle) suggestions that community cohesion can be created by demonstrating loyalty to the nation-state through 'Britishness' tests, which appears to be somewhat misplaced given the emergence of an increasingly hollowed out and multicultural British society (see Waugh 2001). Collectively, these policies can be seen as a way of continually shifting crises out of the political sphere of the state and into society once more.

## CONCLUDING COMMENTS

This chapter has assembled a theoretical framework for making sense of the urbanisation of neoliberalism. In doing this, it has suggested that crisis theory can help urban geographers get at the underlying logic of many of the policy experiments that have shaped Britain's cities over the last four decades. Specifically it has argued that Harvey's work on crisis theory and its three 'cuts', although richly insightful in its geographical analysis, stops short of fully explaining, in a systematic and rigorous manner, the role of the state in the regulation of capitalist accumulation and the internalisation of its inherent contradictions. The state *is* a key actor for *neoliberalising* the city through its influence on the policy machinery and the policy-making process. Building on the work of the RA and the Frankfurt school, the chapter has made a number of suggestive comments on how, when taken a step further through the introduction of a 'fourth-cut', crisis theory as a method of excavating the contradictions of state intervention offers a rich interpretation of contemporary neoliberal British urban policy. Here, crisis-management has become an integral component of a complicated compromise consisting of a restructured scalar architecture of the state, as we appear to be witnessing what Harvey (1999: 431) terms 'a crisis in the co-ordinating mechanisms of capitalism'.

In turn, by structuring empirical analysis around three co-constituted tendencies—the regulatory and scalar geographies of the state, marketisation and the institutionalisation of inter-urban competition, and the rationalisation as the crisis of crisis-management—the chapter has also provided an analysis of urban political *and* policy change (compare Rees and Lambert 1985). This suggests that urban policies pursued by the state in Britain during the 1990s are certainly bound *by design* to intensify the internal contradictions of capital accumulation. Britain's cities are hosts to urban policy experiments that appear to be responses the socio-political and geographical contradictions of *previous* rounds of urban policy and not the underpinning contradictions of accumulation. The state's present approach to addressing urban inequalities is prone to failure simply because no attempt is being made to regulate uneven development and neoliberalism is unable to address the problems of those cities facing acute structural economic problems. As it is currently constituted, Labour's urban policy, by design, can only *increase* the processes of socio-spatial uneven development and territorial injustice occurring in Britain's cities.

# 4. Zones of welfare and workfare

> Employment Zones are areas where the usual national programmes for the unemployed will be *ditched* in favour of running trials of local initiatives. The five areas chosen to pilot the scheme all have high concentrations of the long-term jobless … 'Employment Zones will give communities the flexibility to devise *local solutions* which best meet *local needs*', said the Employment Minister, Andrew Smith. [I]f the programmes are successful the Government will expand the *best features* nationally.
>
> (Denny, 1998: 15, emphasis added)

## INTRODUCTION

Like Denny of *The Guardian*, writing in April 1998, many of us believed the rhetoric of New Labour's Employment Zone (EZ) vision. After continuously criticising the Conservatives for operating a national 'sheep dipping approach' to unemployment, where welfare was handed out in 'big dollops for free', leading to a supposed dependency culture, here *was* a radical alternative and it wasn't the compulsion of New Deal. For those aged 25 and over, who had been out of work more than a year, EZs *were* about stretching the limits of the political and policy imagination-finding progressive, sustainable, and creative ways to manage the unemployment problem. This sounded interesting and worth supporting

EZs represented a potentially bold experiment, central to the New Labour agenda of improving the employability of individuals as part of its welfare-to-work programme. This chapter examines the emergence and evolution of the policy logics behind this radical attempt to blend local welfarism with local labour market policy, which ministers claim represents a major initiative in fostering local flexibilities and local innovation, all aimed at empowering individuals more than ever before in determining how to improve their employability. In particular, the chapter examines how EZs were intended to take forward the search for a 'Third Way' in welfare reform, focusing on the apparently changing policy rationales behind the initial design of prototypes and subsequently the much altered proposals for 'fully-fledged' EZs. The critique suggests that though fully-fledged zones contain much that is innovative, some of the key ingredients that made prototypes such a bold experiment may be lost; changes which may well reflect some of the underlying tensions within the New Labour welfare-to-work project and also, following Chapter 3, reveal how this initiatives exhibits a mechanism for crisis metamorphosis and displacement.

## THE POLICY LOGICS OF THE WELFARE-TO-WORK AGENDA

Welfare-to-work is in many ways a paradigmatic New Labour policy. On the one hand, it reflects the tough-love philosophy of 'rights and responsibility', under which new opportunities for training and work preparation are provided in the context of mandatory participation requirements. On the other hand, preferred methods of delivery incorporate a Third Way combination of pluralistic governance and local partnerships, galvanised by inter-locality competition and national performance targets. Perhaps most importantly, however, Labour's welfare-to-work strategy represents a concrete manifestation of the determination to make the alleviation of poverty, unemployment and social exclusion a central, and in some ways defining, plank of government policy. In place of the indifference and neglect of the Conservative years, when unemployment was simply the price that had to be paid for controlling inflation and when the prevailing governmental response to the existence of poverty was one of denial, Labour has launched a raft of new policies and initiatives in this area while setting itself exacting poverty-alleviation targets.

Labour pledged to create an 'active' benefits system, which requires work of all those who can, to 'make work pay' through measures like the National Minimum Wage and Working Families Tax Credit, and to lubricate transitions into employment by way of the New Deals. The New Deal programmes are particularly important, providing a central plank in the government's efforts to improve the pathways into employment for particular target groups with specific New Deals for the young, the disabled, for those aged 50 and over, for partners of unemployed people and for lone parents. While formally separate from the New Deals, the EZs are definitely part of the same overall concern to improve employability and should be seen as an integral element of the experiments with welfare-to-work reform of which the New Deals are the most public face. The New Deals generally have a strong rhetorical emphasis on local partnership and flexibility, yet have been subject to criticisms of being overly centralist and prescriptive in practice. They represent a supply-side response to the unemployment problem, with a strong emphasis on training and work experience in order to help the unemployed make the transition from benefits to work. In addition to these direct programmes for the unemployed, the welfare-to-work initiative is also tied in with other changes, including tax and benefits reforms, which aim to make employment more attractive for those currently unemployed, plus the introduction of a national minimum wage.

Considerable public resources are being committed to the government's welfare-to-work reforms and the new programmes are markedly more interventionist than their Conservative precursors. While some critics seek to dismiss these as the interfering ministrations of a 'nanny state', ministers insist that they are intended to serve economic as well as social ends. The organising principles here are those of the 'employability agenda', as espoused by David Blunkett, Secretary of State for Education and Employment:

> This is not just a numbers game. The employability agenda is about changing the culture—helping people to gain the skills and qualifications they need to work in a flexible labour market. Our new deal programmes, aimed at tackling systematic disadvantage amongst specific groups in society, are beginning to address this core question of employability and to bring new hope and opportunity. They are also increasing the pool of employable labour available, resulting in a new configuration between inflationary pressures and the ability to get, and to keep, people in work ... This is underpinned by the government's welfare-to-work agenda more generally, which links with the work of the Treasury, the Department for Social Security, the Department of Trade and Industry and our own education, training and employment policies in truly joined-up thinking for a Britain facing the new millennium with increasing confidence ... If we can increase the numbers in work and improve the chances of work for the most disadvantaged, then more vacancies will turn into jobs rather than bottlenecks, skills shortages and inflationary wage pressures. (Blunkett 1999: 25)

Undeniably, there are continuities here with Conservative approaches to labour market policy (see Chapter 3). Labour's rendering of the employability agenda taps into the orthodox strain of economic thinking which has it that both the underlying causes of, and the appropriate remedies to, unemployment essentially lie on the supply-side of the labour market; that the unemployed should be induced to price themselves back into work; that the government has neither the responsibility nor the capability to create jobs, but instead should direct its energies to the supply-side of the labour market. Recall that the Jobseeker's Allowance (JSA), the most conspicuous achievement of Conservative social security reform and still today the foundation stone of the welfare-to-work effort empowers benefit advisers to require specific actions on the part of claimants to 'improve their employability through, for example, attending a course to improve jobseeking skills or motivation, or taking steps to present themselves acceptably to employers' (Employment Department Group/Department of Social Security 1994: 21). In the language of New Labour, Treasury adviser Richard Layard (re)states the policy orthodoxy this way:

> In the very bad old days, people thought unemployment could be reduced by stimulating aggregate demand in the economy . . . But [this] did not address the fundamental problem: to ensure that inflationary pressures do not develop while there are

> still massive pockets of unemployed people. The only way to address this problem is to make all the unemployed more attractive to employers—through help with motivation and job-finding, through skill-formation, and through a flexible system of wage differentials. Nothing else will do the trick. (Layard 1997: 197)

Yet for all the manifest continuities and echoes, Philpott (1999: 2,16), insists that Labour's version of the employability agenda is more ambitious and wide-ranging than that of its predecessor:

> The broad policy objective of 'improving employability' is symbolic of a supply-side approach to raising employment rates and wage levels that, whilst strongly market oriented, identifies a positive role for micro-policy interventions ... The New Deals mark a clear departure by the Labour Government from that of its Conservative predecessor which reduced expenditure on active labour market policy by switching emphasis away from high investment employment and training measures and toward high volume but low cost job search programmes.

Rather than simply being concerned with cost-cutting, Labour's approach seeks to be investment-led (see Giddens 1998). For example, welfare-to-work should be about sustainable transitions to real jobs, rather than simply winnowing down the unemployment register by way of Conservative measures such as the 'stricter benefits regime'. If the new approach calls for investments in education and training, so be it. And alongside this investment-orientated approach sits Labour's macro-economic case for welfare-to-work. This has it that raising the aggregate employability of those on the margins of the labour market will alleviate wage inflation, thereby allowing the economy to function at persistently higher levels of employment. Treasury adviser Richard Layard is a strong advocate of this argument, maintaining that the welfare-to-work strategy will be an effective macro-economic policy in as far as it 'increases the number of employable workers and thus reduces the unemployment needed to control inflation' (Layard 1997: 197). From a US perspective, Solow (1998: 32–33) dismisses this argument as a 'forlorn hope' on the straightforward grounds that inflationary pressures are not especially strong in the low-wage labour market, if indeed they emanate from the job market at all: 'It seems wholly unlikely that unskilled wage-push plays much of an independent inflationary role [so] an influx of former welfare recipients will not give the Federal Reserve much of a cushion against over-heating'.

Instead, more likely economic consequences of welfare-to-work are the crowding of low-wage job markets, downward pay pressure amongst the working poor and the further destabilisation of contingent employment. Given the uneven geography of unemployment, inevitably this policy approach works out differently in areas of high and low labour market demand. In areas of high demand, welfare-to-work reforms may indeed help channel some people into work more effectively. Alternatively, in areas of demand deficit, at best the reforms take people off the unemployment register and engage them in some form of useful job preparation activity. At worst, given the strong coercive element in some programmes, pushing people off benefits into work creates a downward spiral of job insecurity and low pay which harms all those seeking a toe-hold in this precarious segment of the labour market. In other words, this approach may help job seekers in prosperous areas and further harm those in less prosperous areas.

Nevertheless, the employability agenda seems to have been established as a cornerstone of the New Labour approach to economic and social policy. Indeed, Gordon Brown has sought to reformulate the old principle of full employment in terms of a new axiom of full employability, the new rendering of 'full employment for the twenty first century' being based on 'employment opportunity for all in every part of Britain' (*Financial Times*, 30 September 1997: 12). Developments in labour market policy reflect this realignment only too clearly. In the 1970s, when unemployment was regarded primarily as a cyclical problem, a series of 'special employment measures' were deployed as temporary responses to what was seen as a temporary difficulty; the appropriate response to a cyclical downturn in labour demand was to roll out a range of short-term job creation initiatives, some of which would have a skills element. In the 1980s, both the language and the underlying goals of policy changed, as it had become clear that unemployment was at the very least a medium-term problem. In the face of a widespread collapse in the manufacturing jobs base, responsibility for which was effectively denied, the new approach perversely stressed supply-side causes of unemployment, proposing a suite of 'training' measures designed to enhance the adaptability and flexibility of unemployed people in the face of a changing labour market. In the 1990s, the prevailing approach to labour market policy has shifted again, albeit with an established supply-side orthodoxy; improved 'employability' is the underlying goal of an invigorated welfare-to-work offensive, in which 'welfare dependency', as well as deficiencies in the job skills and attitudes of those out of work, is cited as the key policy problem. In Social Security Secretary Alistair Darling's words, the new challenge is to respond to the 'poverty of expectations' of welfare recipients (quoted in *The Guardian*, 11 February 1999: 1).

While there are overlaps and continuities across the recent history of labour market policy, it is important to recognise how far the underlying agenda has shifted since the 1970s. The supply-side orientation of labour market policy has been consolidated, to the point, in fact, that demand-side measures have since the early 1980s been aggressively dismissed as ineffective and even counter-productive (Layard 1998; Turok and Webster 1998, for a critique of the New Deal's lack of attention to demand deficit issues). At the same time, degrees of work compulsion and benefit conditionality within labour market/

welfare policy have been sharpened with each round of reform and new programming, such that many would argue that it is increasingly appropriate to view the UK system as 'workfarist' in orientation (see Dolowitz 1998; Peck 1999b). Yet despite the apparently growing conviction that there is only 'one way' in labour market policy, supply-side programmes continue to yield no more than mixed and modest results, while the problems of unemployment and poverty remain as intractable as ever. As this chapter has already intimated, ironically but hardly surprisingly, supply-side programmes are most effective where jobs are readily available; they tend to flounder in those areas where they are needed most—areas of high unemployment and structural economic decline. The deep-seated unemployment problems of areas like Merseyside or South Yorkshire were not caused by some regional deficit in employability. Here, it was the jobs that disappeared, not the will to work. This is the poverty of opportunity, not the poverty of expectations. The fundamental problems of uneven regional development are unlikely to be met by supply-side labour market interventions alone. They need to be accompanied by measures to skew economic development resources to help expand employment in disadvantaged regions and localities.

Yet while Labour's approach is relatively passive with respect to the demand side of the labour market, it is resolutely active on the supply-side. For Labour, the unfettered operation of markets alone is insufficient to achieve social inclusion through wage labour; instead this requires active policies that promote work values/ethics. The Chancellor of the Exchequer, Gordon Brown, for example, has insisted that the arrival of New Labour marks the end of the 'era of absentee government' in economic policy, as supply-side intervention is to be coupled with gentle redistribution and prudent fiscal management: 'The central thread that runs through our modernization is national economic success achieved through the expansion of individual opportunity' (quoted in *The Guardian*, 12 January 1999: 1).

Clearly, there will be no reversal of the Conservatives' 'deregulation' programme, although there are indications that senior ministers believe this programme has gone more or less as far as it should. Yet Labour promises to build upon the underlying principles of labour market 'flexibility', not to overturn them. Tony Blair (1997) has made much of the competitive virtues of Britain's 'lightly regulated labour market'. As he stated in his Malmo speech of June 1997:

> People criticize some of the right-wing governments of Europe for being too tough. I would criticize them for being old-fashioned and for not having the vision to understand change. For us and Europe, jobs must be the priority; to create jobs we must be competitive; to be competitive in the modern world, knowledge, skills, technology and enterprise are the keys, not rigid regulation and old-style inter-

> ventionism . . . Employability—knowledge, technology and skills, not legislation alone—is what counts'.

So while Labour's welfare-to-work initiative clearly echoes some of the more interventionist policies favoured by 'Old Labour' supporters, the programme is framed within a market-complementing approach which privileges supply-side over demand-side strategies and which accepts the imperatives of 'flexibility' as not simply inevitable but positively desirable. Perhaps the most unequivocal statement of this position came from Peter Mandelson (at that time, Secretary of State for Trade and Industry). Speaking on the occasion of the launch of the Social Exclusion Unit, Mandelson contended in a Fabian Society lecture that 'a permanently excluded underclass actually hinders [economic] flexibility'. Combating social exclusion, he maintained, would be the overriding strategic objective of the Blair Government, but all new initiatives would be premised on the foundation of a flexible labour market:

> flexibility in its own right is not enough to promote economic competitiveness. It is the job of government to play its part in guaranteeing 'flexibility plus'—plus higher skills and higher standards in our schools and colleges; plus partnership with business to raise investment in infrastructure, science and research and to back small firms; plus an imaginative welfare-to-work programme to put the long term unemployed back to work; plus minimum standards of fair treatment at the workplace; plus new leadership in Europe in place of drift and disengagement from our largest markets. This is the heart of where New Labour differs from both the limitations of new right economics and the Old Labour agenda of crude state intervention in industry and indiscriminate 'tax and spend'. (Mandelson 1997: 17)

The strategy would not be about changing the way the labour market operated, but instead would be concerned with ensuring that the excluded should be rendered 'employable' in the context of shifting economic exigencies. Rejecting the canons of redistribution and intervention, New Labour would tackle social exclusion by way of labour market inclusion (backed up with a little coercion). The answers, moreover, would lie not within but beyond the welfare state. As Mandelson emphasised: 'The people we are concerned about will not have their long-term problems addressed by an extra pound a week on their benefits' (1997: 17). The debate over the shape and functioning of EZs very much reflects such thinking.

## CREATING SPACE FOR THE NEW LOCALISM AND THE SEARCH FOR LOCAL FLEXIBILITY

As one of the key policy strands developed by the Labour Party to address its employability agenda, the EZ initiative was designed to explore the advantages and barriers to making 'flexible use of benefit and training money' (David Blunkett, cited in Jarvis 1998: 14). The EZs were to represent the leading edge of the government's attempts to 'think the unthinkable' by piloting local flexibilities in labour market intervention. Introduced before full legislation was feasible to test the boundaries of the existing legislative and bureaucratic parameters, the Prototype Employment Zones (PEZs) placed greater emphasis on localism, voluntarism, and innovation than the national New Deals. The prototypes carried a clear remit of providing ministers and their advisers with lessons, which would inform the subsequent legislation and operational details for fully-fledged Employment Zones (FFEZs).

The early debates and suggested roles for the prototypes represented the progressive end of the emergent welfare-to-work agenda in New Labour, while also clearly illustrating the extent to which New Labour represented a very real break with traditional Labour Party thinking. As the chapter highlights later, the move from the prototypes to fully-fledged zones witnessed an even more radical break, involving a shift away from a relatively progressive attempt at labour market and welfare reform in favour of a more authoritarian stance. However, the chapter focuses first on exploring the ways in which the Labour Party's reorientation of labour market policy were woven together during the period after Tony Blair was elected leader of the party in 1995. The underlying theme here is that the development of the EZ initiative helps shed light on the development of the New Labour agenda, while also illuminating the tensions of a political programme which had internalised a supply-side logic and the wider forces of neoliberalisation highlighted in Chapter 3.

In the face of persistently high levels of unemployment outside the southern half of the UK during the 1980s and 1990s, successive Conservative governments had tinkered with the national structure of unemployment benefits and training provision. However, although many of the changes introduced succeeded in stigmatising unemployed workers, reducing living standards and massaging statistical reporting, it was not until the introduction of the JSA in October 1996 that a sustained assault on the system's underlying assumptions was made (more generally, see Grove 1995). The JSA regime significantly shifted the terrain for the unemployed. It placed the responsibility for getting a job at the core of its policy prescription (implying that unemployment was the fault of the unemployed). Furthermore, emulating the emergent system in the US (Peck 1998a), it proposed a road of welfare reform based on localised solutions to the unemployment problem by creating the space for local experimentation (HM Government 1995b: 24).

The Labour Party was also prepared for a radical reorientation of approach. It had consistently argued during the 1980s and early 1990s that high levels of unemployment, whether nationally or in local and regional economies, were economically wasteful and socially destructive. However, from the mid-1990s the Labour Party increasingly recognised quite how fundamentally the capacity, form and function of the state had changed in the 50 years since Beveridge fashioned the 'Keynesian Welfare State', and began to test the implications of this for future policy regimes. While the Keynesian system had developed a uniform safety net, the (re)emergence of structural unemployment in inner cities and parts of the northern and Celtic fringes of the British state appeared to require targeted local solutions. Drawing selectively on these local approaches, the influential Borrie Commission for Social Justice drew wider lessons from experiments underway in areas of Glasgow, described in Chapter 2, which were creating employment opportunities in the socially useful economy or third sector. The Commission concluded that, faced with the novel challenges of the late twentieth century, an 'intelligent welfare state' must be 'personalised and flexible, designed to promote individual choice and personal autonomy' (Commission on Social Justice 1994: 223). Almost by definition, this would internalise experimentation and emphasise the local.

In this febrile environment, a little noticed report from the Centre for Local Economic Strategies (CLES), the Labour-leaning local authority think-tank, was a key moment in the evolution of EZs. CLES's Regeneration through Work project explored the feasibility of the 'Intermediate Labour Market' model within a Labour Party welfare-to-work programme (Finn 1996). Intermediate Labour Markets (ILMs) had been pioneered in Glasgow by the Wise Group and Glasgow Works and underpinning them was the belief that ILMs can simultaneously engage unemployed people in socially useful activities and satisfy unmet needs within a community (see Chapter 2). Although the details of the two schemes in Glasgow differed, unemployed clients received a higher income than they would have by remaining on benefits (either via a wage or through a supplement to their existing welfare entitlement) in return for carrying out socially useful work. ILMs are not cheap to administer as they combine training, advice and work placements and additional payments to the client. However, they were attractive to the reframers of Labour Party thinking who had concluded that Conservative policy reforms since the 1980s had created a benefits dependency culture and that the national social security system was so inflexible that it restricted the citizenship rights of the unemployed. The CLES report showed how far Labour had already begun to critique the traditional welfare state and embrace the Conservatives' agenda of local experimentation. Subsequently, CLES were to propose that 'local regeneration partnerships' could provide the mechanism with which to combine ILMs, a raft of interventionist labour market policies including social enterprise grants, and benefit transfers to pay wages in order to ensure that funding efforts were synergised to reactivate the long-term unemployed adult (Simmonds and Emmerich 1996).

These strands were brought together by David Blunkett in his pre-election proposal, which maintained that:

> *Regeneration through Work* has focused thinking about intermediate labour markets for moving people from dependence on benefit into regular work through the social economy. They [ILMs] offer the chance of a bridge between social spending meeting need through specific employment programmes on the one hand, and profit-generating work in private enterprise on the other … As we stated in *Getting Welfare-to-work* we will launch a specific pilot scheme to make flexible local use of benefit and training money. Such a pilot scheme would include three options within a personal job account: 1.'Neighbourhood Match'—a job plus training in a local regeneration project. Neighbourhood Match would be delivered through local partnerships involving the private and voluntary/social economy sector as well as public authorities such as the local authority and the local health authority, and Training and Enterprise Councils and the Employment Service, such as Glasgow Works. 2. 'Learning for Work'—education to reach a work-related qualification. 3. 'Business Start'—assistance to start your own business. (Labour Party 1996b)

The proposed labour market interventions combined a critique of the ability of the unfettered market to deliver employability (as opposed to employment) with a frustration over the ways in which labour market interventions were fragmented and ineffectual:

> we do need to break down the 'bamboo walls' between agencies, departments and sectors of the economy … We will therefore examine the potential for new Employment Zones to be established in which all resources available from public and private resources would be combined—including the Benefits Agency—to ensure that funds are available for waged employment as well as programmes in which education and training are the main function … Pulling together all those prepared to play a part with all the resources which would otherwise be disparately spent on different programmes, simply makes good common sense. (Labour Party 1996b)

By early 1997, welfare reform had become a key plank in the New Labour project, as the Party's election manifesto made clear:

> We will be the party of welfare reform. In consultation and partnership with the people, we will design a modern welfare state based on rights and duties going together, fit for the modern world … We favour initiatives with new combinations of available benefits to suit individual circumstances. In new and innovative Employment Zones, personal job accounts will combine money currently available for benefits and training, to offer the unemployed new options—leading to work and independence. We will co-ordinate benefits, employment and careers services, and utilise new technology to improve their quality and efficiency. (Labour Party 1997: 4)

Once in power the new government moved rapidly. PEZs were announced which would allow limited local experimentation with benefit transfer targeted mainly at people unemployed for over 12 months. Although the weight of the legislative programme meant that no immediate changes to benefits and unemployment legislation were made, the government opted to allow limited local experimentation within the existing legislation. In September 1997 the government issued the *Employment Zone Prospectus* (DfEE 1997), which invited competitive bids from eight areas with the aim of establishing five zones. The Prospectus re-emphasised the necessity of joined up government, the central role of partnerships and progression towards a client-centred social security system tailored to local circumstances:

> Employment Zones are a new approach to helping unemployed people move from welfare-to-work … The design and delivery of the menu and its component parts will be a matter for each local partnership to plan. The range and variety of help will need to be in line with local labour market needs. In some areas these options may already be available. Employment Zones will bring them together into a single cohesive package. It is, therefore, for the partners to decide how best to meet these requirements by exploring the range of current provision, as well looking for opportunities to introduce new, high-quality programmes. (DfEE 1997: 6)

A key feature of the PEZs was that they were to be run by local partnerships, which would involve the Employment Service, but not be led by them in order to facilitate the full participation of local government, the voluntary sector, and the business community. Unlike most of the local governance partnerships, which had characterised the Conservative Government's approach, PEZ partnerships had no restrictions placed on the types and numbers of partners involved, nor were the ways in which they were formally constituted prescribed. Little new money was to be attached to the PEZs, around £1–2 million each for administration and related costs. However, the overall amounts involved could be quite substantial, reflecting the mainstream training and unemployment benefit monies, which were being 'bent' through the PEZ framework and the ability of partners to bid for other sources of money, particularly from the European Social Fund (ESF).

EZs would use a system of personal advisers to allow clients to put together their own routes through any combination of the three areas of provision: Learning for Work (which covered training provision); Business Enterprise (to assist people who wanted to become self-employed) and Neighbourhood Match (or intermediate labour market provision). Critical to the provision was the degree of control ceded to the clients, who could work with their advisers to select only those aspects of provision which they felt were appropriate to their needs, rather than being churned through impersonal, mass-production style training courses. In contrast to the usual fare offered under government schemes, with their threat of benefits withdrawal for non-compliance, clients were allowed to veto provision which they felt was inappropriate or providers who had a poor local reputation.

If only for this reason, PEZs very much reflected the progressive end of welfare-to-work policies. But, in addition, in helping to develop intermediate labour market provision and in providing considerable personal advice in tailoring routeways through multiple forms of provision, PEZ provision was genuinely personalised, flexible, and empowering. Although underlying their rationale was an emphasis on the failure of workers to be employable, rather than the failure of the economic structure to provide jobs, the initiative implicitly signalled that employability would be improved by empowering the socially excluded. For example, while the main PEZ client group consisted of people over 25 who had been unemployed for over 12 months, this could be extended to include, from day one, certain categories of non-employed people, such as those on disability allowances, ex-offenders, ex-regulars, lone parents, and those affected by large-scale redundancies. In other words, vulnerable groups were specifically targeted, encompassing some people who were ineligible for JSA but who aspired to paid employment. The clear message was that, at this stage, EZs were prioritising socially excluded groups first and foremost, rather than the usual political priority to reduce the unemployment count first and foremost.

Similarly, and critically, the voluntary nature of PEZ participation was drawn in sharp distinction to the mainstream New Deal for young people programme, where benefits withdrawal could follow refusal to participate. By giving some of the most socially and economically disadvantaged Britons a degree of choice over the content of their job preparations, the scheme allowed them to eschew inappropriate training schemes and to assume greater control over their own lives. However, from a Treasury perspective the voluntaristic approach meant that scheme 'take-up' could not be accurately predicted, leading to some problems in predicting the flow of the funding for the PEZs. Also problematic was that the deep-seated nature of many of the zone client group's disadvantages meant that a successful outcome of 12 months' job preparation for the client may have been the acquisition of basic personal skills rather than a (politician-friendly) job.

Participation in the zones was encouraged by the existence of personal advisers who aimed to form close one-to-one links with clients, developing a personalised programme of activities with them and combining different aspects of the available provision. Clients would also have access to a pool of funds as a 'personal job account', a key Labour Party manifesto commitment. Although average personal job accounts tended to be quite small, the message they gave was that clients would be trusted to make choices about their lives in ways hitherto denied to the unemployed. Moreover, drawing on any budget savings across all personal job accounts, larger amounts could be sanctioned by zone managers, where the circumstances of particular individuals merited them.

## THE EVOLUTION OF THE EXPERIMENT: FROM PEZ TO FFEZ

The national competition for PEZ status resulted in five areas being chosen to take forward their proposals, starting from February 1998, with clients able to start from April 1998. The five selected areas were Glasgow, Liverpool/ Sefton, North West Wales, Plymouth, and Tees South. Each covered an area of high unemployment, though their boundaries tended to be unusual, two covering single local authority areas, the rest covering more complex combinations of local authority and Employment Service area offices. Two of the selected PEZ areas involved partnerships with the local authorities in the lead (Liverpool/Sefton and Plymouth), while the others had the local Training and Enterprise Council (TEC) (North West Wales) or Local Enterprise Company (LEC) (Glasgow) in the lead. It was perhaps inevitable that a large organisation would lead given the need to handle some potentially large and complex cash flows and the payments in arrears, which voluntary organisations for instance would have found difficult to cope with. By and large, leadership and indeed membership of local partnerships have proven uncontroversial locally. Rather than evaluate the performance of the prototype zones, the chapter examines the evolution of the initiative, which has seen major differences in design between the prototypes and the proposals for FFEZs, which were announced in early 1999. The chapter argues that the central importance of this particular transition is that while prototypes had to fit within existing legislative arrangements, fully-fledged zones could operate with the likelihood of legislative change as part of a new bill to be presented to parliament. Attention is paid to the public documentation released by the government, which inevitably tells only a small part of the story about the policy-making processes involved.

## HAIRCUTS AND NEW SUITS: THE ‘RADICAL’ PROGRAMME IN TRANSITION

> The new Zones will enable unemployed people to have the start-up costs to run a business, to pay for a training course or even a suit for a job interview. The long-term unemployed will be able to try anything reasonable which could enable them to get work more quickly than would otherwise be the case. (David Blunkett quoted in DfEE 1999b: 1)

Press releases and conferences at the time of the consultation paper about the creation of FFEZs led to some media praise for the flexibility entailed in this new initiative, with its emphasis on allowing the unemployed to decide how some of their funds will be spent, including on smart haircuts and suits to improve presentability at job interviews (*The Guardian*, Jobs section, 27 February 1999: 36–37). However, in doing so, much of the media attention missed the extent to which the paper (DfEE, 1999a) represented both a radical break with the experiment to date and also the depth of its centralising and prescriptive tendencies. The proposals in the consultation paper may embody a relative disempowerment of clients, a reversion to the priorities, which had become so dominant in the Conservatives' approach to 'partnership politics', and potentially a poorer quality provision. First, while much of the emphasis in the prototypes was to allow socially excluded people to take control over their lives, the fully-fledged zones undermined this. For example, participation in fully-fledged zones would become mandatory and personal advisers would have the ultimate power to compel clients to accept their personal action plans. Only in one major area—the one picked up by the media—were clients to be given greater control over their lives than was the case in the prototypes. Personal job accounts were to be made a more central element of the provision and clients were to be given more control over how the sum of available resources is to be spent—for instance front-loading expensive provision early on in the action plan period. Second, the fully-fledged zones would, effectively, reassert the centrality of 'business priorities' in determining local governance and management in the requirement that at least half the zones would be led by non-public sector bodies. Given the financial resources of the voluntary sector, this is a sophisticated way of reinserting the private sector to the heart of local governance structures. Furthermore, business priorities were asserted because partner organisations could make profits but would have to absorb losses, representing a conceptual leap that even radical Conservative governments were unprepared to make. Third, the duration of provision under the fully-fledged zones is a degraded version of the prototypes. The maximum period of central government funded provision was halved to six months, the requirement for zones to provide training and ILMs had disappeared and, as partner organisations would have to absorb losses, the proposals built in an incentive for them to provide cheap rather than appropriate training or other forms of provision. Just as intriguing as the changes themselves and their limited justification was the fact that some of these major changes in rationale were not offered up for consultation; they were instead treated as predetermined. As such. the key aspects of the changes were not up for challenge, in particular the controversial shifts towards compulsion and privatism. Instead ten questions were set up for consultation, which were bland by comparison, covering largely non-controversial issues (DfEE 1999a):

- How should the action plan and gateway be used?
- What should happen if participants failed to make proper progress on their action plans?
- Given that participation in the zone will be sanctionable, how can the scope for ownership of individual choice of activities be maximised?
- How should the personal job account be used to help people get and keep work?
- How can links be built by zones with the developing national framework of individual learning accounts?
- What guidance on provision should be given to zones?
- Are any types of provision appropriate as key elements for Employment Zones?
- How should those operating the zone evaluate and manage the risk of people not achieving a positive outcome and their personal job account being effectively 'overspent'?
- How can effective synergy be built between different area-based initiatives?
- How can we ensure that Employment Zones remain focused on their key objectives?

It is almost self-evident that such vague questions defy meaningful challenges to the proposals. Indeed most of the key changes between PEZs and FFEZs noted above were simply not up for consultation, nor were the reasons for the shifts spelt out in any detail. Perhaps it was to be expected therefore that the official response would involve very limited changes to the framework set out in the consultation paper, although there were further refinements to the philosophy. Although the specific requirement for half the bids to be private sector led is no longer in evidence, neither is it explicitly dropped. Furthermore, as the successful bidding organisations have to be risk-bearers and the result of the Hammersmith and Fulham, and Allerdale, rulings prevent local authorities from bearing certain forms of risk (Tickell 1998), fully-fledged zones were inevitably going to be dominated by bids involving private sector for-profit entities in a key role. The other major changes to the consultation underscore its original philosophy. For example, there is outright encouragement for organisations running FFEZs to make profits, which do not have to be ploughed back into the zones. Furthermore, the payment structure provides incentives for zones to place clients in work before any substantial training takes place, allowing surpluses and indeed profits to be generated from the savings. However, to counteract this, the (two-tier) final stage payments are only made to the zones if, in the case of the first payment, the client moves into work within four weeks of leaving the zone and, in the case of the second payment, the client remains off benefits for 13 weeks. Higher payments will be made for those who have been unemployed over three years, to provide an incentive to ensure the most disadvantaged do not get left out.

In all other details, however, the fully-fledged zones represent a more coercive labour market approach than the prototype zones. According to advice for those bidding for the zones, 'Activities must be at least as demanding as the current JSA requirements—we expect a lot more' (DfEE 1999c: para 2.7), which raises the spectre of some areas of the country having tougher 'expectations' than others. So although the formal sanctions process for those deemed to be breaching FFEZ expectations is a referral back to the Employment Service and presumably the loss of benefits for a period, what is being required of participants could potentially vary from zone to zone, with some zones potentially making much heavier demands of would-be clients than others. Under the fully-fledged proposals then, there is a requirement to be available for, and preparing for work, but local EZs can apply more stringent requirements of participants if they want. The significance of this dispensation should not be under-estimated. This is potentially a key moment in the history of the post-war welfare state in that local discretion to vary punitive sanctions has been allowed, although as in the case of the United States (Peck 1998a) localities are not allowed to experiment with less harsh regimes. This might allow seaside resorts and other areas that believe that they suffer from 'benefits tourists' to gain a reputation for their tough requirements and stimulate inter-locality competition to make life tougher for the unemployed, while also providing a potential template for further reform to the core infrastructure of the welfare state. Furthermore, while both Employment Training and the PEZs paid additional benefits to clients in recognition that training entailed additional personal costs, under FFEZ only benefits equivalence is to be paid. For clients facing the daily costs of travelling to work and of tea and lunch breaks, for instance, life may well become more penurious than before.

## CONCLUSION: SUPPLY AND DEMAND FOR WORKFARIST POLICIES

In its first incarnation, the EZ initiative epitomised the progressive end of the emergent welfare-to-work programme. Not only was the initiative relatively well-funded, but also partner organisations participated for social welfarist reasons and clients volunteered for EZ provision rather than being coerced on to it. Yet, in exploring the evolution of the EZs, I have shown how these original ideals, which so set the initiative apart from the labour market orthodoxy that developed during the 1980s and early 1990s have been subverted. This chapter has argued that the evolutionary history of the EZs has been one of transformation from a liberal, novel and active approach to labour market intervention into one that resembles the coercive and disempowering policies of the Conservatives.

It also reflects a major shift from open partnerships to local privatism, another favourite Conservative policy approach, a shift confirmed in the announcement of the winning bids for fully-fledged zones. In total, 29 bids were received for the 15 proposed zones: seven were won by Working Links, a partnership between Ernst & Young, Manpower and the Employment Service; three by Reed & Partners (private sector); and one by Pertemps (private sector). The other zones were deemed unsuitable and a new round of bidding invited for them (DfEE 1999b). Clearly the private sector will play a central role in most of the new FFEZs, in contrast to the open partnerships of the prototypes.

The argument here is not that the FFEZs will be in every sense inferior, rather that they represent a highly selective and possibly pre-emptive learning process from the experience of the prototypes. Perhaps inevitably the chapter has focused on the areas where regressive tendencies seem to be dominant, not on the positive advances made to experiment with payment structures which reward long-term job placements and the possible flexibilities, which may emerge with personal job accounts. So in some ways, flexibilities are still being experimented with, yet some of the hallmark flexibilities of the prototypes appear to have been abandoned without adequate testing and thorough evaluation. It is this 'rush to judgement' and 'selective gaze' which has concerned us here, as some of the changes which I have focused on seem to be integral to much wider changes in debates over welfare-to-work reform.

There are three main interpretations to understanding the underlying philosophical shifts reflected in the institutional architecture of the prototype and fully-fledged zones. It is still not clear yet if any of these is a more powerful explanation that the others, or indeed if all have some level of explanatory power. The first interpretation is that the zones were in effect a Trojan Horse for privatism and enforced individual responsibilities, acting initially as a seemingly benign policy regime, behind which more regressive policies could be introduced. This, however, is possibly too glib, abusing the benefits of hindsight by reading too much into events. Even if some people were plotting from early on to subvert the PEZ stage of the initiative, there were others with a vested interest in ensuring that it was not deemed a total failure, creating a more dynamic relationship than the Trojan Horse model implies.

The second possible explanation is that PEZs, as a relatively progressive labour market intervention, were almost pre-ordained to be scripted as a policy failure, having been initially introduced as a sop to certain key groups. In this, reading the changes from the initial PEZ format are seen as reflecting that it was too progressive to be tolerated for long in the absence of strong political commitment and Treasury demands to become more focused on getting people off the unemployment register. One of the main pieces of evidence for this is in fact the lack of a clear rationale for why the changes to the PEZ model were instituted. In particular, the abandonment of voluntarism with little or no published evidence to justify it from the first ten months of the prototypes, when not a single cohort could possibly have passed through the system, suggests that this part of the experiment was unlikely to be carried forward. The formal justification for this pre-emptive move appears to be provided in a summary of evaluation findings in the consultation paper (DfEE 1999a: 4), suggesting that: 'The prototypes have found it difficult to attract the full range of participants who might benefit from help.' The logic appears to be to assume that poor initial recruitment was the fault of non-participants rather than with the design of the benefits systems and the limited flexibilities afforded to the PEZs in terms of benefits transfer and working with whole households. In other words, in spite of having been designed to identify and address problems in the benefits system, in trying to assess how this experiment has fared the first instinct of policy-makers has been to continue to blame the victim rather than the system.

The third form of explanation is to argue that the EZ initiative represents some of the tensions and contradictions within the wider political architecture of New Labour's Third Way approach to welfare-to-work reforms, as it seeks to balance its concerns with enforcing individual responsibility while recognising the difficulties involved for the most socially excluded groups in society. This explanation focuses on how 'joined up' policy thinking becomes undermined by central–local tensions, resistance to radical legislative change, and interdepartmental rivalries. Specifically, central–local tensions are evident in the twin desire to open up the space for local innovation and partnership building while retaining tight central management of both programmes and indeed local partnerships themselves. These tensions have been clearly expressed in the EZ initiative, where the early rhetoric concerning local-level partnership development, programme blending, rule relaxation, policy innovation, and funding flexibility has repeatedly clashed with the 'Mandarin jelly' of entrenched traditions of Whitehall micro-management, close financial scrutiny, bureaucratic inertia, turf politics, and a preoccupation with short-term outcomes. At a more structural level, there are tensions between Labour's activist supply-side measures designed to tackle social exclusion, which not only presume but also are predicated on the ready availability of employment, and its continuing adherence to unyielding, orthodox macro-economic and public expenditure policies. While EZs attempt to tackle exclusion through raising the employability of some of the most disadvantaged people in the UK, that the EZs are located in labour markets, which continue to suffer from endemic structural unemployment, has undermined the ability of the programme to deliver in narrow quantifiable measures. Finally, and building from the previous points, for all the self-evident futility of raising employability-without-jobs in depressed local labour markets, it would seem that programme 'failures' are more likely to be pinned on local delivery agencies and partnerships than on the (central government) architects of the policy itself—a recurrent theme throughout *Cities and Regions in Crisis*, explored in the next chapter in the case of England's new regionalism.

# PART II

# The new regionalism

# 5. Regional Development Agencies

## INTRODUCTION

Regional Development Agencies (RDAs) were formally established in the English regions in April 1999 but have since found it difficult to realise the promise of the new regionalist vision. They owe their origins in large part to the impact of the 'new regionalism' both in academic discourse and in the transfer of institutional design and policy lessons from successful economies elsewhere. This chapter illustrates the growing policy commitment to the new regionalism in the United Kingdom as British policy-makers have moved from observing with interest developments in successful European regions to attempts to implement their alleged lessons at home. Thus, as part of a comprehensive UK-wide devolution agenda, alongside elected Assemblies for Wales, Northern Ireland and London, and a parliament for Scotland, the New Labour government has established eight RDAs. These 'trail blazers' (Hetherington 1998) have been tasked with enhancing economic and social development by promoting global competitiveness through learning and innovation and a rationalised system of local economic governance. It is claimed that RDAs will provide 'new structures and new opportunities ... to enable them [the English regions] to punch their weight in the global market place' (DETR 1997b: 1). Yet, almost since their launch, the RDAs have encountered pressing contradictions. Instead of rationalising the landscape of economic governance, they appear to be adding a new layer of complexity to an already confused institutional arena. But these weaknesses cannot be attributed to the RDAs alone—they stem from key design faults in the overall structure of this experiment in regional economic governance. For England's own brand of new regionalism is heavily steered by political fiat and central government dictate and thus ignores the lessons of successful regional development elsewhere in favour of political prejudice and diktat. Above all, it neglects the complex articulation between differently scaled and territorialised processes that occur within and beyond the national state apparatus. Thus, rather than providing a sustainable basis for 'partnerships for prosperity' (DETR 1997b), it seems that England's new regionalism represents a new (regionalised) scale of state power.

## THE BACKGROUND TO THE NEW REGIONALISM

New regionalism is a useful entry-point for exploring the current 'institutional and scalar turn' in economic development both theoretically and in terms of actual institutional and scalar changes. This dual entry-point is implicit in Lovering's critique:

> The New Regionalism self-consciously represents a new cognitive and normative framework, drawing attention to some issues and policy objectives and away from others. The trouble is that it is based on inadequate foundations. The New Regionalism tells an attractive and persuasive story, but it is largely a fiction. *It fails to explain contemporary regional economic development in general* and correspondingly it is a poor guide to regional policy formation. The analytical, practical and moral advances claimed for it—that it reveals important new dynamics and that it can help empower the peoples of the regions to which it is applied—are spurious. (Lovering 1999: 380, emphasis added)

In the same piece, Lovering relates the new regionalist thinking to four distinct perspectives. First, post-Fordist approaches ground the rise of regions in an economic logic, whereby the vertical disintegration of production promotes the formation of agglomeration economies that encourage, in turn, clusters of industrial districts at a supra-local and sub-national scale (see Scott 1988). Second, theorists of globalisation have suggested the need for 'region states' to overcome the crisis of the national state in economic management by promoting regional competitiveness (Ohmae 1995; also Cooke 1995, 1997). Third, several new regionalist perspectives argue that the region is the most appropriate scale to govern a high-skill, 'knowledge-intensive' economy based on jobs in the research and development sector (compare Leadbetter 1998; Sassen 1994). Fourth, the 'associational economy' model emphasises the contribution of regional or local economic governance to productive success—whether based on 'institutional thickness' (Amin and Thrift 1995), integrated 'regional worlds' (Storper 1997); or 'innovative, learning regions' (Cooke and Morgan 1998). This fourth approach emphasises the role of regions as 'a key, necessary element in the "supply architecture" for learning and innovation' (Storper 1997: 22) and/or as the best site for nesting territorial and scalar fixes based on a nexus of 'untraded interdependencies' (1997: 5).

The influential approach favoured by Cooke and Morgan, who belong to the fourth variant of the new regionalism, emphasises the role of 'innovative, learning regions' grounded in appropriate structures. Drawing on case studies of dynamic regions in Italy and Germany, they recommend policy blueprints to help less favoured regions (such as Wales) increase their economic prosperity (Cooke 1995; Morgan 1997). Their starting point is that a 'region state' can challenge the 'breakup of old uncertainties and established hierarchies' associated with the Fordist–Keynesian institutional compromise (Cooke 1997: 285) because it has a set of reflexive institutions able to combat economic uncertainty and facilitate industrial cooperation through communication structures that monitor and share information. The region state thereby provides a regulatory framework for nurturing the development of robust 'regional innovation systems' which, in turn, help to raise regional economic prosperity (Cooke 1998). Intelligent regions such as Baden-Württemberg depend on public–private provision of collective services, through institutions such as chambers of commerce and RDAs, related to training and technology transfer (Danson et al. 1999). These institutional supports provide a means of collectivising the action of economic agents and preventing market failure.

The regional scale is also considered important because institutional routines and their associated societal conventions—dubbed 'social capital' by Putnam (1993)—'are best developed at the regional level because this is the level at which regular trust-building, can be sustained over time' (Morgan 1997: 501). Cooke further claims that regions are the only scale in and through which a 'system of collective order' could be developed within 'post-Fordist disorder' (or what we have elsewhere termed, following Collinge, the 'relativization of scale'). For regions are:

> increasingly important bases of *economic coordination at the meso-level*. This is conditioned by the globalizing context … post-Fordism, closer interfirm collaboration and, crucially, the soft infrastructure of enterprise support provided by innovative substate governance institutions … [I]t is the institutional capacity to attract and animate competitive advantage, often by the promotion of cooperative practices among economic actors, that gives regions a strong conceptual and real identity. (Cooke 1998: 15, emphasis added)

This orthodoxy has not escaped criticism. Lovering (1996, 1999) sees the new regionalism as yet another academic trend that 'talks up' scale to justify a particular theoretical perspective and policy narrative, and in the process falls foul to institutional functionalism and crude economism. This is similar to his earlier criticism of the 'new localism' (Lovering, 1995) for making claims based on limited empirical evidence and ignoring the non-economic factors (class struggle, the state, social relations, etc.) that help to produce particular geographies of economic development. He now argues that the new regionalism is guilty of 'bad abstraction' because it ignores the role of the multiple and contingent factors (economic and non-economic) that produce regions. This is linked to its mobilisation on behalf of specific political projects. For it is 'a set of stories about how *parts* of a regional economy might work, placed next to a set of policy ideas which *might* just be useful in *some* cases' (Lovering 1999: 384, emphasis original). This critique is essential for getting the new regionalism in perspective. Lovering not only highlights the dangers of using policy borrowing as a method of securing economic growth but also poses important questions for research. What are the connections between economic success, social processes, institutional frameworks, and political context?

## BUILDING 'PARTNERSHIPS FOR PROSPERITY'

It is a commonplace that Britain is 'out of step' with developments in European economic and political governance (Crouch and Marquand 1989). On the issue of devolved tiers of regional administration, Britain operates one of the most centralised state systems in Western Europe. Currently, nine out of the 15 European Union member states can boast a democratic regional tier. While Germany has had democratic regional structures for nearly 50 years, Spain and Italy have been moving towards elected forms of regional governance over the past two decades. Only in the mid-1990s did the (New) Labour Party develop an ambitious programme of constitutional and economic reform for the United Kingdom. It promised a radical break with the entrenched tradition of state centralisation and the primacy of political power over economic life and territorial organisation (Tomaney 1999). This would be achieved, at least if the policy rhetoric were to be believed, through a series of innovative structures of regulation and governance. The genesis of England's RDAs can be traced to the hard-hitting 'Millan Report' produced by the Regional Policy Commission (1996). This sought to advance English regionalism in its *economic* sense. Thus inspired, 'Renewing the Regions' and Labour's election manifesto (Labour Party 1997) proposed that every English region should have a 'one-stop' RDA to promote economic development in the region, within an accountable and strategic framework. No attempts were made, however, to define, or redefine, the 'geographical basis of regions' (Regional Policy Commission 1996). During this period a clear split existed in Labour's policy-making between economic *regionalisation*, driven by the perceived need to respond to globalisation, and the mobilisation of civil society actors by promoting a territorial identity grounded in the principles of democratic *regionalism* (see Chapter 6). In the preface to the RDA White Paper, *Building Partnerships for Prosperity*, the Prime Minister, Tony Blair, for instance remarked:

> We have laid the foundations for our ten-year programme to build a *modern Britain* and a decent society. In this modern Britain I want the people of England's regions to have better opportunities to contribute to the prosperity of their own communities and to the whole nation. The Agencies, working in partnership with central and local government, business and other key regional interests, will bring *fresh vitality to the task of economic development* and social and physical regeneration in the regions. From attracting inward investment to raising people's skills, from improving derelict land to supporting new businesses ... the Regional Development Agencies will *bring coherence and a sharper focus to public resources available to promote*

> *development and regeneration*. I am enthusiastic to see the new Agencies set up and running. I firmly believe their creation will *boost the prospects for enterprise and employment throughout England*: north and south, town and country. (DETR 1997b: 3, emphasis added)

To enact the new regionalist agenda of supply-side fostered growth and competitiveness, these catalytic 'agencies for change' were given five specific objectives: (1) economic development and social and physical regeneration; (2) business support, investment and competitiveness; (3) enhancing skills; (4) promoting employment; and (5) sustainable development. These were all deemed of 'equal importance' as New Labour promised to 'give RDAs the powers and funds they need to achieve them' (DETR 1997b: 17).

Putting their specific genesis in New Labour Third Way discourse and commitment to 'supply-side socialism' to one side, RDAs do indicate the academic and policy-making 'new regionalist' orthodoxy in *rhetoric* and in *action*. First, the regional scale is regarded as a key active ingredient in the 'supply architecture' for fostering social capital, developing regional innovation strategies, and providing a catalyst for enterprise, innovation, and learning—all part of an attempt to reconvert England's rustbelt regions (see Florida 1995; Morgan 1997; Storper 1997). We also find a strong desire to use the region to foster 'economic coordination at *the meso-level*' (Cooke 1998). And, at least rhetorically, RDAs clearly share Cooke's (1995) concern with mobilising—through an associationalist form of coherence—'all a region's assets' (both institutional and economic) to be promoted on the 'international canvas' to foreign direct investors. Second, RDAs also appear to support new regionalist propositions on the importance of 'territorial proximity' (Amin 1999) for capitalising on innovation clusters formed through regional scale economies. In new regionalist policy terms, British policy-makers seem envious of territorial developments elsewhere in Europe (see especially, DETR 2000b). They regard regional scales of intervention as providing the right 'atmosphere' (Cooke 1997) for both business and civil society stakeholders, creating in tandem strong regional partnerships as the foundation of economic growth, democracy, prosperity, and the transition to a 'decent society'. And, third, clear links are made between modernisation, economic prosperity, levels of gross domestic product, and regional levels of representation. At least in rhetoric, this scale is being mobilised to 'help empower the peoples of the regions' (Lovering 1999). Indeed, reinforcing the importance of new scales of democracy, Blair (1999: 1) has subsequently added, 'this government's progressive programme of constitutional reform is now moving us from a centralised Britain, where power flowed top-down, to a devolved and plural state … more regional decentralisation in England makes sense'.

## CONTRADICTIONS AND TENSIONS IN ENGLAND'S NEW REGIONALISM

This section identifies five sources of tension in the new regionalism in England. These are (a) weaknesses in the underlying philosophy that justifies this initiative; (b) lack of clarity about the rationale for the boundaries of the new regions and their relationship to other territorial bases of political representation and state intervention; (c) the complexities of multilevel and multi-scalar governance; (d) the coherence of the Regional Economic Strategy (RES) in the national context of a dominant neoliberal approach; and (e) problems concerning democratic accountability, the viability of associationalism, and the more general drift towards authoritarian statism and populism in the United Kingdom as a whole.

### The Political–Economic Philosophy Underlying New Regionalism

There is a fundamental contradiction in the underlying philosophy of England's new regionalism. In Labour Party accounts, economic failure in the *regions* is allegedly undermining the *nation's* ability to compete in global world markets, 'turning Britain into a nation of regional haves and regional have nots' (Caborn 1996, 2). RDAs—'powerhouses for regional regeneration'—are tasked with reversing this deeply entrenched problem and should succeed in doing so because it is assumed that a strong regional tier is necessary and sufficient to secure sustainable competitive advantage under globalisation. But this belief simply ignores the complex connections between economic, political, and cultural factors that must come together to constitute regions (see MacLeod and Jones 2001; Paasi 1996). 'Talking up' scale in this way without unpacking the multifarious construction of territorially defined collective entities (such as regions) supports Lovering's (1999) argument that the new regionalism is a 'policy tail wagging the analytical dog'. This philosophy is doubly misleading if it goes on to assume that *all* regional governance structures can effectively intervene in the economy, regulate its contradictions, and produce economic growth (for discussions on this, see Harding et al. 1996; Rodríguez-Pose 1996). Indeed recent experience shows the RDAs to be virtually defenceless against a rising tide of capital-initiated regional economic restructuring.

Neglecting the links between scale and economic performance generates a further difficulty for the RDA's economic development mission. In the absence of significant national state intervention, capitalism tends towards spatially uneven development. Yet this tendency is systematically overlooked in the new regionalist faith in the regenerative powers of regional and inter-regional associationalism, collaboration, and trust building (especially

Cooke and Morgan 1998). Even more utopian is the assumption, found in most Labour Party accounts, that *all* regions can win through their regional governance structures (see Bridge 1999; Caborn 1996; DTLR 2002). This belief rests on a one-sided concern with 'micro-economic' design at the expense of 'macro-dynamic' competition and uneven development both within and between regions (Lovering 1999; also Morgan 2002).

Traditional regional policy sought to ameliorate the worst effects of uneven development by blocking the free play of market forces insofar as it regulated capital movements and redistributed resources through public policy (Parsons 1988). The RDAs stimulate the free play of market forces, however, so that, even if the overall rate of growth is raised, some English regions must lose for others to win. Moreover, without a major realignment of national expenditure and fiscal policy, the South East (including London) is probably the only English region that could survive as a fully devolved entity (John et al. 2002). As the Chair of the South East Development Agency (Allan Willett) has remarked:

> The South East is the goose that lays the golden eggs that helps central government fund the rest of Britain ... But it reminds me of a successful company from which the shareholders have extracted unrealistically high dividends for too long. (quoted in Fair 1999: 3)

The first Chair of the North West Development Agency (NWDA) has offered a different analysis, pointing specifically to the inability of RDAs to influence both monetary and fiscal policy:

> Monetary policy CANNOT DIFFERENTIATE BETWEEN REGIONS but there is scope to compensate through fiscal policy. This by its very nature is long-term and it will only be in the longer term that regions below the average GDP per person will be able to catch up with the better regions. They WOULD also then get to where those regions WOULD have developed in the same time span. In the USA it is normal for individual states to have different fiscal policies or incentives to encourage local industries e.g. lower employment taxes or corporation tax or local business taxes or less onerous bureaucratic burdens. The NWDA would like to explore with the Treasury how that could be introduced for North West England and other regions consistently below the average. This should be self-financing since if the GDP was brought up to the national average or to that of the best region, the economy as a whole would benefit. (Thomas 1999: 5, original emphasis)

## Territorial Shape: Whose Boundaries?

A related contradiction of England's new regionalism concerns its territorial basis (see Chapter 6). Because the Regional Policy Commission (1996) made no attempt to define the appropriate 'geographical basis of regions', issues of regional identity are absent from the vision. This is also evident in the recent White Paper on English regional governance, which builds on the territorial structure of the RDAs (DTLR 2002). Policy-makers are taking regional spaces as pre-given and failing to examine their multiple constitutions. Apart from the North West region, the existing boundaries of the Government Offices are being applied on the grounds that noted that long debates on boundaries would only slow the legislative process (see DETR 1997b). For some, however, an important prerequisite of successful economic development is a territorial shape that reflects regional consciousness and provides an economic space with meaning for its inhabitants (Amin and Thrift 1995; Keane 2001; MacLeod and Jones 2001). But New Labour seems to believe that regions can be defined purely by their population size, without reference to cultural or historical coherence: 'a region is defined by a population of five million ... If you've got an identity it's helpful, but not a prerequisite' (Caborn, quoted in Richards 1998: 4). This ignores the fact that there is strong support for regions across England—but not within current RDA boundaries (see MORI 1999). Moreover, those committed to a more radical programme of English regionalism (see Chapter 6) show increasing support for larger regions for economic reasons and on deeply embedded historical cultural grounds (e.g. Wessex Regionalists/Wessex Society/Wessex Constitutional Convention 2002).

## National State Power: The Complexity of Multilevel Metagovernance

The preceding problems are reflected in several tensions in the implementation of the new regional 'Partnerships for Prosperity'. Thus there is a significant gap between the rhetoric and the reality of England's new regionalism. Indeed, the emerging RDA 'spatial architecture' (Robson et al. 2000a) could be read as a mechanism for ensuring national (British) state power. As one RDA Chair put it, 'Whitehall just seems obsessed with keeping as much control as possible' (quoted in Hetherington 2000: 7).

Shortly after the launch of the White Paper, a House of Commons Select Committee considered the proposals for RDAs. It highlighted the 'politically contentious' nature of this regulatory experiment and noted also the beginnings of bloody battles between government departments over RDA functions. The RDAs lost their power to influence economic actors through skills training, a key facet of Cooke and Morgan's (1998) 'associational economy' framework, by ceding power to the Training and Enterprise Councils (TECs) (compare Benneworth 2001; Education and Employment Committee 1998). Likewise, the Business Links retained enterprise and business support functions, another important attribute of a 'learning' region (Florida 1995). Without these functions, the ability to become a proactive one-stop agency and perform 'institutional reflexivity' (Cooke 1997) is clearly restricted.

Thus, even before RDAs were launched, it was clear that they would have limited ownership over the resources currently entering their regional economic space. They were also given control at first over less than 2 per cent of regional public spending (Groom 1999; Jones and MacLeod 1999) and were subject to the rolling-forward of various central government initiatives. Thus, as Hetherington (1998: 23) notes, the 'powers people thought were necessary have been stripped away from these agencies before they have been born'. Central government itself admits to these limitations:

> [A] fair proportion of RDA budgets will already be committed to individual projects. This will allow RDAs to grow into their role of determining priorities and allocating funds. It will also promote the continuity of existing programmes. (DETR 1997b: 51)

> Over 90 per cent of the funding for Regional Development Agencies in 1999–2000 will be in respect of the regeneration programmes which they will inherit from the Government Offices for the Regions, English Partnerships and the Rural Development Commission. (DETR Minister Alan Meale, Hansard WA col. 622, 2 March 1999)

This is reflected in early concern about the restrictions associated with the contractual and financial rules that necessarily accompany government-funded programmes (Benneworth 2001; Pike 2000; Tomaney 2001). This can be seen in a memorandum submitted by RDA Chairs to central government, complaining about nation-state centralisation and the retention of national political–economic power:

> RDAs recognise that it is not sufficient simply to continue to deliver the programmes they inherit. They will, over time, reshape their programmes and budgets in order better to meet the needs of their regions in a coherent, focused and strategic, rather than piecemeal, way. In this, they would be greatly assisted by being given the flexibility by government in terms of the use to which their Grant in Aid can be put, i.e. a move towards a single block grant *rather than a series of programme-specific vote headings with limited, or no, scope for viring between them.* (Chairs of the RDAs 1999: 81, emphasis added)

The Chair of East Midlands RDA reinforces this opinion:

> We have 11 different sources of government funds coming into the RDAs and, even when they are the same Whitehall department, we are not allowed to transfer money between budgets … [T]he future of English devolution is a big talking point in the regions. The continuing uncertainty does not help our attempts to unite regional interests around shared strategies. (quoted in Pike 2000: 15)

Ironically, given the heavy emphasis placed by New Labour on business leadership and regional innovation, RDAs have ended up enacting a less-than-glamorous role as sub-contractor to central government. Like the TECs of the 1990s (see Chapter 2), RDA action about developing modern innovative regions is constrained by strict parameters and incentives set by central government. The balance between executive, advisory, and strategic functions in different policy fields frames the continuing debates over local discretion. For instance, RDAs have an uneven degree of influence over a number of executive functions relating to social regeneration (urban and rural policy), physical regeneration (land management) and the attraction of foreign direct investment—functions previously held by the Department of the Environment, which DETR superseded. They have virtually no influence over advisory functions, which represent battles lost to other government departments, such as skills training and enterprise, or duties carried out by different branches of the state that cut across the economic development remit of RDAs. For these latter functions, problems of ownership and conflict are becoming acute. Since RDAs have been introduced, issues of regional planning (Murdoch and Tewdwr-Jones 1999), sub-regional inward investment strategies (Deas and Ward 2000, 2002), and sub-regional regeneration partnerships (Harding et al. 1999; Robson et al. 2000a)—traditionally the remit of local authorities—have been recurring examples. Despite this, ambitious expectations for the RDAs involve increasing regional competitiveness in line with a number of 'state of the region' core indicators (DETR 2000c). These are:

- Gross domestic product (GDP) per head;
- unemployment rate;
- proportion of the population with above average living conditions;
- percentage of dwellings built on previously developed land;
- labour productivity;
- percentage of 19 year olds with National Vocational Qualification (NVQ) level two qualifications;
- percentage of adults with NVQ level three qualifications;
- percentage of employers with current hard-to-fill vacancies;
- percentage of employees undertaking work-related training in the last 13 weeks;
- business formation and survival rates;
- percentage of medium/large organisations recognised as Investors in People.

In addition, since 1997, the branch of Whitehall Government with overall responsibility for the RDAs has changed several times, adding further to the complexities of economic governance. Following the 2001 General Election, the Department of Environment, Transport and the Regions was restructured into the Department of Transport, Local Government and the Regions (DTLR) with the Department of Trade and Industry (DTI) becoming the sponsoring

Department for the RDAs. From June 2002, a newly created Office for the Deputy Prime Minister (ODPM) took over the responsibility for urban and regeneration policy, the Single Regeneration Budget programmes and European Regional Development Funds from DTLR (which was consequently abolished). This continual reshuffling of the state apparatus and associated changes to ministerial personnel appears to be driven by political contingency or 'muddling through' rather than a genuine post-devolutionary urge to create the best institutional context for securing economic prosperity.

## The Regional Economic Strategy: Distinctiveness or Race to the Bottom?

Although the majority of RDA indicators noted above address policy initiatives *outside* their strategic reach, RDAs have nonetheless been given an overarching strategic function that might enable them to become 'territorial managers' of change. This concerns their responsibility for developing an RES and formulating an 'action plan' for its implementation. Thus it is claimed that RESs are 'the single and most important task facing the RDAs' (Chairs of the RDAs 1999). They represent a one-off chance to 'improve economic performance and enhance the region's competitiveness, addressing the removal of market failures which prevent sustainable economic development, regeneration and business growth in the region' (DETR 1998a: 6). In new regionalist terms, the RES is decisive for developing a system of regional innovation—bringing together the stakeholders to agree on common programmes for action (Morgan 1997). Each RDA has produced an RES to sharpen competitiveness, show local awareness and discretion, and highlight the distinctive contributions they can make to economic development. In the case of Advantage West Midlands' RES 'Creating Advantage', this will lead to a vision where:

> Within 10 years, the West Midlands will be recognised as a premier location in which to live, work, invest and to visit, regarded internationally as world class, and the *most successful region* in creating wealth and benefit for everyone in the area. (Advantage West Midlands 1999: 10, emphasis added)

When viewed in aggregate, the eight RESs are anything but distinctive. RDAs appear to have adopted a lowest common-dominator approach; attempts to address market failure are largely ignored in favour of trumpeting the benefits of neoliberalism, deregulation, globalisation, and the knowledge-based economy. According to a detailed survey: 'They all speak of the challenge of information and communication technologies, of globalization [but] … there is little that suggests variation in approach from one region to another' (Robson et al. 2000a: viii; see also Benneworth 2001). This is not to claim that developments within England's regions are of little interest or note: the East Midlands' integrated regional strategy is currently addressing some of the contradictions discussed in this chapter (see Foley 2002). But such endeavours are isolated and lack any overall coordination to produce an integrated form of economic governance that benefits all England's regions (Goodwin et al. 2002).

This lack of regional distinctiveness is indicative of the minimalist nature of the devolution programme in the English regions. Partly due to this and the above-noted ideological contradictions, the implementation of the RES is causing tensions between the pursuit of competitiveness and the maintenance of social cohesion (Atkinson 1999; Lloyd 1999). During their earliest years one of the RDAs' main revenue sources and policy responsibilities was the Single Regeneration Budget (SRB)—the area-based regeneration programme that seeks to address issues of local deprivation. Together with the Government Offices for the Regions, RDAs were empowered to alter the balance of priorities contained within the SRB Challenge Fund. With RDA Chairs increasingly commanding similar powers to the TECs of the 1990s, they could gradually transfer money from the SRB Challenge Fund for use at their discretion—according to priorities identified within their RES (Townsend 2002). Heavily dependent on public funds and with no statutory role to bring about sustainable economic development, RDAs could take the easy route to competitiveness—that of redirecting public money earmarked for regeneration to attract inward investors. This concern is of utmost importance given the increased flexibility granted to RDAs from April 2002, through the move towards a 'cross-departmental Single Budget', designed to allow them to follow more closely the priorities identified within regional economic strategies (see Tomaney 2001; Townsend 2002).

These criticisms are supported by empirical data on the RDAs' financial capacity (Robson et al. 2000a; Townsend 2002). In their initial stages of operation, 87 per cent of RDA budgets were committed to social and physical regeneration, whereas only 1 per cent was consigned to inward investment. Experience in the case of LG Electronics in Wales shows that allocating public money to attract inward investors is a high-risk strategy (Phelps et al. 1998). At present there are limited mechanisms in place to prevent the development of inter-regional competition (see Morgan 2001), raising the very real issue of whether the RDAs should be allowed to compete for investment in the absence of national and European rules and regulation. The launch of the South East RDA's RES coincided with a push 'for more growth at the expense of others' (Hetherington 1999). If RDAs take full advantage of this regulatory gap, and given the flexibility created through the SRB, there is considerable potential for increased regional inequalities and a race to the bottom (see Crooks 2000). England's RDAs are being 'squeezed between the demands of the centre and the expectations of localities' (Robson et al. 2000a: 31).

## Associational Democracy, or a Lack of Accountability?

These concerns are largely shrouded from public scrutiny because RDAs have only limited accountability to their regional communities (Harding et al. 1999). While peppered with the language of pluralism and collaboration associated with particular new regionalist readings (compare Amin 1999; Hirst 1997), their private sector dominated boards are appointed by, and are directly accountable to, the Secretary of State. Established by political fiat from the centre and charged with economic development in the interests of capital rather than regional communities, this initiative promotes the selective incorporation of interest groups into (and the exclusion of others from) the policy-making arena. To a large extent, governance remains 'in the hands of elite coalitions' (Amin 1999). Given that 'the [RDA] board [should] command the respect of all those operating in the economy of the region' (DETR 1997b: 48), the accountability for RDA (financial) activities are ensured through an annual report and public meeting. Yet the experience of TECs, operating a similar procedure, has shown this to be a highly selective and limited form of accountability (see Jones 1999; Peck 1998b).

Accountability is also secured through voluntary Regional Chambers/ Assemblies, formed to shadow RDAs. Previously at the forefront of Labour's programme for constitutional reform (see Labour Party 1995) these are civil society 'mechanisms through which RDAs can *take account* of regional views and give an account of themselves for their activities' (DETR 1997b: 52, emphasis added). In reality, however, Regional Chambers have limited powers of intervention in the activities of the RDAs and levels of consultation are limited (Robson et al. 2000a). Rentoul argues that, 'in England, Blair does not expect devolution to go beyond regional development agencies and joint boards of local councillors to oversee them' (Rentoul 1996: 467). Thus it is hardly surprising that the Confederation of British Industries (CBI), Institute of Directors, and the Federation of Small Businesses in the North West withdrew their members from the North West Regional Assembly in March 2002, citing, amongst other things, a lack of regional autonomy (see Jones and MacLeod 2002).

The implementation of the recent proposals for elected Regional Assemblies within England's regions over the next few years (see DTLR 2002) will prove critical for any attempt to address these issues and get to the heart of a longstanding historical split within UK policy-making between economic *regionalisation* and democratic *regionalism* (see Chapter 6). Early speculations on this are geographically uneven, depending, in part, on the territorial coherence of RDA boundaries. In the North East, mainstream regionalists have been rather upbeat by the endeavours to revitalise the regions, in part because their territorial identities are largely coterminous with One North

East (compare CFER 2000; MacLeod and Jones 2001). Contrast this with the views of Cornish activists, constrained within the South West RDA's politico-administrative territory:

> The Government should have learnt by now that its 'control freak' tendencies are always destined to failure. Evidence of an obsession with boundaries created to satisfy the administrative needs of unelected Government quangos and departments does not make a sound basis for galvanising public opinion. (Andrew George, MP for St Ives, *Cornish Guardian*, 16 May 2002)

> The White Paper talks about choice, public support and local solutions. But for Cornwall these are empty words. If this about democracy—which it is—the Government has an obligation to allow everyone in Cornwall to fully consider the argument for and against a Cornish Assembly, and then vote in a properly constituted referendum. Denying the people of Cornwall the chance to vote for their own assembly will make a mockery of Labour's devolution programme. (Dick Cole, Leader of Mebyon Kernow, *Cornish Guardian*, 16 May 2002)

## MOVING BEYOND THE NEW REGIONALISM

It is too soon to judge this experiment in regional economic governance or dismiss RDAs' significance for regional devolution (see especially DTLR 2002). But it is already clear that their contribution to economic development is limited. Rather than providing the vanguard of a competitiveness revolution, aimed at resolving England's regional economic problem and increasing community participation by building networks of social capital, the RDAs are actually presiding over a rescaling of the processes that produced England's economic and democratic deficit. Far from simplifying and rationalising the institutional overkill produced by 15 years of local state experimentation, RDAs are adding to the complexity of economic governance and reinforcing its problems. They have been established within a regional space occupied by existing institutions, aggravating a congested set of regional agendas (in political terms) and arenas (in institutional terms). In response New Labour has established a Regional Co-ordination Unit, following a 'hard-hitting' Cabinet Office report that identified the need for 'better Ministerial and Whitehall co-ordination of policy initiatives and communication with Government Offices' (Performance and Innovation Unit 2000, 5). But still more is required. For effective regional governance should promote the integrated economic development 'of', as opposed to political institutional developments 'in', the region (Sayer 1985). This would entail a coherent nested framework of policies and powers that can connect the many sectoral and place-based policy initiatives created by different branches of the state apparatus. This would ensure *both* horizontal and vertical coordination within a given territory (see Chapter 11).

These shortcomings stem not just from a failure in the RDAs' 'strategic capacity' but are also rooted in the institutional conditions in which they were created. For, notwithstanding the new regionalist agenda, the nation-state and national scale still provide the institutional conditions or 'atmosphere' for economic development. Despite the importance attached to inter-organisational alliances involving civil society actors as prerequisites for economic success, the national state still claims the right to orchestrate governance to the detriment of building bottom-up social capital approaches.

Reflecting the risk that 'advocacy can be a surrogate for analysis' (Morgan 1999: 666), it seems that the new regionalism provides 'a poor framework through which to grasp the real connections between the regionalisation of business and governance and the *changing role of the state*' (Lovering 1999: 391, emphasis added). But what is an appropriate framework? If the new regionalism provides no answers, perhaps we should consider the primacy of the political. Thus RDAs could be seen as the realisation of devolution promises made by former Labour leader John Smith—the 'Devolution Minister' under the Callaghan government. RDAs could also signify the reward for the compliance of North East-based MPs with the Scotland and Wales devolution bills, in sharp contrast to their 1977 to 1978 opposition (Tomaney 1999). While this might provide part of the explanation (in terms of the changing balance of forces), we should also consider a political–economic explanation based on the 'changing role of the state' in the political production of scale, interscalar articulation, and providing opportunities for scale jumping, for this chapter highlights the importance of the differently scaled and territorialised processes occurring through the national state apparatus. We find a complex 'tangled hierarchies' of scale as the spatial and scalar division of state labour has emerged, reflecting previous and still ongoing struggles for access to state power, the state apparatus, and its patterns of intervention. The advent of devolution in the English regions has compounded these problems through the ways in which the 'hollowed out' structure of the United Kingdom state is now being 'filled in' without adequate forethought to the interrelationships between the various institutions of governance and government (Goodwin et al. 2005). This requires careful attention to the role of the new regional apparatuses and policies in shaping the spatial and scalar selectivities of the state (Jones 1997b, 1999) and redefining the economy as an object of governance and regulation. In acting upon its recognition that 'something needs to be done about the regions', New Labour is not so much seeking the most effective solution to economic problems as finding a new way to consolidate its political position and legitimate its overall economic strategy and state project. While the justification for the new regionalism is its role in promoting competitiveness and learning, the RDAs have also created a regional scale of government and governance that privileges access by business and Labour Party activists and excludes most popular interests. This supports Paddison's claim that: 'In Britain and elsewhere, the significance of coordination at a regional level has shown itself most clearly in times of national crisis' (1983: 243).

This does not mean that the new regionalism will solve the problems to which it is explicitly addressed or for which it offers a new form of crisis-management. Indeed policy solutions often bring with them new social, political, and geographical contradictions (illustrated above in the case of RDAs). In Hudson's words:

> Rather than resolving policy problems at the economic level, the crisis tendency inherent within the capitalist mode of production is internalized into the state apparatus to appear in *fresh forms*—notably a fiscal crisis (which restricts the state's capacity to manage the economy) and a rationality crisis (a perceived disjunction between the intentions and outcomes of state actions). (Hudson 2000: 60, emphasis added)

As noted in Chapter 3, the more the state intervenes in the economy, the more it introduces economic contradictions and conflicts into its own operations and thereby undermines its capacity to act in a relatively autonomous and unified manner. But it also becomes harder to refuse to intervene because of the disruption this causes to a mode of growth that depends heavily on extra-economic conditions for its expanded reproduction and because of the political fallout of the rolling back of the state. To reiterate from Chapter 3, in short, 'although (arguably) the state aims for crisis-free stabilization and integration in capitalist economies, the *expanded functions* of the state are *themselves* a source of dysfunction and crisis' (Dear and Clark 1978: 179, emphasis added). This leads, in turn, to a crisis of 'administrative rationality' *if* 'the political-administrative system [cannot] achieve a stabilization of its internal disjunctions' (Offe, 1984: 58). The unintended consequences of what might appear to be ostensibly rational state intervention *sharpen* the contradictions of accumulation. But there is no escape from the double-bind of 'to intervene, or not to intervene: that is the question'. Thus the state and its managers are forced to muddle through in the hope of maintaining the political initiative and displacing contradictions and crises at least for another political cycle. The RDAs could well be interpreted as one of the latest twists in this cycle in Britain's flawed political economy, with the political and policy debate shifting, again in the context of crisis displacement, to the issue of 'spaces of regionalism' (territoriality, democracy, and civil society identities), which is discussed in the next chapter.

# 6. Spaces of regionalism

> The English are having a hard time of it these days, if you believe the Press. Derided abroad either as a yob cultural or a heritage theme park; at home, on the verge of divorce from their partners in the United Kingdom of Great Britain and Northern Ireland. For the English, 1997 was what the medievals would have called an *annus mirabilis*. In the year in which we celebrated the 1,400th anniversary of the Roman mission to our island, the New Labour Government launched an ambitious attempt to clear away the baggage of history, to untangle the relations of the English with the Welsh, Scots and Irish, the legacies of 1922, 1707, 1603, and further back still. It has left the English feeling understandable nervous. With the European union already on the horizon, along comes the break-up of Britain.
>
> (Wood 2000: 91)

This chapter suggests that the rescaling of state capacities and competencies associated with economic governance, discussed in Chapter 5, is providing an emerging cultural and political territorial space in and through which grass-roots social justice movements are becoming visible and attempting to gain popular support. The chapter suggests a need to consider two contested processes. In the context of the 'English question', it draws a distinction between a state-driven (and somewhat top-down) *functional regionalisation* and an often pre-existing (and more bottom-up) *civil society regionalism*. The former captures a general set of trends occurring in advanced capitalism and relates to economic globalisation and the scalar and territorial recasting of state power. The latter represents the different historically forged connections between territory and identity, which are geographically specific, typically fragmented, and highly uneven across the English regions—at a general level, interest groups in the North have managed to mobilise a regional identity, whereas with the exception of the Cornish activists, regional consciousness outside this Northern political geometry is weak. The chapter presents this two-fold distinction as a way of analysing the contestation and mobilisation of regions.

In a second section, the chapter explores the emergence of functional regionalisation in England and uses the East Midlands region to ground concerns with social justice. The East Midlands is not known for its coherent regional identity (see Stobart 2001): forged through central government diktat and political fiat, this region has largely acted as an administrative entity and has failed to provide the platform from which to mobilise popular support. The chapter focuses on attempts made by institutions in this region over the last 50 years to promote a state-centred socioeconomic identity. It examines how regionalisation is changing in the context of the Labour Party's devolution and constitutional change programme for England, which is creating an uneven political space for debating issues of justice.

The third section discusses how regionalisation is being contested by *Devolve!*—formerly, as Movement of Middle England (MFME), a Midlands-based regional devolution movement, latterly, as an English devolution movement, still active in the East Midlands. This regional justice movement has been promoting a radical grassroots regionalism since the late 1980s, based on moving power from central government and to the 'people of England' through: regional devolution, democratic devolution, cultural devolution, and economic devolution. For *Devolve!*, this challenge to regionalisation is as much about arbitrary boundaries as about lack of democratic content, although in the case of the East Midlands *parts* of the proposed region do correspond to an historical popular identity (cf. ODPM 2003). This section reveals how movements such as *Devolve!* have struggled to gain support and within the advent of Labour's 'new regional policy' are being drawn into the bargaining process as to how the territorialities of this could be defined. Recent *Devolve!* activities have attracted interest from policy-makers and politicians.

## MOBILISING TERRITORY: NEW REGIONALISMS

As noted in Chapter 5, recent academic debates have been suggesting that regions are becoming central players in economic, social, political and cultural life. On the one hand, some authors see regions as providing the atmosphere for economic prosperity within a forever globalising age (compare Cooke and Morgan 1998; Florida 1995; Ohmae 2001; Porter 2001, 2003; Scott 1998; Storper 1997). Scott and Storper's recent take on some of these debates presents globalisation as challenging the macro-economic planning and development integrity of the nation-state. By focusing on heterodox and endogenous ways of doing economic development, city-region-based 'government agencies, civic associations, private–public partnerships, or a host of other possible institutional arrangements, depending on local traditions and political sensibilities' armed with supply-side innovation strategies are considered appropriate for mobilising and promoting a 'regional economic commons'—i.e. locally specific, territorially embedded, and untraded economic assets—on the international canvas in order to capitalise on the localised agglomeration and the intense clustering of economic activity (Scott and Storper 2003: 587). For these authors, regions are becoming selective 'windows of locational opportunity' for capturing and developing an increasingly specialised reordering and rescaling of economic activity and frequently cited examples often include

Baden-Württemberg, Emilia-Romagna, Silicon Valley, Boston, San Diego, and the Rhône-Alpes (see Scott 2001).

On the other hand, some authors connect the rise of regions to the demands of sub-national groups that are challenging the cultural and political sovereignty of the Westphalian national state system (compare Agnew 2002; Giordano 2000; Harty 2001; Keating 2001; Marks and McAdam 1996; Paasi 1996, 2003; Parks and Elcock 2000). Keating's work on 'new regionalist movements' has been important for drawing our attention to these trends and for highlighting the connections between renewed territorial forms of political mobilisation, social action through cultural expression, and state responses via the institutional frameworks of devolution and constitutional change. For Keating, regions are sites for generating post-national identities and instilling social cohesion in a world increasingly dominated by global and market forces. Cited examples often include Galicia, the Catalan and Basque regions, Brittany, Lombardy, Upper Silesia, and more recently the Celtic fringe of the United Kingdom (Keating 1998, 2001; Keating et al. 2003).

Critical commentators are suggesting an urgent need to bring territorial clarity to these parallel debates and are specifically questioning what is meant by the term 'region' and more importantly *how* region building—i.e. its development and mobilisation— occurs (MacLeod 2001b; Paasi 2002). Within new regionalist literatures there is a reluctance of many scholars to specify their territorial frames of reference, such that regions (mostly those listed above) are becoming slippery and somewhat meaningless concepts for discussing *differently* scaled and territorialised economic, social, cultural, and political assemblages. Three related problems become evident here (Jones and MacLeod 1999, 2004). First, there is the need to be wary of 'territorial functionalism', whereby a necessary relationship is inferred between regions, prosperity, and institutional architecture. Second, the leading edge regions expressed within the new regionalism differ massively in terms of their physical, administrative, scalar, and political form. Third, much discussion lacks an appreciation for how regional territorial, economic, and political channels are institutionalised, i.e. 'the socio-spatial process during which some territorial unit emerges as a part of the spatial structure of society and becomes established and clearly identified in different spheres of social action and social consciousness' (Paasi 1986: 121). By drawing on the work of the 'new regional geography'—where regions are theorised as active and ongoing products of state practices, economic trends, cultural relationships, and senses of place (Gilbert 1988; Paasi 1996)—MacLeod argues that regions need to be seen as multifaceted territorial phenomenon, *forged through points of contact between* economics, culture, political and policy systems, which become institutionalised and layered over time (MacLeod 1998, 2001b).

One way of bringing clarity to these debates is to explore further a recent distinction made elsewhere (see Jones and MacLeod 2004) between 'regional spaces' and 'spaces of regionalism'. The former emphasises the work of mostly economists and economic geographers, who posit an emerging *functional regionalisation* of economic space within globalisation. Functional regionalisation also relates to the practices of political parties and state personnel who construct regions for delimiting particular policy and political problems (Hayward 1969; Kofman 1981)—often to create the conditions for those cluster-based economic developments referred to in the above academic literatures.

By contrast, 'spaces of regionalism' uncovers those political science and political geography concerns with claims to citizenship, cultural expression, and political mobilisation, often associated with the implementation of regional government and governance. Research on 'social capital' has been important here for pointing out that networks of cooperation and trust can foster territorial awareness, civic identity and, in turn, can help to secure prosperity and instil democracy (Putnam 1993). Building on this, authors such as Tomaney use the term 'civic regionalism' to capture a concern with those campaigning (through assemblies and constitutional conventions) for regional government within their regions to provide new spaces of identity, participation, and democracy (Tomaney 2002).

This chapter explores these latter concerns through notions of *civil society regionalism*, to step outside the parameters of the state apparatus and allow my attention to be focused on grassroots regional movements as incipient 'secession groups'—groups which have mostly turned their back on mainstream political parties, operate within the shadow of conventional politics, and prefer to pursue more unconventional ways of making themselves heard (Purcell 2001). This concern partially takes its cue from Agnew's argument that we need to broaden our regional imaginations *beyond* the state to understand the multiple (social) construction, the ongoing scalar reproduction and most importantly in the context of this chapter, the multi-various mobilisations and contestations of regions in geography—with research centring on the often small-scale, localised, and networked micro-geographies of politics, people and place (Agnew 2002; Jones and Desforges 2003). Making this distinction between *functional regionalisation* and *civil society regionalism* importantly allows the chapter to understand regions as socially constructed and political mediated accomplishments, created by a range of 'political, economic, cultural and administrative practices' (Paasi 2001) and frequently revolving around issues of social justice.

## FUNCTIONAL REGIONALISM IN THE EAST MIDLANDS OF ENGLAND

The territories of England are fascinating case studies of regionalisation in action and illustrate Watson's functionalist take on administrative space that 'represents a national or central government way of conceiving and treating the region. The region is denied any policy-making capacity as a political institutional entity ... The problem thereby posed for governments has been seen as basically a technical, economic one and a solution has been sought essentially in the process known as modernization' (Watson 1978: 457–458, cited in Kofman 1981: 174). For Kofman, this implies carving national territories into 'problem zones'—stripping such spaces from a regional identity or 'personality' and 'divorcing' economic and cultural policies from one another.

Academic accounts normally pick up the English regional debate during the 1920s, when an emergency-planning map was constructed following the General Strike (see especially Paddison 1983; Smith 1965a). This was formalised during the 1930s through the appointment of Regional Commissioners, but was later dropped after the Second World War. Civil defence regions became the eight 'Treasury' and then 'standard regions'—deployed to manage the economy and bring a territorial dimension to public policy. During the 1960s era of state modernisation attempts were made to coordinate government policies in the standard regions through Regional Economic Planning Councils and Boards, involving representatives from the civil service, business, trade unions, and local government. Increasing state intervention led to 'economic planning regions', where the state constructed and managed 'problem regions' through the spatial targeting of assistance to address the unevenly developing capitalist space economy. Throughout these *regionalisation* periods, though, little appreciation was given to how spaces of economic development might be democratised or injected with culture through *regionalism* and for critics the English regional project represents 'an extension of the power of central government, not decentralisation' (Banks 1971: 256; see also Fawcett 1919: 23). Or, as Smith chooses to express it in the excellent study of 'regionalism in England 1905–1965':

> [English] regionalism may thus be defined as an attempt to delimit areas usually larger than those of the existing local government structure, with a view to making local and national government and planning more effective and efficient. Regionalism in this sense is essentially concerned with the problem of defining areas for a new, intermediate level of government and administration, rather than with the purely geographical function of delimiting areas of the earth's surface according to physical features. *It refers to the machinery of government rather than geographical analysis*. (1965b: 23, emphasis added)

The East Midlands—now covering the counties of Lincolnshire, Nottinghamshire, Derbyshire, Leicestershire, Northamptonshire, and Rutland—is no different in this regard. With its mixture of medium-sized industrial towns and predominately rural hinterland, Fawcett's early account on this 'Trent province' noted the difficulties of managing this region as an administrative space due to economic fragmentation and disunity (Fawcett 1919). Stobart's work on the industrial geography of this region during the nineteenth century has taken this further by drawing attention to the growth of local specialisms and allegiances in this region rather than the formation of wider integrated regional economic identities found in some other English regions (Stobart 2001). Accordingly, in stark contrast to its industrial neighbour, the West Midlands—which played a leading role in the regional planning movement of the late 1940s due to its position within the national and international division of labour and the territorial coherence of its economic interest groups (Whitehead 2003a)—the East Midlands regional voice was dormant until activated by modernist planners. Smith, importantly, notes that because unemployment was no problem throughout this region at this time—in contrast to developments in Scotland and the North East of England—an East Midlands-wide industrial interest group did not organically develop and argue its case on the national economic stage (Smith 1965a: 81).

Developing instead out of the 'North Midland' town and country planning region (see Massey 1989), an artificial 'East Midlands Standard Region' was created in the early 1960s to house the activities of the East Midlands Regional Economic Planning Council (EMREPC). In contrast, though, to more forward looking regions such as the North East, which fostered an emerging regional consciousness through the (limited) spaces of economic planning and via the political weight of the earlier North East Development Council (MacLeod and Jones 2001; Parsons 1988), EMREPC did little to break out of its functional regionalisation role (Keeble 1980) and rather like its Yorkshire and Humberside neighbour it represented 'a blind alley along the long and slow route towards regionalism' (Pearce 1989: 129).

During the 1980s, the regional planning machinery was swept aside and replaced by local-level experiments in economic governance. The East Midlands received its fair share of unelected local state institutions and policy initiatives, such as Enterprise Zones and Training and Enterprise Councils, which introduced a layer of localisation to the East Midlands' administrative geography (Jones 2004). After the 1992 general election, though, the Conservatives introduced a new round of administrative regionalisation to bring coherence to the activities of government departments operating in the regions and also to control some of the community-based economic developments taking place within the local state. Integrated Government Offices for the Regions came into being as part of the 'new localism' in British urban policy (Whitehead 2003a). The East Midlands Standard Region became home to the Government Office for the East Midlands (GOEM)—bringing together (by 2001) the following functions: transport, regional development, education and skills, culture, media and sport, home office, and environment, food and rural affairs—and also charged with working 'in partnership with local people to maximise the competitiveness, prosperity and quality of life of the region' (GOEM 1996: 3). GOEM became a strategically significant actor in creating an East Midlands regional consciousness within which *central government* has a 'common economic and social purpose at the regional level' (GOEM 1997: 2). These official views are to be compared with critics, who see the Government Offices as the 'regionalisation of injustice' (Robinson and Shaw 1994).

Set within a United Kingdom-wide constitutional change and devolution agenda—alongside elected Assemblies for Wales, Northern Ireland, and London, and a Parliament for Scotland (see above)—a further round of regionalisation arrived with the launch of the Regional Development Agencies (RDAs) under the New Labour administration (Jones 2001; Morgan 2002). In contrast to developments in Scotland and Wales (see above), RDAs have been restricted to the geographical reconstitution of the economy and their genesis can be traced to the desire to have in place 'one-stop' institutions within each region to bring territorial coherence to physical, social, and economic development policies. Echoing some of the 'new regional spaces' (Jones and MacLeod 2004) literature discussed above, politicians presented this endeavour as providing regions such as the East Midlands with 'new structures and new opportunities ... to enable them to punch their weight in the global market place' (DETR 1997b: 1). The East Midland's RDA (EMDA) became active in April 1999 across the East Midlands Standard Region, enacting a series of supply-side policies—such as skills training, enterprise support, cluster-based innovation strategies, and land management—to help raise the wealth and prosperity of this region (Foley 1998, 2002). EMDA's economic strategy presents a socioeconomic vision for this region where, 'By 2010, the East Midlands will be one of Europe's top 20 regions. It will be a place where people want to live, work and invest because of our vibrant community, our healthy, safe, diverse and inclusive communities [and] our quality environment' (EMDA 1999: 2).

Like many other RDAs, EMDA distanced itself from concerns outside promoting economic territorial awareness—such as issues of representation, renewing the civic realm, promoting culture, and building a regional identity (Robson et al. 2000a). This task has been left to regional chambers and regional cultural consortiums, which have been emerging in recent years to increase the participation of the social partners in the region and to act as forums for nurturing a non-economic territorial consciousness. The East Midlands regional chamber (now called an 'assembly') has been important in bringing together the different social partners within this region, but with limited funding and a need to prioritise integrated regional economic strategies, its success has been very uneven (Foley 2002).

With ongoing pressures being exerted on central government by 'civic regional' activists in especially the North East of England—who had been campaigning throughout the 1990s for directly elected regional assemblies (see Tomaney 2002; and below)—and with survey evidence demonstrating an (albeit uneven) desire for devolution across England (ESRC 2003), during their second term in office the Labour Party announced a 'new regional policy' to incorporate the people of England within structures of governance. In the words of *Your Region, Your Choice*:

> For decades the needs and aspirations of the English regions were at best neglected and at worst ignored. The *laissez-faire* and 'Whitehall knows best' approaches of the past created both a widening regional economic decline and regional democratic deficit. By 1997 we had all but abandoned regional policy and had one of the most centralised systems of government in the western world. Right from the word go, this Government has taken a different approach, aiming to bring pride and prosperity back to all our regions … This White Paper carries forward that regional renaissance and puts the regions firmly at the heart of our policies to build a modern and more prosperous society. By devolving power and revitalising the regions we bring decision-making closer to the people and make government more efficient, more effective and more accountable … This is a radical agenda to take us forward fully into the 21st century, where centralisation is a thing of the past. It responds to the desires many regions are already expressing and sets up a framework which can take other regions forward if they wish. Better Government, less bureaucracy and more democracy, and enhancing regional prosperity: proposals from a Government confident that it is people within our regions who know what is best for their region. (Prescott and Byers, quoted in DTLR 2002: foreword)

This White Paper—peppered with connotations of delivering regionalism by providing 'people-led' social justice within regional space—proposes to instil institutional coherence to existing regional arrangements by influencing the activities of the RDAs, the government offices, and the regional chambers/assemblies. With regard to political representation, proposals are dependent on individual regional referendums to test the mood for elected assemblies. According to Blair, 'No region will be forced to have an elected assembly. But where there is public support for one, we believe people should be given the chance to demonstrate this in a referendum' (DTLR 2002: preface). Thus far, it is government intention to only hold referendums in one region—the North East—where there was sufficient 'interest' in regional government (see below). It is an open question whether this move will buck the historical trend of regionalisation: the boundaries relate to 'standard regions'; the membership of the proposed assemblies is limited; their influence over government spend is restricted; and the Government Offices for the Regions are set to be the important players within the regions. Accordingly, in November 2004 the electorate in the North East voted overwhelmingly against a regional assembly and legislation was suspended. However, as I discuss below, this agenda has opened up an emerging 'action space' in English regional civil society for thinking about social justice—albeit with limited success.

## ALTERNATIVES TO FUNCTIONAL REGIONALISATION

### England's Variable (Regional) Geometry

The academic account on England's regionalisation discussed above has been deliberately selective to allow me to chart the main state-centred institutional developments occurring over the past century. Research on regions in England rarely steps out of this historical planning genre to consider English regional cultural politics and more informal socioeconomic development strategies. This is partially because as Peter Taylor (1991, 1993) suggests, England is trapped within a 'territorial enigma': the English generally lack a collective territorial emphasis and have been historically written out of the script. The net outcome of this 'territorial enigma' is that, in contrast to the peoples of Ireland, Scotland, and Wales, who purportedly hold the cultural and institutional resources with which to mobilise against UK state hegemony, the English are unlikely to rebel against their own national identity, even if it does, in effect, exclude them. English regionalism has accordingly remained institutionally and politically fragile, always faced an uncertain future, and has developed an uneven historical and contemporary geography. It is worth pausing momentarily to consider two differing reasons for this and to undertake a deeper reading of the 'English Question'.

First, centralisation is deeply embedded within the territorial practices of the state (see Lefebvre 1976) and the imperialist British/English state system, more than most, has been historically dominated by functional top-down processes, largely instrumental in their goal of securing the best conditions for industrial development, economic strategic planning, and more recently economic regeneration (see above) and within this the fostering of an English regional civil society has *not* been part of the political agenda (compare Linehan 2003; Parsons 1988; Tomaney 2000).

Second, and related to this, regional mobilisation is difficult to achieve given: the frequent conflation of 'Englishness' with a nationalist and right-wing political agenda (compare Colls 2002; Giles and Middleton 1995; Linsell 2000; Paxman 1998); the ambiguous and generally uneven nature and coherence of English regional consciousness and associated identities (see BBC 2002;

MORI 1999); and perhaps more importantly the largely undocumented unevenness of regional interest group formation and their access to the spatially variegated sub-national state apparatus (see below). One illustration of all this is the Labour Government's recent 'sounding exercise' to test the demand for debating the transfer of responsibilities to the English regions through elected regional assemblies. Only in three regions—the North East, North West, and Yorkshire and Humberside—did interested stakeholders (individual and institutional) vote over 50 per cent in favour of holding a referendum in their region. The figure for the East Midlands was 41 per cent (ODPM 2003). However, these figures can be misleading if they are used to gauge identity and consciousness vis-à-vis the demand for English regionalism, without, first, asking individuals if they identify with the territories being offered by the Labour Party (compare Jones and MacLeod 2004; MORI 1999).

Together, then, we have an *unevenly developed and developing English regional civil society*, which from a mobilisation theory perspective makes collectivism difficult to achieve and sustain, and thus the English regions are slippery spaces around which to galvanise and mobilise territorial concerns. For instance, English regional civil society is particularly strong in places such as Cornwall, based on mobilising a Cornish nationalist cultural historical identity (see Deacon et al. 2003). Elsewhere, I have discussed the attempts made by the 50,000+ activists in Cornwall to campaign for a Cornish Assembly (Jones and MacLeod 2004). Regional civil society is also strong in places such as the North East and increasingly important in the North West and Yorkshire and Humberside due to the acquired historical legacies of territorial rivalries revolving around the North–South divide, i.e. the distinct cultural and economic difference found between North and South (see Colls 2002; Taylor 1993; Parsons 1988). In these latter spaces, regional (economic) interest group formation is perhaps more of a driving force than regional identity concerns per se—a point initially made by Smith (1965b) and in serious need of reconsidering at this current conjuncture. Elsewhere, I have also drawn attention to the (at times elite-dominated) nature of regional political mobilisation occurring in the North East since the mid-1990s—leading to the Campaign for the North East Assembly, the formation of the national Campaign for the English Regions (CFER), and its nurturing of cross-party constitutional conventions within the North West, Yorkshire, the West Midlands, and the South West (MacLeod and Jones 2001; Jones and MacLeod 2004; see also Morgan 2002; Sandford 2002; Tomaney and Hetherington 2003). The key point to this discussion is that geographical unevenness helps to explain the variable geometry in and through which English regional devolution is being introduced and developed. Moreover, *outside* regions with markers of cultural and economic difference and histories of (industrial) interest group formation—i.e. Northern territories and peculiar regions such as the South West of England—

regionalism across England has faced, and will continue to face, difficulties in providing a platform for mobilising popular support. The remainder of the chapter turns to discuss England's variable regional geometry by outlining the aims and status, strategies and tactics, and development and achievements of grassroots regional movements in the East Midlands.

## The Movement for Middle England

> Towards the end of 1995 I received a leaflet in the mail, from a group calling itself 'The Movement for Middle England'. Headed 'Middle England Awake' and displaying a quotation from G.K. Chesterton, 'For we are the People of England that have never spoken yet', it announced a conference to be held in Oxford, and invited people to 'work for a society you'll be proud to live in'. The Movement for Middle England was in favour of devolution and autonomous English regions ... Was this the beginning of a genuine resistance movement, I wondered, a grass-roots resurgence in which bamboozled and browbeaten Anglo-Saxons would finally throw off the yoke of the centralised and, as the leaflet put it, Norman British state? Was it a harmless fantasy addressed to the retired colonels and morris dancers of the deep English shires? Or was it a primitive historical cult convened more in the spirit of Goose Green? (Wright 1998: 26–27)

There are those who contest the purported 'territorial enigma' expressed by Taylor (1991, 1993). A number of grassroots regional movements, for instance, emerged during the early 1970s following the Kilbrandon Commission on the Constitution, which sparked an interest in devolution *outside* Scotland and Wales. In 1980 these grouped together as the 'Regionalist Seminar', spreading knowledge of 'what regionalism is about', and a core principle of participating movements signing up to a 'Declaration of Oxford' was to preserve historic community interests (Bennett 1985). In stark contrast to imposed 'standard regions', the Regionalist Seminar advocated governance through traditional territories, in some cases drawing inspiration from Kingdoms of the Anglo-Saxon Heptarchy, with the following connections being made: the Campaign for the North (broadly aligned to Northumbria), the Wessex Regionalists (following Wessex), Mebyon Kernow and Cowenthas Flamank (following Dumnonia), the Orkney Group, and the Shetland Movement. The Regionalist Seminar produced an annual publication, *The Regionalist*, to capture antagonisms against state centralisation and the perils of economic and cultural globalisation. However, with the onset of Thatcherism and an ongoing programme of localisation (see above) these movements lacked the 'action spaces' to become visible and several slipped into insignificance or went into hibernation.

A leading player in the grassroots regionalism field in more recent years has been *Devolve!*—known until year 2000 as Movement for Middle England. This organisation was founded in 1988 initially by three individuals involved with:

grassroots activism; cooperative networks; þa Engliscan Gesiðas (The English Companions) an Anglo-Saxon historical and cultural society; and bottom-up models of 'direct democracy'—associated with diverse neo-distributist and anti-modernist thinkers such as G.K. Chesterton, Robert Blatchford, Peter Kropotkin, and Peter Cadogan (MFME 1989). The winter 1988 edition of *The Regionalist* introduced MFME to the Seminar and detailed its founding aims (*The Regionalist* 1988: 4; also MFME 1988):

1. To be non-party political.
2. To work for the full autonomy of Middle England within a devolved England/Europe.
3. To have power vested in the small appropriate unit (i.e. no decision to be taken at a higher level than necessary).
4. To respect the right of any regional group or area to define its relationship with the whole.
5. To establish 'shadow' institutions outside the present political system, rather than contest elections within that system.

In contrast, then, to regionalist organisations seeking to influence the political system through electoral activity (such as the Wessex Regionalists) or through cross-party support (such as the Campaign for the North)—on which, see MacLeod and Jones (2001)—MFME promulgated the idea of direct democracy divorced from existing political institutions, although in one or two cases local councillors have become members (Banks 1997). As Wright notes above, MFME draw heavily on G.K. Chesterton's political poem 'The Secret People', first published in the campaigning *New Witness* magazine in November 1912, which sees the common folk of England as a people written out of the script of history by a centralised Norman territorial state. Their vision of 'regionalism'—regions 'built on people's own sense of identity'—seeks to devolve power down to the smallest area possible and then to build this up to a regional level within a confederation of regions (MFME 1991). This is to be contrasted with 'regionalisation'—a 'top-down division into administrative areas with fixed boundaries beyond debate'.

The naming of MFME, which 'expresses the "character" of the region and also serves to reproduce it [through] powerful feelings of identification' (Bialasiewicz 2003: 119), originates from a 'third-space'-like identification with both the Greater Midlands area (East and West Midlands combined) and the smaller 'Middle Angles' territory—an Anglo-Saxon Mercian dependency that existed between AD 500 and 700, centred on Leicester (Robyns 1983; Whitelock 1952: 164), but 'rehistoricized and read anew' in the twentieth century (bhabha 1994: 37). For MFME and other members of the Regionalist Seminar, the era before the Norman invasion represents a golden-age of rising material, cultural and artistic confidence, with the English re-forming themselves from Anglian, Saxon, Danish, and other strands and knowing themselves as a people—united, yet with strong regional traditions stemming from the heptarchy period—despite internal conflicts, a centralising Roman Church and increasing attention from ambitious external powers (compare Morton 1948; MFME 1999a). By contrast, the era of the Norman occupation, resulting in the abolition of the Anglo-Saxon Heptarchy, is seen as 'a no-man's-land' of centralisation without an English state system (Urwin 1982; see also Samuel 1998).

The Middle Angles territory of the East Midlands also possesses a unique 'historical and cultural unity' (Fawcett 1919) and for some MFME members this acted as a distinct reminder of a world not touched by globalisation and consumer capitalism. MFME mobilised this consciousness through their literature and emblem—a deliberate subversion of the Cross of St George, with the broken-cross creating four inward pointing arrows: signifying the great regions of England cooperating without being tied in the centre by London. The oak tree in the top left quadrant symbolised the once great forests of Middle England: Sherwood, Charnwood, Needwood, and Arden. This 'cultural regionalism' attracted several members from the historic county of Rutland—'the only example of an ancient Mercian division which has survived the West Saxon shire-ing of the district' (Morton 1933: 226)—and also provided the stimulus for heated debates on English culture within a multicultural and postcolonial world (MFME 1992, 1996).

The initial technique of MFME was to set up stalls in market areas of towns across the Midlands, with literature, badges, car stickers, etc. (MFME 1990). This generated some income, promoted the ideas and more importantly provided direct feedback on the ideas and views of a wide cross-section of people. At this time there was rising membership, various workshop and social events, an open newsletter plus an ideas exchange journal (from 1996) for members only, then called 'Views of Middle England' (see Banks 1997). The membership structures allowed Active members—numbering five by 1998—who were expected to participate in necessary work and meetings, tithe themselves (2.5 per cent of their disposable income) and steer the movement, and Support members (whose main social interests might lie elsewhere) who helped when they wanted to, paid a modest annual subscription, and were kept informed (MFME 1988).

One particularly notable pamphlet, *Wall-to-Wall Democracy*, which received media interest, promotes a model of direct democracy that draws on Anglo-Saxon principals of justice and societal organisation (MFME 1991). In opposition to the rising unelected state of neoliberalism, *Wall-to-Wall* discusses the historical and contemporary virtues of 'moot democracy', with power flowing from the citizen to the 'Regional Witan'—'the hallmark of a liberated England' (MFME 1991: 17). According to Wright's account, 'Spurning party politics, it favoured belonging—taking root in your region and helping to run it.' It wanted to 'encourage local moots of around 50 householders', and to establish them as 'building blocks of future democracy' (Wright 1998: 26). With the launch of EMDA in 1999, MFME issued a *Charter for the Midlands*, with individuals signing a petition to introduce elements of moot democracy and ensure 'regional democracy in the Greater Midlands with true subsidiarity at every level and full representation as a region of Europe' (MFME 1999b: 1). Later internal debates around New Labour's proposals for directly elected regional assemblies (see above) resulted in the moot model being presented for the twenty-first century within a 'new constitution for England' (*Devolve!* 2000a).

## From Movement for Middle England to *Devolve!*

Most social movements and organisations involved in pressure group politics experience a levelling off in their membership numbers—after an early growth in interest—and over time an ageing of membership can also occur, which can alter the dynamics of their policies and politics. Grant's work has shown how this can often lead to tensions and splits, with more radical members wishing to pursue alternative agendas (Grant 1989, 2000). MFME has been no exception to this, with its membership peaking in the mid-1990s with around 40 total members—drawn from across the age group 18 to 75 and with relatively balanced representation according to gender, class, and political affiliation. Frustrations over the limited growth were raised in the *Middle England Newsletter*, but it was recognised that 'time was not yet right for a higher profile' (MFME 1990).

Following a number of heated exchanges on its name, identity, and direction in the mid-1990s (MFME 1993a, 1993b, 1994)—with debating space being provided through an organisational fragmentation occurring in MFME between West Mercian and East Mercian groupings (MFME 1993a)—some members withdrew from MFME, wanting to define a more radical, historical, and 'organic regionalism'—building up a region 'from geology and topography as a counter-modern unit' (Matless 1998: 129). This position advocated outright opposition to developments such as the Government Offices for the Regions. The resulting new Mercia Movement thus offered an anti-modernist manifesto 'for the future inspired by the past' and based on the justice principles of communalism, organic democracy, ecological balance, and the re-creation of Mercia as an autonomous and sustainable bioregion within an English confederation (Mercia Movement 1997). For these organic regionalists, then, 'modern administration violates natural boundaries' (Matless 1998: 130–131). In 1998 the Mercia Movement participated in the formation of the Confederation for Regional England (CfRE), a radical counterpoint to the well-funded CFER (see above). More recently it has sought a broader dialogue in the Mercian Constitutional Convention (MCC) (Mercia Movement 2001), though without wanting to compromise its radical ideals. The MCC has in effect become the new form of the Mercia Movement, gaining local media coverage for its general historical antics and fringe political strategies: in Birmingham on 29 May 2003 it formally declared the whole of Mercia—from Cheshire to the Thames—independent of the United Kingdom and later announced a desire to introduce its own currency!

Meanwhile, the MFME maintained a more pragmatic and sensible stance, with emphasis on empowerment and inter-regional networking rather than history and shock antics. It continued to work at the grassroots, in the shadow of formal electoral politics and, later, of institutions like GOEM and EMDA. A twin strategy of regional moderation and democratic (or social justice) radicalism was just beginning to emerge. And with English regionalism rising high on the political agenda under New Labour, MFME members (now numbering 35) called a special general meeting in June 1999 to discuss their future aims and objectives (MFME 1999c)—with debate focused on either being a straightforward campaign group for a Greater Midlands region, or broadening its activities to promote cultural, democratic and regional devolution *across* England. Members present voted for the latter (a 'triple devolution of power from the centre') and subsequently renamed their organisation *Devolve!* (formerly Movement for Middle England) to: signify a move towards an *inter-territorial* and multidimensional approach to regional politics (dropping its own territorial claim in the Midlands); provide more meaningful engagements with policy-makers, practitioners, and civic regionalists involved in campaigns for elected regional government *across* England (collectively termed 'institutional regionalism'); and pay more attention to local and direction action initiatives for empowerment across Europe (see *Devolve!* 1999a, 1999b, 1999c).

The last issue of the *Middle England Newsletter* offered an honest account of achievements since MFME's formation, recognised the problems it faced in mobilising identity and support in this region, and attempted to clear space for the *Devolve!* project.

> Launched in 1988, a tiny movement with almost no resources committed itself to making a difference on three social issues: English Culture, Direct Democracy, and Regionalism.
>
> *English Culture*: our greatest relative failure. By ten years on we had failed to convince even some of our own members that the English are a people denied. What we have done is to develop our understanding of the problem (two pamphlets published, many debates, letters, stall conversations etc.). We can now see more clearly that the Great British assimilation project is a threat to all cultures, not just

> the English—and that our right to our own heritage, our own future, is truly yet another aspect of devolution. MFME can also claim some credit for helping to change attitudes in England to Scottish, Welsh and Cornish autonomy. In return we should acknowledge our debt to Plaid Cymru and Mebyon Kernow for their moral support and friendship over the year.
>
> *Direct Democracy*: another uphill struggle to convince people that there should be more to democracy than showing who you'd like to be ruled by every few years. Our 'Wall to Wall Democracy' pamphlet seemed like a voice in the wilderness in the early years. More recently the idea seems to be taking hold. There is now constructive debate both inside and outside our movement on the 'how to' of direct or participatory democracy. On top of this, some members continue to work 'hands on' in residents forums and other small groups.
>
> *Regionalism*: victims of our own success? A sea change since the early years, when 'the things we argued seemed too way out even for discussion in many circles'. Yet right from the start our concept of 'Middle England' as both the Greater Midlands and somehow the spirit of England struck a chord with (some of) the people of England who chatted on our Saturday stalls or took our literature. These ripples went wide. It can never be proved whether the media and politicians started to use the term Middle England because it was coming into public thought. What they did do was slant the meaning until our name became a real problem. Regionalism is now centre stage. After years of slog, we and our allies in the Regionalist Seminar can take a little credit for this … In 1988 we were among very few voices for a regional England and in our case this was inseparable from the democracy and identity issues. Now there are many regional advocates (from Westminster itself to e.g. the City Region Campaign) with some very different agendas. This has forces us to seek a new role … Hopefully—if we've got it right—our movement will be able to make a constructive contribution in several areas over the coming years. (MFME 1999a: 1–2)

Since 2000, *Devolve!* has adopted a 'new role' based around four key tenets (see *Devolve!* 2000b, 2001a): *regional devolution* (bringing power closer to people through regionalism to allow and encourage greater diversity); *democratic devolution* (real democracy through rotated delegates within a moot system); *cultural devolution* (nurturing English culture while respecting other cultures and identities); and *economic devolution* (cooperation instead of competition based on local economic networks). With the exception of the fourth tenet—a new angle for these activists and one heavily influenced by the formation of RDA regional economic strategies and only added to the *Devolve!* constitution after long debates and eventual agreements at the 2002 annual general meeting (*Devolve!* 2002)—the origins of this thinking can be found within latter day MFME discussion documents (discussed above) and these tenets involve a degree of maturing and evolution, as well as re-branding for new audiences. For each tenet, steering group members now convene working groups to debate these different dimensions of devolution, with each tenet also covered by several pages on the developing website to attract further recruits (see www.Devolve.org). Working groups in turn report back to the steering group, which meets every three to four months. At the time of writing, *Devolve!* has a membership of 51, comprising 45 ordinary members and a steering group (i.e. Active members) of six. Five of the steering group are involved in income sharing to support each other and to fund the activities of *Devolve!*

## Relational Futures: *Devolve!* as Networked Regional Forum

From the position of mobilisation theory, the most important post-MFME aspect of *Devolve!* has been its role in debating territorial dimensions of social justice by providing a means through which other grassroots civil society regional movements can get their voices heard. *Devolve!* Information Sheet No. 2—'How *Devolve!* Works to Support Regional Movements'—presents this East Midlands-based organisation as: 'an advocate', 'a channel', a 'think tank', and 'a forum'. The importance of *linkage* between these four concepts is expressed by the concern that:

> To further this work, *Devolve!* invites free affiliations with territorial regional/national movements in England and beyond; with other bodies advocating regional devolution; with confederations and associations of regional or pro-regional organisations (in which case the mutual affiliation will be deemed to be with their members also). This 'level thinking' is to indicate no hierarchy of relation. Further, no endorsement of positions or policies is implied on either side. (*Devolve!* 2001b)

In contrast, then, to the historically and geographically based conception of social justice expressed by organisations such as the Mercia Movement, *Devolve!* plugs more into current debates on intergovernmental reforms and relationships, while remaining territorially based by serving as an anchor point for activist networking. *Devolve!* has accordingly hosted three 'Whose Regions' conferences in recent years to debate the future of England. The first was convened as MFME and involved activists from across England and generated a fruitful dialogue with policy-makers involved in RDAs (see MFME 1998). The second created a productive exchange between the CFER—the civic regional movement lobbying for regional assemblies through constitutional conventions (see above), and activists campaigning for a Cornish Assembly (see *Devolve!* 2000c).

A third 'Whose Regions' conference in 2003 debated the future of 'The South' within the Labour Party's programme of English devolution. As noted above, regional assemblies are initially only going to be debated within the North of England and for critics this leaves 'the South' with a democratic deficit. 'Spotlight on the South'—chaired by the godfather of Scottish devolution, Canon Kenyon Wright, involving a presentation by the former Minister for Regions, Alan Whitehead MP, and drawing representation from leading political and cultural stakeholders (such as councillors from several political parties, members of existing regional assemblies, and grassroots regional activists) within the southern political space—granted *Devolve!* a mandate to form a 'Continuing Commission on the South' to discuss: (1) regional representation and funding; (2) resource allocation, planning, infrastructure, and networking across regions; (3) citizen involvement, local government, and very local democracy; and (4) identities and boundaries (see *Devolve!* 2003a, 2003b, 2003c, 2003d). This touches many areas commonly regarded as terrains of social justice and the success of this conference was evidenced by the Office of the Deputy Prime Minister, charged with implementing the White Paper on the governance of England, expressing interest in forming a 'brokering table' to debate the reconfiguring of the southern regional map (see below).

Meanwhile, at the Midlands scale, *Devolve!* has been active in the West Midlands Constitutional Convention—providing research and policy expertise (see Banks 2001; *Devolve!* 2001c) and also participation in forums to debate the constitutional possibilities of this region. More locally and using Leicester in the East Midlands as a pilot, *Devolve!* members have also been both developing and participating in forms of 'very local democracy' including: common ownership and stewardship structures; total and partial income sharing; residents groups and local forums; challenging—in the High Court—electoral destruction of local communities; holding local councillors to continuous account through new ward-based Community Alliances; and lobbying GOEM for community involvement in urban policy and budgets (see *Devolve!* 2003e, 2004).

While admittedly not shaking the very foundations of the Blair government, *Devolve!* has tried to destabilise those organisations programmed to sponsor 'official' visions of economic and social governance. In recent years, though, *Devolve!*—as one of only a few non-territorial regional devolution organisations in England and also the sole grassroots regional movement in the Midlands—is obviously being drawn into the bargaining process, spearheaded by the central state, as to how the regional process, particularly its 'territorial shape' (Paasi 1996), could be defined. According to established member and long-term regional activist Banks, commenting on recent legislation, 'while many aspects of the White Paper urgently need amendment as the Regional Assembly Bill goes through Parliament, there are now positive provisions of which democrats can take advantage' (2003: 15). This emerging position could place *Devolve!* in a catch-22 scenario for the future. It could either lead to an increase in the Support membership, through engagements in more mainstream agendas. Or alternatively, it could alienate some hard-core members, who—in the spirit of the Regionalist Seminar—joined to preserve and celebrate historic English regional cultures and not foster a dialogue with the formal political system.

## CONCLUSION: 'GENUINE RESISTANCE MOVEMENT' OR 'HARMLESS FANTASY?'

This chapter has taken stock of the remaking of state territoriality and the changing scalar contours of the UK state in relation to regional developments within England as a way of exploring social justice. Building on the work of Jones and MacLeod (2004), it has identified two separate processes operating through the English regions. These developments are geographically fragmented because of the legacies of state centralisation and the unevenly developed nature of English regional civil society. This has helped to produce a variable geometry within the English regions, which in turn is influencing the contemporary processes and patterns of post-national state restructuring.

By using the East Midlands region as a case study of state centralisation and disparate regional interests, the chapter has discussed how these two processes are being contested and conditioned by 'regional social relations' and has explored how grassroots movements like *Devolve!* have struggled to challenge the emerging political systems in England's regions. With just over 50 members, it could be written off as a 'harmless fantasy' (Wright 1998). For instance, what leverage do they have as a political movement and is this a curious representation of cultural politics rather than a serious regionalist movement? Moreover, are organisations such as *Devolve!* marginalised from the formal political arena and culturally as well within those spaces in which they operate?

Admittedly *Devolve!* membership is small but they would point out that Plaid Cymru (The Party for Wales) started out in 1925 with six 'eccentrics' sitting round a table. The critical challenge that *Devolve!* faces in future years relates to the ongoing ageing of its membership and the ability to recruit a large enough base of individuals to have sustained credibility as a non-party political lobbying organisation—especially in the thorny context of its shift from informal to more formal political territorial concerns (see above). At present, its views and strategies are not representative of the territorial space and relational networks within which it operates. In this region, grassroots regionalism is fragile, fragmented, and faces a challenging future.

This said, by engaging with the regional state and its apparatus, at a practical level, *Devolve!* has been important in: contributing to the general debate on Englishness and English regional culture since the late 1980s (receiving coverage in the national and local media—see MFME 1999a); promoting alternative forms of democracy at a grassroots urban level in Leicester in recent years and securing a space at ward level for marginalised residents from different ethnic/

cultural backgrounds; and initiating the Continuing Commission on the South in 2003. This latter development is particularly interesting given the desire in certain parts of the Labour Party to redraw the boundaries of the South West and South East, possibly leading to territorial recognition for Cornwall (as a separate region), and a rethinking of the interface between these two regions around the counties of Wiltshire, Gloucestershire, and Hampshire. This project is now chaired by the former Minister for the Regions and given the proposed review of local government boundaries in London—with one proposal being the territorial expansion of London into the South East region (see London Assembly 2003)—this discussion could be given a wider and more legitimate hearing.

# 7. City-region building

> There has been an under-emphasis in the city-region literature on how new territorial forms are constructed politically and reproduced through everyday acts and struggles around consumption and social reproduction. An especially notable lacuna is serious treatment of the role of the state and an associated politics of distribution constructed around various sites, spaces and scales across the city-region. In some respects, this silence on matters of politics and collective social agency arises from a tendency to reify the city-region itself as an agent of wealth creation and distribution. This comes at the expense of knowledge about the people, interests, and socio-political agents who populate and work in city-regions.
>
> (Jonas and Ward 2007: 170)

## INTRODUCTION

This chapter is concerned with city-region building through state and policy interventions. On this new regionalist front, the last few years have witnessed major proposed changes to the regulatory and governance landscape of the learning and skills industry. After a long preoccupation with welfare reform and the raft of welfare-to-work policy initiatives, as a response to continued and deep-seated underperformance in UK vocational education and training (VET), the Leitch Review of Skills was undertaken. To address the current governance system, characterised by 'complexity and bemusement' with 'duplications of institutional responsibilities', and a 'lack of joined up thinking' (HM Treasury 2006), the Government has announced comprehensive changes to the current system of skills governance and policy interventions across a number of geographical scales (see DCSF and DIUS 2008; DWP and DIUS 2008). A UK Commission on Employment and Skills (UKCES) has been established, wholesale restructuring of the Sector Skills Councils (SSCs) is taking place, and Employment and Skills Boards (ESBs) are being implemented at regional and local levels for England. The Learning and Skills Council (LSC) will be replaced with a Young People's Learning Agency, charged with helping local authorities work coherently together, and a Skills Funding Agency (SFA) to administer the flow of £4 billion of public money a year to colleges and training organisations. In addition to this, the 'work skills' component of welfare policy is to be based on local partnerships via multi-area agreements (MAA). This is the biggest shake up to the governance of skills in England for 20 years, repeatedly presented as the right institutional framework for making a higher-skill knowledge-based economy.

Wolf (2007) has provided a general critique of these policy initiatives and highlighted their shortcomings for ensuring 'world class skills'. Research has also highlighted the blurring of the skills and welfare policy framework and speculated on the role this will play in future labour markets (Nunn and Johnson 2008). This chapter is concerned with the implementation, delivery, and the geography of skills governance within the context of city-region building. Governance failure has plagued the skills and employment policy and institutional landscape for the past 35 years. According to commentators, 'the history of vocational education and training policy … is a saga of failure littered with discarded institutions and schemes' (Keep 2003: 14) and 'the institutional context … is by now so complex and constantly in flux that even people who work in it full-time cannot keep up' (Wolf 2007: 112–113). Put simply, we need to know more about how governance works, when and where it is failing, its effects, and what the alternatives are.

This chapter uses Sheffield and the Sheffield City Region specifically as a case study to discuss all this. Sheffield represents a particularly interesting example of a British city struggling with the policy discourses of city-regional competitiveness, because its employment and occupational structure has been transformed over the past 20 years from a high-paid employment economy with a plentiful supply of skilled jobs in the steel and engineering industries, to a de-industrialised economy where many of the new jobs created in the service sector tend to be low paid. Despite this, and like many other rustbelt city-regions in Britain, Sheffield (and its broader Yorkshire and Humberside region—part of the pan-regional Northern Way) is frequently presented as a laboratory for nurturing a sustainable skills and knowledge-based economy (compare Booth 2005; Crouch and Hill 2004; Lee 2002; Robson et al. 2000b; Sheffield One 2005; Sheffield Work and Skills Board 2008; Yorkshire Forward 2003; Work Foundation 2007). Interestingly, Sheffield is ranked 17th in the economic performance table on English city-regions and seventh in the employment performance table (HM Treasury et al. 2006: 26, 30). This, however, hides the qualitative micro-economic and social geographies of this complex city-region and specifically glosses over issues such as the quality and sustainability of the employment base and inequality more broadly. Moreover, in the context of the crisis and contradiction framework presented in Chapter 3, this chapter suggests that city-regions reinforce, and have the potential to increase, rather than resolve, uneven development and socio-spatial inequalities.

The argument is presented in three sections. The chapter first discusses the emerging city-region and skills governance context. This is followed by an analysis of the development of the Sheffield City Region and its strategies, and the chapter outlines how Sheffield's economy and labour market is represented. The chapter then probes labour market policy through the 'Skills Strategy for Sheffield', questions whether this is reinforcing labour market inequalities and, picking up the arguments from Chapter 4, raises the need to analyse the connection between state intervention, economic policy, and social policy.

## THE RETURN OF CITY-REGIONS

The previous two chapters have pointed to the burgeoning literature on the 'new regionalism' in the social and political sciences. Protagonists, both at academic and political levels, have made important arguments on the existence of regions, and city-regions more recently, as successful models of economic development in an increasingly post-national age. Given the increasing context of economic globalisation and the so-called 'borderless' and relational nature of transactions across the contemporary world, the new regionalism captures a belief that site- and place-specific scales of intervention can, first, anchor and, second, nurture nodes of dense economic, social and political activity. It is not hard to see why city-regions, i.e. metropolitan-scaled clusters of socioeconomic importance (Scott 1991b), are being presented as selective 'windows of locational opportunity' for capturing and developing an specialised reordering and rescaling of economic activity (Scott and Storper 2003: 587). In short, city-regions are coming to function as the basic motors of the global economy—a proposition that points as a corollary to the further important notion that globalisation and city-region development are but two facets of a single integrated reality (Scott 1991b, 2001).

In the late 1990s, the Centre for Urban and Regional Development Studies (CURDS) was accordingly commissioned by the Office of the Deputy Prime Minister (ODPM) Core Cities Group to examine the interaction of cities and regions and explore how they could stimulate economic growth within the regions (CURDS 1999). The report discussed the concept of the 'city-region' and its possibilities and constraints for reducing endemic spatial inequalities within the United Kingdom. In state discourse, city-regions are, of course, not new. As Western European experience over the past half a century has demonstrated, this 'metropolitan concept' normally follows in the wake of failed attempts to build stable 'regional units' of state intervention (Dickinson 1967). Following the findings of the CURDS study, and in parallel with other research, the idea of city-region competitiveness was developed further by an ODPM Working Group emphasising certain specific policy areas—in particular, skills, knowledge, innovation, enterprise, and competition—as the drivers of growth (ODPM 2003; see also SURF 2003) as well as advocacy groups (New Local Government Network 2005).

The city-region idea has gained much currency and is now in the vanguard of potential solutions to reducing uneven development and its manifestation as the North–South Divide. In 2004, for instance, the Northern Way was encouraged by the ODPM comprising the three northern Regional Development Agencies (RDAs) One North East, Yorkshire Forward and North West RDA, with the aim of 'bridging the £29 billion output gap' and restructuring the Northern economy on a more competitive footing (see Gonzalez 2006; Goodchild and Hickman 2006). Within this pursuit of reducing regional and urban disparities, the Northern Way identified eight city-regions in the North (Liverpool, Central Lancashire, Manchester, Sheffield, Leeds, Hull and Humber Ports, Tees Valley, and Tyne and Wear) as the basis for fulfilling its strategic growth objectives. The notion of 'city-region' is interpreted in this chapter, then, as 'the area over which key economic markets, such as labour markets as measured by travel to work areas, housing markets and retail markets, operate' (HM Treasury et al. 2006: 8). The city-region is thus the 'economic footprint' of the city; a 'fuzzy' concept that indicates a stretched-out or relational space that does not always correspond to administrative city boundaries (Robson et al. 2006; also MacLeod and Jones 2007; Parr 2005).

The city-region was initially pursued by (the Department of) Communities and Local Government (DCLG 2006a, 2006b, 2007; HM Treasury 2007) as part of a new local state framework, which emphasises a balanced competitiveness agenda of bringing lagging cities/regions to a common baseline without disturbing the strategic and dominant position of leading cities/regions. One grounding of this is City Development Companies—city-wide economic development institutions formed to drive economic growth and regeneration in the English city-regions. More recently and in the context of the review of sub-national economic development and regeneration and the Leitch skills agenda, ESBs represent a parallel solution. Additionally, the Department of Work and Pensions (DWP) introduced City Strategies, which focus on deprived urban centres and invite the key stakeholders from the public, private, and voluntary sectors to come together in a concerted local programme, a 'consortium', to improve the way support for individual jobless people is coordinated and delivered on the ground. In some cases, the two latter developments have been combined in some localities through Work and Skills Boards, which span city-regions and provide an interesting institutional context to examine skills vis-à-vis new regulatory and governance landscapes.

Whether all this reorientation of urban and regional policy, which (as noted in Chapter 2) we might call the 'hollowing out' of regional economic governance (upwards to pan-regionalism, downwards to cities, and outwards to more relational city-regions), will produce positive dividends is an important question for economic development trends more broadly. Critical here are distributional consequences and pivotal inter-linkages of growth strategies with the wider socioeconomic environment, which are never adequately specified in accounts promoting city-regions (Harrison 2007; Jonas and Ward 2007). As Brenner observes, there are limitations and deep contradictory outcomes of city-region building:

> For in their current, market-led forms, metropolitan institutions likewise tend to intensify intra-national sociospatial inequality, uneven development and interspatial competition, and thus to undermine the territorial conditions for sustainable economic development. Moreover, despite their explicit attention to problems of interscalar coordination and meta-governance, metropolitan political institutions cannot, in themselves, resolve the pervasive governance failures, regulatory deficits and legitimation problems that ensue as public funds are spread out ever more thinly among a wide number of subnational entrepreneurial initiatives. (Brenner 2003: 317)

At a political and policy level, commenting on the 'rapid ascent of the city-regions agenda', this observation is supported by Gonzalez et al. (2006: 317):

> The main risk in the particular interpretation of the city-region agenda … is its displacement of issues of uneven development and regional disparities by concentrating only on places that are doing well. This has at least three problematic consequences. First, the emphasis will be mainly on the urban core of the city-regions at the expense of secondary cities, smaller towns and remoter rural areas. Second, it will downplay the importance of the national scale as a frame where regional disparities are still (re)produced. Third, a reified view of scales is being used in this debate, one which assigns different functions to different scales.

Pushing a socioeconomic stance and sensitive to the consequences of this state-promoted uneven development, there is a need to also look at welfare-to-work and employability programmes, alongside the restructuring of skills and training initiatives, to get a handle on labour control and reproduction. This dominance of 'workfare'—where benefits are conditional on unemployed people participating in employment and training schemes—tends to be locked into managing decline and creating the conditions for the creation of surplus value, rather than preparing labour for new and sustainable employment opportunities (see Chapter 4). The effect of these policies, as highlighted in the research of Sunley et al. (2006), is to make labour markets more competitive through enhanced flexibility vis-à-vis minimal regulations and in doing so reinforce their contingent nature. Workfare, because of its regulatory regime and frequent compulsion, removes any (supposed) barriers to employers obtaining a ready supply of labour. Social groups who enter welfare-to-work and training programmes tend to be vulnerable and disadvantaged. The 'work first' principle tends to give prominence to the first job offer and the assumption that work will be sustained and there will be some sort of upward mobility. Workfare, in turn, increases competition, or 'workfare churning', as a result of substitution as subsidised employment is used to replace 'real' jobs. The direction of the unemployed to low-paid work creates a 'crowding' effect on the labour market, which puts even more downward pressures on wages in certain sectors (for perspectives on these issues, see Peck and Theodore 2000a, 2000b; Chapter 4).

## THE SHEFFIELD CITY-REGION AND SKILLS GOVERNANCE

The Sheffield City Region has been in the making over the past five years and encompasses South Yorkshire and North East Derbyshire, thus uniquely cutting across two RDA boundaries (Yorkshire Forward and East Midlands). In addition to the two RDAs and two Sub-Regional Partnerships, there are eight local authorities and the Peak Planning Board. Within these, there are additional numerous strategies and local strategic partnerships/neighbourhood partnerships based around Single Regeneration Programmes.

The initial City Region Development Programme (CRDP) reflected the overall growth orientations as set down by the Northern Way. Four priority interventions were outlined (South Yorkshire Partnership/Alliance Sub-Regional Strategic Partnership 2005: 14):

- Developing knowledge and research on an internationally competitive scale.
- Developing a comprehensive connectivity strategy.
- Providing the skills required by an internationally competitive economy.
- Creating an environment to encourage investment and higher quality of life.

The CRDP identified barriers to growth, economic activity rates were 'patchy', and levels of mobility 'depend upon a package that addresses each of the specific barriers in deprived communities—including public transport, childcare and bridging learning to Learners' (South Yorkshire Partnership/Alliance Sub-Regional Strategic Partnership 2005: 18). Plugging the skills mismatch is also seen as a high priority. The CRDP recognised that 'renewed targeting at the most deprived communities is required to better connect them to the larger pool of jobs and services across the city region' (South Yorkshire Partnership/Alliance Sub-Regional Strategic Partnership 2005: 24).

Linked to this, and with respect to labour market opportunities, the RDA (Yorkshire Forward) had begun to 'talk up' the prospects of the regional economy. To give one example of this, it is claimed that:

> Yorkshire & Humber has a robust, diverse and bullish economy ... Yorkshire's power is its people, our 2.5 million strong workforce leads the country in sectors as varied as advanced engineering, food production, bioscience and digital technologies. Unemployment is at a 30 year low and the same as the national average. (Yorkshire Forward 2005: 1)

Elsewhere, an upbeat tone was evident about how the Sheffield City Region and its knowledge-based economy should be seen and narrated, which reinforces the strategies of the Yorkshire Forward RDA. Repeated statements and discourses on the economy develop an almost scientific truth status with respect to the benefits of market-based growth-orientated strategies, which is in turn used to justify local state intervention (Etherington and Jones 2009). Similarly, the Sheffield City Strategy 2002 to 2005, produced by the Sheffield First Partnership (a city-wide partnership bringing together public, private, voluntary, community and faith sectors to coordinate regeneration activity), for instance, asserted that:

> As late as 1999 it was legitimate to pose the question—'can Sheffield re-discover the inventiveness which previously made it a world wide brand, or is the City locked in a downward spiral in which talented people and organisations will progressively migrate elsewhere?' By 2002 there was convincing evidence that such questions are now irrelevant—the City has turned the decisive corner and is now 'on the up'. (Sheffield First 2003: 10)

In many respects the Sheffield First Partnership (Local Strategic Partnership) and other partnerships within the city-region were responding to increasing economic and development activity by over-hyping progress being made and presenting an 'image' that will attract inward investment.

The Government's agenda in relation to joining up partners with respect to welfare-to-work programmes set in motion an attempt to galvanise partnership working at the city-region level through the submission of a successful City Strategy in 2006 on behalf of the South Yorkshire local authorities. This brought about closer joint working between Job Centre Plus and other partners in the face of increasing economic inactivity and worklessness in the sub-region. In 2007 the South Yorkshire Partnership was dissolved as the Sub-Regional Partnership to be replaced by the City-Region Forum, with the Executive Director appointed in 2008. In addition, following the Leitch Review, a Work and Skills Board was established within the Sheffield First Strategic Partnership in 2007 to take forward the Leitch skills agenda. The

Board has the remit of bringing together the demand and supply-sides of the local labour market in efforts to raise employability and skills levels; putting employer needs at the heart of employability and skills programmes; and ensuring funding agencies align resources in support of employability and skills objectives (Sheffield Work and Skills Board 2007: 1). To enact this, the Board has been allocated seven broad tasks:

- Approve and own a three-year delivery plan to include agreed priorities and performance targets.
- Identify resources and ensure agencies align relevant funding.
- Ensure consistency with partners' plans and the Local Area Agreements (LAAs).
- Oversee performance against the delivery plan.
- Hold partners to account.
- Mobilise employers to commit opportunities/vacancies and to undertake workforce development.
- Identify good practice and champion employability and skills initiatives within the city and the region.

Strategy production is being framed within a wider Yorkshire and Humberside Regional Skills Partnership, which will coordinate the different sub-/city-region and local authority wide strategies in terms of the Regional Economic Strategy and addressing the Leitch targets set down for the region.

## CHALLENGES TO GOVERNING SKILLS

Currently, the skills strategies for the individual local authority area are being formulated in advance of the city-region. For example, the 'Skills Strategy for Sheffield' (the local authority area) is currently being drafted for the Sheffield Work and Skills Board and for taking forward the Leitch ambitions and targets. The vision for this is to produce a city that has 'the highly skilled labour force capable of attracting high-value-added businesses and jobs to the area and one where its businesses and services are highly productive and capable of competing with the best in the global economy'. Moreover, it 'will be a city driven by an overarching conviction that everyone matters, where all are encouraged and helped to develop the skills that will allow them to take full advantage of economic opportunities as they emerge'. These assumptions are largely based on the fact that it 'will be a city that thrives on innovation and an entrepreneurial culture, where businesses are well served with coherent and accessible advice and support where visionary leadership and effective management skills are widespread' (Sheffield Work and Skills Board 2008: 1). Seven skills challenges are then discussed. These are: to improve the skills levels and attainment of young people; develop foundation skills to improve economic inclusion; promote a culture of lifelong learning and encourage progression; build a demand-led training system; cultivate the higher skills needed for economic transformation; lock in high skills; and strengthen partnership (see also CESI 2005).

The skills strategy highlights a number of 'key issues' (although I would prefer to see them as significant challenges) that the Sheffield local authority area needs to address to transform its economy (CESI 2005: 19–20). The central challenge relates to addressing deep-rooted and extensive labour market inequalities and exclusion. For example, a third of the working population has no qualifications at level 2 or higher—more than Manchester or Newcastle—and there is a persistent employment and productivity gap. As it is acknowledged that skills and employment growth are intertwined then the prospects for the city-region in the face of a recession are not positive. Employment growth in South Yorkshire over the past 20 years has been 17 per cent (compared with Humber 23 per cent, and North Yorkshire 35 per cent, in the region), which is at a low level reflecting the high rate of job losses in the early 1990s.

Even before the recession emerged, the prediction for growth in the Sheffield City Region has been lower than other parts of the region (Ekos 2006: 2). Economic growth will depend upon higher qualified and skilled people and the skills gap between the city-region and England in relation to National Vocational Qualification (NVQ) 3 and 4 is significant. For NVQ 4 this is 5 per cent, which translates into about 40,000 more people to obtain NVQ 4 qualifications to catch up with the national average (Sheffield City Region 2006: 13). There are too few high-quality jobs in high-value growth sectors and this discourages those attaining higher skills from being attracted to, remaining in, or returning to the city.

Economic development, inward investment and higher skills are, therefore, mutually dependent and require careful coordination and forward planning. In addition to the 'key issues' raised above, which capture the stubborn problems of the Sheffield City Region low-skills equilibrium, the obvious jobs gap, and the considerable gulf between economic reality and discursive rhetoric, the chapter notes emerging problems of governance complexity and potential failure. With respect to governance complexity, numerous institutional changes and strategies are being produced within a short period of time. Sheffield and its region are now creating Work and Skills Boards for the respective local authority partnerships, and following the Leitch recommendations partners are attempting to create skills pledges committing employers to train people who have low-level skills. Within the Sheffield City Region itself, the Forum is establishing Joint Issue Boards, although it is unclear how these will take the skills agenda forward. Within Sheffield, a Local Employment Partnership has been established in order to develop a sustained commitment by local employers to providing local job opportunities. At the regional level, the RDA, through its convening of the Regional Skills Partnership, is taking on a more proactive role in shaping territorial and sector policies, as the LSC will be phased out. The shift in responsibilities for skills delivery away from the LSC to the local authorities will create a challenge for those seeking to join up and coordinate the proliferation of strategies and programmes at the city-region scale.

A key component of Leitch is its reliance on the market with strategies being predominantly private-sector led, exemplified through the example of Train to Gain. There is considerable evidence that there are problems with engaging with employers and, as the draft skills strategy noted, too few employers invest in the skills of their workforce 'that will be necessary for them to secure a competitive advantage in the knowledge economy'. Furthermore, the focus on private-sector employers tends to ignore the role of the public sector (e.g. local authority and health) in terms of its role in promoting in-work training. Furthermore, coordination issues are apparent in relation to matching demand and supply of the training provision. The supply of education and training is not as responsive to employer and employee demand as is required to meet the Leitch challenge because qualifications are not always fit for purpose, training provision is sometimes too inflexible and employer needs are not always well articulated. At the same time, there is an imbalance in the skills that the local economy needs and those that the city's workforce possesses, with an over-reliance on traditional skills, but with skill gaps and shortages in some buoyant or developing sectors, which threaten to stifle growth (Sheffield Work and Skills Board 2008).

So far, there has been no articulated skills strategy for the Sheffield City Region. City-region local authorities have participated in the Government's LAA process, which could be converted into the production of a possible MAA (around employment and skills) at the city-region level. The LAAs are seen as a possible mechanism by the Government to join up strategies, policies and programmes and improve partnerships in order to enhance outcomes in public service areas. MAAs operate on the same principles, except over a broader geographical area such as the city-region. Such an MAA may galvanise the strategic focus at the city-region level, although whether it will ensure increased employer engagement is open to question. Governance failure arises from market failure in the face of extensive shortfalls and gaps, which can only be 'plugged' by extensive resources and governance models with clearer lines of accountability and transparency. Whether this can be realised at the city-region level is open to question.

The management of local labour markets through city-regions characterised by depressed labour markets is a perpetual challenge in relation to regeneration and upskilling. This is acknowledged by the Sheffield Work and Skills Board:

> [T]o concentrate on the cultivation of high skills in isolation can only lead to the polarisation of our city with those who are most able, best equipped and self-confident benefiting from better paid, more secure employment in high skill, high value sectors, whilst those without these attributes are facing a future of low paid, fragile employment in low value and declining sectors of the local economy and competition from better-qualified individuals attracted to new opportunities in the city. (Sheffield Work and Skills Board 2008: 38)

It is further claimed that the dangers of this strategy of promoting a relational and mobile knowledge-based economy at the expense of nurturing a territorial socioeconomic base and addressing issues of collective consumption will in part be offset by strategies in place to deliver economic inclusion and progression. The key here is the notion of the 'skills escalator', where workforce development needs to be planned, continuous, consistent and responsive to individual need. Other policy mechanisms, though, could undermine and work against sustainable employment and skills objectives. There are over 77,000 on long-term benefits in South Yorkshire alone and there are the dangers of the welfare-to-work programmes reinforcing contingent labour markets (see Fletcher 2007). The Government's welfare reforms (2008) involving the implementation of the 'Flexible New Deal' and policy adjustments relating to lone parents and disabled people place greater emphasis upon conditionality and pressures to accept job offers. This could only serve to reinforce low-paid and low-skill labour markets, which have been a characteristic feature of employment restructuring in the local economy (see Cochrane and Etherington 2007; Etherington and Jones 2009). Chapter 10 returns to Sheffield on this theme.

## CONCLUSIONS

> Improving skills will help individuals to improve their employability, progress in their careers, and secure better wages. It will help employers to secure increased productivity and profitability for their businesses. It will help us reduce unemployment, tackle child poverty and improve social mobility. And it will help to reduce crime, improve health outcomes, and improve civic and community participation. (DIUS 2006: 2)

A lot is being expected of skills in the global economy! In short, skills are becoming the panacea for advanced capitalism. Evidence, though, suggests that part of the 'skills problem' broadly lies with governance, i.e. the nature of state intervention itself and the way policy interventions are arranged and have been devolved and decentralised in recent years (Jones 1999; North et al. 2007). The Sheffield City Region (and its various 'strategies') needs to be viewed within the wider political economy context of state restructuring. The agenda under discussion could be seen as an attempt to displace the economic management of cities to city-regional networked entrepreneurial governance. Here, governance is important for analysing skills on four levels. First, 'images' and discourses allow policy-makers to construct policy problems and then articulate solutions. For example, how the skills problem is defined and linked to employability is critical to understanding the local economy. Second, 'instrumentation' practices allow actors and players to be enrolled into governance arrangements, with some voices left marginal and others afforded dominance. Third, and linked to this, governing 'action' provides the basis for outlining the various roles and responsibilities (i.e. institutions, agencies, non-governmental organisations (NGOs), employers, etc.) for those involved in governance, which can often be a complex arrangement, as the skills agenda is highlighting. Fourth, by virtue of its sub-national spatial focus, governance can create space for policy experimentation and it also provides a way of tackling (or even reinforcing) uneven development and territorial/social inequality.

On this fourth point, this chapter has analysed the emerging city-region approach to the management of labour markets in Sheffield and discussed the links between the interventions of 'active' labour market policies and knowledge-based-economy informed skills strategies, and their potential influences on the local labour market. Sheffield's economy has undergone significant changes and restructuring since the early 1980s, with large-scale job losses occurring in the traditional industries (steel, engineering). Whilst there has been some improved performance in the local economy, low pay, skills and high levels of worklessness characterise the labour market. There is little evidence, though, that upskilling to achieve upward mobility of the kind inferred in recent government documentation on city-regions and, in turn, constructing the sustainable basis for a 'global city region' based on localised agglomeration (Scott 2001) occurs to any significant degree within the Sheffield City Region labour market. The chapter has highlighted that there is also a substantial skills gap to accompany the employment gap within the Sheffield economy, which current strategies appear to be unable to plug.

Yes, the causes of the problem are deeply economic, and supply-side initiatives can make a difference in the right context, but they are also deeply political; they relate to the shortcoming of the neoliberal model of city-regional competitiveness, its 'everyone's a winner' discourse (Bristow 2005), and multiple rounds of market failure, government failure, government-induced market failure, and market-induced government and governance failures. The key to UK (and Sheffield) success in an expanding global economy will be the ability to innovate and apply technology, and control an increasingly intellectual property portfolio. This requires an economy able to produce, absorb, and reproduce highly skilled people, which policies in the Sheffield City Region appear to be unable to provide in a sustainable manner. Future research is encouraged on the consequences of the scenarios outlined here for: the future of labour markets without a growing and sustainable stock of 'good' jobs; social exclusion geographies stemming from this; and those local people and place characteristics mentioned above with respect to unevenly developing cultures of (un)employability.

# PART III

# The new new localism

# 8. Locality making

> Our approach recognises that places have specific geographic, historic, environmental and economic circumstances that help to determine the prospects for growth and the most suitable approach to support the private sector and residents' opportunities … Policy should therefore recognise that the situation will be different for each place and is likely to be particularly affected by factors such as the inherent skills mix or entrepreneurial tradition of the population; business confidence; quality of infrastructure provision; and proximity of trading markets. There has in recent years been a strong focus on the role that agglomeration effects—the contribution of people and businesses within a defined areas—can have on economic performance.
>
> (HM Government 2010: 7)

## INTRODUCTION

Welcome to the new new localism. The quotation above is taken from the *Local Growth* White Paper, launched in November 2010 in the wake of the UK's election of a new Conservative-led Coalition Government, which also marked the end of the Labour administration (1997–2010). Underpinning the White Paper was the argument that previous attempts at promoting economic and social development had been too centralised and there was a need to curtail top-down initiatives that had ignored the varying needs of different areas. In England, institutions such as the 'bureaucratic' and 'rigid' Regional Development Agencies (RDAs) were to be swept aside and replaced by 'flexible' and 'tailored' Local Enterprise Partnerships (LEPs) and Enterprise Zones. As the then Deputy Prime Minister continued, this was to mark an end to the 'culture of Whitehall knows best' and create the conditions for 'meaningful decentralisation' (Clegg 2010, cited in HM Government 2010: 3). The Coalition Government of 2010–15, and the Conservative Government from May 2015–, has purported to offer a radically different approach to spatially based economic and social development policy, but did it deliver?

This chapter offers a contextual framework to explore some of the somewhat *silent geographies* of the 'new new localism' (Jones and Jessop 2010; Jones 2013). In doing so, the chapter seeks to offer theoretical insights into the rhetoric of decentralist discourses and the geographical complexities and contradictions of local state remaking on-the-ground (cf. Clarke 2014; Clarke and Cochrane 2013; Mohan 2012). The new localism is an old concept (see Peck

1995)—and one that will doubtless recur (see Ward and Hardy 2013). The latest variant of localist thinking draws extensively on some key antecedents. According to the 'Big Society' guru, Jesse Norman MP, localism 'is a coherent and logistical expression of a conservative tradition which goes back to the 18th century' (Norman 2011: 201). Edmund Burke's 'little platoons' pepper this literature and are presented as progressive enablers for a democratic form of civil society-centred economic and social policy (Willetts 1994). The reanimation of civil society is in turn viewed as a means of stimulating localist economic development. As one LEP leader has argued, 'growth programmes and policies seem focused more on social re-engineering than growth' (Alex Pratt, Chair of Buckingham Thames Valley LEP, quoted in HoC and BIS, 2013: 56). The chapter argues that by attempting to link economic and social policy in local contexts, the Government's new localism is profound and needs to be more fully theorised in undertaking geographical political economy research. In the words of Jesse Norman (2011: 197) again, the Conservative's new localism stresses a:

> three way relationship between individuals, institutions and the state. It is when this relationship is functioning well that societies flourish. This requires each element in the triad to be active and energised in its own right … Societies should be thought of as ecosystems.

The chapter explores the conceptual significance of this notion of 'ecosystems' for geography and beyond. It suggests that there is considerable mileage in the notion of 'locality' to advance critical policy analysis and build political economy theory, shedding particular light on the 'agglomeration booster' (Haughton et al. 2014) discourses offered by the Conservatives since 2010. During the mid to late 1980s, 'locality' was *the* spatial metaphor deployed to describe and explain the shifting world of regional studies (Cooke 2006). Building on previous research (Jones and Woods 2013; Jones 2011), the chapter argues that the resulting 'localities debate' saw a potentially important concept prematurely abandoned. It urges a 'return to locality' to enlighten studies of economic and social development. It offers three new readings of locality, which, when taken together, constitute the basis for thinking about geography through the lens of *new localities*. The chapter suggests that, first, locality can be seen as bounded territorial space, recognised politically and administratively for the discharge and conduct of public services, and for the collection and analysis of statistical data. Second, locality represents a way of undertaking comparative research analysis, linked to processes occurring within and outside localities and also connecting them. Third, locality can be used to read spaces of flows for numerous policy fields, which in turn exhibit spatial variations due to interaction effects. Additionally, and building on notions of cultural political economy (Chapter 1), the chapter suggests that for locality to have analytical value it must also have both an imagined and material coherence. Last, the chapter draws on these constructs to argue that uneven development within the context of the crisis of crisis-management is an integral feature of this new new localism.

## WHAT IS LOCALITY? THE RISE AND FALL OF SPATIAL METAPHORS

'What is locality?' asked Simon Duncan (1989) when commenting on the locality debates of the previous five years. 'Locality' was that buzz-word of the mid-1980s, even a 'new geography' (Cochrane 1987), used to frame research on economic geography. It filled the pages of human geography journals and contributed to the intellectual development of regional studies (see also Cooke 1990). Reflecting on this, Cooke has gone as far as to argue that debates around localism were 'the most heated yet illuminating wrangles in human geography since those over "environmental determinism" in the 1950s and the "quantitative revolution" in the 1960s. The soul of the discipline seemed to be at stake' (Cooke 2006: 1). For Duncan, locality was being used as a misleading catch-all term, an 'infuriating idea' used imprecisely to describe the local autonomy of areas, case study areas, spatially affected process (social, political, economic, cultural), spaces of production and consumption, the local state, and so on.

Massey's (1984) text *Spatial Divisions of Labour* was pivotal to starting what became the locality debate. This was written during an era of intense economic restructuring and challenged how geographers thought about 'the local' in an increasingly internationalising and globalising world in which Fordist and Keynesian certitudes were perceptibly unravelling. The tangible impact of all this was an acceleration of uneven development, with acute job loss in some areas juxtaposed with accelerating growth in others, as distinctive localities began to emerge in the context of globalisation and economic restructuring (see also Lovering 1989).

The intellectual goal in this was to tease out the dialectic between space and place by looking at how localities were being positioned within, and could themselves help to reposition, the changing national and international division of labour. For Massey (1991), 'the local in the global' was not simply an area around which a line can be drawn; instead, localities were defined in terms of sets of social relations or processes under consideration. This highly influential 'new regional concept of localities' (Jonas 1988) influenced two government-sponsored research initiatives in the UK, delivered through the Economic and Social Research Council—the Social Change and Economic Life programme and the Changing Urban and Regional Systems (CURS) programme. Both were given substantial funding and remits to uncover the effects of international and global economic restructuring on local areas, exploring why different responses and impacts were reported in different places. Locality research, independent of these programmes, was already taking place in Lancaster University (Murgatroyd et al. 1985) and Sussex University (Duncan 1989), which fuelled an interest in this important topic (although as Barnes (1996) notes, notions of 'locality' differ across all these interventions and focusing on the CURS programme is most helpful to get behind the meaning of locality).

In seeking to put 'the local' into 'the global', the CURS initiative set out to undertake theoretically informed empirical research in seven localities between 1985 and 1987. The goal was to examine the extent to which localities themselves could shape their own transformation and destiny as agents and not be passive containers for processes passed down from above. Two edited books documented the fortunes of a series of mainly metropolitan de-industrialising towns/regions and rural areas, tracking the impacts of globalisation and economic restructuring on 'the local' and the considering the complex and variable local–global interplay that conditioned locality experiences (Cooke 1989a; Harloe et al. 1990).

Particularly worthy of note here was the work of Hudson and Beynon (see Beynon et al. 1989), whose research closely followed Massey's theoretical and interpretative framework. Their account of economic change in Teesside seemed to demonstrate a 'locality effect' of local particularities in global times: the different ways in which 'rounds of investment' can impinge on the local economic landscape, how local politics played a role in international investment decisions, and, in turn, how attempts to cope with de-industrialisation (by either building a service-based economy or using state-sponsored local economic initiatives to create employment opportunities) were expressed on the ground.

As argued by Gregson (1987), Duncan and Savage (1991), and Barnes (1996), there is a fundamental difference between locality research (the CURS findings) and the resulting 'locality debate' across human geography and the social sciences. The latter was fuelled by a desire to rethink the theorisation of socio-spatial relations across disciplines, within the context of a broader transition from Marxist to poststructuralist research enquiry. The localities debate was also informed by shifting research methodologies, and practices, such as the rise and fall of critical realism (see Pratt 2004). In this febrile intellectual context, the journal *Antipode*, between 1987 and 1991, published a series of often-heated exchanges on the conceptual and empirical value of localities (for summaries, compare Cooke 2006; Pratt 2004). The initial assault came from North America by Smith (1987, 63), who bemoaned the perceived shift away from (Marxist) theory to a critical realist-inspired regional world of empirics, worthy of nothing more than a 'morass of statistical data'. Smith's memorable dismissal of localities research had it that 'like the blind man with a python in one hand and an elephant's trunk in the other, the researchers are treating all seven localities as the same animal'. This was supported, to a differing degree, by Harvey (1987), who saw these projects as refusing to engage in any theoretical or conceptual adventures. The consequences, for Scott (1991a: 256–257), was to encourage 'a form of story-telling that focuses on dense historical and geographical sequences of events, but where in the absence of a strong interpretative apparatus, the overall meaning of these events for those who live and work in other places is obscure'.

Duncan (1989) offered a more sympathetic critique, which saw locality—in the wrong hands—as a form of reified uniqueness and 'spatial fetishism': in what sense can localities act, or is it the social forces within these spaces that have this capacity? In two influential papers with Savage, Duncan made the first serious interventions on the relationships between spatial scales (Duncan and Savage 1990; Savage and Duncan 1990). Duncan concluded with some thoughts on three ways forward for research on locality: considerations of spatially contingent effects (processes contained in places), propositions on local causal process (locally derived forces of change), and the notion of locality effects (the combination of the previous two, affording a capacity to localities to act). Warde (1989) recognised the value of locality for empirical research but also argued that the scale of locality changes according to the object of analysis under question. Cooke (1987, 1989b), the Director of CURS, took a more defensive and ultimately pragmatic line, arguing that CURS was about seeking to make some general claims from multi-site case study research, even if this was about nothing more than local labour markets and its boundaries. The CURS findings were, therefore, empirical and not empiricist (see Cooke 2006).

A special issue of *Environment and Planning A* offered further critique and extension, and contended that locality was still a valuable concept to be grappled with. For Jackson (1991), the danger was that cultural change and political change were overly attributed to economic factors, at odds with a reality in which each was embedded in the other. Pratt (1991) took a similar line and suggested a need to look at the discursive construction of localities and their material effects. Paasi (1991), much inspired by the 'new regional geography' material that the locality debate uncovered and which helped rekindle interest in regions, encouraged scholars to take 'geohistory' more seriously and offered the idea of 'generation' to distinguish between the concepts of locality, place and region. Duncan and Savage (1991, 1989) pushed what they saw as the missing agenda of place-formation and class formation and the interconnections of these within and between localities. Cox and Mair (1991; see also Cox 1993) offered an agenda-setting account of localities in the United States as arenas for economic development coalitions, and as ways of the fixing and scaling socio-spatial relations. Their research took debate forward and brought agency and scale to the fore through notions of 'local dependency', the 'scale division of labour' and the 'scale division of the state'—concepts that highlighted the location and mobility of actors at different times. Cox and Mair claimed this avoided 'spatial fetishism' (a criticism levelled by Sayer 1991) as locality is seen not in physical terms but as a 'localised social structure'. Finally, Massey's (1991, 1994) interventions offered some sensible qualifiers on what CURS had initially set out to achieve, shifting the scale of debate from locality to 'senses of place'.

As Cooke's (2006) subsequent retrospective commentary notes, because CURS and the locality debate became so quickly mired in these debates, the potentially useful notion of locality was jettisoned somewhat prematurely. Debates moved on and during the mid-1990s economic geographers became preoccupied not so much with localities per se but with the links between space and place as a way of looking at the 'local in the global'. Massey (1994) argued that globalisation is happening but that the extent of time–space compression is socially and spatially uneven due to the variable mobility potential of people in place. 'Power geometries', a metaphor for capturing geographies of power, exist and therefore constrain some and enable others. This makes generalisations about the powerlessness of 'the local' in a globalising world unwise (compare Harvey 1989). The argument here was that localities need to be understood in terms of 'global senses of place'—as interconnected nodes in spaces of flows, stretching back and forth, ebbing and flowing according to how they are positioned by, and positioning, socio-spatial relations. Two distinctions are then made to get a handle on 'the local in the global'. The first is a 'regressive sense of place', based on rejection of the potentials of globalisation and the embrace instead of heritage and other forms of 'romanticised escapism'. The second is a more 'progressive sense of place', based on harnessing and making the most of difference and diversity through those stretched-out connections. Massey discusses this through her own experiences of living in Kilburn (a cosmopolitan area of North London) and her approach has no truck with locality perspectives that stick to administrative boundaries or tightly drawn labour market areas. Localities as 'global senses of place' are *relational* in the sense of seeing the local as an unbounded mosaic of different elements always in a process of interaction and being made. In short, one cannot explain locality or place by only looking inside it, or outside it; the 'out there' and 'in here' matter *together* and are dialectically intertwined (see Massey 2005, 2007).

## BRINGING THE METAPHOR BACK: TOWARDS 'NEW LOCALITIES'

In the early 1990s, 'region' replaced locality as the spatial descriptor around which economic and political geography cohered. Academic trends tend to closely mirror political and policy events (see Cooke and Morgan 1998) and economic geographers began increasingly to focus on the perceived re-emergence of regional economies and new spaces of economic governance across the globe (Chapters 5 and 6). These spaces had been initially flagged by writers talking about post-Fordism and the geographies of flexible accumulation. From these initial efforts came wider attempts to delimit the contours of a 'regional world' (Storper 1997). Scott, for instance, in the text *New Industrial Spaces* (1988), offered a new way of looking at agglomeration and the development of distinct local territorial production complexes or industrial districts. Whereas Fordist accumulation was favoured by and grew in accordance with economies of scale and vertical integration, economic development after-Fordism was seen to be linked to spatially specific economies of scope resulting from the vertical disintegration of production and the development, amongst other things, of flexible working practices and shared support mechanisms. The geographical extent of this phenomenon and its reproducibility and sustainability was discussed at length in various edited collections (see Storper and Scott 1992). Inspired by this, debates gradually shifted throughout the 1990s to examine the governance of local economies in global contexts through a 'new regionalist' perspective—as part of a broader 'institutional-turn' in economic geography. A parallel set of debates, also drawing on 'new regionalist' thinking, took place in political science on 'multilevel governance', driven by the so-called hollowing out of the national state and the 'Europe of the Regions' thesis (Keating 1998; Scott 2001). For Cooke this was important for locality studies:

> Probably the longest-lasting legacy of locality studies has been the rise of so-called 'new regionalism'. Already spotted around the time of his return from Australia by Nigel Thrift (1983) this theorised regional political economy analysis was gaining ground rapidly as we have seen, in the new times of 'global localisation'. The locality studies themselves and the comparative methodology that allowed spatial variety to be explained within a coherent and satisfying theoretical framework furthered this impulse. (Cooke 2006: 10)

This orthodoxy and alleged theoretical coherence referred to above by Cooke has, of course, been subjected to piercing academic critique. In a similar manner to some of the critiques of locality, philosophically (via critical realism) the new regionalism is deemed guilty of 'bad abstraction' in that it ignores the role of multiple and contingent factors (both economic and non-economic) that produce regions. For this reason Lovering argues that the region is becoming a 'chaotic conception'; generalised claims are being made based on selective empirical evidence to support the centrality of this scale for stimulating economic growth. Consequently, he argues, this approach is a theory led by selective empirical developments and recent public policy initiatives. It is 'a set of stories about how *parts* of a regional economy *might* work, placed next to a set of policy ideas which *might* just be useful in some cases' (Lovering 1999: 384, emphasis original). These arguments have been developed and extended by others (see MacLeod 2001b; Hadjimichalis 2006; Harrison 2010; Painter 2008).

New regionalist thinking has been, in turn, challenged by relational approaches to space, where—building on the work of Massey (1994) above—geographies are made through unbounded relations influenced by global flows and local nodal interactions. Space here is a reflection of networked, nodal and open place-based relationships, rather than merely a container or independent backdrop for existence. This argument, of course, has been clearly articulated by those advocating that space is a relational concept (Amin 2004, 2007; see also Marston et al. 2005). 'Unbounded' or 'relational' regions need not be territorially coherent or contiguous. 'Alternative regional geographies' involve spatial configurations and boundaries that are no longer necessarily or purposively territorial or scalar, since social, economic, political, and cultural processes are constituted through actor networks which are becoming increasingly dynamic and varied in spatial constitution (Massey 2007: 89, 2011; Amin 2004).

Radical open-ended politics and economics of *place* are proposed, in opposition to frameworks of so-called bounded territorial economic development, to create spaces of opportunity for localities under globalisation. This perspective is evidenced in the text *Cities: Reimagining the Urban*, where Amin and Thrift (2002) view localities as unbounded, fuzzy, fluid, complex, and mixed entities, formed through recurring practices, movements, and experiences. They claim this has implications for developing successful economies in a context of economic globalisation, building institutional and policy frameworks for economic governance, nurturing civic participation, and delivering radical democracy (compare Massey 2007). Putting 'the local into the global' has 'far less to do with territorial properties (such as localized linkage, local identity and identification, scalar politics, and governance) than with *the effects of spatial and temporal exposure and connectivity* (such as continual and open-ended change, juxtaposition of difference, overlap of networks of different global connections)' (Amin 2002: 391, emphasis added).

This is a perspective that stretches the imagination of economic geography, but those working within state theoretic frameworks and more grounded approaches to economic geography have taken issue with the *realpolitik* of 'the local' grappling with the challenges of globalisation. For example, it is important to consider the ways in which cities and regions can be categorised as problematic by the state and those seeking to direct resources to different geographical areas. It is also important not to lose sight of the ways in which contentious politics are being played out across the globe. One instance of this in recent years has seen campaigns for devolved government and cultural rights linked to territorially articulated spaces (see Jones and MacLeod 2004; Keating 2013). For Tomaney (2007), localities, then, are more than the local articulation of global flows, and concerns with territorialised culture need not necessarily be atavistic, archaic or regressive.

Commentators on the territorial–relational debate suggest several ways forward. Jonas (2012a) suggests that the distinction between territorial and relational can be 'registered obsolete' if critical attention is paid to matters of territory and the nature of territorial politics, both of which are products of bounded and unbounded forces. Moreover, he argues, the form this takes is contingent, and requires empirical investigation. The way forward, then, is 'further examples of both relational thinking about territorial politics and of territorial thinking about relational processes' (Jonas 2012a: 270; see also Allen and Cochrane 2014).

## 'NEW LOCALITIES' RESEARCH AGENDAS

Some 25 years on, in the wake of long-running debates about the new regionalism and glocalisation and about relational and bounded territoriality, how useful is the concept of locality? Can it be energised by these debates and developed in order to begin to answer the challenges thrown up by Jonas (2012a)? In this respect, it is worth revisiting Duncan's (1989) claim:

> Localities in the sense of autonomous subnational social units rarely exist, and in any case their existence needs to be demonstrated. But it is also misleading to use locality as a synonym for place or spatial variation. This is because the term locality inevitably smuggles in notions of social autonomy and spatial determinism, and this smuggling in excludes examination of these assumptions. *It is surely better to use terms like town, village, local authority area, local labour market or, for more general uses, place, area or spatial variation.* These very useable terms do not rely so heavily on conceptual assumptions about space vis-à-vis society. (Duncan 1989: 247, emphasis added)

Counter to this analysis, the chapter suggests that locality has the capacity to capture those spatial categories deemed by Duncan (1989) to be more useful units of analysis. It is exactly those 'conceptual assumptions', which render locality free of charges of 'spatial determinism'. *Locality is a meaningful term.*

This stance, however, requires some hard thinking and the introduction of a new conception of locality: that of 'new locality'.

Savage et al. (1987: 30) argue that '[g]reater clarification of the concept "locality" should start with an analysis of the significance of space in general'. In response, three readings of 'new locality' can be formulated from the three commonly understood notions of space used in the physical and social sciences—absolute, relative and relational—which, as Harvey (1969) has highlighted, can coexist.

This coexistence can be illustrated in relation to the conceptual treatment of local areas in a global context. In *absolute* understanding of space, the local is treated independently; locality is a discrete space around which a line can be drawn and where a loose spatial determinism has some purchase. Concerns with relative space, by contrast, lead us to consider the relationship between localities in an increasingly internationalising world of processes and patterns. The notion of *relational space*, by way of further contrast, is a truly radical attempt to collapse analysis into networked concerns such that there is no global and local to talk about, only unbounded and networked geographies of 'jostling' (Massey 2007), 'throwntogetherness' (Massey 2005) and becoming (Woods 2007). Sites become the sources of analysis, but how they relate to each other is not clear, such that research needs to pay attention to power and policy relations flowing through localities. These three notions of space therefore inform different ways of identifying localities as objects of research, each of which can be found employed in the social science literature, viz:

1. From the perspective of *absolute space*, localities can be presented as bounded territories, such as local authority areas, which are recognised politically and administratively for reasons of electoral accountability, for the discharge and conduct of public services, and for the collection and analysis of statistical data. They are not naturally occurring entities (though some may be contiguous with natural features such as islands), but they do have a stable and precisely delimited materiality that can form the focus for traditional, single-place-based or comparative case study research (Bennett and McCoshan 1993).
2. From the perspective of *relative space*, localities can be seen as connected containers for spatial analysis. Here localities are identified by their cores, not their edges, and are not necessarily consistent with formal administrative geographies. In this perspective, the boundaries of localities are relative, fuzzy, and sometimes indeterminate, contingent on the processes and phenomena being observed, and shaped by dynamics within, outside, and between localities. Such a notion of locality forms the basis for research sensitive to connective forms of enquiry, including, for example, work on city-regions and nested hierarchies (Etherington and Jones 2009).

3. From the perspective of *relational space*, localities are nodes or entanglements within networks of interaction and spaces of flow. They are not bounded in any conventional understanding of the term, but have a topography that is described by lines of connectivity and convergence. Localities transgress inscribed territories and are not necessarily discrete, sharing points of coexistence. Such a conceptualisation of locality lends itself to counter-topographical research (Katz 2001; see also Heley and Jones 2012), or the practice of a 'global ethnography' (Burawoy 2000).

Unlike earlier locality debates, the 'new localities' approach does not seek to adjudicate between these different representations of locality, but rather recognises that all are valid ways of 'talking about locality', and each captures a different expression of locality. New localities are, therefore, multifaceted and multidimensional. They are 'shape-shifters' whose form changes with the angle from which they are observed. As such, the identification of localities for research can be freed from the constraints of the rigid territoriality of administrative geography and should move beyond the reification of the local authority scale that was implicit in many previous locality studies. Warde's comments of twenty plus years ago on this remain critical:

> Deciding on an appropriate spatial scale depends initially on the research problem. If we want to know about foreign policy we might choose states; if voting behavior, constituencies; if material life, perhaps the labour market; if everyday experience, maybe the neighbourhood. Greater difficulty arises if we want to know about the intersection of several of these, the burden of the restructuring thesis. Concepts with substantive spatial properties ought to be theoretical predicates. Conscripting the concepts of locality requires that a theoretical decision be made. (Warde 1989: 277)

In recognising the contingency and impermanence of localities, and acknowledging Warde's (1989) plea for notions of 'intersection', the new localities approach also focuses attention on processes of 'locality making', or the ways in which stable and popularly recognised representations of locality are brought into being through the moulding, manipulation, and sedimentation of space within ongoing social, economic, and political struggles (see Jonas 2012a; Pierce et al. 2011). Indeed, it is in these acts of locality making that localities are transformed from mere points of location (a description of where research was conducted) to socio-economic-political creations that provide an analytical framework for research. For the concept of locality to have analytical value, it must be possible to attribute observed processes and outcomes to social, economic, and political formations that are configured in a given locality, and this, it can be argued, requires a locality to possess both material and imagined coherence.

Material coherence refers to the particular social, economic, and political structures and practices that are configured around a place. Thus, material coherence may be provided by the territorial ambit of a local authority, by the geographical coverage of an economic development initiative, by the catchment area of a school or hospital, by a travel-to-work area, by the reach of a supermarket or shopping centre, or by any combination of the above and other similar structures and practices. Material coherence hence alludes to the institutional structures that hold a locality together and provide vehicles for collective action.

Imagined coherence relates to collective resident consciousness and the sense of shared identity and affinity with a place, resulting in a perceived community with shared patterns of behaviour and common geographical reference points. Imagined coherence therefore makes a locality meaningful as a space of collective action. There are territorial units that exhibit material coherence but lack a strong imagined coherence (such as artificially amalgamated local authority areas) and there are territories with an imagined coherence but only a weak material coherence (for example, where institutional boundaries bisect contiguous urban areas or where areas with strongly developed popular consciousness exist within much larger institutional units). Areas falling into either of these categories could not be considered coherent functioning localities.

Both material coherence and imagined coherence are also important in fixing (through multiple intersections) the scale at which localities can be identified (Jones and Woods 2013). The imagined coherence of a locality is framed around perceived shared forms of behaviour, whether linked to common patterns of collective consumption, shared affinity with sporting or cultural institutions, or common geographical/historical reference points. However, this imagined coherence is not founded on direct inter-personal connection between residents (compare Anderson 1991). In this sense it differs from the social coherence of a neighbourhood—which may share some of the above attributes but is framed around the probability of direct interaction between members. It also differs from the imagined coherence of a region—which is a looser affiliation that draws more on perceived cultural and political identities and economic interests.

Similarly, the material coherence of a locality should be denser and more complex than that found at a neighbourhood or regional scale. The material coherence of a neighbourhood will be restricted by its situation within a larger geographical area for employment, administrative and many service provision functions, whilst the material coherence of a region could be fragmented by the inclusion of several different labour markets, local authority areas, sub-regional shopping centres, and so on. Savage's (2009) work on 'granular space' is illustrative of these concerns:

> People do not usually see places in terms of their nested or relational qualities: town against country: region against nation, etc. but compare different places with each other without a strong sense of any hierarchical ordering. I further argue that the culturally privileged groups are highly 'vested' in place, able to articulate intense feelings of belonging to specific fixed locations, in ways where abstract and specific renderings of place co-mingle. Less powerful groups, by contrast, have a different cultural geography, which hives off fantasy spaces from mundane spaces. (Savage 2009: 3)

The attributes of localities outlined above do not easily translate into discrete territorial units with fixed boundaries. Labour market areas overlap, as do shopping catchment areas; residents may consider themselves to be part of multiple localities for different purposes and at different times; the reach of a town as an education centre may be different from its reach as an employment centre; and so on. The boundaries that might be ascribed to a locality will vary depending on the issue in question (Warde 1989).

All this has a bearing on how localities are identified, defined and constructed for case study research. The argument of Beauregard (1988) on the 'absence of practice' in locality research is important here in calling for both methodological and political interventions. The application of the approach discussed logically leads us to start by identifying localities by their cores—whether these be towns or cities or geographical areas—rather than as bounded territories, and working outwards to establish an understanding of their material and imagined coherence. This process will necessarily require mixed methods, combining cartographic and quantitative data on material geographies with qualitative evidence of imagined coherence and performed patterns and relations. This is more than just an exercise in boundary drawing. Whilst it may be possible to identify fixed territorial limits for the reach of a locality with respect to certain governmental competences or policy fields, applying proxy boundaries to imagined localities must necessarily assume a degree of permeability, and localities may be configured differently depending on the object of inquiry.

## CODA … DON'T FORGET UNEVEN DEVELOPMENT

This chapter has proposed a new approach to thinking about localities in the context of the new new localism in the UK. This recognises that localities not only exist in absolute space as bounded territories but also have expression in relative and relational space where boundaries are at best 'fuzzy' and permeable. Whilst each representation may be legitimately employed to frame localities in particular contexts, taken together they point to a new understanding of localities as multifaceted, dynamic and contingent entities that change shape depending on the viewpoint adopted. Constructing localities as frames for the analysis of social, economic, or political phenomena, therefore, requires investigation of both their imagined and material coherence, which in combination make a locality meaningful and create a capacity for action.

This chapter has proposed that the 'new localities' approach has at least three implications for case study-oriented geographical research. First, it provides a revised model for understanding locality effects that does not take localities as given bounded spatial units, but instead emphasises the contingency and relationality of localities. Second, the new localities approach therefore requires identification and description of the locality to be incorporated as an intrinsic part of the research process, rather than treating locality as a taken for granted backdrop. This approach further recognises that the shape, reach, and orientation of a locality might differ according to the research questions being examined. Third, the new localities notion consequently demands a new body of research concerned with establishing the material and imagined coherences of localities, employing mixed-method strategies. Through these mechanisms, 'locality' can be reclaimed as a meaningful and useful concept in social and economic research. In its resurrected guise, 'locality' can be freed from the shackles of fixed boundaries. As such, whilst locality research can be spatially focused, it should not be spatially constrained, and needs to be prepared to follow networks and relations across scales and spaces in order to reveal the full panoply of forces and actors engaged in the constitution of a locality (Jones and Woods 2013).

All of this raises the issue of relationships within and between localities in the new new localism, constituted in and as the landscapes of combined and uneven development. On the one hand, there are statements from the UK Government such as:

> We think that the best means of strengthening society is not for central government to try and seize all the power and responsibility for itself. It is to help people and their locally elected representatives to achieve their own ambitions. This is the essence of the Big Society … The Localism Act sets out a series of measures with the potential to achieve a substantial and lasting shift in power away from central government and towards local people. (Greg Clark MP, Minister of State for Decentralisation, Foreword, DCLG 2011)

These 'atomist' localist ideologies are being echoed in turn by the actors involved in institutional developments, such as LEPs:

> As a City Region, *collaboration* is our trump card. The networks, the relationships and our strong history of partnership working are the envy of other LEPs and will

be a *comparative advantage* as we close the gap on rival LEP areas. Collaboration has been a driving principle of our LEP and will be key to transforming our local economy. (James Newman, Chair Sheffield City Region LEP, quoted in Sheffield City Region LEP 2013a, emphasis added)

Such sentiments, though, explicitly ignore the complex and contradictory relationships within and between places and regions. Expressed simply, everywhere cannot win, everywhere cannot raise performance above the average (because it is the average), and everywhere cannot mobilise the so-called local agglomeration forces into temporary permanent fixes for economic success, social cohesion, and democratic renewal (compare Blond 2010; Cheshire et al. 2014). The landscape of England's localities is a story of competition hot-spots and not-spots; a tapestry of some places developing out of control, boom to bust, and other places stagnating and witnessing little in the way of sustained economic development (see Ward and Hardy 2013). Drawing parallels with literature in development studies, it remains the case that 'by focusing so heavily on "the local" … manifestations tend to underplay both local inequalities and power relations as well as national and transnational economic and political forces' (Mohan and Stokke 2000: 247). This is due not just to the historical long-run dynamics of British capitalism and a macro-economic policy environment that favours finance-led accumulation in London and the South East. The institutions of economic governance simply lack the regulatory capacity to correct market or governance failure. The regulation approach sentiments of Goodwin and Painter remain relevant here:

The geographical differentiation of local governance is as much a hindrance as a help to regulation. The contradictions thrown up by capitalist uneven development, which continue to lead to problems of political legitimation and economic performance, seem less amenable to constrain through a system of governance than they did through a system of government. If anything, these contradictions are exacerbated by the emerging system of local governance, which actively promotes uneven development. (Goodwin and Painter 1996: 646)

Actors involved in the new new localism acknowledge some of this and also highlight serious issues of blurred accountability and outright confusion:

The LEP boundaries and sizes seemed sometimes to be politically driven under the camouflage of functional economies—insufficient strategic consideration was given to the LEP coverage of the Country; and little serious consideration seemed given to the confusing impact of allowing overlapping LEP areas. This has resulted in an overcomplicated network of massively different LEPs based more on political geographies, rather than sub-regional economic areas. *Localism is an interesting concept but if applied to my car, if all four wheels were allowed to be different sizes, shapes and positions, it wouldn't aid the car much in its progress.* (Alex Pratt, Chair of Buckingham Thames Valley LEP, quoted in HoC and BIS 2013: 15, emphasis added)

**Chair (Adrian Bailey MP)**: I need to conclude fairly quickly but I have a couple of questions to finish with on accountability. Very briefly, who do you feel you are accountable to as a LEP?

**Linda Edworthy (Tees Valley Unlimited)**: local business and local residents.

**Mark Reeve (Chair Grt Cambs & Grt Peterb LEP)**: both public and private sector within the LEP.

**James Newman (Chair Sheffield City Region LEP)**: to a certain extent to the Ministers who appoint us as well, in terms of their expectations of us—very much so.

**Adrian Shooter (Chair Oxford LEP)**: I would add to that to the people who we are supposed to be finding jobs for, which is why we are there.

**David Frost (Chair LEP Network)**: There is a wide range, but of course we are also accountable, where there are funding streams, to those Departments that are providing it. (quoted in HoC and BIS 2013: 12)

Where next for the new localism, or even the new new localism? With 'English votes for English laws' presented at the heart of the Conservative Party campaign for the 2015 General Election (see Redwood 2014), following the rejection of Scottish independence and the subsequent 'devo-max' settlement to consolidate devolution to Scotland, issues of 'locality making' (Jones and Woods 2013) are of increasing importance to state spatiality and state territoriality.

# 9. Devolution dynamics

> Political and economic elites always advertise their successful policies during phases of prosperity, but try to deny their responsibility in cases of crisis, using internal or external causes as explanations.
>
> (Hadjimachalis 2018: 4)

## INTRODUCTION

As noted in the previous chapter, since 2010 the UK Government has sought to reshape the ways in which economic development takes place and, although this shift in governmental delivery began under New Labour, there has been a continuing emphasis on developing the city-region scale to unlock economic growth. It was much vaunted by the Coalition Government elected in 2010 (Deas 2014), whereby they replaced the Regional Development Agencies (RDAs) with Local Enterprise Partnerships (LEPs) and latterly the morphing of LEPs into Combined Authorities (CAs). These policies were subsequently continued by the Conservative administrations (Conservative Party 2015) through a variety of locality-specific devolution deals. However, despite the rhetoric of the 'Northern Powerhouse' as a flagship policy for delivering economic growth for the North of England (Lee 2016), it has sat alongside a severe austerity programme that has seen Local Authority (LA) budgets cut significantly. This, therefore, raises difficult questions with regards to the ability of CAs and LAs to address the current and future needs of their populations (Etherington and Jones 2016b). Finally, although the context of 'Brexit' and the changing leaders of the Conservative Party means the future of the Northern Powerhouse remains uncertain, the political territorialisation and regionalisation (Harrison 2014) of the city-region has problematised the position of civil society actors working in their respective city-regions.

Concurrently to this and historically within geography as well as more broadly the social sciences, there have been a series of parallel debates simmering away for the past decade (see Jonas and Ward 2007 for one such example). These debates have revolved around a well-developed series of discussions that consider the ways in which such spatial fixes either foster economic development through agglomeration (Harding 2007) or continue to exacerbate uneven development and spatial disparities (Etherington and Jones 2009). This chapter seeks to connect these themes with the *realpolitik* concerns of delivering devolution. To do this, I follow the development of city-regionalism through these different discourses and unfolding city deals to allow us to ask: within a language of localism, devolution and austerity, how have civil society actors in Sheffield and Greater Manchester City-Regions (SCR and GMCR) sought to deal with city regional development approaches and the new governance structures that have been created? These are two key city-regions in the North; thus, focusing on their cases is central to comprehending what kind of Northern Powerhouse growth is being built, and whose interests are being represented, if this to be more than an empty policy husk (Lee 2016). In turn, the chapter is interested in mapping out the missing elements from the Northern Powerhouse recipe book for economic growth and social democracy. By looking at Manchester and Sheffield, if the Northern Powerhouse is a coordinating frame for city-regions in the North of England in terms of their interaction with each other, the chapter is interested in understanding how these bodies are being shaped by devolution.

The chapter accordingly sheds light upon the ongoing processes of LA restructuring in Greater Manchester and Sheffield towards combined authority (city-region) approaches. Therefore, it will highlight how 'policies are not, after all, merely being transferred over space; their form and their effects are transformed by these journeys' (Peck and Theodore 2015: 29). This will be done by engaging with the views of civil society actors on the ground, in terms of how they have responded to a shifting governance framework at the local state-/city-region scale. The chapter will, therefore, address the positioning of civil society within these processes by, first, giving greater context to the development of city-regions as a process of regionalisation. Regionalisation captures the process by which 'new regions' are created territorially through changes in governance structures, i.e. the territorial (re-)creation of GMCR and SCR. In following this, it will also consider how austerity has impacted upon these processes. It will, second, highlight how this repositions civil society due to the economic rationale of city-regions, the changes in governance scale and the creation of new 'citizenship regimes' (Jenson and Saint-Martin 2010). By focusing upon the positioning of civil society actors, the chapter highlights how city-regionalism and the Northern Powerhouse, more broadly, raises serious queries towards developing notions of an 'inclusive growth' approach (RSA 2016a). The question becomes whether failure to deliver inclusive growth at the city-region scale will reflect a failure to deliver equitable growth within the Northern Powerhouse.

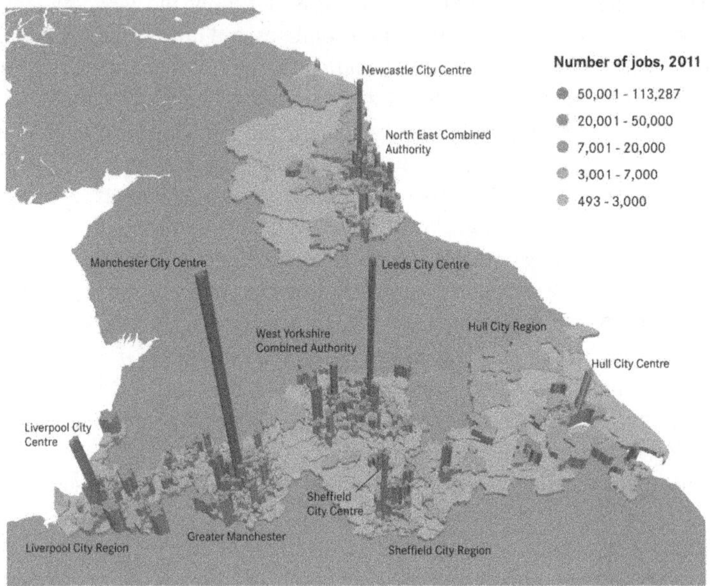


*Source:* Centre for Cities (2015: Figure 9).

*Figure 9.1 The geography of jobs across the Northern Powerhouse*

## BUILDING THE CITY-REGIONS OF THE NORTHERN POWERHOUSE

The UK Government has sought to reshape the map of governance in England. One part of the solution to this has been the creation of the 'Northern Powerhouse'. The Northern Powerhouse can be seen as a policy-framing device, in which a series of ongoing projects have been placed (Lee 2016). The powerhouse represents what Jessop (2016a: 38) would call a 'spatial imaginary'—a discursive phenomenon that distinguishes, by carving out distinctiveness, specific places and spaces 'from the inherently unstructured complexity of a spatialized world'—and is well represented rhetorically in Figure 9.1, whereby economic success and growth is emphasised by the role Northern Powerhouse cities have in providing employment in their metropolitan centres.

The Northern Powerhouse agenda, has therefore framed the more substantial restructuring of (some) local authorities into combined authority city-regions. This has been based upon a city first approach whereby, to date, city-region devolution has focused around the existing metropolitan footprints of the core UK cities (G. Jones et al. 2015; Harrison and Heley 2014). The momentum for this has been developed due to a number of factors, which the UK State has attempted to deal with. First, it was very much a post-crisis reaction in order to stimulate economic growth with the city-region vaunted as the de facto scale for growth (Overman 2012). This reflected both a dominant policy discourse in urban development (see Storper 2013 for such an example) and a perceived failure of RDAs (Pugalis and Townsend 2012).

Second, it has sought to address the longstanding issue of spatial balance within the UK economy, whereby an overheating South is contrasted by an underperforming North (Clarke et al. 2016; Martin et al. 2016; Gardiner et al. 2013). Third, the UK State (with specific reference to England) is renowned for being the most centralised in Western Europe, hence, with the failure of regional devolution (beyond Wales, Scotland and London) under New Labour (Goodwin et al. 2005), devolution to a suitable scale within England has been sought (Pike et al. 2012). Fourth, via the deal-making approach, it has attempted to embed and deliver austerity into the reformulation of CAs through a process of block grant reduction and rationalisation.

Relatedly, as noted in Chapters 5, 6, and 7, the city-region scale has become the dominant discourse in urban development policy and this has developed due to a number of reasons and analytical frames such as the rise of new regionalism (Brenner et al. 2003; Keating et al. 2003) and the influence of new economic geography (NEG), both placing specific emphasis upon the growing of regions for economic purposes (MacLeod 2001b). Within both these accounts of economic and regional geography, there is an implicit understanding given that the city-region is both the 'natural' and 'functional' scale for economic development. It is suggested that where nation-states have failed to deal with macro-economic shifts in the global economy, city-regions represent the suitable scale whereby they are small enough but big enough to deal with this challenge (Scott 2001).

Central also to this has been a belief in neo-classical variants of agglomeration theory (Overman et al. 2007; Overman 2012; compare Haughton et al. 2014) as the driver to economic development, whereby city-regions open themselves up to attract as much investment as they can, so that growth trickles down in turn to their populations. The city-region, therefore, represents a governance strategy that seeks to harness agglomeration and share this geographically. According to an important account of this logic:

> The policy implication of theories of agglomeration is that enabling people and firms to benefit from proximity to centres of activity, bring beneficial economic outcomes … This implies empowering and incentivising local government, firms and people across economic centres and natural economic geographies [cities] to promote growth and correct the market and government failures which are acting as barriers to economic development. (BIS 2010: 25)

The BIS quote neatly highlights this underpinning to government rhetoric and the role it sees local government and business having in to order to address the past failures of both the market and government. Key to this, from their thinking, is to create an agglomerative economy in each of the city-regions; quite simply, everyone can win. As Figure 9.1 suggests, this then links up, or agglomerates, to form the Northern Powerhouse, which is presented as the 'spatial imaginary' to eventually match London in economic terms (HM Government and Transport for the North 2015).

In placing a primarily economic focus upon the Northern Powerhouse agenda, which is emphasised by the development of soft-institutional organisations (Haughton et al. 2013) such as LEPs, this importantly rescales the 'representational regime' of the city-region (Jessop 2016a; MacLeod and Goodwin 1999; Cox 1998), in spatially specific and strategic ways, linked in turn to creating new 'citizenship regimes' for the governance of city-regions. This notion captures:

> Who qualifies and is recognized as a model citizen is under challenge. The legitimacy of group action and the desire for social justice are losing ground to the notion that citizens and interests can compete equally in the political marketplace of ideas. (Jenson and Phillips 1996: 112)

In the context of GMCR and SCR, the new business-oriented representational regime, by design, places civil society on the outside. This means that what could broadly be termed as the 'social reproduction of the city', is given secondary status to its economic drivers (Jonas and Ward 2007). This, in turn, positions civil society actors as no longer directly and centrally relevant within the context of chasing agglomerative growth. Some have been critical to this approach for a number of reasons, with three important areas of critique to consider for the Northern Powerhouse going forward: (1) for continuing uneven regional and city regional development (Etherington and Jones 2009, 2016b), in terms of the failure for agglomerative approaches to trickle down to those that need it most; (2) how this pitches city-regions against each other in a competitive race to capture investment (Harrison 2007), questioning the potential of the Northern Powerhouse as represented in Figure 9.1; and (3) who such strategies empower and disempower within the city-region (see Rutherford 2006). The final point is central to the continuing aim of this chapter, in terms of thinking what such an economically driven strategy means for those who sit outside of this rubric for growth. The representational regime of the city-region is central to this and to date, city-region devolution has only sought to strategically engage business communities in terms of dealing with government and market failure. This raises difficult questions for those that operate within what could be broadly termed 'civil society', who are often working with those who benefit least from agglomerative strategies. This also reflects a failure to properly integrate a social or inclusive dimension into devolution, due to its narrow focus on economic development. Despite many devolution deals having been put in place, this is only now starting to be discussed as a concern, in the continuing process of implementing devolution. An example of this can be seen in the RSA's Inclusive Growth Commission, which is seeking to identify practical ways to make local economies across the UK more economically inclusive and prosperous (RSA 2016a). The next section frames devolution in Sheffield and Manchester, before addressing the position of civil society more directly within this rescaling of governance.

## PLACING CIVIL SOCIETY IN THE CITY-REGION

Civil society is used as a catch-all term for a number of different types of organisation, which are separate from both the state and business. This includes organisations such as charities, those termed third sector, voluntary groups, community groups (of both place and identity), social enterprises, and housing associations. They all have very different relationships with both the local state and business in terms of how they operate. Some have contractual relationships, whereby they deliver specific services, others act to give specific representation to minority groups, and different groups work on very different spatial scales. From across a city-region to very localised, neighbourhood development. What ties them together as a set of groups is their individual organisational remit to produce or engender some form of social benefit for their perceived communities? The research interviews were not discussing the development of the Northern Powerhouse specifically, but more broadly the development of the city-region building agenda. However, as has been previously stated, the development of city-regions is central to development of the Northern Powerhouse as a 'spatial imaginary' and GMCR and SCR are two key cases in point in this respect. Hence, the following responses should be viewed in the context of what such approaches to city-regions mean for discourses surrounding the Northern Powerhouse.

In framing current developments in devolution from a UK State perspective and from within both SCR and GMCR, it is important to consider the ways in which civil society actors are dealing with this changing governance structure. G. Jones et al. (2015) highlight how, in Liverpool and Bristol, the changing governance landscape and the reduction in funding opportunities through austerity has made things more difficult for groups that sit within what is broadly termed civil society. This has been reflected in both GMCR and SCR, as austerity has impacted those hardest, in the most deprived areas of each city-region (Beatty and Fothergill 2016), often where such groups are more active and needed. However, civil society members have also highlighted a number of opportunities to mitigate this (despite being problematic) within the context of devolution and in spite of the difficulties of austerity. Below I analyse how civil society actors have struggled with devolution, but also have attempted to find new positions and strategies on which to see their social agendas addressed against the economic framework.

## Struggling with the Economic Rationale

For many groups, there have been a number of problems that devolution and the rhetoric of the Northern Powerhouse have failed to address. These issues initially focus upon the economic emphasis of city-regions, which places civil society on the outside but also misses the need to help those who are most disadvantaged within city-regions. According to one source:

> I think of Greater Manchester as having a ring donut economy, it's a lot like a North American city. So you have thriving city centre, which it didn't have twenty-five years ago. The suburbs actually doing ok and then the middle bit. If they do not do something about that is really meaningful in that ring donut, the powers that be will never achieve their economic goals of achieving a fiscal balance for this conurbation. (Interview 7, Salford Social Enterprise, 2016)

The above highlights how from the outset there is a perception that the growth model proposed for GMCR fails to address the broader problems faced by the city-region. This is caused by the ongoing geo-history of inequality but also how this is compounded by pursuit of an agglomerative growth strategy. This is also reflected in views held in Sheffield:

> Trickledown doesn't work for the most vulnerable and disadvantaged and you have to have strategies around social regeneration (for want of a better word) alongside economic regeneration. Those two things should come together and I don't think they do because the LEP is very purely focused on the economic policy ... Feels like I'm in a rowing boat and my colleagues are in a rowing boat and we're trying to turn round this big tanker. (Interview 1, Sheffield Community Development Group, 2015)

For both respondents, one a social enterprise, primarily focused upon projects in Salford, and the other a community development organisation in a deprived area of Sheffield, the urban growth machine strategy (Logan and Molotch 1987; Jonas and Wilson 1999) is deeply problematic. They pick out how the 'trickledown' approach, which implies a strategy of developing high-level gross value added (GVA) uplift by bringing people to jobs within the city-region (Etherington and Jones 2016b), does little for the disadvantaged citizens they are attempting to support. This means that because they question the rhetoric of this growth model, they are left on the periphery of its strategic delivery. This is also reflected in the above quote, which highlights how such groups, operating at a local level, have little ability or remit in the context of devolution to act at the city-region level and there is an ongoing lack of accountability that marginalises local civil society through institutions such as the LEP. According to one source:

> What opportunity will there be to genuinely involve civil society in the process? Because I think the LEP has been and I know it is an economic driver, fine and it's about inward investment, economic growth and the private sector is at the heart of that but there is very little in terms of any wider involvement. And maybe that's ok but when it comes to the combined authority, there needs to be more direct lines of accountability into localities and into local areas. (Interview 3, Sheffield Community Development Group, 2015)

Therefore, the construction of a new 'representational regime' for the city-region based upon economic interests purposefully excludes civil society actors from the outset, which in turn allows for an uncontested agglomerative growth model to be developed. The following section addresses this by thinking further through how civil society is being positioned and marginalised differently at different scales.

## Dealing with Scale?

The difficulty to have a voice within such processes, due to the failure for civil society groups to be integrated into the representational regime of the city-region, has left some squeezed between the 'scale jump' (Cox 1998) of the city-region and austerity occurring at the same time. According to one interviewee:

> At one point they talk about localism but if you look at regionalisation, it's huge, it's huge and actually the local voluntary community sector can't even hope to engage with, let alone deliver against that agenda. Therefore civil society is finding itself squeezed behind/between a rhetoric that emphasises its importance but a reality, which mitigates against its ability to capture the resources to deliver against that agenda. (Interview 12, Bolsover Voluntary Organisation, 2016)

This highlights the difficulties for civil society organisations to deal with austerity and devolution at the same time. It also shows the way in which civil society groups are co-opted and recast into a neoliberal growth model. In short, civil society groups are both needed for the continuing function of the city-region, but at the same time they are marginalised within rescaling processes too. There is also appreciation of how LAs are struggling to deal with this rescaling process too within the context of austerity:

> To be honest, they are holding what they can, both in Tameside and Oldham, they are holding everything that they can. We are predominantly funded through the local authorities, Tameside get us a fair bit from their CCG [Clinical Commissioning Group] but actually, we don't, as an organisation the make-up is a much greater split for local authorities. So they are doing all they can to protect us. I think the voluntary organisations with smaller grants are dwindling, the smaller amounts of funding for the sector are dwindling, which is in itself a risk and that's something that we fight hard against. But strategically they do view us as important in terms of achieving their public service reform and in fact it has been said by the cabinet portfolio holders around in Oldham and others, that we are their answer to that, that's how they see the change in the relationships between citizens and the wider population and the public services. (Interview 3, Oldham Voluntary Organisation, 2016)

The end of this quote from the Oldham interviewee also touches on the important shifts within the positionality of civil society; it acknowledges how the local state is a deeply contradictory 'agent and obstacle' (Duncan and Goodwin 1988). Civil society is, first, drawn into the local state as a necessity of funding. Second, it is somewhat powerless in the context of restructuring and cuts, as civil society groups are further distanced from having a strategic voice. Here, the paradox of austerity in the context of scale suggests that at local level, civil society actors are needed more than ever, stepping into the austerity void (DeVerteuil 2016; Dear and Wolch 1987) and increasingly being relied on to deliver public services. However, at a city-region level they are being afforded a minor voice. This is especially true within GMCR, due to the devolved nature of health and social care, but this is also noted in Sheffield:

> I think it's probably changed enormously actually. I think—well there's a number of pros and cons, I think with the current government policy and the austerity measures everything that's going on in terms of shrinking the states, promoting using third sector organisations and growing civil society has brought some opportunities for the third sector. There's definitely, for example, funding streams that the third sector can access that statutory organisations can't access so having said that, they are highly competitive. (Interview 6, Sheffield Youth Development Organisation, 2015)

As illustrated above, within the context of austerity, opportunities have arisen for civil society groups, even despite the highly competitive nature of funding. However, the jumping of scale to the city-region and realignment of governance alongside austerity has also been creating destabilising experiences. This is discussed below.

## Responding and Repositioning within City-Regions

Within GMCR, this terrain has articulated a response from civil society groups via the Greater Manchester Voluntary, Community and Social Enterprise (VCSE) Devolution Reference Group (VCSE 2016). The group was formed in response to devolution due to the failure of Greater Manchester Combined Authority (GMCA) to engage such organisations. This represents an attempt by the various actors to find a voice and influence the direction of devolution (and potentially in turn the Northern Powerhouse) by their collective knowledge and access to different parts of GMCA. According to one account:

> The reference group was set up when we realised that all this was going on around us and nobody was going to come banging down our door … So from that a little coalition of the willing emerged, completely undemocratically but again I think that's part of it. Stop waiting for permission; stop feeling like you have to get every detail right. Because actually things are moving so fast, we have to trust each to advocate for what our sector wants to collectively achieve. (Interview 4, Manchester Voluntary Organisation, 2016)

Although the group does not give full democratic representation for civil society at large, it represents an attempt to jump scales by organisations that for the most part do not exist on a city-region scale. The above quote also highlights the failure of the GMCA to address the needs of civil society within the context of devolution and the group's desire to be part of the processes, conversations, and the representational regime of the city in the context of devolution. One interviewee develops this further:

> The pace of change of devolution has been about the public sector thinking about the public sector and their internal mechanism ways of working override that belief that we're important partners. I think we are a group, I'm going to use your term, 'civil society' but voluntary sector and social enterprises. By having that collective group that is able to in some part have representative round tables, to have the ability to talk to some of the key individuals, as a collective to be able to do that, that is important. (Interview 3, Oldham Voluntary Organisation, 2016)

In contrast to the LEP and its privileged position for business leaders, who work in conjunction with city-region CAs, groups like the VCSE have had to find other ways to reposition themselves within the devolved CA. This represents how the UK Government, with its emphasis upon economic development has sought to shape devolution from the centre. By its very structure, it has defined who is and who is not involved and although each city-region will implement its city deal differently, the 'rules of the game' have been initially shaped in one direction in terms of creating a new 'citizenship regime' under devolution. This raises serious questions around representation and recognition in the pursuit of economic growth and this is something that all respondents from civil society backgrounds have recognised. In identifying this, they have attempted to find ways to try and place their agendas towards inequality and the social reproduction of the city-region back into the processes of city-region building. These processes are currently unfolding and the success of such positioning will only become clear as the city-region is delivered in the coming years.

## CONCLUSIONS

This chapter has addressed the changes being created by the unfolding process of devolving power to two of the Northern Powerhouse's key city-regions. Within this, it has attempted to understand how civil society is being positioned. The aim has been to think through the ways in which, if the Northern Powerhouse is to be successful and be more than just a 'spatial imaginary' (Sum and Jessop 2013) in which a 'rag bag' set of policies fall (Lee 2016), it needs to deal more seriously with issues surrounding inequality and uneven development in each of its constitutive city regions.

The Northern Powerhouse is supposed to be a project that will bring prosperity to the North of England, but evidence suggests that its model of agglomerative economic growth, fostered on trickledown economics, will only continue to exacerbate uneven development and undermine the project of spatial rebalancing. In conducting interviews with civil society actors, this chapter has highlighted how in the context of city-region building, the current approach to city regional economic development and governance is falling short of its promises. The chapter has suggested that this is due, in part, to who has been enabled within the Northern Powerhouse city-region agenda and who has been marginalised in this process. Further to this, the new citizenship regimes implemented within city-regions place civil society outside decision-making processes, whilst expecting civil society to deal with the fallout from continuing uneven development, socio-spatial inequalities and austerity.

The Northern Powerhouse faces an uncertain future as a result of Brexit due to the switch towards an industrial strategy for the UK and the largely repacking of existing committed expenditure with little new to create regional distinctiveness (compare Berry 2016; HM Treasury 2016). The pendulum of UK economic development may have turned away from the spatial imaginaries of the Northern Powerhouse and the city-region to focus on the national level again, but the spatial dimensions and sub-national dynamics of this remain unclear. Moreover, as I have argued here, there remains a need to re-balance relationships between the economy, state, and civil society, so that a more representational form of devolution can be delivered. I would suggest that this requires a much stronger attempt to integrate 'the social' alongside the economic within devolution if a more inclusive growth strategy is to be achieved.

# 10. Devolution depoliticisation

> The precipitants are to be found in the crises of capitalism—crises which are bound to become more and more acute owing to the objective dynamics of the capitalist system.
>
> (Jessop 1972: 29)

> [T]he simplest questions are the real ones, they are also the most complex. In order to avoid losing ourselves in the maze, we must keep hold of the guiding thread …
>
> (Hall 2014: 1)

## POST-POLITICS AND CITY-REGIONS

There has been an increasing focus in recent years on the devolution of economic environment and social policies through city-region building endeavours (see Deas 2014; While et al. 2013). The context to this is, first, seeing city-regions as the 'scale at which principal economic interactions occur' (Storper et al. 2015: 230) and appropriate for territorially demarcating and anchoring functional economic areas, and, second, as Storper (2013: 4) boldly puts it, '[c]ity-regions are the principal scale at which people experience lived reality' such that collectively city-regional development is 'more important than ever'. Within this literature there has been a debate around neoliberalism where state restructuring involves major changes in organisational forms and structures with an increasing role for non-state or quasi-state agencies (see Swyngedouw 2011). This is often referred to as a 'destatisation' of a series of former (central) state domains, with the transfer of responsibilities to civil society organisations that redefines the state–civil society relationship 'through the formation of governance beyond the state' (Swyngedouw 2005: 1998). This involves increasingly networked forms of governance in policy fields, with an externalisation process comprising privatisation, contracting-out and deregulation, and service delivery and public–private partnerships to ensure policy coordination.

Relatedly, according to 'post-political' approaches, this 'regime' of governance, which operates at different spatial scales and territorial reaches, is increasing the actors in policy implementation. An array of players, stakeholders and organisations are playing active roles in the transformation of relations between state and market economy by also involving and increasing the influence of corporate interests and the privatisation of public services therein (Haughton et al. 2013; MacLeod 2013). Also related to this, power is often being transferred to, or captured, by an elite formation in terms of political, social, and cultural influences (Crouch 2004). Rather than promoting democracy, this new 'regime' of politics can undermine it; governance per se has bypassed direct elected and representative democracy. Accordingly, the 'status, inclusion or exclusion, legitimacy, system of representation, scale of operation and internal or external accountability of such actors takes place in non-transparent, ad hoc, context dependent ways and differs greatly from those associated with egalitarian pluralistic democratic rules and codes' (Swyngedouw 2010: 6). One of the key elements to this approach, then, is the parallel role of *depoliticisation*—the narrowing of the boundaries of democratic politics, the displacement strategies used by the state to frame engagement, and the emergence of technocratic and delegated forms of governance (see Flinders and Buller 2006; Wood and Flinders 2014). In the context neoliberalism, this process reinforces dominant ideologies and imaginaries around what is possible and required, restricting or foreclosing avenues for debate around alternative and critical discourses (Darling 2016).

In the context of the new new localism, this chapter suggests that 'post-political' approaches downplay or ignore forms of crisis-management, governance failure, and state failure, and the way state policies and institutions are sites themselves of political mobilisation and conflict. The 'post-political' literatures can reduce the state to 'the police' (Rancière 1999, 2010) and consequently the state is no longer directly seen as a key arena for struggle and political contestation (see Dikeç and Swyngedouw 2017; Swyngedouw 2017). The chapter challenges this closure and contends that the state should continue to be seen as a productive arena for performing politics, even, as Harvey points out, 'in the midst of immense contemporary skepticism, on both the left and right of the political spectrum' (Harvey 2013: 153). The state is the 'theatre for the contestation of ideologies', it is the place of the public, and there is no (as yet) credible alternative forum for mass representation, organised accountability, and the expression and enactment of collective solidarity (Glaser 2015: 30). Put simply, the state's matters and its theorisation is absent from these debates and exchanges; the state needs to be brought back into urban and regional studies and demonstrated empirically.

The chapter addresses this lacuna with a grounded focus on politics and struggles of economic development in and across the city-region, especially the economic forces acting upon them and the people engaged in struggles to shape such forces in different ways within the state. Following Cumbers et al. (2010: 55), it is 'interested not just in the overt forms of resistance that emerge at the level of individuals and groups, but also in the daily struggles of workers and their families to ensure their own social reproduction'. A key element of the politics of city-region building, in particular in the older industrial areas, has been to give scant recognition to the underlying trend towards declining growth and productivity, the ongoing brutal logic of labour market segmentation, marginalisation, and flexibilisation. Related to these labour market changes, and an outcome of them, are the shifts in power relations between capital and labour vis-à-vis the weakening of collective bargaining and employment rights, which is creating the conditions for control over work arrangements and the casualisation of employment through part-time, temporary, and zero-hour jobs (Etherington and Jones 2016b).

Analysis traces the localisation of welfare restructuring and the new geographies of austerity, alongside the evolving and more media-friendly devolution of skills and other employment initiatives. Returning to the Sheffield city-region (South Yorkshire, England), and the strategic shifts in governance and politics embraced by devolution, the chapter explores the politics of welfare reform and employment policy. It undertakes this analysis against a backdrop and context of social inequalities and austerity policies, identifying and analysing emerging social struggles and their conflicts. It discusses city-regions as 'post-political contested spaces' and makes connections between the new new localism, the state, depoliticisation, and neoliberalism.

## THE INSTITUTIONAL MATERIALITY OF THE STATE

This chapter advocates an approach to analysing the state that provides nuanced insights into political agency, actor relations, and interest groups to provide insights into the way depoliticisation occurs as a consequence of the complex interaction between reflexive subjects. Jessop's strategic–relational approach (SRA) to the state can both accommodate and operationalise this. As noted in Chapter 1 and Chapter 3, drawing on the contributions of Gramsci, Poulantzas, and Offe, Jessop (1985, 1990a, 2008, 2016a) sees the state not as an instrument of capital or class, but as a social relation; the state is a site, product, and generator of struggle itself, and its spatial form is determined by the condensation of political forces that are represented in and through the state apparatus. The state can thus be understood as follows: first, it has varied natures, apparatuses, and boundaries according to its historical and geographical developments as well as its specific conjunctures. However, there is a strategic limit to this variation, imposed by the given balance of forces at a specific time and space. Thus, second, the state has differential effects on various political and economic strategies in a way that some are more privileged than others, but, at the same time, it is the interaction amongst these strategies that results in such exercise of state power. Extending Jessop's analysis, depoliticisation is an increasingly important governing strategy for exercising state power, removing the political character of decision-making by privileging certain interests in the state-making process, in turn framing politics and shaping political opportunities.

Burnham provides a useful insight into this when he contends that depoliticisation was central to Marx's critique of capitalism and is a key mechanism for the political management of economy. The existence of the state being, amongst other things, a 'political' sphere, which presupposes the possibility of a depoliticisation of civil society, makes it 'clear that the depoliticisation of civil society could only be achieved through bloody legislation against the expropriated—producing a "class" free from the means of production and "free" to sell their labour power—a process that could not in essence be more political' (Burnham 2014: 191). This is contemporised by Wood and Flinders (2014: 152), who emphasise that depoliticisation is a contingent neoliberal political strategy for managing conflicts and rationalising urban governance, which exhibits three forms:

- *Governmental depoliticisation*: focusing on the switching of issues from the governmental sphere through the 'delegation' of those issues by politicians to arm's-length bodies, judicial structures or technocratic rule-based systems that limit discretion.
- *Societal depoliticisation*: involving the transition of issues from the public sphere to the private sphere and focusing on the existence of choice, capacity deliberation and the shift towards individualised responses to collective challenges.
- *Discursive depolitisisation*: the role of language and ideas to depoliticise certain issues and through this, define them as little more than elements of fate.

Allmendinger and Haughton also consider that neoliberal state agents deploy three patterns of intervention across these forms for deferring, displacing, and transferring the political moment and containing, albeit temporarily, crises further. By *deferring* the political, the state can enact strategies of deferral of conflict to some future point in time. By *displacing*, the state can shift political problems to other arenas and groups. By *transferring* the political, conflict can be removed from immediate community and representative processes into new, fuzzy communities of interest and democratic processes that may not align or map onto experiences of change 'on the ground' (Allmendinger and Haughton 2015: 44).

In short, depoliticitisation characterises the neoliberal political-administrative state system, the operation of which requires a careful unpacking of the 'organizational form and sociopolitical bases of the state' (Jessop 1990a: 345). The above accounts offered by Wood and Flinders (2014) and Allmendinger and Haughton (2015) are helpful in signposting the key issues, trends, and emerging dynamics of state intervention, but they give limited conceptual insights into the *processual* operation of the depoliticised state. By contrast, for Jessop, the state is a 'medium and outcome' of *processes* that constitute its many interventions and the terrain of the state is forged through the ongoing engagements between agents, institutions, and concrete political and policy circumstances (Jessop 2008, 2016a). In this approach, there is a need to not only examine where it takes place (e.g. sites of government and governance), but also how policy and politics are defined by their contents and in situations where choice, capacity for agency, deliberation, and social interaction prevail. In short, depoliticisation, as Jessop points out, can only be guaranteed through a process of 'repoliticisation' and an assertion of the 'political' in and through the state—underlying the point that both are integral to each other (Jessop 2014). For Jessop, this covers, inter alia:

> (1) the forms and stakes of normal and/or exceptional politics; (2) the thematisation of issues as controversial, negotiable or consensual; (3) the subjective identity as well as material and ideal interests of political agents; (4) their location within, on the margins of, or at a distance from the state's institutional architecture; and (5) their positioning relative to the front-or back-stage of the political scene … [Governance projects then] may become objects of political contestation as attempts occur to establish, deny, or reframe their relevance to the political field and changing policy agendas. These attempts may involve *reorganising the integral state* in the shadow of hierarchy and, indeed, serve to enhance state power by exercising influence indirectly and/or at a distance from the state. (Jessop 2014: 214, emphasis added)

Jessop's (2016a) 'integral state in the shadow of hierarchy' has six dimensions, summarised and extended in Table 10.1, which points to how the city-region–state nexus operates not just in relation to the state's organisation form and socio-political bases, but also how crises, contradictions, depoliticised politics, and struggles can emerge within a devolved governance framework and create opportunities (see MacLeavy 2007).

As noted in Table 10.1, the first three dimensions capture the state's institutional relations within the political and policy system. This SRA approach identifies a *mode of representation* to delimit patterns of representation and the state in its inclusive sense. This uncovers the territorial agents, political parties, state officials, community groups, para-state institutions, regimes, and coalitions that are incorporated into the state's everyday policy-making practices. Alongside this, Jessop (2016a: 66) identifies *modes of articulation*. This is the institutional embodiment of the above and it underscores the distribution of powers through different geographical divisions and departments of the state and its policy systems. This explores the ways in which political strategy helps to create spaces and scales of policy intervention and delivery. Last, Jessop (2016a: 70) introduces *modes of intervention* to analyse the different political and ideological rule systems that govern state intervention. In effect, through depoliticisation as a governing strategy, read across these three dimensions of the state, state managers are able to spatially reorganise the state apparatus to retain arm's-length control over crucial economic and social processes, whilst simultaneously benefiting from the distancing effects of depoliticisation. As a form of politics, depoliticisation also seeks to change market expectations by rationalist assumptions regarding the effectiveness and credibility of policy-making in addition to shielding the government from the consequences of unpopular policies.

The second set of three dimensions captures the state's 'inner-dwelling' (Jessop 1990a: 345) and the overarching forces in the political and policy system (see Table 10.1). As any substantive unity that the state possesses only derives from (but can never be guaranteed through) specific political projects, the state's wider social relations are key for securing integration and cohesion. Jessop (2016a: 71) introduced the *social basis of the state* to draw attention to the consolidation of the representational regime through civil society, i.e. those social forces outside the political system. Jessop (2016a: 84) adds that just as accumulation strategies are needed to bring a coherence and direction to the circuit of capital, *state projects* are required to bring some guidance and coherence to the manifold activities of the state. Discursive domains are also important for uncovering the internal unity and modes of policy-making and in terms of the state's purpose for the wider society. Jessop notes the importance of *hegemonic visions* to examine language and other semiotic codes that enact ideological programmes of action, i.e. how forms of knowledge and discourses become codified and mobilised to advance particular interests (2016a: 86). The effort to construct a particular *hegemonic project* (in part through the mobilisation of a social base of support) can prove decisive in resolving (albeit temporally and unevenly) the conflicts between particular interests. Depoliticisation, read across these three dimensions of the state, thus operates through hegemony-seeking 'discursive institutions' (Fuller 2017), which establish semantic links between the discursive aims of those seeking to control, and the pragmatics of the everyday lives of those subject to such institutions. As these are socially constructed by particular actors and involve the utilisation of particular broader societal values, these dimensions stress the contingency and flux of political decisions and the pervasive power relations that are involved in depoliticising contexts (Jessop 2016a: 88–90).

As Newman, however, demonstrates, the construction of 'hegemonic projects' is a highly contested process within and between localities. Negotiating

*Table 10.1 Six dimensions of the state, crisis tendencies, and depoliticisation processes*

| State dimension | Definition | SRA linkage | Crisis aspects | Depoliticisation processes: strategies, tools and tactics |
|---|---|---|---|---|
| *Governmental dimensions capturing institutional relations within the political and policy system* | | | | |
| Mode of Representation *(representational regime)* | These give social forces access to the state apparatus and to its capacities | Unequal access to state<br>Unequal ability to resist at distance from state<br>Unequal capacity to shape, make and implement decisions | Crisis of representation | Reordering of representational regimes, differentially incorporating new interests (forms of 'on the scene') into the state apparatus to promote and rework forces and capacities to exclude interests |
| Mode of Articulation *(internal structures of the state)* | Institutional architecture of the level and branches of the state | Unequal capacity to shape, make and implement decisions | Crisis of institutional integration | Reorganising the state apparatus through administration/self-administration, government/governance, hollowing-out/filling-in, re- and decentralisation, and steering the distribution of power via institutional fixes and balancing geographical divisions (forms of 'collibration') |

| State dimension | Definition | SRA linkage | Crisis aspects | Depoliticisation processes: strategies, tools and tactics |
|---|---|---|---|---|
| Modes of Intervention *(patterns of intervention)* | Modes of intervention inside the state and beyond it | Different sites and mechanisms of intervention for deferring, displacing and transferring crisis from the economic to the political form (from the market to the administrative system) and political moments thereafter | Rationality crisis | Reworking state intervention and the policy field by delimiting mechanisms: public/private and (reprivatising), universal/selective, quality/competition, and inclusive/exclusion, etc. Using spatio-temporal fixes to alter patterns of state intervention and policy-making repertoires spatially and temporally |
| *Societal dimensions capturing the wider social relations and discursive domains* | | | | |
| Social Basis of the State *(social bases of state power)* | Institutionalised social compromise | Uneven distribution of material and symbolic concessions to the 'population' in order to secure support for the state, state projects, specific policy sets, and hegemonic visions | Crisis of the power bloc<br>Disaffection with parties and the state<br>Civil unrest, civil war, revolution | Changes to the state's social and 'spatio-temporal selectivity' to include/exclude or privilege/disprivilege some coalition possibilities and interest groups, promote or ameliorate uneven development |

| State dimension | Definition | SRA linkage | Crisis aspects | Depoliticisation processes: strategies, tools and tactics |
|---|---|---|---|---|
| State Project *(accumulation strategy and state strategies)* | Secures operational unity of the state and its capacity to act | Linked to modes of intervention Overcomes improbability of unified state system by orienting state agencies and agents | Legitimation crisis | Reworking the balance between forms of government, governance, and 'meta-governance' (the governance of governance) to provide compromise coherences or flexible policy-making repertoires/shifting policy paradigms |
| Hegemonic Vision *(hegemonic project)* | Defines nature and purpose of the state for the wider social formation | Provides legitimacy for the state, defined in terms of promoting common good, etc. | Crisis of hegemony | 'Semiosis' (sense- and meaning-making), 'construal' through 'spatial imaginaries' (identification of problems/goals/blame and mobilisation of solutions/visions) Scientisation, use of think-tanks, assemblages of 'experts', new intellectuals |

*Source:* Columns 1–4, Jessop (2016a: 58), column 5, author's analysis.

neoliberalism, in what Newman terms ‘landscapes of antagonism’, thus needs to be contextualised within a ‘contradictory field of political forces’ where:

> the vibrancy of local democracy can serve as a challenge to hegemonic projects … Landscapes of antagonism are formed (and reformed) through the discursive constitution of new subjects and the orchestration of new lines of antagonism, resistance and alignment … [and] local governments are both actors in such landscapes of antagonism, with their own interests and political projects, and the mediators of wider struggles in which they seek to privilege some and mitigate others. (Newman 2014: 3298–3299)

The challenge is to demonstrate these processes in empirical instances, in doing so analysing the complex mechanisms and processes shaping emergent forms of regional and urban governance. Focusing on the Sheffield City Region, I undertake this below, emphasising the processual dynamics of structure and struggle (compare Bonefeld 2003) taking place within the internal organisation of the state and state policy formation to re-state the post-political.

## THE POLITICS OF DEVOLUTION AND WELFARE-TO-WORK

In the 1980s, as a result of a prolonged economic crisis, rising unemployment, and extensive de-industrialisation that was an outcome of the Thatcher Government monetarist and free market *accumulation strategies*, Sheffield became a focal point of resistance to the Conservative Government’s national *state project*, with several Labour-controlled local authorities taking a proactive role in developing alternative *modes of intervention* by privileging local economic initiatives (employment and training) to promote a more redistributive and inclusive strategy (see Chapter 7). Between 1979 and 1982, for instance, 45,000 jobs were shed in the core engineering and steel industries within the Sheffield local authority area alone. Added to this, the damaging effects of the 2008 economic and financial crisis (Townsend and Champion, 2014) and weak economic growth has led to a further ‘prosperity gap’ of over £1.1 billion due to a combination of economic inactivity, unemployment, and low productivity sectors. Policy-makers have calculated that Sheffield needs to create around 120,000 jobs to close the gap with the national average by 2024 and ‘nowhere in the UK grows at this rate for such a sustained period of time’ (Sheffield City Region LEP 2014: 22).

Depoliticisation processes have been at work throughout the 1980s and 1990s, deferring, displacing, and transferring the crisis of this economy into more politically manageable *state projects* to promote regional and local economic development. This has been crucial for seeking to manage spatial uneven development and deal with the political problems arising from this. Sheffield has witnessed an ongoing reworking of neoliberal *modes of articulation*, spatially reorganising the internal structures of the state and patterns of intervention to give unequal access and capacity to shape, make, and implement *state strategy*. Issues of economic management have been effectively displaced from the governmental sphere through the 'delegation' of those issues by politicians to arm's-length bodies, judicial structures or technocratic rule-based systems that limit discretion. Shifts within the *mode of representation* saw a raft of private sector-led initiatives being developed, including Training and Enterprise Councils, as devolved bodies to cities and sub-regions charged with making the skills and training market. Despite there being evidence-based limits to creating an employer-led training market, New Labour continued with supply-side and market-driven *accumulation strategies* through further skills policies—a discursive depoliticisation process by a *hegemonic vision* of ignoring history and promoting employer interests at all costs. Local Skills Councils (LSCs), along with Regional Development Agencies (RDAs) and Sector Skills Councils, were variously charged with coordinating skills strategies across the regions (see Chapter 7). The transitions within and between these new governing arrangements have lacked clarity, coordination, and accountability (Pike et al. 2015) and have formed part of a broader depoliticised *mode of intervention* aimed at normalising neoliberalism through the institutionalisation of economic paradigms (such as the primacy of the market, deregulation, and privatisation) and with Central Government state managers retaining control and distancing themselves from unpopular policies.

A central element of depoliticisation is the rescaling of *modes of intervention* to localities for the 'management' of the social reproduction of labour, reorganising class alliances amongst dominant class fractions and disorganising subordinate classes and forces, whether through divide-and-rule tactics or through a national-popular interest that transcends particular class interests (Jessop 2014: 214). Sheffield's *state strategy* for tackling unemployment and 'worklessness' is indicative of this and how the depoliticisation of the unemployment problem operates. The City Strategy Pathfinder (CSP) pilot, established in major de-industrialised conurbations, was accordingly established in 2006 with the primary aims of devolving welfare-to-work programmes for tackling worklessness and integrating employment and skills strategies. The CSP was seen as a vehicle to promote an element of devolved responsibility to local partnerships in delivering Pathways and presented as a bottom-up process—partnerships and consortia were formed by local employment services along with local authorities, and the private, voluntary, and community sectors where there was some discretion given to develop their own priorities and innovate with project development. In many respects, a wider Sheffield City Region (SCR) building project was to emerge from the CSP, which was initially geographically confined to South Yorkshire local authorities and then expanded beyond South Yorkshire to nine local authorities covering the North-east Derbyshire coalfield. In terms of Jessop's (2016a) *social basis of the state*, a new institutionalised social compromise was emerging, based around 'multi-city regionalism' (Wachsmuth 2016). Instead of addressing uneven development in these localities, changes were taking place to the state's 'spatial selectivity', in effect depoliticising inequality by widening the local authority spatial coalition and drawing local government into the economic agenda for the further normalisation of neoliberalism.

This depoliticisation through *modes of representation* was embodied further in the Sheffield City Region Development Programme, which set out how the local authorities believed that by working together, and with the business-sector as a city-region, they could increase the economic output of the area by 12.6 per cent by 2016. The economic context to city-region governance building is important to understand; one of increasing labour market inequalities and socioeconomic exclusion as a result of the 2008 recession. Within the SCR, for instance, there are 85,640 people claiming Employment Support Allowance/Incapacity Benefit (ESA/IB) and 16,090 claiming Disability Benefits. Furthermore, in-work poverty has become a major issue with significant numbers of people paid below the Living Wage (currently £8.45 an hour). It is not only the rates of pay that are important but also the hours of work. As a result of the scale of (full-time) manufacturing job losses, the SCR has created fewer new full-time jobs in the last growth period when compared to other leading city-regions. As highlighted by the Sheffield Independent Economic Review, this difference in the balance of full-time to part-time job creation is one of the key defining features of low-performing city-region areas (Sheffield City Region LEP 2013b, 2016).

Against this low-skills equilibrium backdrop, Sheffield's post-2015 'Devolution Agreement' has been concerned with locally making more with skills and employment—local councils and businesses have been promised the control of a £150 million skills budget (2015–21) for 'building a new skills system' (HM Government 2015). This 'Devolution Deal' builds on previous City Deals as dealing-making *state projects* for orienting state agencies and agents, with the difference being the requirement to elect a Metro-Mayor (a representational instance of depoliticisation through the rise of populism) to access devolved economic development budgets. For Wharton, writing as the Conservative Party Minister for the wider Northern Powerhouse initiative, this positioned places like Sheffield as:

> local areas [which could] now look forward to real control … devolution has arrived and is here to stay. It will require local business and civic leaders to take ownership … and maintain the momentum of growth. (2016: 8–9)

Attempts made to secure further operational unity of the state and its capacity to act for this saw the introduction of new *state projects*, Local Enterprise Partnerships (LEPs), superseding the Yorkshire Forward RDA, without an evaluation of the success of the RDA model of governance (see Pike et al. 2015). To give legitimacy through local government by widening the *social basis of the state* and anchoring support within the local state system, albeit 'an unstable equilibrium of compromise' (Jessop 2016a: 72), as I discuss below, this *state project* subsequently became the Sheffield LEP Combined Authority (SCRCA).

'SCR2040' is the epitome of a consensual depoliticised call-to-arms vision for the SCR. Launched in February 2016, education and health bosses unite, booster-style, around the digital, creative, and logistics sectors, 'fab-labs', opportunities for a 'fourth industrial revolution' based on apprenticeships and innovation districts, and better internal and external connectivity to facilitate agglomeration through competition. This represents a powerful, no-discussion, *hegemonic vision* to legitimise state intervention by framing policy problems and mobilising support behind a *spatial imaginary* vision (in this case Sheffield as a high-skills knowledge-based economy). As this defines the nature and purpose of the state for the wider social formation, though, the state apparatus is still the conduit for neoliberalism via 'post-politicizing processes … channeled into post-democratic forms of consensual policy-making [which] cannot be questioned' (Haughton et al. 2016a: 477). SCR2040 argues that 'we cannot leave it to our elected representatives' (SCR Vision 2017: 24), such partisanship must be cast aside for the 'common good'. Sheffield's residents are asked *not* to question or debate these issues, but to 'read it, decide how they can help … and make a pledge of support' (Moore 2017: 5) and 'back bold decisions' (Mothersole 2017: 18). By depoliticising economic choice, SCR2040 further normalises neoliberalism. There is no mention of distribution, inequality, or poverty; the liberation of markets and privatisation continues at pace. Put bluntly:

> The new devolution arrangements are not the product of wider public debate in the areas to be affected by them, but instead are the outcomes of 'secret deals' (City Deals, 'Devolution Deals', etc.) between the political and business elites at the national and local levels … [T]he model of devolution currently on offer is one designed to advance a narrowly defined set of business interests with very little democratic scrutiny. (Tomaney 2016: 550)

A key element of this Devolution Agreement, which has involved little public discussion or debate, is the emerging *mode of intervention* between the Central Government Department of Work and Pensions (DWP) and SCRCA partners in piloting changes to and co-designing the future of welfare-to-work programmes to operate at the city-region scale replacing the current Work

Programme (WP) from the end of 2017. The WP was established in 2011 by the former Coalition Government and designed to deliver personalised services via 'private contractor market actors' (Dean 2009: 3) to people who have significant barriers to work or who are on long-term sickness benefit. The WP 'contract areas' territorially cut across SCRCA administrative boundaries (as the WP covers the South Yorkshire contract area and part of the East Midlands contract area), which in effect serves to reinforce fragmentation of the welfare market in cities and regions, and this also shapes the *internal structures of the state* and *patterns of intervention* to 'facilitate the process of neoliberalism through flexibility and variability' (Haughton et al. 2013: 217).

The welfare reform localisation agenda now involves bringing more target groups into employment including people on long-term sickness benefits and with disabilities. This involves a tough medical Work Capability Assessment (WCA) designed to determine eligibility for sickness benefits such as ESA. Local authorities are also key in the development of their own employment and welfare *modes of intervention* to support more marginalised groups including at a city-region scale. Sheffield City Council operates an Apprenticeship Programme across the SCRCA and other local authorities run a city-region-wide programme (Ambition) targeting young people and providing support into employment and training.

Moreover, the roll out of Universal Credit (UC), involving merging benefits and a tapering system linked to in-work benefits and wages designed to 'make work pay', involves a more disciplinary and conditional welfare system through a tougher claimant regime in which sanctions are an integral feature (see below). Furthermore, in-work conditionality is a central feature of UC in terms of 'making work pay' with the requirement for claimants to attain an 'earning threshold' set at the level of effort it is reasonable for an individual to undertake. Working-age adults will be subject to conditionality until they are working full-time (35 hours) at National Minimum Wage. If someone is earning below the conditionality cut-off point they will be expected to 'look for work, more work or better paid work' (see HM Government 2016b). In short, as argued in Chapters 4 and 7, the localisation of welfare is a national *state project* and neoliberal *modes of intervention*, exercising societal depoliticisation by transferring aspects of social policy from the (collective) public to the (individualised) private sphere, articulated locally through the changing *internal structures of the state*. Devolution and city-region building is being implicitly used to implement welfare cuts and austerity. As I highlight below, although 'the politics of austerity can be interpreted as a long-term strategic offensive designed to reorganize the institutional matrix and balance of forces in favour of capital' (Jessop 2016a: 235), challenges to this are occurring within the state, 'exploiting the bloc's fragilities' (2016a: 237).

## SHEFFIELD CITY REGION DEVOLUTION: DEPOLITICISATION REACTIONS

The dynamic interrelationship between the two processes of depoliticisation and repoliticisation is appearing in the contemporary rolling out of devolution, which has in turn generated open political conflict and opposition. Three examples demonstrate the role of agency with respect to the state as a social relation, arena of struggle, and the 'theatre for the contestation of ideologies' (Glaser 2015, 24). First, Sheffield City Council organised an event on devolution (March 2016), attended by civil society leaders, to provide opportunities for critical voices to express concerns around the Northern Powerhouse *state project* (see Sheffield City Region LEP 2016). A roundtable discussion and panel session noted the limits to the clustering forces of agglomeration and pointed to geographies of uneven development:

> The first unanimous issue raised was that of social inequalities, with delegates noting the economic emphasis of the deal and the devolution debate in general, and wondering how devolution will serve to combat inequalities and increase fairness. In particular there were concerns that in discussions on the economy the question of how growth alleviates poverty is often lost. Though delegates agreed that growth is an important contributory factor in improving people's lives, it is not the only one and the links between economic growth and lessening of inequalities need to be drawn more clearly. Relatedly, concerns exist that action is required to address some of the structural inequalities that exist in Sheffield in order to make the most of the opportunities of devolution. Growth will be best achieved if citizens have the opportunity and skills to participate but there is a sense that this is not the case at the moment; for example, delegates asked whether we will create an Advanced Manufacturing Innovation District only to import employees? (Sheffield City Region LEP 2016: 10)

The voluntary and community sector expressed a similar viewpoint in their response to the devolution deal. According to one source:

> We also believe there is a case for constructing a 'social deal' to sit alongside the present economic, employment, planning and infrastructure deal. Without this, we are concerned that growth will not be inclusive, and that we may see growing inequalities and the risks that emanate from this despite overall better economic performance. (Voluntary and Community Sector, Interview, 2016)

Second, the closure of Government's Business Innovation and Skills (BIS) offices in Sheffield is creating Civil Service redundancies and transfers, with demonstrations and strikes (organised by the Employment Services trade union Public and Commercial Services Union) against this cost-cutting endeavour (under the banner of 'Northern Poor House, Not Powerhouse'—see RSA 2016b: 6). The links and tensions between austerity and devolution have more than surfaced in the SCR and this has brought into sharp focus how the 'devolution revolution' (HM Government 2016a) underpins, manages, and at the same time is threatened by, austerity.

Third, the implementation of an extensive welfare market within the SCR has raised further issues and tensions around *modes of representation* accountabilities with respect to employment and skills programmes, in particular the WP. The lack of transparency and engagement by WP providers with local actors and partnerships has been seen as a key source of tensions in the decentralisation of welfare-to-work programmes in the UK (Finn 2015). This is certainly the case within the SCR, as there is evidence (raised in Chapter 4) of widespread technocratic criticism, which is indicative of how this 'output-centred' contractual governance *mode of intervention* 'limits' certain forms of 'political engagement' (Raco et al. 2016), by agencies of the performance of the WP providers and local actors, with some local authorities and agencies expressing a view that the DWP is not fully aware of what the providers actually do in localities. As one local authority officer stated:

> There is no published data on the volume of referrals made to these learning providers, on what their geographic coverage is, or the nature of skills provision and outcomes. The policy-making process and its evaluation aren't known locally within this city-region. (Interview, 2016)

## Welfare, Conditionality, Employment, and Skills Systems

The impact of welfare reforms on poverty and social inequality has been an intensely contested issue at the national level (see HM Government 2016b) and these tensions have been deeply experienced in the SCR. Several initiatives illustrate the importance and impact of struggle and contestation in and against the neoliberal *mode of intervention*. First, the action taken by the Unite trade union against Sports Direct, a mass production sportswear company, whose headquarters are located in Shirebrook (in the Bolsover District). This has been against low-pay, zero-hours contracts and poor working conditions, which has had major national impacts, as both local and national actors and campaigns have successfully brought the company to account through the Government's Select Committee evidence process (see Goodley and Ashby 2015). Second, local authorities, advice organisations, and anti-poverty coalitions have been very outspoken, seeking to mobilise advocacy on behalf of residents within the welfare system. According to one particularly vocal organisation:

> The circumstances of people coming through our doors are far worse than those of the 1980s. Reliance on Foodbanks, Benefit Sanctions on a massive scale, sick or disabled workers, without a hope of being employed, found 'fit for work' are some of the issues that our team of advisers have dealt with this year. Policies which are

> supposed to be about helping people to move closer to the labour market are in many cases damaging to health, self-defeating, and at their very worst, causing deaths and contributing to suicides. (Derbyshire Unemployment Workers Centre, Interview, 2015)

As noted above, one of the features of government localisation welfare reforms is the increasing use of benefit sanctions (Webster, 2015) as a national *state project* of disciplining benefit claimants, whilst at the same time depoliticising the unemployment and job-gap problem and undermining the safety net provided by social benefits (Fletcher et al. 2016). The significant number of benefit sanctions implemented in the SCR (at approximately 70,000 sanctions, between 2012 and 2015) has been the subject of intense criticism amongst local authorities, advice services, and welfare workers. Local authorities have borne the brunt of the sanctions in terms of the pressures on their welfare and support services and have accordingly articulated opposition to the use of sanctions and the way other tools of benefit conditionality are leading to the increasing impoverishment of claimants. For example Rotherham MBC (Rotherham MBC 2014), Sheffield Citizens Advice Bureaux, and Derbyshire network of advice centres (Needham 2015) have all voiced concerns about claimants in many cases being unfairly (incorrectly against the DWP guidelines) sanctioned and benefits ceased.

Disability rights organisations, trade unions, and community coalitions have run campaigns against such benefit sanctions, involving picketing the Job Centre network and seeking to raise the profile of the issue through publicity campaigns, as the impact of sanctions combined with benefit cuts is creating serious financial hardships for vulnerable groups (see Involve Yorkshire and Humberside 2014). At the same time, Derbyshire Unemployed Workers Centre has successfully won tribunals and appeals on benefit sanctions decisions through representation, which underlines the importance of advocacy via the formal political system for those negotiating the benefit system from within the state. This illustrates how policy implementation happens as a consequence of the 'complex interaction between reflexive subjects involved in multiple relations of power and objective factors that present opportunities and constraints on actions' (Prior and Barnes 2011: 267; see also Williams et al. 2012) and how the unemployed and the social excluded exercise purposeful agency in '*collective* practices' (Wright 2012: 316, emphasis original). According to one source:

> Each year we deal with over 9,000 enquiries at our Centres and outreach venues. We have recovered over £3 million in lump sum payments and increased weekly benefits for the people of Derbyshire. This money is vital both for the recipients, but also for the regeneration of the local economy. Money gained is mostly spent locally

> helping to preserve jobs and aid local businesses. (Derbyshire Unemployed Workers Centre, Interview, 2016)

The *hegemonic project* and policy debate, though, is largely construed around unemployed and disadvantaged groups becoming 'employable' and obtaining the 'right skills' to obtain employment. The views of stakeholders consider that employers as well as the employment services have an important role to play. The evidence submitted to the Sheffield Fairness Commission (2013: 42) indicates, 'that people from deprived communities are often trapped in "poor" work with low pay, poor working conditions, long hours and job insecurity'. Once people have obtained qualifications, there are no guarantees of progression in employment, given the nature of pay, work organisation, job design, casualisation and the increasing use of zero-hours contracts (Industrial Community Alliance 2015). This is indicative, on Jessop's terms, of a depoliticisation transference shift occurring towards individualised responses to collective challenges in the state's *mode of intervention*: 'a further move from national welfare states to more postnational workfare regimes in advanced capital states and a reinforcement of current tendencies towards enduring states of austerity' (2016a: 246).

## The Politics of 'States of Austerity' in the City-Region

As noted above, and building on Chapter 7, an underlying tension exists in the SCR between the somewhat consensual *hegemonic vision* of promoting growth (see SCR Vision 2017) within a context and backdrop of a *state project* of austerity and welfare cuts. Beatty and Fothergill (2016) demonstrate that the greatest loss in the income of working-age adults occurred in the more deprived local authorities. For example, two local authority districts within the SCRCA, Bolsover and Barnsley, are in the top 50 districts in the UK worst affected by the reforms. Also, as Table 10.2 shows, the largest loss in income occurs through the changes in tax credits, which has implications for those on low wages. Collectively, the stark reality of the SCR financial context reveals cuts of £1,109 billion over a four-year period set against the trumpet-like fanfare of the £900 million total 'devolution deal' (over 30 years). Within the expanded nine local authority *social basis* of the SCRCA state form, the gaps between devo-rhetoric and austerity-reality could not be further apart. Despite this, the Sheffield LEP Chair has reinforced a neoliberal participatory inclusiveness strategy, where the 'let's get it done work-ethic in Sheffield City Region harnesses drive and ambition [and] with everyone pulling together, and a significant sense of community, we are achieving transformational change' (Walsh 2017: 61).

*Table 10.2 Sheffield City Region income changes*

| Local authority area | Total spending 2010 (£ million) | Total spending 2014 (£ million) | Reductions 2010–14 (£ million) | Total estimated annual welfare cuts (2015) (£ million) |
|---|---|---|---|---|
| Barnsley | 196 | 167 | 29 | 86.6 |
| Bassetlaw | 20.8 | 12 | 8.8 | 35 |
| Bolsover | 13.3 | 10.3 | 3 | 27.0 |
| Chesterfield | 21.7 | 13.5 | 8.2 | 35.1 |
| Derbyshire Dales | 11.8 | 7.7 | 4.0 | 13.6 |
| Doncaster | 528 | 371 | 157 | 104.8 |
| North-east Derbyshire | 16.8 | 10.4 | 6.4 | 13.6 |
| Rotherham | 484 | 399 | 85 | 86.8 |
| Sheffield | 970 | 829 | 141 | 162.6 |
| Totals | | | 442.4 | Approx. 577 |

*Sources:* For local authority spending (2010–14): https://ig.ft.com/sites/2015/local-cuts-checker/#E09000028%23 (accessed 14 June 2016). For welfare reforms: Data provided by Christina Beatty relate to annual changes.

The role and nature of local authorities (all are represented on the SCRCA Board) has been diverse and their relationship with the city-region building process in some cases has been ambivalent. On the one hand, local authorities are managing austerity (but in different ways) by moving towards a more 'facilitating' and enabling role in terms of provision of services (CLES 2014). SCRCA and its local authorities are 'discursive institutions' (Fuller 2017), relaying depoliticisation through the ongoing savage cuts in public sector budgets, which contribute directly to their economic agenda by providing opportunities for private profit (outsourcing and privatisation), as well as, on the other hand, providing a critical voice in relation to increasing poverty and social inequalities.

This highlights the contradictory 'agent and obstacle' (Duncan and Goodwin 1988) nature of the state as a social relation and the multiple roles that *modes of representation* can have for opening up political engagement. Sheffield Fairness Commission (see above) is further illustrative of this, as it promotes inclusion discourses and politics around alternatives to benefit and welfare cuts, but is also a site of tensions and struggles itself. Stakeholders witness how Sheffield City Council, as well as promoting the growth agenda through its involvement in the SCRCA, despite being integral to the Fairness Commission, bows to the dominant narrative of the necessity of cuts and is actively part of their implementation.

Pessimism is toxic and I am certainly not conceding ground to the TINA mantra of 'there is no alternative'. Analysis highlights 'the fractures and frictions that create the space for alternative' (Jessop 2016a: 246). The SCR is witness to an increasing lack of buy-in to the neoliberal growth discourse, which is coalescing around the local state and the SCRCA local authorities as key agents for counteracting depoliticisation and becoming a space for repoliticisation.

First, the Sheffield-centric location of the proposed HS2 transport connection stations has created territorial tensions between South Yorkshire councils. Added to this, the cross-border city-region involvement of Chesterfield and Bassetlaw local authorities in a South Yorkshire deal has led Derbyshire County Council to seek a (successful) judicial review (on the breadth of the consultation, on its fairness, on the means used to consult, and on the complexity of the information surrounding transfer of powers) of the Sheffield devolution process, effectively putting back the mayoral election timetable to run the city-region's development corporation. These 'custody battles' and 'regional rows' (Perraudin 2016), illustrating that 'the power of the state is the power of the forces acting in and through the state' (Jessop 1990a: 270), have increased during 2017 through the ambitions of Barnsley and Doncaster's local authorities to be part of a wider Yorkshire Devolution deal, culminating on 18 September 2017 with their withdrawal from, and 'derailing' of, the SCR devolution process (Burn 2017). This triggered Central Government to withdraw the £900 million financial offer, with a possible mayor de facto penniless, whilst austerity romps on and the welfare cuts bite deeper.

Second, trade unions, in particular Unite Community, have played a key role in making connections with, recruiting, and involving unemployed people with 'local' campaigns around benefit sanctions and austerity policies. Third, Barnsley Borough Council has also developed an alternative employment and skills strategy around 'more and better jobs', recognising the limits to the city-region growth model and the low-pay, low-skills cycle that is a dominant feature of this economy.

## CONCLUSIONS

This chapter has highlighted the trajectories of a 'post-political' economic and social development approach to city-region building. 'The post-political condition' is clearly seen not to be a coherent institutional fix that supports this neoliberal growth project. City-region building frameworks are clearly incapable of addressing the dilemmas associated with uneven growth and the failure of policies to address deep-rooted problems of labour market inequalities that are integral to market and governance failures. The chapter thus concurs with Darling (2016: 230) that when 'combined with a market-oriented transfer of responsibilities, depoliticisation acts to constrain the possibilities of political debate and to predetermine the contours of those policy discussions that do take place'. The chapter has discussed how the SCR is being depoliticised through *state projects* and *hegemonic visions*, continually generating discourses and narratives on the economy (the *shaping of context*, according to Jessop 2016a). Our analysis has stressed the importance of considering trends and counter-trends and there has been a failure to build a broad *social basis* for devolution *spatial imaginary* initiatives such as the Northern Powerhouse. Devolution deals are concerned with arrangements for individual city-regions and, beyond the aspiration for a larger collective contribution to national economic output, there is no focus on the relationships with and between city-regions and hence the overall functioning of the economy is bereft of strategic planning. In effect, there is an asymmetric distribution of powers: the devolution deals encourage competition over collaboration between city-regions, which exacerbates existing inequalities, whereas, the fantasy of 'neoliberalism promises that everyone will win' (Dean 2009: 72). This is heightened by the welfare and local authority cuts identified in our research, set to be amplified, as many of the policies that previously distributed the proceeds of the UK's finance-centric economic model have been ended by the broader austerity agenda. Public sector and public investment should play key roles in supporting and leading growth, but I have highlighted that 'this is being directly hampered by a big withdrawal of state funding for this purpose' (RSA 2016a: 6).

It is essential to continue to find ways of working for change from *within* our research situations, jobs, and our private as-residents-lives, ways of developing effective, organised oppositional action, which comes directly out of exposing these contradictions of neoliberalism (Etherington and Jones 2016b). In contrast to 'post-political' approaches, which tend to stand outside the state, the goal is to 'advocate participation within the mechanisms of power to intensify their internal contradictions and conflicts' (Jessop 1985: 129). In this chapter, by focusing on Jessop's state as a social relation—not as a static 'black box' (compare Swyngedouw 2017) but continually materialising as an institutional ensemble and one where any power distributed through the state only constitutes the power of particular agents (and their practices) incorporated into its *social bases*—the chapter has highlighted how different forms of agency are shaping and politicising the SCR governance landscape.

Building on Chapter 2, the chapter has also highlighted how a number of 'bottom-up' initiatives have served to develop counter-*hegemonic visions* by directly engaging with the city-region devolution agenda, all of which are forming part of an important repoliticising of the local state. The task is to identify further counter-discourses and ideas about a more inclusive city-region (see RSA 2017) and consider how these might be 'scaled up' from the locally specific to the general, to mobilise a broader social base of support

(Haughton et al. 2016a; RSA 2016a: 11). Addressing these would, paraphrasing Larner (2014: 203), allow for 'new political formations [to] emerge', and empower grassroots democracy via a repoliticised civil society to recast the 'integral state'.

The chapter is certainly not arguing that political organisation has to be modelled only on the state within capitalism—a challenge made by Amin and Thrift (2013: 113) in their promotion of what they call 'liquid models of political organization', some of which are akin to the more libertarian and revolutionary frameworks advocated by 'post-political' commentators that see limited viability or desirability of these forms of institutionalisation (see Swyngedouw 2017). It has argued that Jessop's SRA approach allows for just this—the state 'an institutionally diverse form of political organization that can be more open and flexible than the standard state form' (2016a: 113)—and the chapter encourages constructive discussion and debate on advancing this and other frameworks to get a handle on the 'post-political' depoliticised state in, and of, contemporary capitalism.

# PART IV

# Alternatives to neoliberalism

# 11. Developing inclusive growth

## INTRODUCTION

The city-region building agenda appears to be showing more of an interest in the voluntary and third sector as partners for economic and social development. A Green Paper on the interfaces between employment and health, for instance, calls for an understanding of how to best support people with health conditions or those deemed disabled to return to or stay in work. This includes finding ways 'to extend the reach of Jobcentre Plus into third sector support groups which are already well established' (DWP 2016: 29–30). The Greater Manchester (GM) model is particularly interesting here and its specifics are influencing new trials in Sheffield and the West Midlands. There are further developments in the inclusive growth policy-fields stemming from the limits to the Metro-Mayor model, which are advocating the repositioning of civil society, the third sector, and the voluntary sector in local and regional economic and social development (see RSA 2016a, 2017). This chapter bridges these concerns and focuses on developments and potentials in the Greater Manchester City Region (GMCR), with lessons for other localities.

Devolution to the GMCR to date has been a centrally led process with only minimal and piecemeal consultation (Waite et al. 2013). The process of devolution is creating a variety of new policy opportunities for the city-region, but the initial variety of devolution has been geared more towards economic growth for sure (Bailey and Budd 2016). In doing this and especially given the opportunities provided by the devolution of health and welfare, there is a recognised need to bring together the appropriate voices within the city-region to address the problems of inequality faced by the region (on the scale of which, see Etherington and Jones 2016b). Devolution, to date, has been framed and shaped by Central Government in terms of what politicians see as the appropriate pathway to growth, activated in turn through a deal-making process of negotiation (O'Brien and Pike 2015). As noted in Chapter 9, this pathway is largely dependent on an economic model predicted and focused on enhancing processes of agglomeration, which in turn only serves to further create uneven development within the city-region (see Haughton et al. 2016b). If growth is to be inclusive, this model has to change and devolution has to find ways to offer new opportunities that significantly move beyond the limited options offered by Central Government (Beel et al. 2016; Jonas 2012b).

Based on a study of the GM Voluntary, Community and Social Enterprise (VCSE) Devolution Reference Group, this chapter suggests a need to bring third and voluntary sector organisations into processes of devolution and city-region building and also shows the limits to achieving this. The work of Dear and Wolch (1987) represents an important framing point here, as they followed a similar trajectory of neoliberalisation of inner-city welfare provision in the United States during the 1980s, charting the rise of what was then termed ‘the shadow state’. This referred to the variety of civil society groups that stepped in to provide welfare, as the state rolled-back and increasingly absolved itself of its social responsibility. This led though to a disintegration in the third sector’s ability to deliver such services in North American (United States) cities, as they could not cope with the demands being placed upon them. This partially stemmed from a lack of engagement by the state with civil society and a similar sense of non-engagement, particularly with third sector groups, is being conveyed within the GMCR. As argued in Chapter 10, successful devolution will ultimately rely on the sector being better engaged with the state and policy-making processes. An important first hurdle for inclusive growth models, therefore, is the requirement for a stronger form of representation within the governance structures of devolution for VCSE groups. This is to not only acknowledge the important role such organisations have in the GMCR, but also to think through the ways in which, moving forward, the sector will be further required to deliver different aspects of devolution. This is critical in the context of a significant reduction in Central Government spending on local economic growth as part of the Government’s deficit reduction programme. The National Audit Office reports that over the five-year period 2010/11 to 2014/15 the Coalition Government will have spent £6.2 billion on local growth programmes, including that spent via Regional Development Agencies (RDAs) and their legacy and the spend on new funds and structures. By comparison the RDAs spent £11.2 billion over the preceding five-year period 2005/06 to 2009/10 (National Audit Office 2013). This is, of course, within the context of ongoing austerity measures, which will reportedly cost the GMCR between 2015 to 2020 an estimated £1.4 billion from their welfare budgets (see Beatty and Fothergill 2016; Etherington and Jones 2017).

Despite the difficult environment surrounding devolution, discussed at length in Chapters 9 and 10, VCSE groups, although cautious, are also interested to see what devolution to city-regions may offer and how they can play an important role within shaping this. This chapter discusses four key drivers that can position the sector as an appropriate interface through which a more inclusive economy might be delivered: the need for inclusive governance; addressing issues related to operational scales and modes of representation;

probing into how inequality hinders growth; and, finally, the need to harness the multifaceted thinking and social innovation of VCSE in order to deliver inclusive growth.

## INCLUSIVE GOVERNANCE FOR AN INCLUSIVE CITY-REGION

The parallel contexts of devolution and austerity have created a number of challenges, which in turn raise a series of questions about how governance structures will deal with this and how resources will be effectively deployed to create economic development in GM. This raises questions about what economic development in GMCR should look like and who should benefit from future economic growth. To date, within the context of city-region devolution across England and GMCR included, devolution has sought to primarily privilege business interests (Pike et al. 2015). As noted in Chapter 8, this can be seen in the development of Local Enterprise Partnerships (LEPs) as strategic bodies to shape combined authority economic planning. In the context of inclusive growth, there is a risk that when such city-region governance arrangements do not involve 'civil society' groups, decision-making processes accordingly lack local legitimacy in terms of transparency, scrutiny, and accountability. This points towards issues whereby from an instrumental perspective, the processes of devolution are missing out on opportunities to glean social capital and local knowledge, engage with communities, support local social innovation, and build suitable partnerships. The following section highlights the ways in which the VCSE communities have responded to devolution within the GMCR through organisations such as Greater Manchester Centre for Voluntary Organisations (GMCVO) and the nascent Devolution Reference Group. Taking forward the argument in Chapter 10, this illustrates how inclusive governance models can be developed in city-regions by engaging with the state apparatus, so that devolution can begin to address the stubborn geographies of uneven development and inequality.

In the context of this, the VCSE Devolution Reference Group grew out of a desire for the civil society sector to more actively engage and help shape the city-region in a way that this sector had not seen with previous economic and social development policy initiatives. Devolution represents a different moment in time, where new working relationships are being developed, both reactively and more interestingly, proactively through new geographies of negotiation and engagement. The VCSE Devolution Reference Group represents a new form of collaborative working, which sits alongside existing institutions in the city-region such as GMCVO. GMCVO has a long history of voluntary (or third) sector representation across the city-region and is also deeply active within the VCSE Devolution Reference Group in continuing to represent the concerns of its members. The scale and pace of devolution and the mechanisms by which the Greater Manchester Combined Authority (GMCA) and the UK Government have negotiated such deals has meant that further forms of representation have been sought to find ways to address the new governance structures that are being created within the city-region. According to one source:

> The reference group was set up when we realised that all this was going on around us and nobody was going to come banging down our door … So from that, a coalition of the willing emerged, completely undemocratically but again I think that's part of it. Stop waiting for permission, stop feeling like you have to get every detail right. Because actually things are moving so fast, we have to trust each other to advocate for what our sector wants to achieve collectively. (Interview, Voluntary Service Leader 1)

The purpose of the VCSE Devolution Reference Group has, therefore, been to find the appropriate ways in which to influence processes of devolution through sectoral collaborations and partnerships. This has been in order to push city-region agendas towards more inclusive approaches that attempt to acknowledge the different ways in which the voluntary sector is positioned throughout GM's structures. This is further reflected by another respondent, which highlights how, by focusing on the restructuring of the public sector alone, analysis misses the bigger picture with regards to what could be achieved with a more inclusive governance framework:

> The pace of change of devolution has meant a strong inclination towards the public sector thinking about [only] the public sector … their internal mechanisms and ways of working can override the belief that we're important partners. By having a collective group that is able to rapidly make the case for what we are about and could be about is particularly important at this time. (Interview, Voluntary Service Leader 2)

The VCSE Devolution Reference Groups, then, represent one model, which, within the context of devolution, can bring a broad coalition of diverse groups together alongside pre-existing organisations. The group aims to be representative of (rather than represent), and connect to, the broad spectrum of VCSE activity in GMCR. This takes in how such groups are positioned in different ways with very different approaches. The VCSE Devolution Reference Group, in its current form is not perfect and the group recognises that it will always need to evolve. Its ability to develop partnerships across a multifaceted range of organisations highlights a model that can be moved forward with devolution to create parallel forms of representation and governance. Such groups involved are at the hard end of delivering and enabling citizens to thrive in the very difficult circumstances of austerity. They have clear social purposes with regards to helping or enabling those in the most difficult circumstances to achieve, in order to 'eradicate' inequality in the GMCR. They also have a strong innovative spirit for delivery in a time of limited resources. This innovation could be harnessed more directly by including such organisations earlier in commissioning processes rather than just as respondents to funding opportunities. In doing this, there could be more attuned responses to inequality whilst giving the processes of commissioning more transparency. In the context of devolution, such activities should be folded into the processes of delivering devolution, rather than being a reaction to what is unfolding around VCSE members. This, though, raises questions of scale and representation and of the wider positioning of civil society as either an agent or obstacle to the development of city-region policy. As 'agent', they risk being complicit in policy, which promotes agglomerative economic growth. Whereas an 'obstacle' positioning could see them marginalised further from the representational regime of the city-region which could be precarious for organisations that can often be reliant on various forms of local state funding.

## SCALE AND REPRESENTATION

The creation of the GMCA could paradoxically shift some forms of governance further away from individuals and communities. Although devolution offers potentially more powers at a city-region scale, it could also take powers and control away from those operating at a local authority scale. Consequently, this can leave many VCSE groups, who often (not always) work within a specific locality, place-based community or LA, further away from the processes of decision-making and commissioning. This, in turn, potentially reduces their capacity to be an effective advocate for the areas. According to one commentator:

> My concern would be, as a medium sized organisation based and working predominately in Salford, and for other organisations who are smaller than ourselves, what happens if you've got a brilliant, cost effective service and the combined authority wants to commission that service across all of the localities. If you are only delivering in Salford and not in the other nine localities, does that mean they are going to commission you on the understanding that you would need to build your organisation's capacity to be able to deliver across the other localities or would they not commission as they would be worried about scaling up and would want to use one of the bigger organisations. (Interview, Place-based Community Leader 1)

The description above highlights how devolution can potentially be disempowering for locality actors. As noted in Chapter 9, city-region building creates a 'jumping of scale' (Cox 1998) whereby policy direction and commissioning will reflect combined authority policy decisions. 'Scale jumping', in this context, is the redefining of territorial relations from the local authority to the city-regional scale in such a way that it circumvents, where possible, certain locality 'politics of turf' (Cox 1989). Scale jumping is, therefore, a process through which new networks of association can be built to prioritise practices of capital accumulation (Smith 1990). This potentially leaves smaller and more localised providers further away from decisions that may greatly impact upon their organisation's future viability, which in turn creates a series of questions for GMCA in terms of how policy can be filtered and interpreted down to the local level. The VCSE sector already has a variety of different organisations working at and delivering across different geographical scales, whether this is at the community, local authority or city-region scales. They have been consistently able to find ways to engage those individuals and groups, which are often hardest to reach or most in need, though this ability is becoming continually strained in the current era of austerity. For a more centralised form of 'the local', city-regional governance not to appreciate the local could lead to a number of valuable services being lost.

Devolution processes also need to think through ways in which the processes of city-region rescaling also miss, by exclusion, different formations of community, which are not necessarily place-based, such as those concerned with black and minority ethnic (BME), disability, lesbian, gay, bisexual, and transgender (LGBT), homeless and mental health. Such groups exist across city-regions, with specific needs that should be taken into consideration. Considerable work has gone into the processes of locality planning in GM for health provision, but this needs to ensure that it does not miss the needs of different minority groups across the city-region. According to one source:

> My other worry about devolution from an equality perspective is that: in terms of the localism model that everybody is talking about and working on, is that for some people locality isn't their community of identity … That's what many disabled people would say, 'I'm not interested in being disabled, I am a disabled person' and that's it. Now that also might mean that your need or your interface with a service or organisation won't be geographically defined. And also for some people you might actively move away from the geography, in terms of young people who are homeless, young people with mental health problems. (Interview, Community of Interest Leader 1)

There is, therefore, a need to find ways in which individuals and groups can see appropriate representation within processes of governance. One such approach is to have more involvement of different VCSE groups who form a broad form of representation to different types and forms of communities, who have a history of advocacy within the city-region:

> I think it's also about working on different levels. I was very involved in working with colleagues in looking at a voluntary sector response … There is something very compelling about not doing this just for ourselves and on our own and actually

> building a coalition of the willing and recognising that we have much more power doing something together and articulating similar arguments with a range of our colleagues. (Interview, Community of Interest Leader 2)

In terms of equality, then, the city-region footprint potentially offers the opportunity for a stronger exploration of how to engage, support and champion communities of identity. It also allows space to develop a more sophisticated understanding of how scale, engagement, representation and subsidiarity should interrelate:

> The risk is, what's happening is either within GM or moving into GM are big corporate bodies and you could see in the middle of Manchester, big corporates moving in. Big public sector structures being created and indeed the big charities moving in. The third sector is as guilty of this stuff as anybody else. So we at least need to balance some of that stuff because it's probably going to happen anyway or possibly replace some of that stuff, I think with a much more diverse, smaller medium scale stuff that actually engages the people who need to be engaged. (Interview, Social Enterprise Leader 1)

This system is not without its limits, but the scale of operations provided by VCSE groups represents the multifaceted ways in which different organisations work with different communities of geography (city-region through to neighbourhood) and with different communities of identity (disabled groups, LGBT, BME).

## INEQUALITY AND GROWTH DYNAMICS

Inequality and social disadvantage actually hinders growth (see Etherington and Jones 2016a, 2016b; Jonas and Ward 2007; Lee 2016) or, at best, creates the wrong kind of growth due to it not being distributed evenly (see Bowmen et al. 2014). The converse is that those policies, which actively promote labour market inclusion, will contribute to sustainable growth and also assist with maintaining productivity. The current model of growth, though, restricts access to employment and skills initiatives and hence the city-region will accordingly struggle to meet targets. This is identified in the quote below as it spatially impacts upon the development of the GMCR:

> I think of Greater Manchester as having a ring donut economy, it's a lot like a North American city. So you have thriving city centre, which it didn't have 25 years ago. The suburbs actually doing ok and then the middle bit. If they do not do something about that, the powers that be will never achieve their economic goals of achieving a fiscal balance for this conurbation. (Interview, Social Enterprise Leader 1)

This quote highlights that, despite the successes of the GM economy over the last 30 years, it has still failed to address core problems of uneven development. As argued in Chapter 9, neo-classical economic informed agglomeration focuses growth in specific places; it does not worry about how that growth is then evenly spread, other than for the ideological belief that trickledown will no doubt occur (Peck 2012). Chapter 3 highlighted that the latter principles certainly do not occur in the long history of urban and regional policy. There is a disconnect then taking place not just with city-region planning across GM but also across the entire process of city-region devolution in the UK (see Chapter 8). According to one perspective on this:

> So one of the challenges we've got at the minute, and that's part of the discussion that has just happened in the meeting today, is this dilemma—or not a dilemma, this disconnect rather, between the VCSE and the work that goes in the whole economy plan around LEPs and everything else that's going on. And there's—social care and the VCSEs are quite well connected, usually through contract and commissioning but then you've got this whole world around economy, employment and skills that spins close to it but never—rarely collides or isn't connected. (Interview, Community of Interest Leader 2)

The two previous quotes also highlight a continuing mismatch in the logic of city-region agglomeration, which focuses on gross value added (GVA) uplift, rather than finding ways to provide across the existing populations of GM. The second quote also highlights an important disconnection in current thinking—the need for a stronger consideration, at a strategic economic level, towards a more holistic approach for employment and skills training (see also Chapter 2). The absence in mainstream discourse about how inequality can be addressed offers an opportunity for voluntary and community sectors to alter the terms of the debate. Members of the VCSE Devolution Reference Group recognise this opportunity and would like to have a stronger voice in order to deliver a more inclusive growth strategy. The social innovation already shown by the VCSE sector in delivering on employment and skills training, which attempts to integrate health and social needs within such training strategies, suggests there is wealth of pre-existing knowledge that needs to be accessed by GMCA. The VCSE sector has a strong record in terms of providing pathways back to work and has been successful in being able to react to changes in economic circumstances.

## SOCIAL INNOVATION, MULTIFACETED THINKING AND ECONOMIC GROWTH

VCSE Devolution Reference Group members note how the increased devolution offered to GMCR offers real opportunities to do things differently from the supposed model of growth offered by Central Government, but this opportunity has to be negotiated. The devolution of health and social care in GM (unlike in other city-regions) is one such opportunity, but this again needs radical rethinking if it is to fulfil its potential (see Etherington and Jones 2017). The sector has been one of the most dynamic in terms of thinking through how to deliver services to people and communities that are hardest to reach. The opinion below highlights how the voluntary sector is already involved in taking a multifaceted thinking approach:

> We need to look at where are the skills and knowledge and solutions to fix any particular problem. Some of it may lie with the people who apparently have the problem, so if you want to solve homelessness, you've got to involve people who have experienced homelessness or who are currently homeless because it would be stupid not to take their … so they would have knowledge that no-one else has. You've got to involve a whole range of other agencies who have touched with that problem in one way or another. And those who have got the overview. Collectively you might then start to come up with an answer to that. (Interview, Voluntary Services Leader 3)

This desire to socially innovate by connecting different agents to tackle problems, such as homelessness, exemplifies how new approaches can be found that are very much in tune with public sector partner thinking. VCSE groups can play a key strategic role due to their on-the-ground knowledge and their flexibility in delivering services. Indeed, understanding that the current inequality present in the GMCR is more than just an economic concern and that it is linked to a variety of other multifaceted problems is key to thinking about how groups within VCSE can have a very strong impact in terms of addressing these problems. The VCSE community represents one way in which complex activity and thinking (from small to large, from person to community and from place to identity) can allow for a stronger response to social inequality and build a more inclusive economy.

## CONCLUSIONS

There is a risk, moving forward, that, as devolution is delivered across GM and in other city-regions, not appropriately integrating VCSE groups and arrangements like this into governance structures will miss an excellent opportunity to redraw the relationships between VCSE, state, business and communities. Combined Authorities and LEPs could do worse than listen and then take stock of the knowledge, expertise, and innovative ways of working with communities and individuals that the VCSE sector has developed. They also need to think through, if inclusive growth is to be achieved, how this expertise can be deployed strategically.

The VCSE Devolution Reference Group is very much a response to the conditions of devolution in GM but, in that response, there is a model alluded to that, with further development, could address many of the gaps that have developed in the economic-led thinking of city-regions. Therefore, in the context of inclusive growth, there needs to be stronger acknowledgement of the expertise this sector can bring and they should be a voice, alongside business and the public sector, in terms of future devolution processes.

As a final caveat to the above and the potential VCSE groups offer devolution and an inclusive economy approach, there is also a need to take a step back and think through, in the context of austerity and devolution, some of the pitfalls that could undermine a more inclusive economy. Here, the earlier discussion with regard to Dear and Wolch (1987) on the neoliberalisation of welfare policy in the United States is important. Here, the scale of problems that faced 'the shadow state' was well beyond its means to deal with and, as such, a whole variety of social problems 'spun-out' from this failure to provide a sufficient social welfare safety net. If this similar turn is taking place in the UK, within the context of city-region devolution and austerity, the UK state, at national, combined authority and local state levels alongside business, has to continue to play its part in balancing and supporting the VCSE sector, so that it can have the opportunity to deliver on its aims.

# 12. Beyond withered local states

[P]olicy can succeed only if this corresponds to an expansion of the alliances and mechanisms of integration on which it is to be based.

(Offe 1984: 72)

## INTRODUCTION

One of the key purposes of comparative work in the social sciences and its policy studies sub-discipline is to develop critical insights into particular models of policy-making, which would not be developed otherwise from a purely national or sub-national analysis, and to construct frameworks for assessing the scope for policy transfer and learning (see Castles 1989; Cochrane and Clarke 1993; Coates 2000; Pickvance and Preteceille 1991). With this in mind, this chapter explores some trends and developments in the role of local government in labour market policy in the UK and Denmark during the 1990s, which it is argued still remain relevant today.

During the 1990s, two 'Third Way' Social Democratic governments have embarked on quite contrasting strategies for local government and local state restructuring more broadly. In the United Kingdom, state intervention has tended to continue (although with important modifications) the path of marginalising the role of local government in terms of urban policy and the provision of local welfare state services relating to collective consumption. As outlined initially in Chapter 3, a greater emphasis is placed on market-making, with non-elected institutions and the private sector taking on increasing responsibilities for policy formation and its implementation. In the sphere of employment and labour market policy its role in the various welfare-to-work strategies is relatively peripheral compared with the private and voluntary sectors. In Denmark, by contrast, the former Social Democratic Government prescribed an expanded role for local government in the provision of employment and vocational training programmes, and as a 'social partner' in local labour market policy partnerships.

The chapter compares and contrasts developments and changes in the two countries with the aim of addressing some of the issues, concerns and critiques generated by UK local government interest associations (see LGA 2001; LGIU 2002) about state strategy, and the possibilities for an expanded role in local employment and social development. The chapter is structured as follows. The next section provides a brief discussion on ways of conceptualising and comparing the dynamics and trajectories of the Danish and UK state apparatus and its policy fields. This is followed by a discussion on trends in the United Kingdom. The chapter then analyses the basic principles of a 'welfare-*through*-work' (Etherington and Jones 2004a, 2004b) strategy and the positioning with this of local government in Denmark. The concluding section offers critical reflections on the Danish model and makes connections with developments in the United Kingdom.

## WELFARE REGIMES AND THE GEOGRAPHY OF LABOUR MARKET REGULATION

DiGaetano (2001) provides a useful starting point for thinking about comparative developments within the welfare state by focusing on ideological relations with respect to the growing and hegemonic influence of the new right, the shifts in international political economy, the more overt influences of 'globalisation', the accompanying reorientation from welfare to workfare, and changes within the mix of government and governance through the creation of partnerships. Drawing on the class and power relations theory (Huber and Stephens 2001), it is argued that two further aspects need to be taken into account within comparative thinking. First, welfare regimes or settlements often embody institutionalised class relations and policies are also contingent on the balance of social forces and specific forms of political struggle—in other words struggle plays an important role in the remaking of labour markets (see Esping-Andersen 1992, 1999). These debates have been covered elsewhere, where it has been suggested that the key reason for comparing policies' trajectories is to understand the role and strategic particularities of *political mobilisation* in the context of welfare-to-work policy formation (Etherington 1998; Etherington and Jones 2004a, 2004b; see also Compston and Madsen 2001). Discussion here builds on this by stressing the importance of scale—political mobilisation can be analysed with respect to the geographical dynamics and territorial specificities of state restructuring (see Chapters 2 and 3).

In this context, Jessop (1999b, 2002c) suggests that changes in welfare regimes comprise of a shift from a Keynesian Welfare National State (KWNS) to a Schumpeterian Workfare Post-National Regime (SWPR). This is related to crises in the traditional post-war welfare settlement of redistribution and social accords, and a more contradictory and unstable regime is now prevailing that is more orientated to the market in terms of economic and social policy by promoting structural and economic competitiveness through supply-side policies. It is workfare in the sense that it subordinates social policy to labour market flexibility and relies on private sector training provision. The political-economic logic of workfare, then, is to incorporate labour into an increasingly commodified labour market (Peck 2001).

For Jessop (2002c), a central dimension to state restructuring is its modus operandi—i.e. shifts within the mixture of government and governance. This involves different non- or para-state organisations in coalition building and partnerships. The nature and forms of these partnerships is again contingent on political struggle and social relations at a variety of different spatial scales. In Jessop's analysis, the move to a SWPR is accompanied by a hollowing-out process, which involves the devolution of responsibilities to the sub-national actors. Thus social and activation programmes are increasingly locally based (see Chapter 2). In relation to local government and the public sector in general, the SWPR involves a de-commodification of their functions—i.e. bringing in the private sector through privatisation and contracting out. This manifests itself in the various structures of governance and partnerships, which exert an influence over the policy-making process, its implementation, and policy outcomes. These trends are, of course, more prominent in neoliberal welfare regimes (such as the United States and United Kingdom) than in social democratic settlements (see below).

As noted in Chapters 2, 3 and 10, Jessop's categorisation is useful in that it also provides a framework for comparing the geography of the state apparatus within and between welfare regimes. For Jessop, the SWPR emphasises the significance of other spatial scales and 'horizons for action' where the national territory is no longer the sole power container. Policy-making functions are in effect being shifted upwards, outwards, and downwards, and the devolution to localities is important because policies are designed close to their sites of implementation. Thus, sub-national politics are important in the shaping of labour market regulation and the different trajectories that this shift embodies is influenced by the balance of political forces, institutional legacies, and changing economic and political conjunctures therein. Such scalar shifts, however, do not necessarily mean a radical devolution of power, but often involve a reordering of relations between different levels and responsibilities for socioeconomic governance (Jessop 2002c). In some contexts this increases the centralising and control functions of the state, with respect to labour market governance (see Jones 1999). In other contexts, a space is provided for a more progressive and negotiated work–welfare policy regime (see Amin and Thomas 1996). Thus, when comparing and analysing local government economic strategies, this has to be set within the context of the mixture of institutions, their scalar/territorial relations, and the associated dynamics of class and political struggle.

## RESTRUCTURING THE UK LOCAL STATE: MARGINALISING LOCAL GOVERNMENT

The 1980s and 1990s were significant periods in the history of British local government in terms of the initiatives, innovations, and debates about the possibilities of local economic development programmes and the different ways in which unemployment and economic restructuring could be tackled at the local level (Duncan and Goodwin 1988; Eisenschitz and Gough 1993; Moon and Richardson 1985). The Conservative 'attacks' on local government are well documented—they curtailed local authority employment policies through wider welfare state restructuring involving cuts in finance and the transfer of economic development functions to non-elected institutions (Cochrane 1993; Stoker 1991; Ward 2000). Such changes formed part of a neoliberal political strategy, which involved 'rolling back' the structures and patterns of intervention associated with the Keynesian welfare state, and 'rolling forward' single-minded institutions, which were embedded within a more market-based and post-welfare ethos (discussed in Chapters 2 and 3).

For academics and policy commentators, the policies implemented by the Labour Party since 1997 embody both continuity and change with respect to economic development (cf. Colenutt 1999; Hay 1999; Hill 2000; Jones 1999). According to Atkinson and Wilks-Heeg (2000), attempts made by Central Government to marginalise the local state have been uneven (see also Imrie and Raco 1999a, 1999b). Far from being 'defenceless' victims of Central Government, Atkinson and Wilks-Heeg (2000) explore the ways in which local authorities have devised strategies to protect their independent policy-making role. Local government, then, is very much alive and kicking, and under New Labour is being positioned and responding in a proactive way to a wide range of social, political, and economic initiatives. The authors cite the increasingly strategic roles played by local authorities in new forms of finance, devolution and regional institution building, and sustainable development (see also Bennett and Payne 2000).

This more upbeat perspective should be compared with those offering a more critical reflection. In Taylor's (2000) analysis on local government, the Labour Party has modified rather than replaced the contract culture introduced by the Conservatives. The changes made through initiatives such as Best Value have provided little new resources and central control has generally increased through a lottery-based funding system with applications being made to over 50 separate streams of money, which is heavily policed by a 'new culture of audit, inspection and challenge' (Stoker 2002). This introduces new players to the local state and creates risk and unpredictability. Likewise, by analysing the 1998 'modernisation' White Paper, Snape argues that there is little evidence to suggest that local government is being put back into the driving seat at the local level. 'Quangocrats still outnumber councillors and many new quangos have been created over the last three years' (Snape 2000: 125) and the pattern of central–local relations underway since the 1980s is unlikely to change.

These claims are extended in Diamond's (2001) work, which traces the transfer of welfare services to a number of Zone-based area-regeneration partnership initiatives. Here, as discussed in Chapter 4, urban managers are still in a powerful position when dealing with local groups but the scope for locally driven renewal is somewhat restricted due to the continued imposition of tight performance targets and externally defined strategies (see also Edwards et al. 2001; Jones and Gray 2001). For Diamond, Labour's 'Third Way' approach to local state restructuring is a continuation of the neoliberal state strategy implemented during the 1980s and 1990s. The responsibility for capacity building is being shifted from the state and into the community, often through increasing the roles played by the voluntary sector in 'neighbourhood management', who are blamed for the failings of economic and social initiatives. Elements of this strategy are evident in the discourses and tactics being used within Labour's 'Neighbourhood renewal' programme (see Jones and Ward 2002, 2004).

Building on this literature, within labour market governance and associated shifts in social policy, *Cities and Regions in Crisis* has argued that there has been increasing central control over local policy-making within Britain. Critical research undertaken on welfare-to-work and the various New Deal programmes, for instance, has also highlighted the entrenched neoliberal basis of policy initiatives introduced since 1997, which have focused on furthering supply-side initiatives through incorporating the private sector into the state apparatus and rescaling the unemployment problem by displacing risk and insecurity to the individual (see Peck 1999b, 2001; Peck and Theodore 2000a, 2000b; Theodore and Peck 1999, 2001). These commentators have also touched on the marginal roles played by local government in employment policy formulation and its delivery. For instance, in their early survey of the New Deal Units of Delivery, Herd et al. (1998) note that local government was in the driving seat in only 16 per cent of New Deal Partnerships and, whilst numerical representation is not an accurate picture of quality, this figure presented somewhat of concern for a Central Government preaching a discourse of democracy, citizenship, and political engagement.

Many of the New Deal Partnerships are being subsumed by Local Strategic Partnerships (see below), which are embracing the local delivery of the New Deal and also acting as coordinators for other area-based regeneration strategies (such as forms of governance associated with the National Strategy for Neighbourhood Renewal). This additional layer of governance within employment and social programmes represents a challenge for local government (Foley and Martin 2000). On this point, research by the Local Government

Association (LGA) has claimed that if 'the government also wants to move to full employment and effectively tackle the deep seated problems of long-term and hidden unemployment … a *new approach* is needed in which local authorities will have a key part to play' (LGA 2001: 1, emphasis added). For the LGA, this new approach should exhibit three strategies: more effective coordination between the key agencies involved at local and sub-regional levels; coordinated implementation of demand-side job creation policies and supply-side skills and training measures; and a range of measures to make better use of the totality of public funds going to deprived areas and to retain this investment in the local economy. These proposals are not falling on deaf ears—they have received support from a wide range of influential audiences (see Home Office 2001; LGIU 2002; Nathan et al. 2001; National Audit Office 2002; Performance and Innovation Unit 2001) and the Local Government Act 2000 has placed much emphasis on local authorities as important key players within socioeconomic regeneration. Developments in Denmark provide an interesting insight into how these strategies can be realised at the local level.

## DENMARK'S WELFARE-THROUGH-WORK STRATEGY

### Making Local Welfare States

The Danish welfare state in its current form evolved from a bitter struggle at the turn of the twentieth century between capital and labour over social rights and representation. Labour won important concessions in relation to employment rights, social provision and access to participation within state policy forums. As a result, the national trade union movement has evolved alongside a 'social democratic' redistributive/universal model of welfare provision. The administration and delivery of welfare also needs to be located in the traditions and culture of local self-governance, which were prominent features of a radical agriculture-based movement during the nineteenth century, which through religious organisations created networks of poor relief, education, and political organisation (Christiansen 1994). A highly decentralised system of local government has consequently developed and been charged with major welfare functions: 275 local councils (municipalities) operate, which carry out planning, social services, care for the elderly, childcare, social security provision, and primary education, and manage utilities (water, energy, waste). Above this, 14 county councils (regions) provide regional planning, transport, secondary education, environmental policy and health (see Etherington 1995; Jørgensen 2002).

It is also important to understand the local government system in terms of interest articulation and political struggle. There are several aspects to this.

First, there is a highly developed system of service user-groups, which act as 'watch dogs' in relation to how services are delivered. Second, the public sector trade unions are organised to resist marked-based reforms and other neo-liberalising tendencies, which undermine the collective and social solidarity principles of welfare provision (Scheur 1998; Taylor-Gooby 1996). Third, the local government organisations (such as the Kommunernes Landsforegningen (KL)—National Association of Local Government) are represented in the corporatist networks and act as important pressure groups around local government issues (Etherington 1997). Gender dimensions of welfare provision also need to be considered. Women have individual status in terms of eligibility to benefits and, through comprehensive childcare provision, have structured access to the labour market. There is also an active women's movement, closely connected to the Danish labour movement, which possesses a powerful voice in shaping welfare debates. This movement has played a significant role in defending the social and universal rights commonly associated with the Danish welfare settlement (Siim 1998).

Until the 1980s, local government did not play a proactive role in relation to intervening in the local economies. This changed during the global downturn and the consequent unemployment crisis that followed major economic restructuring in the cities and rural areas (Keane 2001). Interestingly, a Conservative–Liberal Government (1985–93) responded to pressure from the local government organisations and trade unions for more local powers to tackle local unemployment. Local authorities were given legal powers to provide work-related training for those unemployed claiming social assistance. Furthermore, the local and county councils in the peripheral regions developed local economic and technology policies framed by European Union (EU) structural fund programmes (Etherington 1995). These processes reflect an emerging spatial rescaling/restructuring of the Danish state both 'upwards' with increasing influence of EU policy agendas (which have become more prominent in the 1990s) and a 'downwards' or decentralised shift in the responsibilities for economic and social policies (Amin and Thomas 1996; Etherington 1998).

## Labour Market Reforms: Decentralisation and Increasing Local Government Responsibilities

Building on this legacy, and increasing pressures to tackle rising unemployment, the 1993 Social Democratic Government implemented wide-ranging reforms of the welfare state (see Etherington 1998). Under the 1994 Labour Market Reforms, policies were introduced to ensure that social security benefits were conditional on accepting various offers of educational leave and employment training. A training and job placement package was also introduced with paid leave schemes comprising educational, sabbatical, and childcare initiatives. The educational leave scheme provides opportunities for unemployed aged 25 years and over that are members of the Unemployment Insurance (UI) system to participate in educational and training programmes for a maximum of 12 months. They receive an income that is equivalent to the maximum unemployment benefit. This is available for those in employment and is often used to implement job-rotation, whereby those undertaking leave are replaced by unemployed individuals, with the employed being provided with employment training and vocational education to increase their skills. Local government provides employment training for those claiming social assistance from the local authority. The government's Employment Service organises job placement and training for those claiming unemployment insurance. Eligibility for the UI system is tied to previous employment. Many people in the insurance system, however, find work placements in local government (Goul Andersen 2002).

In stark contrast, then, to the UK state strategy, since 1994 the Danish Social Democratic Government's 'welfare-*through*-work' model (Etherington and Jones 2004a, 2004b) has focused on three key areas. First, social partnerships have been strengthened in policy formulation and implementation at all scales of governance. The public sector and local government are allocated major functions in both the delivery of programmes and in the strategic policy-making process. Second, financial planning and decision-making has been decentralised to regional and local-based institutions, which involve representation from local government. Third, the unemployed have been given rights to counselling, an individual action plan, and, more importantly, access to a comprehensive package of job training, job-rotation, education, and childcare leave schemes. Local government again plays a key role here.

The 1998 Social Policy Act and 1999 Finance Act placed increasing responsibilities on local government for the most vulnerable groups in the labour market, i.e. those claiming social assistance (see Rosdahl and Weise 2000). This was due to an increasing drop-out rate from the UI system because of tightening eligibility rules and also due to increasing barriers for certain groups such as young people, immigrants, and ethnic minorities to gain access to employment. As a consequence, an increasing proportion of the unemployed are claiming social assistance and individual job training schemes are offered to those who cannot be placed in ordinary job placements and require special training and supervision. In addition to job training, 'flex jobs' have been created for people who have a 'reduced capacity' for employment. These are special employment schemes geared to people with health and social problems. Both the public and private sectors can employ people in the so-called 'flex' jobs but, in cases where people are experiencing severe social problems, local government acts as the employer. In addition, local councils are required to produce Individual Action Plans for those on social assistance and the unemployed have a choice from a menu of job training and other vocational orientated training. More recent reforms have promoted an important campaign around 'socially inclusive' labour market policies, because local authorities are legally required to coordinate social inclusive programmes with the other social partners through the establishment of local social coordinating committees (see Keane 2001; Ploug 2002; and below).

It is also important to emphasise four additional areas of local government responsibility following the 1998–99 legislation that have increased access to work (Pedersen et al. 2000). One is transport, which, although subject to privatisation and outsourcing in recent years, remains primarily within local government control in terms of planning and subsidy arrangements. Second, the availability of subsidised childcare has important consequences in relation to women's and men's access to the labour market. The third relates to education, where special initiatives have taken place to promote post-16 school study. Fourth, the system of financial compensation established during the 1930s—whereby richer local authorities subsidise poorer authorities via a system of financial transfers (including additional transfers from Central Government to pay for social assistance and subsidise childcare)—remains in operation. Hansen and Jensen-Butler (1996) argue that this has been crucial in combating uneven development and the worst effects of economic restructuring in urban areas. Last, the retention of public sector employment levels throughout the 1990s has been an important dimension of sustaining labour demand in urban areas (Danish Government 2000).

## Re-Regulating the Representation of Interest Groups

The administration of labour market programmes is undertaken by the 14 Regional Labour Market Councils (RLMCs) (whose boundaries are coterminous with the county council system). The RLMCs are corporatist-style institutions with planning and implementation undertaken by the 'social partners'—local government, trade unions, and the employers—who have equal representation within the 14 regions. This mirrors the composition of the Central Labour Market Council (LMC), where local government is represented by the KL (National Local Government Association). RLMC boards have executive status, are supervised by the Central Government Labour Market Authority, and their policies and plans are subject to approval by Central Government. The RLMCs are allocated responsibilities to produce labour market plans and submit these to the national council. These set targets and identify labour market priorities for the respective region (or county council). The RLMCs are accordingly allocated substantial budgets for priority labour market measures (see Keane 2001). Labour market policy, therefore, reflects the geographies of local labour markets in Denmark in that a trend towards selective decentralisation and intervention in local and regional economies by the state, which actively involves social partners, has been implemented (Ploug 2002). The increasing role and power allocated to the RLMCs in terms of labour market policy decision-making, then, is an important feature of Denmark's rescaled state apparatus. In many respects the regionalisation of politics through the LMC and associated networks is a defining feature of the welfare reforms. The Danish state regulates interest representation and this provides a space for influencing both the form and function of public policy (Etherington and Jones 2004a, 2004b).

The second area of significant development in relation to labour market governance is the establishment of local social coordination committees (*koordineringudvalg*) for each local authority area. Although these are legally required by the Active Social Policy Act and its emphasis on the 'socially inclusive labour market', such committees had previously been established informally as a result of the 1994 reforms by some local authorities (see Keane 2001). Post-1999 legislation, however, places a legal responsibility on local authorities to establish committees with relevant representation from the social partners (trade unions, employers, and local authorities, as well as from the health and social sectors). These social committees are allocated budgets in order to establish projects and initiatives, which seek to facilitate labour market integration by creating more socially inclusive forms of governance (Danish Government 2000; Ploug 2002).

Evaluation research on the first phase of this programme (see Andersen and Torfing 2002; Kommunernes Landsforegningen 2001; compare Keane 2001) suggests that in most cases the committees have achieved better coordination between the various 'actors' in the local labour market policy arena, and they have strengthened involvement from local politicians and senior managers in the socially inclusive labour market. Andersen and Torfing (2002: 17) argue that the committees have contributed to building local democracy because of the 'bottom-up' and territorially focused orientation of much of their work. Another key success, and perhaps the main stimulus for the reforms, has been to develop closer involvement from the private sector in the various programmes to integrate those on social assistance into longer-term employment. The lesson here is that the social partnership model and its 'steering reform' mechanisms (Keane 2001) can benefit employers by identifying skill bottlenecks, moulding state policy to meet local needs, and generally increasing cooperation within the local labour market (Ploug 2002).

## CONCLUSIONS: REFLECTIONS ON THE DANISH MODEL

There are, of course, problems with exaggerating the positive aspect of certain 'models' and underplaying some of the internal contradictions and instabilities, which are endemic features of Keynesian and social democratic strategies (Coates 2000). The Danish model has never been wholly social democratic and there are strong neoliberal components within the collective bargaining system, where wage controls are tied to 'international competitiveness' (as opposed to profits), which has been successfully bargained by the employers (Lind 2000). The 1990s reforms may represent a Schumpetarian Workfare Post-National Regime shift in terms of Jessop's terminology, but it may be more appropriate to analyse them as reflecting a reordering of the post-war Keynesian settlement with an increasing influence of neoliberal market politics within the context of internationalisation and globalisation (compare Torfing 1999). In turn, the changing modes of intervention as reflected in the creation of the RLMCs and other socially inclusive partnership structures within labour market policy can be interpreted as a paradigm shift from a 'top-down' state-driven regional policy to a decentralised politics of the regions, or a 'new spatial order' (Fosgaard and Jorgensen 1996). The contradictions and conflicts of this development involve a number of interrelated elements, which have lessons for the United Kingdom:

1. Problems relating to the technical competence of the partners to plan and steer labour market policy because of the complexity of rules and institutional coordination. The planning process can be undermined by the lengthy time-scales involved in producing the plans through negotiated governance and the relevance of these plans can be subject to question because of a volatile and rapidly changing local labour market (Keane 2001).
2. Problems of accountability and representation of elected politicians active within the corporatist institutions. Key decisions about the labour market are undertaken by an organisation which is not directly elected by local people and therefore not accountable to the local electorate (Hansen and Hansen 2000).
3. A conflict exists between planning for economic growth within and between regions and planning for equality. There has been a paradigm shift towards spatial competition and a more market-driven urban policy, shaped by the EU neoliberal market agendas as reflected in a 'planning for inequality'.

Added to this, Denmark faces similar problems to those previously identified in the work of Offe (1984): state intervention in social and economic infrastructure can act as a barrier to accumulation—primarily because by the time policies are implemented, capital has new requirements and needs in relation to the socialisation of production and reproduction. Furthermore, there are problems in relation to financing social benefits by local government because of the shift towards dependency on social assistance, rather than unemployment insurance, as highlighted above. This creates fiscal problems for the local state because local government partly finances the costs of social assistance through locally levered taxation.

These issues are particularly pertinent given the shift from a rights-based to a workfare-based benefits system, which represented something of a retreat by the Centre-Left Parties from full employment policies, controlling capital and confronting dominant neoliberal explanations of unemployment, skill shortages, and employment problems (see Coates 2000). The shifting political dynamics that shape dominant discourses towards a more neoliberal workfare strategy and a more polarised class conflict/offensive regime are embodied in the Liberal Conservative Government. Privatisation and the outsourcing of local government services, which were actively pursued by the former Social Democratic Government, are now centre stage agendas. There is also more emphasis now on the 'duties' within activation measures, which has given rise to a more 'disciplinary' mode of policy implementation within local government (Goul Andersen 2002). During the early 2000s, the Danish Government launched a discussion document with the slogan 'Flere I Arbejde' (More in Work) with the intention of rationalising the organisation of labour market policy, adjusting access to unemployment insurance, and making education and training initiatives more work specific (see Regergingen 2002). This said, how the new government's strategy will ultimately unfold is hard to predict and will depend on the balance of social and political forces and future patterns of mobilisation. If the experience of the last Conservative–Liberal Government is anything to go by, resistance to fundamental policy changes could be fierce from both within and outside the Danish Parliament, and the gap between the rhetoric and reality of this strategy could be wide (see Goul Andersen 2002). There *is* continuing wide support for redistribution and a consensus around defending the most durable and socially progressive aspects of the welfare system (Ploug 2002).

Outside these reflections and tensions, there are a number of guiding principles within the Danish model that are important for re-engaging local authorities in the United Kingdom. The first of these relates to the sphere of responsibilities and functions. In the Danish model, local government has been *prescribed* a central role in the delivery of labour market policies. In relation to schemes for the unemployed, local government implements over twice as many schemes as the private sector. Local authorities (local and county councils, including the health service) manage 31,545 unemployed people (the private sector dealt with 9,364) in the various schemes. In 2001 this rose to 32,716 for local authority and 12,002 for private sector placements. By comparison, for the United Kingdom and with a significantly larger number of claimants, local councils activated 2,144 unemployed people through the New Deal and by 2001 this had fallen to 1,639. Without figures for the health service, direct comparisons are difficult, but the figures nevertheless expose startling contrasts between the uneven roles of the public sector within welfare reforms.

Yet the Danish experience also demonstrates that a large public sector involvement will also sustain labour demand in areas where local economies are subjected to economic restructuring. It is no coincidence that regional inequality in Denmark has in fact been reduced in recent years (Hansen and Jensen-Butler 1996), whilst regional differences within the United Kingdom remain marked by the dominance of the South East over other regions (see John et al. 2002). Local government is still the major employer in most urban and rural economies in the United Kingdom, yet its role in labour market programmes depends on a contract and bidding process that, as I suggested above, involves risk and uncertainty. This leads to a point where local government is restricted as the focus for a strategic form of labour market development involving both the unemployed and employed.

Given the still innovative way UK local government works (see Atkinson and Wilks-Heeg 2000), a *deeper* involvement in welfare-to-work could have important implications for 'social inclusion' programmes as well as addressing some of the deficiencies in labour demand in local labour markets. This point has been made by the Social Security Advisory Committee (SSAC), which has argued for a new institutional framework to promote 'social inclusion within work-focused agendas' (SSAC 2002). One of its key recommendations is for the provision of a 'local support infrastructure' to integrate those who are marginal and at risk into the labour market. It would seem logical for local government to plug this gap (in partnership with others). This could bring a 'value-added factor' to welfare-to-work and answer some of the criticisms of dead-weight and displacement that were raised in the National Audit Office's (2002) report on this programme for the New Deal for young people.

Second, following recent debates on the need to rationalise the tangled nature of UK local and regional economic governance—where for a number of years partnership overkill and 'too much institutional tinkering' (Blair 2001: 3) has created an imbroglio of actors and responsibilities—the Danish experience holds lessons for the implementation, operation, and success of Local Strategic Partnerships (LSPs) within the coordination of welfare-to-work. At the time of writing, the English New Deal partnership map is currently being redrawn to take into account the overlapping territorial responsibilities of other areas of socioeconomic governance. LSPs—the partnership of partnerships (compare DETR 2001)—are being introduced as a form of 'meta-governance' (see Jessop 2002c) to bring coherence to area-based regeneration and also reposition local government alongside the myriad of other actors involved in the formulation and implementation of public policy (see LGA 2002). Whether this represents a genuine rationalisation of the partnership scene, or a 'containing process of muddling through' (Jessop 2002c: 242), remains an open question. The Danish lesson regarding this form of coalition building relates, first, to the need to have in place coterminous boundaries and a clear division of 'nested' policy responsibilities between various spatial scales. As Keane suggests:

> A strength of the Danish system is the remarkable consistency with which administrative boundaries are defined. This helps to alleviate some of the potential difficulties that can arise in local development when the territory is crowded with many actors and institutions. (2001: 371)

These points are central to the arguments on LSPs of Russell (2001), whose research points to the significance of institutional boundaries, but I would, second, wish to add that the Danish system also brings with it a representative and regulated system of interest group representation and this has direct consequences for the modes of policy intervention therein and the nature of policy outcomes thereafter (Russell 2001). Within LSPs, even if coordination is achieved, this does not necessarily provide for the re-articulation of interests within labour market policy—i.e. local government and the community sector/trade unions—and the strategic incorporation of local territorial concerns. The Danish model regulates and *guarantees* systems of representation to strategically involve the relevant interests within policy arenas. This chapter has argued that local government, far from being marginalised in labour market policy-making, plays an *active* role. Danish labour market partnerships, despite their problems, are transparent and simple. By contrast, the increasingly complex nature and fragmented nature of UK partnerships does not guarantee the political space to challenge polarisation and counterbalance the more powerful groups such as local business interests (also Foley and Martin 2000; Russell 2001).

Given arguments that there is much to learn from corporatist models of economic development for addressing the contradictions of neoliberalism (Lawson 2002), the role of local government in Denmark's welfare-*through*-work system still has much to offer Britain.

# Postscript: the Stoke road to Brexit

> Saturday, February 6, 1965. An early start to Stoke with Molly in the official car. As I was driving through it, I suddenly felt, 'here is this high, ghastly conurbation of five towns—what sense is there in talking about urban renewal here?' … I felt even more strongly that it was impossible to revive Britain without letting places such as Stoke-on-Trent decline. Indeed, I began to wonder whether it wasn't really better to let it be evacuated: renewal is an impossibility or alternatively a fantastic waste of money.
>
> (Crossman 1975: 58)

> If you go around Stoke these days there is [sic] lots of bare land where things have been demolished. I've no idea what it looks like in Helmand Province, But I get the feeling it would look a little like here.
>
> (Rice, MD Emma Bridgewater, quoted in Tappin 2010: 1)

> After 40 years of ideological assault, the state is in trouble.
>
> (Toynbee and Walker 2017: 9)

> A richer and deeper understanding of capitalism can generate more successful approaches to economic policy, aimed at achieving more innovative, inclusive and sustainable forms of growth and prosperity.
>
> (Jacobs and Mazzucato 2016: 2)

Born in Cheshire (England) but resident in Stoke-on-Trent and Staffordshire for my formative years, I returned to Stoke in May 2017 to take up the post of Deputy Vice-Chancellor at Staffordshire University—a role which involves regular networking events and meetings with civil leaders, pitches to Central Government for funding opportunities, etc., given the place of this (applied research) university as an 'anchor institution' in the landscape of regional and local economic and social development (Jones 2018). In a sense, as Gordon MacLeod regularly reminds me, I am 'poacher turned gamekeeper'. My arrival corresponded with interesting geopolitical and geoeconomic times; some would say a reaction against the political elites' perceptions of Stoke in 2016—not a million miles away from the 1965 statement above by the Minister of Housing and Local Government under the Wilson Labour Government. Unlike Crossman, I do not have an official car.

It is not difficult to see why Stoke-on-Trent (often abbreviated to Stoke)—a polycentric federation of six towns (Stoke, Burslem, Tunstall, Longton, Fenton, and Hanley) created in 1910—has been dubbed by the media as the 'Brexit Capital': 69.4 per cent of the voters voted to leave, which triggered Paul Nuttall, then leader of the ferociously anti-European UK Independence Party (UKIP), to decide to run for Parliament in Stoke-on-Trent Central in the February 2017 by-election. Nuttall eventually lost to the Labour Party candidate Gareth Snell, but picked up one-quarter of the votes, pushing the Conservatives into third place. Stoke-on-Trent, home of the pottery industry in England and known as the Potteries with its local residents known as Potters, is surely the archetypal heartland of the 'left-behind people and places'. Stoke is an isomorphic space of dsyfunctionalism, best captured by Tappin (2010: 1) as a textbook 'study of system, economic and political failure'. This is where geography, class, and heritage frequently meet economics, globalisation, state intervention and its failure, and national and local politics in a series of head-on collisions, with the most important being around the Brexit vote of 23 June 2016—in short, a 'conjunctural event' of multiple crises and contradictions (Clarke 2018; MacLeod and Jones 2018).

Stoke's economic geography is a classic tale of the rise and fall of resource-based economies and the links between this, state intervention, parliamentary democracy, and their failure. The North Staffordshire Coalfield and 'clay outcrops' framed industrial activity and community in unique ways akin to the 'genre de vie' (Vidal de La Blache 1918) sentiments of Vidalian regional geography. Clusters of small towns with 'pot banks' rapidly developed into the driver of a pottery and ceramics world alongside dense back-to-back houses collectively producing 'universal littleness' and impressions of 'provincial remoteness' (Beaver 1964: 28), all reinforced by being sandwiched betwixt and between the West Midlands and the North West of England. Diversification of industry (through Michelin Tyres and later ICL) was slow due to relative economic buoyancy, which later backfired into economic dependency, and the lack of Assisted Area designated status by successive governments, with Ball (1993: 198) depicting the Potteries as an 'intervention backwater' in comparison to the spatially selective West Midlands and North West regions for state intervention in the economy.

The world-class home to 90 per cent of the UK's ceramics base in the nineteenth and early to mid-twentieth centuries, between 1971 and 1981 Stoke's pottery industry shed just over 13,000 employees (with 60 per cent being female). Like British manufacturing in general, there was a failure in the pottery industry to invest its way out of trouble throughout the 1970s (Warren et al. 2000) and a predominance of export markets (80 per cent) left the pottery industry vulnerable to monetary policy shifts in the 1980s—deflation, spending cuts, and shifts to exchange rates resulted in the collapse of export markets (see Imrie 1989). Added to this, the state's role in reworking the international spatial division of labour through privileging privatisation and neoliberal growth models had a catastrophic impact on Stoke with the closure of the Shelton steelworks and various coal mines, despite these being profitable and advanced in technology (see Rodgers 1980). In short, Stoke never recovered from this recession and the opportunities for the ceramic industry to develop artisan-style into England's Third Italy at-scale was hampered by local economic fragmentation and a shortage of mobile capital (compare Imrie 1991; Tomlinson and Branston 2017).

Following the central themes of *Cities and Regions in Crisis*, processes have been at work throughout the 1980s and 1990s, deferring and displacing the crises of the Stoke-on-Trent economy into more politically manageable economic development projects. Issues of economic management were serially displaced through a raft of private sector-led initiatives. Staffordshire Training and Enterprise Council (TEC), based on the site of the 1986 Etruria Garden Festival, for instance, played a key role in normalising neoliberalism in relation to labour market and skills initiatives, as well as supplying a flexible workforce to fuel the growth of the burgeoning low-skills and low-value-added services and distribution sector economy (Jones 1998). Alongside this, attempts were made by Stoke City Council (backed by Staffordshire TEC and other agencies such as Business Link—see Chapter 2) to create a creative economy through the leverages of the European Regional Development Fund, presenting the town of Hanley as the metro-centre for agglomeration. Between 1989 and 1993, 32 Urban Pilot Projects were funded, with the Cultural Quarter being the flagship project for Hanley. Jayne's (2000, 2004) devastating critique of these interventions provides a bridge to the disenfranchised Brexit present:

> Substantial funding has supported creative industries development initiatives in Stoke-on-Trent for the past fifteen years. However, the impact of this development on the regeneration of the city has been minimal. This is the result of both a flawed creative industries strategy, and associated failings of the city to overcome its structural conditions so as to compete in an urban hierarchy dominated by post-industrial and middle-class consumption cultures. Unlike many other Western cities, Stoke-on-Trent remains overly dominated by working-class production and consumption cultures. The city is thus, in a sense, rendered illegible to post-industrial businesses, tourists, and to many young people who leave the city in search of the more dynamic economic and cultural opportunities offered in other cities. I argue that, unless such inadequacies are addressed, the city will continue to fail to generate a thriving cultural economy. (Jayne 2004: 208)

The advent of New Labour in 1997 saw the arrival of the Advantage West Midlands (AWM) Regional Development Agency, which took over responsibility for urban policy and the regeneration of brownfield industrial sites. North Staffordshire Regeneration Partnership followed a few years later to work in partnership with AWM, covering Newcastle-under-Lyme and the Staffordshire Moorlands local authorities as well as the six towns of Stoke-on-Trent. The transitions within and between these new governing arrangements lacked clarity and accountability, with North Staffordshire Regeneration Partnership (NSRP) experiencing a history of board resignations, public interest requests over highly paid consultants, and geographical tensions between the Stoke-on-Trent players (wanting development in Hanley at all costs) and Newcastle-under-Lyme Borough Council keen to spread investment spatially. NSRP implosion (losing 70 jobs) corresponded with the Coalition Government's arrival and localism agenda in 2010, with Stoke-on-Trent and Staffordshire Enterprise Partnership (SSLEP) replacing the space left by AWM, but without the target urban funding for deprivation (see Crowley et al. 2012). In return, Stoke received the 'New Labour apparatchik' Tristram Hunt MP—after a career as an author, academic, and TV face (Harris 2017: 7).

Noted as the 'sick city' (see Whitehead 2003b), with half the men in 20 of the poorest wards expected to die before they reached retirement age, Stoke-on-Trent is a case study in working-class disaffection connected not just to economic circumstances stemming from restructuring and the politics of uneven development, but linked also to political 'disaffected consent' (Gilbert 2015). The characteristics of political parties, and in this case the Labour Party and the dynamics around local government, is an important part of the Stoke-on-Trent story. On the latter, similar to other post-industrial cities such as Burnley (see Rhodes 2009), the Potteries local government had been predominately Labour Party controlled but suffered from criticisms during the 1990s of mismanagement and an identity crisis caused by the local election successes of the British National Party (BNP) in the working-class council ward of Bentilee after focusing on immigration and a 'flood' of asylum seekers into the city (Jayne 2012: 37). In October 2002, stimulated by criticism of Labour's failure to achieve post-industrial success and depictions of the city as culturally backwards, Mike Wolfe (Independent) became the first elected mayor of Stoke-on-Trent, beating pre-election favourite George Stevenson (Labour) into second place. This posting was short-lived: Wolfe lasted three years and his replacement was elected on a pledge to modify representation from a Mayoral to a Cabinet system, which the electorate approved in 2008. Since then, a perceived paralysis of decision-making has taken place due to the political parties cross-checking each other at the Cabinet table in the context of austerity and deepening budget cuts and with the private provider Serco running the Stoke education authority after Audit Commission criticisms and now amidst an academy landscape 'splintering the school system' and blurring issues of ownership and accountability (Toynbee and Walker 2017: 56).

On the former, the Labour Party held all three seats in Stoke between 1950 and 2017 (losing the Stoke South seat then) but with the city's 'old economic base evaporating' (Morris 2017: 2) the party has struggled in the past decade due to far right parties attacking its working-class base, campaigning around immigration, and Labour being seen to be radically out of touch with the needs of the locality. Though local Labour people were energetically campaigning in 2016 for Remain, whole neighbourhoods and streets were set on voting the other way. For *The Guardian* journalist Harris (2017: 7), 'Leave was doing a brisk trade amongst not just white voters but also British-Asian people. There was a sense of a long-dormant political relationship between party and people that had now reached the point of an indifference tinged with bitterness.' The perceived 'parachuting in' of Hunt in 2010 only made this allegation worse and, having presided over the Brexit result of 2016, Hunt resigned in January 2017 to take up the post of Director, Victoria and Albert Museum—retreating back to the elite London high-culture, as some local residents saw it. Hunt's (2017) resignation letter detailed the 'harrowing effects of poverty and inequality' he had seen during his work as an MP. Job losses were equated to having 'Detroit-style impacts', with one in 12 (7,235) of the city's private homes empty (Jones 2018). *The Guardian's* 'Made in Stoke' series of six articles and episode video interviews published during the preparation of the Stoke bid to become City of Culture in 2017 make equally harrowing reading and offer a critical insight into what McKenzie (2017) calls 'Brexit and the land of no-hope and glory' and the 'zombie democracy'—living dead categories that are not able to capture the contemporary milieu—metaphors of Koch (2017).

*The Guardian* journalist Domokos charts the rise and fall of the Potteries, the city that voted so heavily for Brexit in the context of having the lowest turnout in Britain at the last election and the 13th most deprived local authority on the 2015 index of multiple deprivation, with 30 per cent of its neighbourhoods in the bottom of all wards nationally. In the first episode in the series, titled 'We Have Lift-off', a 21-year-old man leant out of a council block window to shout: 'They don't give a shit about us. I'm not voting for anyone.' Further episodes expose the harsh realities of unemployment, low-skilled work, drug-use, and the failures of state intervention nationally and locally (Domokos 2017). The analysis is supported by data from Stoke City Council, where their Employment and Skills Strategy (City of Stoke-on-Trent Council 2017) details 16,000 (10 per cent of the workforce) people on Employment Support Allowance and Incapacity Benefit, which has risen 15 per cent in a decade, and with half these cases being linked to mental illness. Stoke-on-Trent would need to support 8,917 unemployed adults into work in order to reduce the city's workless levels to a national average. State policy, though, is heading in the opposite direction: from 13 June 2018, 25 per cent of the workforce will be impacted by the changes in benefits as part of Universal Credit, which will take £73 million out of the Stoke-on-Trent economy per year.

Residents of Stoke were invited to respond to the series via *The Guardian* website, with one reply being:

> The people of Stoke are not racist monsters. I was born there and lived there for 22 years and go back now and again even after living out of Stoke for 30 years and outside the country for 25. The place is dead on its feet following the demise of the pot banks the mines and the steel. All no fault of the people who live there. The Brexit vote was just a kick against the status quo that has done nothing for the City. (SingStokie, posted 9 January 2018: https://www.theguardian.com/cities/2018/jan/08/made-in-stoke-on-trent-documentary-guardian-readers (accessed 11 June 2018))

Another said:

> I lived in the Potteries through the 1990s. It's clear that many of the problems that existed then have only grown worse in the two decades that have followed. It's such a terrible shame because the city is a unique place with masses of potential—I always liked its human scale, being made up of six towns. And yet despite the chronic neglect the films show that many warm and determined people live there—I found several of them to be hugely admirable … There are many fine people in Stoke. I voted Remain; I don't care if the city voted for Brexit. It deserves better than this. (Grimscribe, posted 8 January 2018: https://www.theguardian.com/cities/2018/jan/08/made-in-stoke-on-trent-documentary-guardian-readers#comment-110565595 (accessed 11 June 2018))

Moved by these comments and experiences, Domokos returned to Stoke and surmised that it is a city that defies expectation and rewards the time you spend looking. It is fighting back against its stereotype of a depressed Brexit heartland. 'It's a place that has been high on political apathy and anger, but where people of many backgrounds are building something exciting with enterprise, passion and creativity.' Domokos adds that the story of Stoke-on-Trent gets to the 'heart of modern Britain—with our high streets and industries changing fast, how do our towns and cities move forward in the 21st century? How do we rebuild and support communities? And what is the "culture" of a place, in the deepest most human sense?' (Domokos 2018: 7). For Jack Brereton MP, the future lies in leaving Europe, although the economic basis of his arguments on ceramics-vitality would appear to defy the export-orientated economic history lessons of Stoke:

> My constituents were very clear in the referendum: they voted 70% to Leave. They think Brexit should indeed mean Brexit, something manifestly different to the status quo. Many felt membership of the EU had not benefited traditional working-class areas, that it had not brought improvements to their own quality of life, that it had not realised the huge potential for a major revival of our world-class ceramics indus-

> try. This need—and the entirely realistic desire—for an increased number of skilled manufacturing jobs is why so many in Stoke-on-Trent voted so overwhelmingly to Leave ... (Brereton 2017: 1)

At the Hay Festival 2018, I had the pleasure of listening to Will Hutton and Andrew Adonis launch talk their book *Saving Britain: How We Must Change to Prosper in Europe* (2018). The former *Observer* editor and the politician writer suggest that the EU is a success story, despite its spatio-temporal frailties. For most, it has guaranteed fundamental human freedoms and provided economic prosperity and order. They argue that Britain is abandoning four centuries of being part of the European diplomatic order for illusory gains and actual losses. No gains in trade from deals with protectionist China and the United States can compensate for what is being lost in Europe. Britain is weakening a pillar of the world's diplomatic and trade order at the same time as weakening itself—an 'act of self-harm', especially when so many countries are retreating from democracy, free trade, and progressive value. With my office based in Shelton (Stoke) off Leek Road, this is provocative stuff.

I came home committed to thinking that Stoke-on-Trent needs a modern economic strategy to improve the lives and communities shut out from growth and prosperity. This arena is the subject of discussions between our civic and business leaders, with the timing never being so urgent. Local debate, such as interventions by the British Ceramics Confederation and Michelin, is revealing the nervousness around dumped imported applied materials (tyres and ceramics) entering into our markets, which could undercut and destabilise employment prospects in our localities (Jones 2018). Set against this fear, the opportunities for thinking differently about our economy through Local Industrial Strategies (compare DBEIS 2017; Fai 2018) are critical and the Local Enterprise Partnerships (LEPs) are starting to take the lead here and our civil leaders sit on the LEP boards.

The Stoke-on-Trent electorate debated and rejected some of Hutton and Adonis's points. What comes next is critical and new economic thinking is needed. 'Reinventing England's cities' is a central thesis of their book for taking back real control. They write that apart from London and perhaps Birmingham and Manchester/Salford, England's cities quickly fall behind the population threshold to support the full array of public and private institutions of a diversified urban economy. Where possible—they claim—the opportunity should be taken to create city-regions that are big. Scale matters: not for administrative convenience, but because it enables the city-regional leaders to get the best from interlinking their urban areas thereby boosting growth—'agglomeration' as economists call it (Hutton and Adonis 2018) and discussed in Chapters 8 and 9.

So the argument goes, agglomeration is essential because most of England's cities are just too small. Whether it's the density of transport links, the range of healthcare or the demand needed to support company start-ups or viable cultural and sporting institutions, the international evidence is that successful cities need to serve substantial populations. Cities, like nations, rise and fall much faster than is commonly appreciated. Stoke-on-Trent has seen a loss in population throughout the years. Stoke-on-Trent's 2018 population is now estimated at 383,000. In 1950, the population was 400,000. However, the census taken in 2011 showed that the population was on the upswing for the first time since 1931. Stoke-on-Trent has grown by 6,000 since 2015, which represents a 0.53 per cent annual change. The challenge is how to grow this further and agglomerate Stoke-on-Trent, scaling economic, cultural, and social ambition in the process.

Stoke needs a progressive and credible economic and industrial strategy, backed by strong civic leaders. Within this, a transformational agenda for jobs, infrastructure, and quality of life is integral to rebalance the damage caused by cuts to local state funding (Jones 2018). Part of 'Left-behind Britain', Stoke is also not just isolated by poverty and lack of opportunity. It is also left behind by poor (mainly internal) transport links. The High-Speed Rail (HS2) project has the opportunity to begin to address some of these challenges of regional connectivity. The Stoke Station Masterplan developments, currently in discussion with politicians, will be important here, if it can help to develop an infrastructure to drive a creative economy.

More fundamentally, some serious 'spatial rebalancing' of economic activity is also needed (Gardiner et al. 2013). The Treasury's Green Book sets out the rules of engagement for departments and government bodies when formulating policy interventions (see HM Treasury 2018). This states that policies that aim to spread growth spatially amongst the regions run counter to the agglomeration growth process of going beyond market failure corrections and are difficult to justify on efficiency grounds. They incur costs and create economic distortion for agglomeration. This thinking needs to be challenged by our politicians and civic leaders, especially in the context of the movement towards the Shared Prosperity Fund (DBEIS 2018). Prosperity needs to be shared across the United Kingdom and not just held in London and the South East. Currently stuck between the Northern Powerhouse and the West Midlands Combined Authority, with the Manchester and Birmingham Mayors gaining 'consolidated' powers through 'strengthened LEPs' (HCLG 2018), Stoke-on-Trent needs targeted investment to back any transformational economic agenda coming from our leaders. Alongside this, policy-makers could do worse than looking at the impact of endogenous and exogenous development factors and undertaking the obvious reality check on governance and the succession of failed policy interventions for future generations. Here, coordinated multispatial metagovernance will matter to provide the effective spatio-temporal fix to hold down the global and produce effective local and regional economic development. Ball's previous words still hold and *Cities and Regions in Crisis* has given insights into how and why the tinkering process of regeneration has been taking place:

> As local economic and land-use planners have long realized, the area needs to diversify but not to deny its manufacturing specialism. Just as Rodgers [1980] argued back in the late 1970s, the area needs something to spearhead its growth. Not a new town as it was suggested at the time, but an industrial and infrastructure-led solution and one that must involve the private sector as well as the public. In these terms, the area is perhaps a strong candidate for an injection of public infrastructure support over a finite period, something that might act as a catalyst for private industrial investment and, in such terms, *stimulate rather than tinker with the process of regeneration*. (Ball 1993: 211, emphasis added)

The impacts of this on the neighbourhoods across Stoke-on-Trent remains a challenge, set within a context of not just governance failure, but now with Universal Credit across the city and the branding of Stoke as 'debt capital of England' due to the highest rate (more than double the national average) of personal insolvencies in 2017 (Partington 2018: 20). According to the Hardship Commission:

> There is no over-arching strategy aimed at poverty. Instead, there is a multiple array of initiatives and organisations working to address aspects of poverty—sometimes in collaboration with others and sometimes in competition—with the commissioning and funding process not that effective. (City of Stoke-on-Trent Council 2015: 4)

In the midst of a world of polka dot economic governance and its failures, the need for new spatial frameworks and ways of coupling governance with regulation to hold down the global and ensure some level of social cohesion via applying the brakes on combined and uneven development has never been so urgent. Without this, to use the metaphor from Offe (2015), local and regional economic development will remain 'entrapped' in neoliberalism with all the accumulated political and economic contradictions being played out across space. As I have argued elsewhere (see Etherington and Jones 2016b; Etherington and Jones 2017; Etherington et al. 2018), some key principles of sub-national economic and social development apply, which 'challenge the common sense on which the process of neoliberalism relies' (Rogers 2015: 398).

1. Promote inclusive governance at the city region level:

    - Ensure that disadvantaged groups and organisations that represent them (such as the voluntary sector—Chapter 11) are actively involved in decision-making processes.
    - Trade unions have important roles to play (Chapter 12) and should be represented equally alongside local authorities and business leaders.
    - Establish joint spatial working relationships across the local state and *between* LEPs, the Department for Work and Pensions (DWP), Work Programme providers, and local authorities, to tackle governance boundary problems and also facilitate the integration of employment and skills policies.

2. Design a new 'growth model' (Hay 2013) and strategies to address poverty reduction:

    - Highlight the financial case for social and economic inclusion by undertaking a cost–benefit analysis of anti-poverty initiatives and the public expenditure savings that can be accrued.
    - Promote the role of a holistic and 'foundational' local state (Foundational Economy Collective 2018), where local authorities and the public sector are equal creators of jobs, alongside the promotion of private sector activity. It is *not* the case that 'businesses pay the taxes, create the economic growth that deliver the ultimate outcomes of the Industrial Strategy: higher living standard and higher levels of productivity' (HCLG 2018: 17) *alone*.

3. Redesign welfare-to-work programmes for target groups:

    - Redesign the claimant agreement so as to reduce the incidence of benefit sanctions, such as incorporating a role for advice services to support the customer journey through the welfare-to-work system.
    - Ensure that welfare-to-work programmes are appropriately resourced so that interventions can be sustained.

4. Increase emphasis on in-work support, skills acquisition, and progression:
    - Develop ‘skills creation cycles’ that recognise pipeline high-skills progressions, seek to address skills shortages, and challenge low-skills equilibriums (compare Sheffield City Region LEP 2017).
    - Increase access to apprenticeships for disadvantaged groups—learning from best practice.
    - Promote high-quality apprenticeships in the context of expanding numbers, rather than deliver a target-chasing culture.
    - Promote the employee voice in the city region through initiatives such as the Unionlearn model, which involves greater union engagement in promoting learning and skills development in the work place to disadvantaged groups.
    - Pilot a job-rotation model across the localities of England, drawing on the Danish and wider European experience (see Chapter 12).
5. Promote employment rights and employee voices within the city region:
    - This should include adopting initiatives developed by the various Fairness Commissions and Living Wage Campaigns.
    - Ensure that trade unions are actively involved with employment and training in city-regions, building on the Unionlearn proven track record of achieving this.

By contrast, the following direction of neoliberal policy-churn is predicted with the announcement (December 2018) of Skills Advisory Panels – another talking shop with few levers to affect change. Reading like a carbon copy of the *Employment for the 1990s* White Paper (of December 1988), and with those historically inbuilt crises and contradictions of markets, governance, and their failures set to continue beyond 30 years:

> Skills Advisory Panels aim to bring together local employers and skills providers to pool knowledge on skills and labour market needs, and to work together to understand and address key local challenges. This includes both immediate needs and challenges and looking at what is required to help local areas adapt to future labour market changes and to grasp future opportunities. (DfE 2018: 1)

As noted throughout *Cities and Regions in Crisis*, assumptions around this employer-led and market-driven local capacity to act are deeply flawed.

# References

Advantage West Midlands (1999), *Creating Advantage: The West Midlands Economic Strategy*, Birmingham: Advantage West Midlands.

Aglietta, M. (1979), *A Theory of Capitalist Regulation: The US Experience*, London: New Left Books.

Aglietta, M. (1998), 'Capitalism at the turn of the century: Regulation theory and the challenge of social change', *New Left Review*, 232, 41–90.

Agnew, J. (2002), *Place and Politics in Modern Italy*, Chicago: Chicago University Press.

Allen, J. and Cochrane, A. (2014), 'The urban unbound: London's politics and the 2012 Olympic Games', *International Journal of Urban and Regional Research*, 38, 1609–1624.

Allmendinger, P. and Haughton, G. (2015), 'Post-political regimes in English planning: From third way to big society', in J. Metzger, P. Allmendinger and S. Oosterlynck (eds) *Planning Against the Political: Democratic Deficits in European Territorial Governance*, London: Routledge, 29–53.

Amin, A. (1994), *Post-Fordism: A Reader*, Oxford: Blackwell.

Amin, A. (1999), 'An institutional perspective on regional economic development', *International Journal of Urban and Regional Research*, 23, 365–378.

Amin, A. (2002), 'Spatialities of globalisation', *Environment and Planning A*, 34, 385–399.

Amin, A. (2004), 'Regions unbound: Towards a new politics of place', *Geografiska Annaler*, 86B, 33–44.

Amin, A. (2007), 'Rethinking the urban social', *City*, 11, 100–114.

Amin, A. and Thomas, D. (1996), 'The negotiated economy: State and civic institutions in Denmark', *Economy and Society*, 25, 255–281.

Amin, A. and Thrift, N. (1995), 'Institutional issues for the European regions: From markets and plans to socioeconomics and power of association', *Economy and Society*, 24, 41–66.

Amin, A. and Thrift, N. (2002), *Cities: Reimagining the Urban*, Cambridge: Polity.

Amin, A. and Thrift, N. (2013), *Arts of the Political: New Openings for the Left*, Durham, NC: Duke University Press.

Andersen, K.L. and Torfing, J. (2002), *Netvaerksteering I velfaerdsamfundet: de lokale koordinationsudval* [Network steering in the welfare society: The local coordination committees], Mimeograph, Aalborg: CARMA, Aalborg University Centre.

Anderson, B. (1991), *Imagined Communities: Reflections on the Origin and Spread of Nationalism*, Verso: London.

Atkinson, H. and Wilks-Heeg, S. (2000), *Local Government from Thatcher to Blair: The Politics of Creative Autonomy*, Cambridge: Polity.

Atkinson, R. (1999), 'Developing a regional and local institutional capacity for urban regeneration: The case of Regional Development Agencies and the Single Regeneration Budget', paper presented to the Regional Studies Association Conference, Bilbao, 18–21 September.

Atkinson, R. (2000), 'Narratives of policy: The construction of urban problems and urban policy in the official discourse of British government 1968–1998', *Critical Social Policy*, 20, 211–232.

Atkinson, R. and Moon, G. (1994), *Urban Policy in Britain: The City, the State and the Market*, London: Macmillan.

Atkinson, H. and Wilks-Hegg, S. (2000), *Local Government from Thatcher to Blair: The Politics of Creative Autonomy*, Cambridge: Polity.

Audit Commission (1989), *Urban Regeneration and Economic Development: The Local Government Dimension*, London: HMSO.

Ayers, S. and Stafford, I. (2009), 'Deal-making in Whitehall: Competing and complementary motives behind the Review of Sub-national Economic Development and Regeneration', *International Journal of Public Sector Management*, 22, 605–622.

Bachtler, J., Berkowitz, P., Hardy, S. and Muravska, T. (eds) (2016), *EU Cohesion Policy: Reassessing Performance and Direction*, London: Routledge.

Bailey, D. and Budd, L. (eds) (2016), *Devolution and the UK Economy*, London: Rowman & Littlefield.

Bakker, K. (2010), *Privatising Water: Governance Failure and the World's Urban Water Crisis*, Ithaca: Cornell University Press.

Ball, R.M. (1993), 'Economic and industrial diversification: Changing policies, technologies and locations', in A.D.M. Phillips (ed.) *The Potteries: Continuity and Change in a Staffordshire Conurbation*, Stroud: Alan Sutton, 191–212.

Banks, J.C. (1971), *Federal Britain? The Case for Regionalism*, London: Harrap.

Banks, J.C. (1997), *Grass-roots Regional Movements in England 1974–1996*, Mimeograph, Cheltenham: Secretary of the Wessex Regionalists.

Banks, J.C. (2001), *Government of the West Midlands: Part 1, 2, and 3*, Mimeograph, Cheltenham: Secretary of the Wessex Regionalists.

Banks, J.C. (2003), 'Regional government—a foot in the door?', *Views on a Devolved England*, 19, 13–15.

Barnekov, T., Boyle, R. and Rich, D. (1989), *Privatism and Urban Policy in Britain and the United States*, Oxford: Oxford University Press.
Barnes, T.J. (1996), *Logics of Dislocation: Models, Metaphors, and Meanings of Economic Space*, New York: Guilford Press.
Bassett, P. (1994), 'Heseltine hits at Business Link ventures', *The Times*, 4 June, 21.
BBC (2002), 'How devolution is changing our identity', report on March 2002 poll, London: BBC.
Beatty, C. and Fothergill, S. (2016), *The Uneven Impact of Welfare Reform: The Financial Losses to Places and People*, Sheffield: Sheffield Hallam University.
Beauregard, R.A. (1988), 'In the absence of practice: The locality research debate', *Antipode*, 20, 52–59.
Beaver, S. (1964), 'The Potteries: A study in the evolution of a cultural landscape. Presidential Address', *Transactions and Papers (Institute of British Geographers)*, 45, 1–31.
Beel, D., Jones, M. and Jones, I.R. (2016), 'Regulation, governance and agglomeration: Making links in city-region research', *Regional Studies, Regional Science*, 3, 509–530.
Begg, I. (1999), 'Cities and competitiveness', *Urban Studies*, 36, 795–809.
Bennett, R.J. (1985), 'Regional movements in Britain: A review of aims and status', *Environment and Planning C: Government and Policy*, 3, 75–96.
Bennett, R.J. and McCoshan, A. (1993), *Enterprise and Human Resource Development: Local Capacity Building*, London: Paul Chapman.
Bennett, R.J. and Payne, D. (2000), *Local and Regional Economic Development: Renegotiating Power Under Labour*, Aldershot: Ashgate Publishing.
Bennett, R.J., Wicks, P. and McCoshan, A. (1994), *Local Empowerment and Business Services: Britain's Experiment with Training and Enterprise Councils*, London: UCL Press.
Benneworth, P. (2001), *Regional Development Agencies: The Early Years*, London: Regional Studies Association.
Berry, C. (2016), 'Industrial policy change in the post-crisis British economy: Policy innovation in an incomplete institutional and ideational environment', *The British Journal of Politics and International Relations*, 18, 829–847.
Betrand, P.H. (1986), 'Modernisations et pietinements', in R. Boyer (ed.) *Capitalismes fin de Siecle*, Paris: PUP, 67–108.
Bewick, T. (1996), 'Training and jobs in the social economy', *Training Tomorrow* (November), 5–8.
Beynon, H., Hudson, R., Lewis, J., Sadler, D. and Townsend, A. (1989), '"It's all falling apart here": Coming to terms with the future in Teesside', in P.

Cooke (ed.) *Localities: The Changing Face of Urban Britain*, London: Unwin Hyman, 267–295.

bhabha, h.k. (1994), *The Location of Culture*, London: Routledge.

Bialasiewicz, L. (2003), 'Upper Silesia: Rebirth of a regional identity in Poland', *Regional and Federal Studies*, 12, 111–132.

BIS (2010), *Understanding Local Growth*, BIS Economics Paper 7, London: Department for Business, Innovations and Skills.

Blackman, T. (1995), *Urban Policy in Practice*, London: Routledge.

Blair, T. (1997), 'Speech to the Party of European Socialists' Congress, Malmo, 6th June', Labour Party, London.

Blair, T. (1999), 'Speech on Britishness', Address by the Prime Minister, 28 March.

Blair, T. (2001), 'Foreword', in Performance and Innovation Unit (eds) *In Demand: Adult Skills in the 21st Century*, London: Cabinet Office.

Blond, P. (2010), *Red Tory: How Left and Right Have Broken Britain and How We Can Fix It*, London: Faber and Faber.

Blunkett, D. (1999), 'Pessimistic pundits put on notice', *The Guardian*, 11 August, 25.

Bonefeld, W. (2003), 'The capitalist state: Illusion and critique', in W. Bonefeld (ed.) *Revolutionary Writings: Common Sense Essays in Post-Political Politics*, New York: Automedia, 201–218.

Bonefeld, W. and Holloway, J. (eds) (1991), *Post-Fordism and Social Form: A Marxist Debate on the Post-Fordist State*, London: Macmillan.

Booth, P. (2005), 'Partnerships and networks: The governance of urban regeneration in Britain', *Journal of Housing and Built Environment*, 20, 257–269.

Bourdieu, P. (1998), *Acts of Resistance: Against the Tyranny of the Market*, New York: The New York Press.

Bowley, G. (1996), 'Rate of business failures steadies', *Financial Times*, 31 December, 4.

Bowmen, D., Froud, J., Joha. S., et al. (2014) *The End of the Experiment? (Manchester Capitalism)*, Manchester: Manchester University Press.

Boyer, R. (1979), 'Wage formation in historical perspective: The French experience', *Cambridge Journal of Economics*, 3, 99–118.

Boyer, R. (1988), 'Technical change and the theory of regulation', in G. Dosi, C. Freeman, R. Nelson, G. Silverberg and L. Soete (eds) *Technical Change and Economic Theory*, London: Pinter, 67–96.

Boyer, R. (1990), *The Regulation School: A Critical Introduction*, New York: Columbia University Press.

Boyer, R. (2001), 'Introduction', in R. Boyer and Y. Saillard (eds) *Regulation Theory: The State of the Art*, London: Routledge, 1–10.

Boyer, R. and Saillard, Y. (2001), 'Glossary', in R. Boyer and Y. Saillard (eds) *Regulation Theory: The State of the Art*, London: Routledge, 334–345.

Brenner, N. (1998), 'Between fixity and motion: Accumulation, territorial organization and the historical geography of spatial scales', *Environment and Planning D: Society and Space*, 16, 459–481.

Brenner, N. (2000a), 'Building "Euro-Regions": Locational politics and the political geography of neoliberalism in post-unification Germany', *European Urban and Regional Research*, 7, 319–345.

Brenner, N. (2000b), 'The urban question as a scale question: Reflections on Henri Lefebvre, urban theory and the politics of scale', *International Journal of Urban and Regional Research*, 24, 361–378.

Brenner, N. (2003), 'Metropolitan institutional reforms and the rescaling of state space in contemporary Western Europe', *European Urban and Regional Studies*, 10, 297–324.

Brenner, N. (2004), *New State Spaces: Urban Governance and the Rescaling of Statehood*, Oxford: Oxford University Press.

Brenner, N. and Theodore, N. (eds) (2002a), *Spaces of Neoliberalism: Urban Restructuring in North America and Western Europe*, Oxford: Blackwell.

Brenner, N. and Theodore, N. (2002b), 'Cities and the geographies of "actually existing neoliberalism"', *Antipode*, 34, 349–379.

Brenner, N., Peck, J. and Theodore, N. (2012), *Afterlives of Neoliberalism: Civic City Cahier 4*, London: Bedford Press.

Brenner, N., Jessop, B., Jones, M. and MacLeod, G. (eds) (2003), *State/Space: A Reader*, Oxford: Blackwell.

Brereton, J. (2017), 'Brexit must refresh parts of the UK like Stoke which the EU has failed to reach', https://brexitcentral.com/brexit-must-refresh-parts-uk-like-stoke-eu-failed-reach/ (accessed 11 June 2018).

Bridge, J. (1999), 'Regional competitiveness: How will the RDAs make a difference', presentation by the Chair of One NorthEast, Local Economic Policy Unit Conference on Regional Development Agencies: Shaping the New Regionalism, LEPU, London.

Bristow, G. (2005), 'Everyone's a winner: Problematising the discourse of regional competitiveness', *Journal of Economic Geography*, 5, 285–304.

Burawoy, M. (2000), *Global Ethnography*, Berkeley: University of California Press.

Burn, C. (2017), 'How station saga helped to derail devolution hopes', *Yorkshire Post*, 22 September, 17.

Burnham, P. (2014), 'Depoliticisation, economic crisis and political management', *Policy & Politics*, 42, 189–206.

Business, Innovation and Skills Committee (2013), *Local Enterprise Partnerships: Ninth Report of Session 2012–13, HC 598*, London: DBIS.

Business Link Staffordshire (1996), *Who? What? Why? A Summary of the Staffordshire Business Link Business Plan*, Staffordshire: Business Link Staffordshire.

Cabinet Office (1988), *Action for Cities*, London: Moore & Matthew.

Caborn, R. (1996), *A New Deal for the English Regions*, Labour Party Statement on Regional Economic Policy, London: Labour Party.

Castles, F. (1989), *The Comparative History of Public Policy*, Cambridge: Polity.

CDP (1977), *Gilding the Ghetto: The State and Poverty Experiments*, London: CDP Inter-Project Team.

Centre for Cities (2015), 'Northern Powerhouse', Factsheet, 2 June, Centre for Cities, London.

CESI (2005), *More Jobs, More Skills—the Future for Sheffield's Labour Market*, London: Centre for Economic and Social Inclusion.

CFER (2000), *Policy Statement*, Newcastle: Campaign for the English Regions.

Chairs of the RDAs (1999), 'Memorandum by the Chairmen of the Regional Development Agencies', in *Tenth Report: Regional Development Agencies, Volume II, Memorandum Relating to the Inquiry*, London: Stationery Office, 80–83.

Cheshire, P.C., Nathan, M. and Overman, H.G. (2014), *Urban Economics and Urban Policy: Challenging Conventional Policy Wisdom*, Cheltenham, UK and Northampton, MA, USA: Edward Elgar Publishing.

Christiansen, N.F. (1994), 'Denmark: End of an idyll?', in P. Andersen and P. Camiller (eds) *Mapping the Western European Left*, London: Verso, 77–101.

City of Stoke-on-Trent Council (2015), *Hardship Commission Stoke-on-Trent: Initial Report*, Stoke: City of Stoke-on-Trent Council.

City of Stoke-on-Trent Council (2017), *Employment & Skills Strategy*, Stoke: City of Stoke-on-Trent Council.

Clark, G. (2010), 'Stylised facts and close dialogue: Methodology in economic geography', *Annals of the Association of American Geographers*, 88, 73–87.

Clark, G. and Dear, M. (1984), *State Apparatus: Structures and Languages of Legitimacy*, London: Allen & Unwin.

Clarke, G., Martin, R. and Tyler, P. (2016), 'Divergent cities? Unequal urban growth and development', *Cambridge Journal of Regions, Economy and Society*, 9, 259–268.

Clarke, J. (2018), 'Find place in the conjuncture: A dialogue with Doreen', in M. Werner, J. Peck, R. Lave and B. Christophers (eds) *Doreen Massey: Critical Dialogues*, Newcastle upon Tyne: Agenda Publishing, 201–213.

Clarke, J. and Newman, J. (1997), *The Managerial State: Power, Politics and Ideology in the Remaking Social Welfare*, London: Sage.

Clarke, N. (2014), 'Locality and localism: A view from British human geography', *Policy Studies*, 34, 492–507.

Clarke, N. and Cochrane, A. (2013), 'Geographies and politics of localism: The localism of the United Kingdom's coalition government', *Political Geography*, 34, 10–23.

Clarke, S. (1994), *Marx's Theory of Crisis*, London: Macmillan.

Clarke, S.E. and Gaile, G.L. (1998), *The Work of Cities*, Minneapolis: University of Minnesota Press.

CLES (2014), *Austerity Uncovered Report to TUC*, Manchester: CLES.

Coates, D. (2000), *Models of Capitalism*, Cambridge: Polity.

Cochrane, A. (1987), 'What a difference the place makes: The new structuralism of locality', *Antipode*, 19, 354–363.

Cochrane, A. (1989), 'Britain's political crisis', in A. Cochrane and J. Anderson (eds) *Politics in Transition*, London: Sage, 34–66.

Cochrane, A. (1993), *Whatever Happened to Local Government?*, Buckingham: Open University Press.

Cochrane, A. (1994), 'Restructuring the local welfare state', in R. Burrows and B. Loader (eds) *Towards a Post-Fordist Welfare State*, London: Routledge, 117–135.

Cochrane, A. (1999), 'Just another failed urban experiment? The legacy of the Urban Development Corporations', in R. Imrie and H. Thomas (eds) *British Urban Policy: An Evaluation of the Urban Development Corporations*, London: Sage, 246–258.

Cochrane, A. and Clarke, J. (eds) (1993), *Comparing Welfare States: Britain in International Context*, London: Sage.

Cochrane, A. and Etherington, D. (2007), 'Managing local labour markets and making up new spaces of welfares', *Environment and Planning A*, 39, 2958–2974.

Cohn, D. (1997), 'Creating crises and avoiding blame: The politics of public service reform and the new public management in Great Britain and the United States', *Administration and Society*, 29, 584–616.

Colenutt, B. (1999), 'New deal or no deal for people-based regeneration', in R. Imrie and H. Thomas (eds) *British Urban Policy: An Evaluation of the Urban Development Corporations*, London: Sage, 233–245.

Collinge, C. (1999), 'Self-organization of society by scale: A spatial reworking of regulation theory', *Environment and Planning D: Society and Space*, 17, 557–574.

Colls, R. (2002), *Identity of England*, Oxford: Oxford University Press.

Commission on Social Justice (1994), *Social Justice: Strategies for National Renewal*, London: Vintage.

Compston, H. and Madsen, P.K. (2001), 'Conceptual innovation and public policy: Unemployment and paid leave schemes in Denmark', *Journal of European Social Policy*, 11, 117–132.

Conservative Party (1992), *The Best Future for Britain: The Conservative Manifesto 1992*, London: Conservative Central Office.

Conservative Party (2009), *Control Shift: Returning Power to Local Communities*, London: Conservative Party.

Conservative Party (2015), *Strong Leadership, A Clear Economic Plan, A Brighter, More Secure Future*, Conservative Party Manifesto, London: Conservative Party.

Cooke, P. (1987), 'Clinical inference and geographical theory', *Antipode*, 19, 69–78.

Cooke, P. (ed.) (1989a), *Localities: The Changing Face of Urban Britain*, London: Unwin Hyman.

Cooke, P. (1989b), 'Locality-theory and the poverty of "spatial variation"', *Antipode*, 21, 261–273.

Cooke, P. (1990), *Back to the Future: Modernity, Postmodernity and Locality*, London: Unwin Hyman.

Cooke, P. (1995), 'Introduction—regions, clusters and innovation networks', in P. Cooke (ed.) *The Rise of the Rustbelt*, London: UCL Press, 1–19.

Cooke, P. (1997), 'Institutional reflexivity and the rise of the region state', in G. Benko and U. Strohmayer (eds) *Space and Social Theory: Interpreting Modernity and Postmodernity*, Oxford: Blackwell, 285–301.

Cooke, P. (1998), 'Introduction: Origins of the concept', in H.J. Braczyk, P. Cooke and M. Heidenreich (eds) *Regional Innovation Systems: The Role of Governances in a Globalized World*, London: UCL Press, 2–25.

Cooke, P. (2006), *Locality Debates*, Mimeograph, Cardiff: Centre for Advanced Urban Studies, Cardiff University.

Cooke, P. and Morgan, K. (1998), *The Associational Economy: Firms, Regions, and Innovation*, Oxford: Oxford University Press.

Corry, D. and Stoker, G. (2003), *New Localism: Refashioning the Centre-Local Relationship*, London: New Local Government Network.

Costello, N., Michie, J. and Milne, S. (1989), *Beyond the Casino Economy: Planning for the 1990s*, London: Verso.

Cox, K. (1989), 'The politics of turf and the question of class', in M. Dear and J. Wolch (eds) *The Power of Geography: How Territory Shapes Social Life*, London: Unwin Hyman, 61–90.

Cox, K. (1993), 'The local and the global in the new urban politics: A critical view', *Environment and Planning D: Society and Space*, 11, 433–448.

Cox, K. (1998), 'Spaces of dependence, spaces of engagement and the politics of scale, or: Looking for local politics', *Political Geography*, 17, 1–24.

Cox, K. (2008), *Political Geography: Territory, State and Society*, Chichester: Wiley.

Cox, K. and Mair, A. (1991), 'From localised social structures to localities as agents', *Environment and Planning A*, 23, 197–213.

Crooks, E. (2000), 'Economists urge Labour to mind the growing gap', *Financial Times*, 21 August, 3.

Crossman, R.H. (1975), *The Crossman Diaries. The Diaries of a Cabinet Minister, Volume 1*, London: Hamish Hamilton and Cape.

Crouch, C. (2004), *Post-Democracy*, Cambridge: Polity.

Crouch, C. and Hill, S. (2004), 'Regeneration in Sheffield: From council dominance to partnership', in C. Crouch, P. Le Galès, C. Trigilia and H. Vorlzkow (eds) *Changing Governance of Local Economies: Responses to European Local Production Systems*, Oxford: Oxford University Press, 180–196.

Crouch, C. and Marquand, D. (eds) (1989), *The New Centralism: Britain Out of Step in Europe*, Oxford: Blackwell.

Crowley, L., Balaram, B. and Lee, N. (2012), *People or Place? Urban Policy in the Age of Austerity*, London: The Work Foundation.

Cumbers, A., Helms, G. and Swanson, K. (2010), 'Class agency and resistance in the older industrial city', *Antipode*, 42, 46–73.

CURDS (1999), *Core Cities: Key Centres for Regeneration*, Newcastle: Centre for Urban and Regional Development Studies.

Curran, J. and Blackburn, R. (1994), *Small Firms and Local Economic Networks: The Death of the Local Economy*, London: Paul Chapman.

Curry, J. (1996), 'Business Link hit by redundancies', *Staffordshire Newsletter*, 6 December, 3.

Danish Government (2000), *National Action Plan for Employment 2000*, Copenhagen: Ministry of Labour/Ministry of Economic Affairs.

Danson, M., Halkier, H. and Cameron, G. (1999), *Governance, Institutional Change and Regional Development*, Aldershot: Ashgate Publishing.

Danziger, N. (1996), *Danziger's Britain: A Journey to the Edge*, London: HarperCollins.

Darling, J. (2016), 'Privatising asylum: Neoliberalisation, depoliticisation and the governance of forced migration', *Transactions of the Institute of British Geographers*, 41, 230–243.

Davis, H. and Stewart, M. (1993), *The Growth of Government by Appointment: Implications for Local Democracy*, Birmingham: Institute for Local Government Studies.

DBEIS (2017), *Industrial Strategy: The 5 Foundation*, London: DBEIS.

DBEIS (2018), *UK Position Paper on the Future of Cohesion Policy*, London: DBEIS.

DCLG (2006a), *Strong and Prosperous Communities: The Local Government White Paper Cmn 6939-1,* London: DCLG.

DCLG (2006b), *The Role of City Development Companies in English Cities and City-Regions: A Consultation*, London: DCLG.

DCLG (2007), *The Role of City Development Companies in English Cities and City-Regions: Summary of Responses to the Consultation Paper Published by Communities and Local Government*, London: DCLG.

DCLG (2011), *A Plain English Guide to the Localism Act*, London: Department for Communities and Local Government.

DCSF and DIUS (2008), *Raising Expectations: Enabling the System to Deliver*, London: Department for Children, Schools and Family and Department for Innovation, Universities & Skills.

Deacon, B., Cole, D. and Tregidga, G. (2003), *Mebyon Kernow and Cornish Nationalism*, Cardiff: Welsh Academic Press.

Deakin, N. and Edwards, J. (1993), *The Enterprise Culture and the Inner City*, London: Routledge.

Dean, J. (2009), *Democracy and Other Neoliberal Fantasies: Communicate Capitalism and Left Politics*, Durham, NC: Duke University Press.

Dear, M. and Clark, G. (1978), 'The state and geographical process: A critical review', *Environment and Planning A*, 10, 173–183.

Dear, M. and Wolch, J.R. (1987), *Landscapes of Despair: From Deinstitutionalisation to Homelessness*, Cambridge: Polity.

Deas, I. (2014), 'The search for territorial fixes in subnational governance: City regions and the disputed emergence of post political consensus in Manchester England', *Urban Studies*, 51, 2285–2314.

Deas, I. and Ward, K. (1999), 'The song has ended but the melody lingers: Regional development agencies and the lessons of the urban development corporation "experiment"', *Local Economy*, 14, 114–132.

Deas, I. and Ward, K. (2000), 'From the "new localism" to the "new regionalism"? The implications of regional development agencies for city-regional relations', *Political Geography*, 16, 273–292.

Deas, I. and Ward, K. (2002), 'Metropolitan manoeuvres: Making Greater Manchester', in J. Peck and K. Ward (eds) *City of Revolution: Restructuring Manchester*, Manchester: Manchester University Press, 116–132.

DeGroot, L. (1992), 'City Challenge: Competing in the urban regeneration game', *Local Economy*, 7, 196–209.

Denny, C. (1998), 'Go-go for no-go zones—jobs', *The Guardian*, 11 August, 15.

Department of Trade and Industry (DTI) (1992), *Business Link: A Prospectus for OneStop Shops*, London: DTI.

Department of Trade and Industry (DTI) (1995), *Business Link Development and Funding: Internal Audit Report*, London: DTI.

Department of Trade and Industry (DTI) (1996), *Business Link Regional Supply Network Management Information: April 1995 to March 1996*, London: DTI.

DETR (1997a), *Regeneration Programmes—The Way Forward*, Discussion Paper, London: Department of the Environment, Transport and the Regions.

DETR (1997b), *John Prescott Promises a Radical Approach to the Regions*, Press Notice 194/ENV, London: Department of the Environment, Transport and the Regions.

DETR (1998), *Community-based Regeneration Initiatives*, Working Paper, London: Department of the Environment, Transport and the Regions.

DETR (2000a), *Our Towns and Cities: The Future. Delivering an Urban Renaissance*, Cm 4911, London: Department of the Environment, Transport and the Regions.

DETR (2000b), *Regional Government in England: A Preliminary Review of Literature and Research Findings*, London: Department of the Environment, Transport and the Regions.

DETR (2000c), *Regional Development Agency Core Indicators*, London: Department of the Environment, Transport and the Regions.

DETR (2001), *Local Strategic Partnerships: Government Guidance*, London: Department of the Environment, Transport and the Regions.

DeVerteuil, G. (2016), *Resilience in the Post-Welfare Inner City: Voluntary Sector Geographies in London, Los Angeles and Sydney*, Bristol: Policy Press.

*Devolve!* (1999a), *Annual General Meeting: Proposal on Change of Name*, Leicester: *Devolve!*

*Devolve!* (1999b), *Constitution*, Leicester: *Devolve!*

*Devolve!* (1999c), *Notes for New Contacts*, Leicester: *Devolve!*

*Devolve!* (2000a), *A Constitution for England*, Leicester: *Devolve!*

*Devolve!* (2000b), 'Continuity in change', *Open Newsletter*, 32, Autumn.

*Devolve!* (2000c), *Whose Regions? 2. Report of a Conference Held at Lanceston, Kernow, on 17th June 2000*. Leicester: *Devolve!*

*Devolve!* (2001a), *Information Sheet: Objectives*, Leicester: *Devolve!*

*Devolve!* (2001b), *How* Devolve! *Works to Support Regional Movements*, Information Sheet No. 2, Leicester: *Devolve!*

*Devolve!* (2001c), *Report on the Launch Conference of the West Midland's Constitutional Convention*, Leicester: *Devolve!*

*Devolve!* (2002), *Constitution (Revised)*, Leicester: *Devolve!*

*Devolve!* (2003a), *Continuing Commission on the South: Proposal*, Leicester: *Devolve!*

*Devolve!* (2003b), *Continuing Commission on the South: Letter of Confirmation*, Leicester: *Devolve!*

*Devolve!* (2003c), *The Third Whose Regions? Conference—Your Regions, Your Choices, Spot on the South. Report on the Conference*, Leicester: *Devolve!*

*Devolve!* (2003d), *From March to November: Establishing a Continuing Commission on the South. Report-Back by* Devolve!, Leicester: *Devolve!*

*Devolve!* (2003e), 'Very local democracy', *Open Newsletter*, 36, November.

*Devolve!* (2004), *Community Alliance, Stoneygate Ward. Report to Steering Group, January*, Leicester: *Devolve!*

DfE (2018), *Skills Advisory Panels: Guidance on the Role and Governance*, London: Department for Education.

DfEE (1997), *Employment Zone Prospectus*, Sheffield: Department for Education and Employment.

DfEE (1999a), *Employment Zones Consultation Paper*, Sheffield: Department for Education and Employment.

DfEE (1999b), 'News release 53/99', 23 November, 1–3.

DfEE (1999c), *Bidding for Employment Zones*, Sheffield: Department for Education and Employment.

Diamond, J. (2001), 'Managing change or coping with conflict? Mapping the experience of a local regeneration partnership', *Local Economy*, 16, 272–285.

Dicken, P. (1992), *Global Shift: The Internationalisation of Economic Activity*, London: Paul Chapman.

Dickinson, R.E. (1967), *The City Region in Western Europe*, London: Routledge & Kegan Paul.

DiGaetano, A. (2001), 'The changing nature of the local state: A comparative perspective', *Policy and Politics* 30, 61–78.

Dikeç, M. and Swyngedouw, E. (2017), 'Theorizing the politicizing city', *International Journal of Urban and Regional Research*, 41, 1–18.

DIUS (2006), *World Class Skills: Implementing the Leitch Review of Skills in England*, London: Department for Innovation, Universities & Skills.

Dixon, D. and Hapke, H. (2003), 'Cultivating discourse: The social construction of agricultural legislation', *Annals of the Association of American Geographers*, 93, 142–164.

DoE (1980), *Urban Renaissance: A Better Life in Towns*, London: Department of the Environment.

DoE (1991), *Michael Heseltine Outlines New Approach to Urban Regeneration*, Press Release 138, 11 March, London: Department of the Environment.

Dolowitz, D.P. (1998), *Learning from America: Policy Transfer and the Development of the British Workfare State*, Brighton: Sussex Academic Press.

Domokos, J. (2017), 'Made in Stoke-on-Trent', *Transcript of the Made in Stoke-on-Trent Series*, made available by John Domokos, *The Guardian*, London.

Domokos, J. (2018), 'Made in Stoke-on-Trent: Local people inspired our documentary, tell us what you think', *The Guardian*, 8 January, 7.

DTLR (2002), *Your Region, Your Choice: Revitalising the English Regions*, Cm 5511, London: The Stationery Office.

Duncan, S. (1989), 'What is locality', in R. Peet and N. Thrift (eds) *New Models in Geography: Volume Two*, London: Unwin Hyman, 221–254.

Duncan, S. and Goodwin, M. (1988), *The Local State and Uneven Development: Behind the Local Government Crisis*, Cambridge: Polity.

Duncan, S. and Savage, M. (1989), 'Space, scale and locality', *Antipode*, 21, 179–206.

Duncan, S. and Savage, M. (1990), 'Space, scale and locality: A reply to Cooke and Warde', *Antipode*, 22, 67–72.

Duncan, S. and Savage, M. (1991), 'New perspectives on the locality debate', *Environment and Planning A*, 23, 155–164.

Dunford, M. and Perrons, D. (1983), *The Arena of Capital*, London: Macmillan.

Dunford, M. and Perrons, D. (1992), 'Strategies of modernisation: The market and the state', *Environment and Planning C: Government and Policy*, 10, 387–405.

Dunsire, A. (1993), *Manipulating Social Tensions: Collibration as an Alternative Mode of Governance Intervention*, MPFIFG Discussion Paper 93/7, Koln: Max Planck Institut fur Gesellschaftsforschung.

DWP (2016), *Improving Lives: The Work, Health and Disability Green Paper*, London: HM Government.

DWP and DIUS (2008), *Work Skills*, London: Department for Work and Pensions and Department for Innovation, Universities.

Education and Employment Committee (1998), *The Relationship Between TECs and the Proposed Regional Development Agencies*, London: The Stationery Office.

Edwards, B., Goodwin, M., Pemberton, S. and Woods, M. (2001), 'Partnerships, power, and scale in rural governance', *Environment and Planning C: Government and Policy*, 19, 289–310.

Eisenschitz, A. and Gough, J. (1993), *The Politics of Local Economic Policy: The Problems and Possibilities of Local Initiative*, London: Macmillan.

Ekos (2006), *Strategic Economic Assessment South Yorkshire Summary City of Sheffield: Emerging Policy Priority Areas*, Glasgow: Ekos.

Elliott, L. (2017), 'No wonder the north is angry. Here's a plan to bridge the bitter Brexit divide', *The Guardian*, 16 November, 12.

Ellis, H. and Henderson, K. (2013), *Planning Out Poverty: The Reinvention of Social Town Planning*, London: TCPA.

EMDA (1999), *Prosperity Through People: Economic Development Strategy for the East Midlands 2000–2010*, Nottingham: EMDA.

Emmerich, M. and Peck, J. (1992), *Reforming the TECs: Towards a New Training Strategy*, Manchester, England: CLES.

Employment Department Group/Department of Social Security (1994), *Jobseeker's Allowance*, Cm 2687, London: HMSO.

English, R. and Kenny, M. (eds) (2000), *Rethinking British Decline*, Basingstoke: Macmillan.

Ernst & Young (1996), *Evaluation of Business Links*, London: Ernst & Young.

Esping-Andersen, G. (1992), 'The emerging realignment between labour movements and welfare states', in M. Regini (ed.) *The Future of Labour Movements,* London: Sage, 133–149.

Esping-Andersen, G. (1999), *Social Foundations of Post Industrial Economies*, Oxford: Oxford University Press.

ESRC (2003), 'The English regions debate: What do the English want?', *Devolution Briefings*, 3, July.

Etherington, D. (1995), 'Decentralisation and local economic initiatives: The Danish free local government initiative', *Local Economy*, 10, 246–259.

Etherington, D. (1997), 'Local Government and labour market policies in Denmark: Is there an alternative to free market policies?', *Local Government Studies*, 23, 48–58.

Etherington, D. (1998), 'From welfare to work in Denmark: An alternative to free market policies?', *Policy and Politics*, 26, 147–161.

Etherington, D. and Jones, M. (2004a), 'Beyond contradictions of the workfare state: Denmark, welfare-*through*-work, and the promises of job-rotation', *Environment and Planning C: Government and Policy*, 22, 129–148.

Etherington, D. and Jones, M. (2004b), 'Beyond neoliberal workfare: Welfare-*through*-work and the re-regulation of labour markets in Denmark', *Capital and Class*, 83, 19–45.

Etherington, D. and Jones, M. (2009), 'City-regions: New geographies of uneven development and inequality', *Regional Studies*, 43, 247–265.

Etherington, D. and Jones, M. (2016a), 'The city-region chimera: The political economy of metagovernance failure in Britain', *Cambridge Journal of Regions, Economy and Society*, 9, 371–389.

Etherington, D. and Jones, M. (2016b), *Devolution and Disadvantage in the Sheffield City Region: An Assessment of Employment, Skills, and Welfare Policies*, Sheffield Solutions Policy Briefing, September, Sheffield: University of Sheffield.

Etherington, D. and Jones, M. (2017), *Devolution, Austerity and Inclusive Growth in Greater Manchester: Assessing the Impacts and Developing Alternatives*, Policy Briefing, CEEDR, Middlesex University and Staffordshire University.

Etherington, D. and Jones, M. (2018), 'Restating the post-political: Depoliticization, social inequalities, and city-region growth', *Environment and Planning A*, 50, 51–72.

Etherington, D., Jeffery, B., Thomas, P., Brooks, J., Beel, D. and Jones, M. (2018), *Forging an Inclusive Labour Market: Empowering Workers and Communities*, Interim Report on Low Pay and Precarious Work in Sheffield, Sheffield: Sheffield TUC.

Fai, F. (ed.) (2018), *Place-based Perspectives on the UK Industrial Strategy*, IPR Policy Brief, March, Bath: Institute for Policy Research, University of Bath.

Fainstein, S. (2001), 'Competitiveness, cohesion, and governance: Their implications for social justice', *International Journal of Urban and Regional Research*, 25, 884–888.

Fair, J. (1999), 'Region is failing to reach potential, agency claims', *Planning*, 30 July, 6.

Fairburn, J. and Pugh, G. (2010), *The Dismantling of the Regional Innovation System*, Staffordshire Business School Briefing Paper, Stoke-on-Trent: Staffordshire University.

Farnsworth, K. (2015), *The British Corporate Welfare State: Public Provision for Private Businesses*, SPERI Paper 25, Sheffield: Sheffield Political Economy Research Institute.

Fawcett, C.B. (1919), *Provinces of England: A Study of Some Geographical Aspects of Devolution*, London: Hutchinson.

Fawcett, P., Finders, M., Hay, C. and Wood, M. (eds) (2017), *Anti-Politics, Depoliticization and Governance*, Oxford: Oxford University Press.

Finn, D. (1996), *Making Benefits Work: Employment Programmes and Job creation Measures*, Manchester, England: CLES.

Finn, D. (2015), *Welfare to Work Devolution in England*, York: Joseph Rowntree Foundation.

Fletcher, D.R. (2007), 'A culture of worklessness? Historical insights from the Manor and Park area of Sheffield', *Policy and Politics*, 35, 65–85.

Fletcher, D.R., Flint, J., Batty, E. and McNeill, J. (2016), 'Gamers or victims of the system? Welfare reforms, cynical manipulation and vulnerability', *Journal of Poverty and Social Policy*, 24, 171–185.

Flinders, M. and Buller, J. (2006), 'Depoliticisation: Principles, tactics and tools', *British Politics*, 1, 293–318.

Florida, R. (1995), 'Toward the learning region', *Futures*, 27, 527–536.

Florida, R. and Jonas, A. (1991), 'U.S. Urban policy: The postwar state and capitalist regulation', *Antipode*, 23, 349–384.

Foley, P. (1998), 'The impact of the regional development agency and regional chamber in the East Midlands', *Regional Studies*, 32, 777–782.

Foley, P. (2002), 'Regional strategy development in the East Midlands', in J. Tomaney and J. Mawson (eds) *England: The State of the Regions*, Bristol: Policy Press, 147–158.

Foley, P. and Martin, S. (2000), 'A new deal for the community? Public participation in regeneration and local service delivery', *Policy and Politics*, 28, 479–491.

Fosgaard, M. and Jorgensen, I. (1996), 'Recent tropisms of regionalisation—as observed in Denmark', Paper to the European Urban and Regional Studies Conference *A Changing Europe in a Changing World: Urban and Regional Issues*, Exeter, 11–14 April.

Foundational Economy Collective (2018), *Foundational Economy: The Infrastructure of Everyday Life*, Manchester: Manchester University Press.

Frost, D. (2017), 'LEP Chair introductory remarks: The skills problem', *The Skills Challenge in Stoke-on-Trent and Staffordshire LEP Skills: A Round Table Discussion*, Stafford Place, 13 December.

Fuller, C. (2017), 'City government in an age of austerity: Discursive institutions and critique', *Environment and Planning, A* 49, 745–766.

Fuller, C. and Geddes, M. (2008), 'Urban governance under neoliberalism: New Labour and the restructuring of state-space', *Antipode*, 40, 252–282.

Gamble, A. (2014), *Crisis Without End? The Unravelling of Western Prosperity*, London: Palgrave Macmillan.

Gardiner, B., Martin, R. and Sunley, P. (2013), 'Spatially unbalanced growth in the British economy', *Journal of Economic Geography*, 13, 889–928.

Geddes, M. (1994), 'Public services and local economic regeneration in a postFordist economy', in R. Burrows and B. Loader (eds) *Towards a Post-Fordist Welfare State*, London: Routledge, 154–174.

Giddens, A. (1998), *The Third Way: The Renewal of Social Democracy*, Cambridge: Polity.

Gilbert, A. (1988), 'The new regional geography in English and French-speaking countries', *Progress in Human Geography*, 12, 208–228.

Gilbert, J. (2015), 'Disaffected consent: That post-democratic feeling', *Soundings*, 60, 29–41.

Giles, J. and Middleton, T. (eds) (1995), *Writing Englishness*, Routledge: London.

Giordano, B. (2000), 'Italian regionalism or "Padanian" nationalism—the political context of the Lega Nord in Italian politics', *Political Geography*, 19, 445–471.

Glaser, E. (2015), 'Post politics and the future of the left', *Juncture*, 22, 23–31.

GOEM (1996), *Government Office for the East Midlands: Annual Report 1996/97*, Nottingham: GOEM.

GOEM (1997), *Government Office for the East Midlands: Summary Operational Plan, April 1997–March 1998*, Nottingham: GOEM.

Gonzalez, S. (2006), *The Northern Way: A Celebration or a Victim of the New City-regional Government Policy?*, ESRC/DCLG Postgraduate Research Programme Working Paper 28, Swindon: ESRC.

Gonzalez, S., Tomaney, J. and Ward, N. (2006), 'Faith in the city-region?', *Town and Country Planning*, November, 315–317.

Goodchild, B. and Hickman, P. (2006), 'Towards a regional strategy for the North of England? An assessment of the "Northern Way"', *Regional Studies*, 40, 121–133.

Goodley, S. and Ashby, J. (2015), 'Revealed: How Sports Direct effectively pays below the minimum wage', *Guardian*, 9 December 2015.

Goodwin, M. and Painter, J. (1996), 'Local governance, the crises of Fordism and the changing geographies of regulation', *Transactions of the Institute of British Geographers*, 21, 635–648.

Goodwin, M., Jones, M. and Jones, R. (2005), 'Devolution, constitutional change and economic development: Explaining and understanding the new institutional geographies of the British state', *Regional Studies*, 39, 421–436.

Goodwin, M., Jones, M. and Jones, R. (2012), *Rescaling the State: Devolution and the Geographies of Economic Governance*, Manchester: Manchester University Press.

Goodwin, M., Jones, M. and Jones, R. (2017), *Rescaling the State: Devolution and the Geographies of Economic Governance*, Manchester: Manchester University Press. [New preface for the 2017 paperback edition.]

Goodwin, M., Jones, M., Jones, R., Pett, K. and Simpson, G. (2002), 'Devolution and economic governance in the UK: Uneven geographies, uneven capacities?', *Local Economy*, 17, 200–215.

Gottdiener, M. (1986), *Cities in Stress: A New Look at Urban Crisis*, London: Sage.

Gottdiener, M. (1987), *The Decline of Urban Politics: Political Theory and the Crisis of the Local State*, London: Sage.

Gottdiener, M. and Komninos, N. (eds) (1989), *Capitalist Development and Crisis Theory: Accumulation, Regulation and Spatial Restructuring*, New York. St Martin's Press.

Gouge, E. (1996), 'Local and regional economic development', in D. Coates (ed.) *Industrial Policy in Britain*, Basingstoke: Macmillian, 182–211.

Gough, J. and Eisenschitz, A. (1996a), 'The construction of mainstream local economic initiatives: Mobility, socialization, and class relations', *Economic Geography*, 72, 178–195.

Gough, J. and Eisenschitz, A. (1996b), 'The modernization of Britain and local economic policy: Promise and contradictions', *Environment and Planning D: Society and Space*, 14, 203–219.

Goul Andersen, J. (2002), 'Work and citizenship: Unemployment and unemployment policies in Denmark, 1980–2000', in J. Goul Andersen and P.H. Jensen (eds) *Changing Labour Markets, Welfare Policies and Citizenship*, Bristol: Policy Press, 59–84.

Gramsci, A. (1971), *Prison Notebooks*, London: Lawrence & Wishart.
Grant, W. (1989), *Pressure Groups, Politics and Democracy in Britain*, Hemel Hempstead: Philip Allan.
Grant, W. (2000), *Pressure Groups and British Politics*, London: Macmillan.
Gregson, N. (1987), 'The CURS initiative: Some further comments', *Antipode*, 19, 364–370.
Grimes, A. (1996), 'Unemployment: A modest proposal', *Economic Report*, May, London: Employment Policy Institute.
Groom, B. (1999), 'A federal England?', *Financial Times*, 31 March, 9.
Grove, M. (1995), *Michael Portillo: The Future of the Right*, London: Fourth Estate.
Gurr, T.R. and King, D.S. (1987), *The State and the City*, London: Macmillan.
Habermas, J. (1976), *Legitimation Crisis*, London: Heinemann.
Hackett, P. and Hunter, P. (2017), *Devo-Work: Trade Unions, Metro Mayors and Combined Authorities*, London: The Smith Institute.
Hadjimichalis, C. (2006), 'Non-economic factors in economic geography and in "new regionalism": A sympathetic critique', *International Journal of Urban and Regional Research*, 30, 690–704.
Hadjimichalis, C. (2018), *Crisis Spaces: Structures, Struggles and Solidarity in Southern Europe*, London: Routledge.
Hall, P. (1989), *Urban and Regional Planning*, London: Routledge.
Hall, S. (2014), 'Introduction', in N. Poulantzas (ed.) *State, Power, Socialism*, London: Verso, 1–7.
Hall, S. (2016), 'The rise and fall of urban policy in England, 1965 to 2015', in F. Weber and O. Kühne (eds) *Fraktale Metropolen*, Wiesbaden: Springer, 313–330.
Hall, S. and Weir, M. (1996), *The Untouchables: Power and Accountability in the Quango State*, London: Charter 88 Trust.
Hansen, C. and Hansen, A. (2000), *Democracy and Modern Governance Exemplified by the Danish Labour Market Steering System*, Mimeograph, Aalborg: CARMA/Aalborg University Centre.
Hansen, F. and Jensen-Butler, C. (1996), 'Economic crisis and the regional and local economic effects of the welfare state: The case of Denmark', *Regional Studies*, 30, 167–187.
Harden, I. (1992), *The Contracting State*, Buckingham: Open University Press.
Harding, A. (2007), Taking city regions seriously? Response to debate on 'City-Regions: new geographies of governance, democracy and social reproduction', *International Journal of Urban and Regional Research*, 31, 443–458.
Harding, A., Wilks-Heeg, S. and Hutchins, M. (1999), 'Regional Development Agencies and English regionalisation: The question of accountability', *Environment and Planning C: Government and Policy*, 17, 669–683.

Harding, A., Evans, R., Parkinson, M. and Garside, P. (1996), *Regional Government in Britain: An Economic Solution?*, Bristol: Policy Press.

Harloe, M. (2001), 'Social justice and the city: The new "liberal formulation"', *International Journal of Urban and Regional Research*, 25, 889–897.

Harloe, M., Pickvance, C. and Urry, J. (eds) (1990), *Place, Policy and Politics: Do Localities Matter?*, London: Unwin Hyman.

Harris, J. (2017), 'Stoke-on-Trent is the Brexit heartland that could be Corbyn's Waterloo', *The Guardian*, 13 January, 5.

Harrison, J. (2007), 'From competitive regions to competitive city-regions: A new orthodoxy, but some old mistakes', *Journal of Economic Geography*, 7, 311–332.

Harrison, J. (2010), 'Networks of connectivity, territorial fragmentation, uneven development: The new politics of city-regionalism', *Political Geography*, 29, 17–27.

Harrison, J. (2014), 'Rethinking city-regionalism as the production of new non-state spatial strategies: The case of Peel Holdings Atlantic Gateway strategy', *Urban Studies*, 51, 2315–2335.

Harrison, J. and Heley, J. (2014), 'Governing beyond the metropolis: Placing the rural in city-region development', *Urban Studies*, 52, 1113–1133.

Harrison, P. (1983), *Inside the Inner City: Life Under the Cutting Edge*, London: Penguin.

Harty, S. (2001), 'The institutional foundations of substate national movements', *Comparative Politics*, January, 191–210.

Harvey, D. (1969), *Explanation in Geography*, London: Arnold.

Harvey, D. (1978), 'The Marxian theory of the state', *Antipode*, 8, 80–89.

Harvey, D. (1982), *The Limits to Capital*, Oxford: Blackwell.

Harvey, D. (1985a), 'The geopolitics of capitalism', in D. Gregory and J. Urry (eds) *Social Relations and Spatial Structures*, London: Macmillan, 128–163.

Harvey, D. (1985b), *The Urbanization of Capital*, Oxford: Blackwell.

Harvey, D. (1987), 'Three myths in search of a reality in urban studies', *Environment and Planning D: Society and Space*, 5, 367–376.

Harvey, D. (1989), 'From managerialism to entrepreneurialism: The transformation in urban governance in late capitalism', *Geografiska Annaler*, 71b, 3–17.

Harvey, D. (1999), *The Limits to Capital, New Edition*, London: Verso.

Harvey, D. (2000), *Spaces of Hope*, Edinburgh: Edinburgh University Press.

Harvey, D. (2001), *Spaces of Capital: Towards a Critical Geography*, London: Routledge.

Harvey, D. (2005), *A Brief History of Neoliberalism*, Oxford: Oxford University Press.

Harvey, D. (2011), 'Roepke lecture in economic geography—crises, geographic disruptions and the uneven development of political responses', *Economic Geography*, 87, 1–22.

Harvey, D. (2013), *Rebel Cities: From the Right to the City to the Urban Revolution*, London: Verso.

Harvey, D. (2016), *Abstract from the Concrete*, Cambridge, MA: Sternberg Press.

Hatcher, R. (2017), *The West Midlands Combined Authority has Turned its Back on Inclusive Economic Growth to Tackle Inequality*, Mimeograph, Birmingham: Birmingham City University, https://bcu.ac.uk/Download/Asset/7d156976-8a1f-e711-80cf-005056831842 (accessed 26 June 2018).

Haughton, G., Allendinger, P. and Oosterlynck, S. (2013), 'Spaces of neoliberal experimentation: Soft spaces, postpolitics, and neoliberal governmentality', *Environment and Planning A*, 45, 217–234.

Haughton, G., Deas, I. and Hincks, S. (2014), 'Making an impact: When agglomeration boosterism meets antiplanning rhetoric', *Environment and Planning A*, 46, 265–270.

Haughton, G., Gilchrist, A. and Swyngedouw, E. (2016a), '"Rise like lions after slumber": Dissent, protest and (post-) politics in Manchester', *Territory, Politics, Governance*, 4, 472–491.

Haughton, G., Deas, I., Hincks, S. and Ward, K. (2016b), 'Mythic Manchester: Devo Manc, the Northern Powerhouse and rebalancing the English economy', *Cambridge Journal of Regions, Economy and Society*, 9, 355–370.

Haughton, G., Hart, T., Strange, I., Thomas, K. and Peck, J. (1995), *TECs and Their Non-Employer Stakeholders*, Sheffield: Employment Department.

Hay, C. (1995), 'Re-stating the problem of regulation and re-regulating the local state', *Economy and Society*, 24, 387–407.

Hay, C. (1996), *Re-Stating Social and Political Change*, Buckingham: Open University Press.

Hay, C. (1999), *The Political Economy of New Labour: Labouring Under False Pretences?* Manchester: Manchester University Press.

Hay, C. (2013), 'Treating the symptom not the condition: Crisis definition, deficit reduction and the search for a new British growth model', *British Journal of Politics and International Relations*, 15, 23–37.

Hayman, K. (1997), 'Local businesses deserve better', *Sheffield Telegraph*, 31 January, 6.

Hayton, K. (1989), 'The future of local economic development', *Regional Studies*, 23, 49–57.

Hayward, J.S. (1969), 'From functional regionalism to functional representation: The battle for Brittany', *Political Studies*, 17, 48–75.

HCLG (2018), *Strengthened Local Enterprise Partnerships*, London: Ministry of Housing, Communities and Local Government.

Held, D. (1996), *Models of Democracy*, Oxford: Polity.

Held, D. and Krieger, J. (1982), 'Theories of the state: Some competing claims', in S. Bornstein, D. Held and J. Krieger (eds) *The State in Capitalist Europe*, London: Allen & Unwin, 1–20.

Heley, J. and Jones, L. (2012), 'Relational rurals: Some thoughts and relating things and theory in rural studies', *Journal of Rural Studies*, 28, 208–217.

Herd, D., Peck, J. and Theodore, N. (1998), *Union Representation in New Deal Partnerships*, A Briefing Paper Prepared for the TUC, Manchester: University of Manchester, School of Geography, New Deal Monitoring Project.

Heseltine, M. (1990), *Where There's a Will*, London: Arrow Books.

Heseltine, M. (2013), *No Stone Unturned: In Pursuit of Growth*, London: Department for Business, Innovation and Skills.

Hetherington, P. (1998), 'Prescott gets half a cake', *The Guardian*, 20 November, 23.

Hetherington, P. (1999), 'Wealth seekers', *The Guardian*, 3 November, 7.

Hetherington, P. (2000), 'Nudge and fudge', *The Guardian*, 13 March, 7.

Hetherington, P. (2013), 'England's lack of urban policy blights the nation', *The Guardian*, 29 October, 11.

Hill, D. (2000), *Urban Policy and Politics in Britain*, London: Macmillan.

Hirst, P. (1997), *From Statism to Pluralism: Democracy, Civil Society and Global Politics*, London: UCL Press.

HM Government (1994), *Competitiveness: Helping Business to Win*, Cm 2563, London: HMSO.

HM Government (1995a), *Competitiveness: Forging Ahead*, Cm 2867, London: HMSO.

HM Government (1995b), *Jobseekers Act 1995, Chapter 18*, London: HMSO.

HM Government (2010), *Local Growth: Realising Every Place's Potential*, London: HM Government.

HM Government (2015), *Sheffield City Region Devolution Agreement*, London: HM Government.

HM Government (2016a), *Devolution: The Next Five Years and Beyond*, First Report of Session 2015–16, London: House of Commons, Communities and Local Government Committee.

HM Government (2016b), *The Local Welfare Safety Net*, Fifth Report of Session 2015–16, London: House of Commons, Work and Pensions Committee.

HM Government and Transport for the North (2015), *The Northern Powerhouse: One Agenda, One North*, Manchester: TfN.

HMSO (1965), *The National Plan*, Cmnd. 2764, London: Her Majesty's Stationery Office.

HMSO (1977), *Policy for the Inner Cities*, Cmnd. 6845, London: Her Majesty's Stationery Office.

HM Treasury (2006), *Prosperity for all in the Global Economy—World Class Skills*, London: HM Treasury.

HM Treasury, DTI and ODPM (2006), *Devolving Decision Making: 3—Meeting the Regional Economic Challenge: The Importance of Cities to Regional* Growth, London: Stationery Office.

HM Treasury (2007), *Review of Sub-national Economic Development and Regeneration*, London: HM Treasury.

HM Treasury (2016), *Northern Powerhouse Strategy*, London: HM Treasury.

HM Treasury (2018), *The Green Book: Central Government Guidance on Appraisal and Evaluation*, London: HM Treasury.

HoC and BIS (2013), *Innovation and Skills Committee, Local Enterprise Partnerships: Ninth Report of Session 2012–13*, HC 598, London: HM Government.

Home Office (2001), *Community Cohesion: A Report of the Independent Review Team Chaired by Ted Cantle*, London: Home Office.

Hoogerwerf, A. (1990), 'Policy and time: Consequences of time perspectives for the content, processes and effects of public policies', *International Review of Administrative Sciences*, 56, 671–692.

Huber, E. and Stephens, J.D. (2001), *Development and Crisis of the Welfare State: Parties and Policies in Global Markets*, Chicago: University of Chicago Press.

Hudson, R. (1989), *Wrecking a Region: State Policies, Party Politics, and Regional Change in North East England*, London: Pion.

Hudson, R. (2000), *Production, Places and Environment: Changing Perspectives in Economic Geography*, London: Prentice Hall.

Hudson, R. (2001), *Producing Places*, New York: Guilford Press.

Hughes, A. (1996), *Small Firms and Employment: Economic Report*, London: Employment Institute.

Hunt, T. (2017), 'Letter to Members of the Stoke-on-Trent Central Labour Party', House of Commons, London.

Hutton, W. and Adonis, A. (2018), *Saving Britain: How We Must Change to Prosper in Europe*, London: Abacus.

Imrie, R. (1989), 'Industrial restructuring, labour, and locality: The case of the British pottery industry', *Environment and Planning A*, 21, 3–26.

Imrie, R. (1991), 'Industrial change and local economic fragmentation: The case of Stoke-on-Trent', *Geoforum*, 22, 433–453.

Imrie, R. and Raco, M. (1999a), *Urban Renaissance? New Labour, Community and Urban Policy*, Bristol: Policy Press.

Imrie, R. and Raco, M. (1999b), 'How new is the new local governance? Lessons from the United Kingdom', *Transactions of the Institute of British Geographers*, 24, 45–64.

Imrie, R. and Thomas, H. (1999), 'Assessing urban policy and the Urban Development Corporations', in R. Imrie and H. Thomas (eds) *British Urban Policy: An Evaluation of the Urban Development Corporations*, London: Sage, 3–39.

Industrial Community Alliance (2015), *Whose Recovery? How the Upturn in Economic Growth is Leaving Older Industrial Britain Behind*, Barnsley: Industrial Community Alliance.

Institute of Directors (1996), *Business Link: Preliminary Findings of the IoD Research Programme*, London: IoD.

Involve Yorkshire and Humberside (2014), *Rapid Review of Foodbanks in Sheffield*, Sheffield: Sheffield City Council.

Jackson, P. (1991), 'Mapping meanings: a cultural critique of locality studies', *Environment and Planning A*, 23, 215–228.

Jacobs, M. and Mazzucato, M. (2016), 'Rethinking capitalism: An introduction', in M. Jacobs and M. Mazzucato (eds) *Rethinking Capitalism: Economics and Policy for Sustainable and Inclusive Growth*, Chichester: Wiley Blackwell, 1–27.

Jarvis, T. (1998), 'Innovation the key in new Employment Zones', *Working Brief*, August, 14–17.

Jayne, M. (2000), 'The cultural quarter: (Re)locating urban regeneration in Stoke-on-Trent—a city in name only', in T. Edensor (ed.) *Reclaiming Stoke-on-Trent: Leisure, Space & Identity in the Potteries*, Stoke: Staffordshire University Press, 19–41.

Jayne, M. (2004), 'Culture that works? Creative industries development in a working-class city', *Capital and Class*, 28, 199–210.

Jayne, M. (2012), 'Mayors and urban governance: Discursive power identity and local politics', *Social & Cultural Geography*, 13, 29–47.

Jenson, J. and Phillips, S. (1996), 'Regime shift: New citizenship practices in Canada', *International Journal of Canadian Studies*, 14, 111–136.

Jenson, J. and Saint-Martin, D. (2010), 'New routes to social cohesion? Citizenship and the social investment state', *Canadian Journal of Sociology*, 28, 77–99.

Jessop, B. (1972), *Social Order, Reform and Revolution*, London: Macmillan.

Jessop, B. (1982), *The Capitalist State: Marxist Theories and Methods*, Oxford: Martin Robertson.

Jessop, B. (1985), *Nicos Poulantzas: Marxist Theory and Political Strategy*, London: Macmillan.

Jessop, B. (1990a), *State Theory: Putting Capitalist States in their Place*, Cambridge: Polity.

Jessop, B. (1990b), 'Regulation theories in retrospect and prospect', *Economy and Society*, 19, 153–216.

Jessop, B. (1991), 'Thatcherism and flexibility: The white heat of a post-Fordist revolution', in B. Jessop, H. Kastendiek, K. Nielsen and O.K. Pedersen (eds) *The Politics of Flexibility*, Aldershot, UK and Brookfield, VT, USA: Edward Elgar Publishing, 135–161.

Jessop, B. (1992), 'Fordism and post-Fordism: A critical reformulation', in M. Storper and A.J. Scott (eds) *Pathways to Industrialisation and Regional Development*, London: Routledge, 46–69.

Jessop, B. (1993), 'Towards a Schumpeterian workfare state? Preliminary remarks on post-Fordist political economy', *Studies in Political Economy*, 40, 7–39.

Jessop, B. (1994a), 'Post-Fordism and the state', in A. Amin (ed.) *Post-Fordism: A Reader*, Oxford: Blackwell, 251–279.

Jessop, B. (1994b), 'The transition to post-Fordism and the Schumpeterian workfare state', in R. Burrows and B. Loader (eds) *Towards a Post-Fordist Welfare State*, London: Routledge, 13–37.

Jessop, B. (1995), 'Towards a Schumpeterian workfare regime in Britain? Reflections on regulation, governance, and welfare state', *Environment and Planning A*, 27, 1613–1626.

Jessop, B. (1997a), 'Survey article: The regulation approach', *The Journal of Political Philosophy*, 5, 287–326.

Jessop, B. (1997b), 'A neo-Gramscian approach to the regulation of urban regimes: Accumulation strategies, hegemonic projects, and governance', in M. Lauria (ed.) *Reconstructing Regime Theory: Regulating Urban Politics in a Global Economy*, London: Sage, 51–73.

Jessop, B. (1999a), 'Globalisation and the nation state', in S. Aaronowitz and P. Bratsis (eds) *Rethinking the State: Miliband, Poulantzas and State Theory*, Minneapolis: University of Minnesota Press, 185–220.

Jessop, B. (1999b), 'The changing governance of welfare: Recent trends in its primary functions, scale, and modes of co-ordination', *Social Policy and Administration*, 33, 348–359.

Jessop, B. (2000), 'Governance failure', in G. Stoker (ed.) *The New Politics of British Local Governance*, London: Macmillan/ESRC, 11–32.

Jessop, B. (2001), 'Institutional (re)turns and the strategic relational approach', *Environment and Planning A*, 33, 1213–1235.

Jessop, B. (2002a), 'The political scene and the politics of representation: Periodizing class struggle and the state in The Eighteenth Brumaire', in M. Cowling and J. Martin (eds) *Marx's Eighteenth Brumaire: (Post)modern Interpretations*, London: Pluto, 179–194.

Jessop, B. (2002b), 'Liberalism, neoliberalism, and urban governance: A state-theoretical perspective', *Antipode*, 34, 452–472.

Jessop, B. (2002c), *The Future of the Capitalist State*, Cambridge: Polity.
Jessop, B. (2008), *State Power: A Strategic-Relational Approach*, Cambridge: Polity.
Jessop, B. (2011), 'Metagovernance', in M. Bevir (ed.) *The Sage Handbook of Governance*, London: Sage, 106–123.
Jessop, B. (2014), 'Repoliticising depoliticisation: Theoretical preliminaries on some responses to the American fiscal and Eurozone debt crises', *Policy and Politics*, 42: 207–223.
Jessop, B. (2016a), *The State: Past, Present, Future*, Cambridge: Polity.
Jessop, B. (2016b), 'Territory, politics, governance and multispatial metagovernance', *Territory, Politics, Governance*, 4, 8–32.
Jessop, B. (2018), 'Neoliberalization, uneven development, and Brexit: Further reflections on the organic crisis of the British state and society', *European Planning Studies*, DOI: 10.1080/09654313.2018.1501469.
Jessop, B. and Peck, J. (2001), 'Fast policy/local policy', *Mimeograph*, Lancaster: Department of Sociology, University of Lancaster.
Jessop, B., Brenner, N. and Jones, M. (2008), 'Theorizing sociospatial relations', *Environment and Planning D: Society and Space*, 26, 389–401.
Jessop, B., Bonnett, K., Bromley, S. and Ling, T. (1988), *Thatcherism: A Tale of Two Nations*, Cambridge: Polity.
John, P., Musson, S. and Tickell, A. (2002), 'England's problem region: Regionalism in the South East', *Regional Studies*, 36, 733–741.
Johnstone, C. and Whitehead, M. (2004), 'Horizons and barriers in British urban policy', in C. Johnstone and M. Whitehead (eds) *New Horizons in British Urban Policy: Perspectives on New Labour's Urban Renaissance*, Aldershot: Ashgate Publishing, 3–21.
Jonas, A.E.G. (1988), 'A new regional concept of localities', *Area*, 20, 101–110.
Jonas, A.E.G. (1994), 'United States urban policy: A question of scale?', *Urban Geography*, 15, 395–405.
Jonas, A.E.G. (2012a), 'Region and place: Regionalism in question', *Progress in Human Geography*, 36, 263–272.
Jonas, A.E.G. (2012b), 'City-regionalism: Questions of distribution and politics', *Progress in Human Geography*, 36, 822–829.
Jonas, A.E.G. and Ward, K. (2002), 'A world of regionalisms? Towards a US–UK urban policy framework comparison', *Journal of Urban Affairs*, 24, 377–402.
Jonas, A.E.G. and Ward, K. (2007), 'Introduction to a debate on city-regions: New geographies of governance, democracy and social reproduction', *International Journal of Urban and Regional Research*, 31, 169–178.
Jonas, A.E.G. and Wilson, D. (eds) (1999), *The Urban Growth Machine: Critical Perspectives, Two Decades Later*, Albany: SUNY Press.

Jonas, A.E.G. and Wood, A. (eds) (2012), *Territory, the State and Urban Politics*, Farnham: Ashgate Publishing.

Jones, A. (2010), 'Here we go again: The pathology of compulsive re-organisation', *Local Economy*, 25, 373–378.

Jones, G., Meegan, R., Kennet, P. and Croft, J. (2015), 'The uneven impact of austerity on the voluntary and community sector, *Urban Studies*, 53, 2064–2080.

Jones, M. (1996a), 'New-style chambers for Britain: A critical Review', *Regional Studies*, 30, 194–199.

Jones, M. (1996b), 'Business Link: A critical commentary', *Local Economy*, 10, 71–78.

Jones, M. (1996c), 'The trouble with Business Links', in *Trade and Industry Committee Report: Business Links, Volume II, Memoranda*, London: HMSO, 91–92.

Jones, M. (1996d), 'Full steam ahead to a workfare state: Analysing the UK Employment Department's abolition', *Policy and Politics*, 24, 137–157.

Jones, M. (1997a), 'The degradation of labour market programmes', *Critical Social Policy*, 17, 91–104.

Jones, M. (1997b), 'Spatial selectivity of the state? The regulationist enigma and local struggles over economic governance', *Environment and Planning, A*, 29, 831–864.

Jones, M. (1998), 'Partnerships as modes of economic governance: A regulationist perspective', in N. Walzer and B. Jacobs (eds) *Public–Private Partnerships for Local Economic Development*, Westport: Praeger, 205–226.

Jones, M. (1999), *New Institutional Spaces: Training and Enterprise Councils and the Remaking of Economic Governance*, London: Routledge.

Jones, M. (2001), 'The rise of the regional state in economic governance: "Partnerships for prosperity" or new scales of state power?', *Environment and Planning A*, 33, 1185–1211.

Jones, M. (2004), 'Critical realism, critical discourse analysis, concrete research', in J. Joseph and J.M. Roberts (eds) *Realism, Discourse, and Deconstruction*, London: Routledge, 43–67.

Jones, M. (2008), 'Recovering a sense of political economy', *Political Geography*, 27, 377–399.

Jones, M. (2009), 'Political geography: State', in R. Kitchin and N. Thrift (eds) *International Encyclopaedia of Human Geography, Volume 10*, Oxford: Elsevier, 409–415.

Jones, M. (2010), '"Impedimenta state": The anatomy of neoliberal penality', *Criminology and Criminal Justice*, 10, 393–404.

Jones, M. (2011), 'The local in the global', in A. Leyshon, R. Lee, L. McDowell and P. Sunley (eds) *The Sage Handbook of Economic Geography*, London: Sage, 121–134.

Jones, M. (2013), 'It's like déjà vu, all over again', in M. Ward and S. Hardy (eds), *Where Next for Local Enterprise Partnerships*, London: Smith Institute, 86–94.

Jones, M. (2018), 'City's economic strategy must change after Brexit', *The Sentinel*, 4 June, 10.

Jones, M. and Gray, A. (2001), 'Social capital, or local workfarism? Reflections on Employment Zones', *Local Economy*, 16, 178–186.

Jones, M. and Jessop, B. (2010), 'Thinking state/space incompossibly', *Antipode*, 42, 1119–1149.

Jones, M. and MacLeod, G. (1999), 'Towards a regional renaissance? Reconfiguring and rescaling England's economic governance', *Transactions of the Institute of British Geographers*, 24, 295–313.

Jones, M. and MacLeod, G. (2002), 'Regional tensions: Constructing institutional cohesion?', in J. Peck and K. Ward (eds) *City of Revolution: Restructuring Manchester*, Manchester: Manchester University Press, 176–189.

Jones, M. and MacLeod, G. (2004), 'Regional spaces, spaces of regionalism: Territory, insurgent politics and the English question', *Transactions of the Institute of British Geographers*, 29, 433–452.

Jones, M. and Ward, K. (1997), 'Crisis and disorder in British local economic governance: Business Link and the Single Regeneration Budget', *Journal of Contingencies and Crisis Management*, 5, 154–165.

Jones, M. and Ward, K. (2002), 'Excavating the logic of British urban policy: Neoliberalism as the "crisis of crisis-management"', *Antipode*, 34, 479–500.

Jones, M. and Ward, K. (2004), 'Capitalist development and crisis theory: Towards a fourth-cut', *Antipode*, 36, 497–511.

Jones, M. and Woods, M. (2013), 'New localities', *Regional Studies*, 47, 29–42.

Jones, M., Orford, S. and Macfarlane, V. (eds) (2015), *People, Place and Policy: Knowing Contemporary Wales Through New Localities*, London: Routledge.

Jones, R. and Desforges, L. (2003), 'Localities and the reproduction of Welsh nationalism', *Political Geography*, 22, 271–292.

Jørgensen, H. (2002), *Consensus, Cooperation and Conflict: The Policy Making Process in Denmark*, Cheltenham, UK and Northampton, MA, USA: Edward Elgar Publishing.

Judd, D. and Parkinson, M. (1990), 'Introduction: Urban leadership and regeneration', in D. Judd and M. Parkinson (eds) *Leadership and Urban Regeneration: Cities in North America and Europe*, London: Sage, 7–30.

Katz, C. (2001), 'On the grounds of globalization: A topography for feminist political engagement', *Signs*, 26, 1213–1234.

Keane, M.J. (2001), 'Tripartism, partnership and regional integration of policies in Denmark', in OECD (eds) *Local Partnerships for Better Governance: Territorial Economy*, Paris: OECD, 341–373.

Keating, M. (1998), *The New Regionalism in Western Europe: Territorial Restructuring and Political Change*, Cheltenham, UK and Northampton, MA, USA: Edward Elgar Publishing.

Keating, M. (2001), *Nations Against the State: The New Politics of Nationalism in Quebec, Catalonia and Scotland*, London: Palgrave.

Keating, M. (2013), *Rescaling the European State: The Making of Territory and the Rise of the Meso*, Oxford: Oxford University Press.

Keating, M., Loughlin, J. and Deschouwer, K. (2003), *Culture, Institutions and Economic Development: A Study of Eight Regions*, Cheltenham, UK and Northampton, MA, USA: Edward Elgar Publishing.

Keeble, D. (1980), 'East Anglia and the East Midlands', in G. Manners, D. Keeble, B. Rodgers and K. Warren (eds) *Regional Development in Britain*, Chichester: Wiley, 177–199.

Keep, E. (2003), 'No problem', *The Guardian*, 16 December, 14.

King, D.S. (1995), 'Government beyond Whitehall: Local government and urban politics', in P. Dunleavy, A. Gamble, I. Holliday and G. Peele (eds) *Developments in British Politics 4*, London: Macmillan, 194–218.

Koch, P. (2017), 'When politicians fail: Zombie democracy and the anthropology of actually existing politics', *The Sociological Review*, 65, 105–120.

Kofman, E. (1981), 'Functional regionalism and alternative development programmes in Corsica', *Regional Studies*, 15, 173–181.

Kommunernes Landsforegningen (2001), *Lokal Politik for et mere Rummeligt Arbejdsmarked* [A Local Policy for a more Social Inclusive Labour Market], Copenhagen: Kommunernes Landsforegningen.

Labour Party (1995), *A Choice for England*, Consultation Paper on Labour's Plans for English Regional Government, London: Labour Party.

Labour Party (1996a), *Opportunities to Earn: Labour's Proposals to Tackle Long-Term Unemployment*, London: Labour Party.

Labour Party (1996b), 'Getting welfare-to-work: A new vision for social security', speech by David Blunkett MP, Shadow Secretary of State for Education and Employment to the Centre for Local Economic Strategies and Employment Conference, Labour Party, London.

Labour Party (1997), *New Labour: Because Britain Deserves Better*, London: Labour Party.

Larner, W. (2014), 'The limits of post politics: Rethinking radical social enterprise', in J. Wilson and E. Swyngedouw (eds) *The Post-Political and its Discontents: Spaces of Depoliticisation, Spectres of Radical Politics*, Edinburgh: Edinburgh University Press, 189–207.

Lawless, P. (1986), *The Evolution of Spatial Policy: A Case Study of Inner-Urban Policy in the United Kingdom 1968–1981*, London: Pion.

Lawson, N. (2002), 'Why we should bring back corporatism', *New Statesman*, 29 July, 15.

Layard, R. (1998), 'Getting people back to work', *CentrePiece*, Autumn, 24–27.

Layard, R. (1997), 'Preventing long-term unemployment', in J. Philpott (ed.) *Working for Full Employment*, London: Routledge, 190–203.

Le Galès, P. (2016), 'Neoliberalism and urban change: Stretching a good idea too far?', *Territory, Politics, Governance*, 4, 154–172.

Leadbetter, C. (1998), 'Who will own the knowledge economy?', *Political Quarterly*, 69, 375–386.

Lee, N. (2016), 'Powerhouse of card? Understanding the "Northern Powerhouse"', *Regional Studies*, 51, 478–489.

Lee, S. (2002), 'Yorkshire (and the Humber)', in J. Tomaney and J. Mawson (eds) *England: The State of the Regions*, Bristol: Policy Press, 45–62.

Lefebvre, H. (1969), *The Explosion: Marxism and the French Upheaval*, New York: Monthly Review Press.

Lefebvre, H. (1976), *The Survival of Capitalism: Reproduction of the Relations of Production*, London: Allison & Busby.

Lefebvre, H. (1991), *The Production of Space*, Oxford: Blackwell.

Leitner, H. and Sheppard, E. (2002), '"The city is dead, long live the net": Harnessing European interurban networks for a neoliberal agenda', *Antipode*, 34, 495–518.

LGA (2001), *Opportunity to Prosper Beyond the New Deal: A New Approach to Local Employment Policy*, London: Local Government Association.

LGA (2002), *We Can Work it Out: In-depth Research into Development and Policies Issues for Local Strategic Partnerships*, London: Local Government Association.

LGIU (2002), *Free to Differ: The Future of Local Democracy*, London: Local Government Information Unit.

Lind, J. (2000), 'The social pact in Denmark under a neoliberal regime', in J. Lind and D. Mortimer (eds) *Worlds of Employment*, Aalborg: Aalborg University Press, 259–288.

Lindblom, C.E. (1968), *The Policy-Making Process*, Englewood Cliffs: Prentice Hall.

Linehan, D. (2003), 'Regional surveys and the economic geographies of Britain 1930–1939', *Transactions of the Institute of British Geographers*, 28, 96–122.

Linsell, T. (ed.) (2000), *Our Englishness*, Hockwood-cum-Wilton: Anglo-Saxon Books.

Lipietz, A. (1987), *Mirages and Miracles: The Crises of Global Fordism*, London: Verso.

Lipietz, A. (1989), 'Three crises: The metamorphoses of capitalism and the labour movement', in M. Gottdiener and N. Komninos (eds) *Capitalist Development and Crisis Theory: Accumulation, Regulation and Spatial Restructuring*, New York: St Martin's Press, 59–95.

Lipietz, A. (1994), 'The national and the regional: Their autonomy vis-à-vis the capitalist word crisis', in R.P. Palan and B. Gills (eds) *Transcending the State-Global Divide: A Neostructuralist Agenda in International Relations*, London: Lynne Rienner, 23–44.

Lloyd, P. (1999), 'The Regional Development Agencies and social inclusion: Widening the agenda', *Environment and Planning C: Government and Policy*, 16, 701–713.

Logan, J.R. and Molotch, H.L. (1987), *Urban Fortunes: The Political Economy of Place*, Berkeley: California University Press.

Lojkine, J. (1976), 'Contribution to a Marxist theory of capitalist urbanization', in C. Pickvance (ed.) *Urban Sociology: Critical Essays,* London: Tavistock, 119–146.

London Assembly (2003), *Local Government in London. Report of the Chair of the Business Management and Appointments Committee*, 15 October, London: London Assembly.

Lorenz, A. and Smith, D. (1992), 'Heseltine aims for an industrial revolution', *Sunday Times*, 19 April, 7.

Los, B., McCann, P., Springford, J. and Thissen, M. (2017), 'The mismatch between local voting and the local economic consequences of Brexit', *Regional Studies*, 51, 786–799.

Lovering, J. (1989), 'The restructuring approach', in R. Peet and N. Thrift (eds) *New Models in Geography: Volume One*, London: Unwin Hyman, 198–233.

Lovering, J. (1995), 'Creating discourses rather than jobs: The crisis in the cities and the transition fantasies of intellectuals and policy makers', in P. Healey, S. Cameron, S. Davoudi, S. Graham and A. Madani-Pour (eds) *Managing Cities: The New Urban Context*, Chichester: Wiley, 109–126.

Lovering, J. (1996), 'New myths of the Welsh economy', *Planet: The Welsh Internationalist*, 116, 6–16.

Lovering, J. (1999), 'Theory led by policy: The inadequacies of the new regionalism (illustrated from the case of Wales)', *International Journal of Urban and Regional Research*, 23, 379–395.

Macintosh, M. (1992), 'Partnership: Issues of policy and negotiation', *Local Economy*, 7, 210–224.

MacLeavy, J. (2007), 'The six dimensions of New Labour: Structures, strategies, and languages of neoliberal legitimacy', *Environment and Planning A*, 39, 1715–1734.

MacLeod, G. (1996), 'The cult of enterprise in a networked, learning region? Governing business and skills in lowland Scotland', *Regional Studies*, 30, 749–755.

MacLeod, G. (1997), 'Globalizing Parisian thought-waves: Recent advances in the study of social regulation, politics, discourse and space', *Progress in Human Geography*, 21, 530–553.

MacLeod, G. (1998), 'In what sense a region? Place hybridity, symbolic shape, and institutional formation in (post-)modern Scotland', *Political Geography*, 17, 833–863.

MacLeod, G. (2001a), 'Beyond soft institutionalism: Accumulation, regulation and their geographical fixes', *Environment and Planning A*, 33, 1145–1167.

MacLeod, G. (2001b), 'New regionalism reconsidered: Globalization, regulation, and the recasting of political economic space', *International Journal of Urban and Regional Research*, 25, 804–829.

MacLeod, G. (2013), 'New urbanism/smart growth in the Scottish highlands: Mobile policies and the post-politics in local development planning', *Urban Studies*, 50, 2196–2221.

MacLeod, G. and Goodwin, M. (1999), 'Reconstructing an urban and regional political economy: On the state, politics, scale, and explanation', *Political Geography*, 18, 697–730.

MacLeod, G. and Jones, M. (1999), 'Reregulating a regional rustbelt: Institutional fixes, entrepreneurial discourse, and the "politics of representation"', *Environment and Planning D: Society and Space*, 17, 575–605.

MacLeod, G. and Jones, M. (2001), 'Renewing the geography of regions', *Environment and Planning D: Society and Space*, 19, 669–695.

MacLeod, G. and Jones, M. (2007), 'Territorial, scalar, networked, connected: In what sense a "regional world"?', *Regional Studies*, 41, 1177–1191.

MacLeod, G. and Jones, M. (2018), 'Explaining "Brexit Capital": Uneven development and the austerity state', *Space and Polity*, 22, 111–136.

Main, D. (1990), 'Local economic development and TECs', in R.J. Bennett, G. Krebs and H. Zimmerman (eds) *Local Economic Development in Britain and Germany*, London: Anglo-German Foundation, 85–89.

Mandel, E. (1981), 'Introduction', in K. Marx, *Capital: A Critique of Political Economy. Volume Three*, London: Penguin/New Left Review, 9–26.

Mandelson, P. (1997), 'A lifeline for youth', *The Guardian*, 15 August, 17.

Marks, G. and McAdam, D. (1996), 'Social movements and the changing structure of political opportunity in the European Union', *West European Politics*, 19, 249–278.

Marston, S.A., Jones, J.P. III and Woodward, K. (2005), 'Human geography without scale', *Transactions of the Institute of British Geographers*, 30, 416–432.

Martin, R. (1986), 'Thatcherism and Britain's industrial landscape', in R. Martin and B. Rowthorn (eds) *The Geography of Deindustrialisation*, London: Macmillan, 238–290.

Martin, R. (1989), 'The political economy of Britain's north–south divide', in J. Lewis and A. Townsend (eds) *The North–South Divide: Regional Change in the 1980s*, London: Paul Chapman, 20–60.

Martin, R. (2001), 'Geography and public policy: The case of the missing agenda', *Progress in Human Geography*, 25, 189–210.

Martin, R. and Sunley, P. (2001), 'Rethinking the "economic", in economic geography: Broadening our vision or losing our focus?', *Antipode*, 33, 148–161.

Martin, R., Sunley, P., Tyler, P. and Gardiner, B. (2016), 'Divergent cities in post-industrial Britain', *Cambridge Journal of Regions, Economy and Society*, 9, 269–299.

Marx, K. (1919), *Capital: A Critique of Political Economy. Volume 1. The Process of Capitalist Production*, Chicago: Charles H. Kerr & Company.

Massey, D. (1984), *Spatial Divisions of Labour; Social Structures and the Geography of Production*, London: Macmillan.

Massey, D. (1989), 'Regional planning 1909–1939: The experimental field', in P.L. Garside and M. Hebbert (eds) *British Regionalism 1900–2000*, London: Mansell, 57–76.

Massey, D. (1991), 'The political place of locality studies', *Environment and Planning A*, 23, 267–281.

Massey, D. (1994), *Space, Place and Gender*, Cambridge: Polity.

Massey, D. (2002), 'Geography, policy and politics: A response to Dorling and Shaw', *Progress in Human Geography*, 26, 645–646.

Massey, D. (2005), *For Space*, London: Sage.

Massey, D. (2007), *World City*, Cambridge: Polity.

Massey, D. (2011), 'A counterhegemonic relationality of place', in E. McCann and K. Ward (eds) *Mobile Urbanism: Cities and Policy-making in the Global Age*, Minneapolis: University of Minnesota Press, 1–14.

Matless, D. (1998), *Landscape and Englishness*, London: Reaktion Books.

Mattick, P. (1981), *Economic Crisis and Crisis Theory*, London: Merlin.

Mawson, J. (2009), 'Local economic development and the sub-national review: Old wine in new bottles?', *Local Government Studies*, 35, 39–59.

Mazier, J., Baslé, M. and Vidal, J-F. (1999), *When Economic Crises Endure*, London: ME Sharpe.

McArthur, A. and McGregor, A. (1991), 'Regenerating public sector housing estates: The role of community enterprise', *Local Economy*, 4, 29–43.

McCann, P. (2016), *The UK Regional–National Economic Problem: Geography, Globalisation and Governance*, London: Routledge.
McKenzie, L. (2017), 'The class politics of prejudice: Brexit and the land of no-hope and glory', *The British Journal of Sociology*, 68, 265–280.
Mercia Movement (1997), *The Mercia Manifesto: A Blueprint for the Future Inspired by the Past*, Cotes Heath: Witan Books.
Mercia Movement (2001), *A Draft Constitution for Mercia*, Cotes Heath: Witan Books.
MFME (1988), *Movement for Middle England: Constitution (first edition)*, Leicester: Movement for Middle England.
MFME (1989), *Movement for Middle England: A Brief History*, Leicester: Movement for Middle England.
MFME (1990), 'Progress', *Middle England Newsletter*, 7, December.
MFME (1991), *Wall to Wall Democracy: The View from Middle England*, Leicester: Movement for Middle England.
MFME (1992), *Race, Culture & Identity: The View from Middle England*, Leicester: Movement for Middle England.
MFME (1993a), 'Developments', *Middle England Newsletter*, 15, May/June.
MFME (1993b), 'Debate over name and identity', *Middle England Newsletter*, 16, September/October.
MFME (1994), 'The name and identity debate', *Middle England Newsletter*, 17, February/March.
MFME (1996), *Replies to Middle England: Alternatives Views on Race, Culture and Identity*, Leicester: Movement for Middle England.
MFME (1998), *Whose Regions? Report of a Conference held at Dr Johnson House, Birmingham on 27 June 1998*, Leicester: MFME.
MFME (1999a), 'Then and now', *Middle England Newsletter*, 31, December.
MFME (1999b), *Charter for the Midlands*, Leicester: Movement for Middle England.
MFME (1999c), *Special General Meeting*, First Minute to Members, Leicester: Movement for Middle England.
Mohan, G. and Stokke, K. (2000), 'Participatory development and empowerment: The dangers of localism', *Third World Quarterly*, 21, 247–268.
Mohan, J. (2012), 'Geographical foundations of the Big Society', *Environment and Planning A*, 44, 1121–1129.
Moon, J. and Richardson, J.J. (1985), *Unemployment in the UK: Politics and Policies*, Aldershot: Gower.
Moore, A. (2017), 'We need to get together to give the region a better future', *Sheffield Telegraph*, 23 February, 4–5.
Morgan, K. (1997), 'The learning region: Institutions, innovation and regional renewal', *Regional Studies*, 31, 491–503.

Morgan, K. (1999), 'Editorial: England's unstable equilibrium. The challenge of RDAs', *Environment and Planning C: Government and Policy*, 17, 663–667.

Morgan, K. (2001), 'The new territorial politics: Rivalry and justice in post-devolution Britain', *Regional Studies*, 35, 343–348.

Morgan, K. (2002), 'The English question: Regional perspectives on a fractured nation', *Regional Studies*, 36, 797–810.

MORI (1994), *Business Link: The Business Advice Market Among Small and Medium Sized Enterprises*, London: DTI.

MORI (1999), 'Attitudes towards regional government', paper presented to the June meeting at the *North West Regional Constitutional Convention*, Wigan New Town Hall, Wigan.

Morris, I. (2017), 'Left behind Brexit capital', http://worldview.stratfor.com/article/left-behind-brexit-capital (accessed 12 June 2018).

Morton, A.L. (1948), *A People's History of England*, London: Lawrence & Wishart.

Morton, H.V. (1933), *In Search of England*, London: Methuen.

Mothersole, J. (2017), 'Why city punches at a new weight as the challenges of Brexit approach', *Sheffield Telegraph*, 23 March, 18.

Mulgan, G. (2010), 'RDA demise', https://www.placemakingresource.com/article/1015255/rda-demise (accessed 11 June 2018).

Murdoch, J. and Tewdwr-Jones, M. (1999), 'Planning and the English regions: Conflict and convergence among the institutions of regional governance', *Environment and Planning C: Government and Policy*, 17, 715–729.

Murgatroyd, L., Savage, M., Shapiro, D., Urry, J., Walby, S., Warde, A. and Mark-Lawson, J. (1985), *Localities, Class, and Gender*, London: Pion.

Nathan, M., Ward, M., Roberts, H. and Jones, S.P. (eds) (2001), *Welfare to Work: Where Next?*, Manchester: Centre for Local Economic Strategies.

National Audit Office (2002), *The New Deal for Young People: Report by the Comptroller and Auditor General, HC 639*, London: Stationery Office.

National Audit Office (2013), *Funding and Structures for Local Economic Growth*, London: Stationery Office.

National Audit Office (2017), *Investigation to the Governance of Greater Cambridge Greater Peterborough Local Enterprise Partnership, HC 410*, London: Stationery Office.

National Audit Office (2018), *Rolling Out Universal Credit*, London: Stationery Office.

Needham, E. (2015), *The Impact of Benefit Sanctions Policy in Derbyshire*, Matlock: Rural Action Derbyshire.

New Local Government Network (2005), *Seeing the Light: Next Steps for City Regions*, London: NLGN.

Newman, J. (2014), 'Landscapes of antagonism: Local governance, neoliberalism and austerity', *Urban Studies*, 51, 3290–3305.

Ney, M. (2017), *Review of Local Enterprise Partnership Governance and Transparency*, London: Department for Communities and Local Government.

Nicholls, W., Miller, B. and Beaumont, J. (eds) (2013), *Spaces of Contention: Spatialities and Social Movements*, Farnham: Ashgate Publishing.

Norman, J. (2011), *The Big Society*, Buckingham: The University of Buckingham Press.

Norris, E. and Adam, R. (2017), *All Change: Why Britain is Prone to Policy Reinvention and What Can Be Done about It*, London: Institute for Government.

North, D., Syrett, S. and Etherington, D. (2007), *Devolution and Regional Governance: Tackling the Economic Needs of Deprived Areas*, York: Joseph Rowntree Foundation.

Nunn, A. and Johnson, S. (2008), 'Labouring and learning towards competitiveness: The future of local labour markets after Harker, Leitch and Freud', *Local Economy*, 23, 122–137.

Oatley, N. (1998), 'Cities, economic competition and urban policy', in N. Oatley (eds) *Cities, Economic Competition and Urban Policy*, London: Paul Chapman, 3–20.

O'Brien, P. and Pike, A. (2015), 'City deals, decentralization and the governance of local infrastructure funding and financing in the UK', *National Institute Economic Review*, 233, 14–26.

O'Brien, P. and Pike, A. (2018), '"Deal or no deal?" Governing urban infrastructure funding and financing in the UK City Deals', *Urban Studies*.

O'Connor, J. (1973), *The Fiscal Crisis of the State*, San Jose: California University Press.

O'Connor, J. (1987), *The Meaning of Crisis: A Theoretical Introduction*, Oxford: Blackwell.

ODPM (2003), *Your Region, Your Say*, London: Office of the Deputy Prime Minister.

Offe, C. (1975), 'The theory of the capitalist state and the problem of policy formulation', in L.N. Lindberg, R. Alford, C. Couch and C. Offe (eds) *Stress and Contradiction in Modern Capitalism*, London: Lexington Books, 125–144.

Offe, C. (1984), *Contradictions of the Welfare State*, London: Hutchinson.

Offe, C. (1985), *Disorganized Capitalism: Contemporary Transformations in Work and Politics*, Oxford: Polity.

Offe, C. (1996), *Modernity and the State: East, West*, Cambridge: Polity.

Offe, C. (2015), *Europe Entrapped*, Cambridge: Polity.

Ohmae, K. (1995), *The End of the Nation State*, London: HarperCollins.

Ohmae, K. (2001), 'How to invite prosperity from the global economy into a region', in A. Scott (ed.) *Global City-Regions: Trends, Theory, Policy*, Oxford: Oxford University Press, 33–43.

Omstedt, M. (2016), 'Reinforcing unevenness: Post-crisis geography and the spatial selectivity of the state', *Regional Studies, Regional Science*, 3, 99–113.

Orwell, G. (1940), *The Lion and the Unicorn*, London: Grangrel.

Orwell, G. (1946), *Why I Write*, London: Grangrel.

Overman, H.G. (2012), 'Investing in the UK's most successful cities is the surest recipe for national growth', *LSE Politics and Policy Blog*, 12 December, http://spatial-economics.blogspot.com/2012/01/cities-and-economic-growth.html (accessed 27 November 2018).

Overman, H., Rice, P. and Venables, A.J. (2007), *Economic Linkages Across Space*, London: Centre for Economic Performance, LSE.

PA Cambridge Economic Consultants (1996), *Wise Group Evaluations*, Cambridge: PCEC.

Paasi, A. (1986), 'The institutionalization of regions: A theoretical framework for understanding the emergence of regions and regional identity', *Fennia*, 164, 105–146.

Paasi, A. (1991), 'Deconstructing regions: Notes on the scale of spatial life', *Environment and Planning A*, 23, 239–256.

Paasi, A. (1996), *Territories, Boundaries and Consciousness: The Changing Geographies of the Finnish-Russian Border*, Chichester: John Wiley.

Paasi, A. (2001), 'Europe as social process and discourse: Considerations of place, boundaries and identity', *European Journal of Urban and Regional Studies*, 8, 7–28.

Paasi, A. (2002), 'Place and region: Regional worlds and words', *Progress in Human Geography*, 26, 802–811.

Paasi, A. (2003), 'Boundaries in a globalizing word', in K. Anderson, M. Domosh, S. Pile and N. Thrift (eds) *Handbook of Cultural Geography*, London: Sage, 462–472.

Pacione, M. (ed.) (1999), *Britain's Cities: Geographies of Division in Urban Britain*, London: Routledge.

Paddison, R. (1983), *The Fragmented State: The Political Geography of Power*, Oxford: Blackwell.

Painter, J. (2008), 'Cartographic anxiety and the search for regionality', *Environment and Planning A*, 40, 342–361.

Painter, J. and Goodwin, M. (1995), 'Local governance and concrete research: Investigating the uneven development of regulation', *Economy and Society*, 24, 334–356.

Painter, J. and Goodwin, M. (2000), 'Local governance after Fordism: A regulationist perspective', in G. Stoker (ed.) *The New Politics of British Local Governance*, London: Macmillan, 33–53.

Parks, J. and Elcock, H. (2000), 'Why do regions demand autonomy', *Regional and Federal Studies*, 10, 87–106.

Parr, J.B. (2005), 'Perspectives on the city-region', *Regional Studies*, 39, 555–566.

Parsons, W. (1988), *The Political Economy of British Regional Policy*, London: Routledge.

Partington, R. (2018), 'Stoke is debt capital of England and Wales—followed by Plymouth', *The Guardian*, 13 July, 20.

Paxman, J. (1998), *The English: A Portrait of a People*, London: Michael Joseph.

Pearce, D.C. (1989), 'The Yorkshire and Humberside economic planning council 1965–1979', in P.L. Garside and M. Hebbert (eds) *British Regionalism 1900–2000*, London: Mansell, 129–141.

Peck, J. (1995), 'Moving and shaking: Business elites, state localism and urban privatism', *Progress in Human Geography*, 19, 16–46.

Peck, J. (1996), *Work-Place: The Social Regulation of Labour Markets*, New York: Guilford Press.

Peck, J. (1998a), 'Postwelfare Massachusetts', *Economic Geography*, special AAG meeting edition, 62–82.

Peck, J. (1998b), 'Geographies of governance: TECs and the neoliberalism of local interests', *Space and Polity*, 2, 5–31.

Peck. J. (1999a), 'Editorial: Grey geography?', *Transactions of the Institute of British Geographers*, 24, 131–135.

Peck, J. (1999b), 'New Labourers: Making a New Deal for the "workless class"', *Environment and Planning C: Government and Policy*, 17, 345–372.

Peck, J. (2000), 'Jumping in, joining up and getting on', *Transactions of the Institute of British Geographers*, 25, 255–258.

Peck, J. (2001), *Workfare States*, New York: Guilford Press.

Peck, J. (2010), *Constructions of Neoliberal Reason*, Oxford: Oxford University Press.

Peck, J. (2012), 'Austerity urbanism', *City*, 16, 626–655.

Peck, J. and Jones, M. (1995), 'Training and Enterprise Councils: Schumpeterian workfare state, or what?', *Environment and Planning A*, 27, 1361–1396.

Peck, J. and Miyamachi, Y. (1994), 'Regulating Japan? Regulation theory versus the Japan experience', *Environment and Planning D: Society and Space*, 12, 639–674.

Peck, J. and Theodore, N. (2000a), 'Work first: Welfare-to-work and the regulation of contingent labour markets', *Cambridge Journal of Economics*, 24, 119–138.

Peck, J. and Theodore, N. (2000b), 'Beyond "employability"', *Cambridge Journal of Economics*, 24, 729–749.

Peck, J. and Theodore, N. (2001), 'Exporting workfare/importing welfare-to-work: Exploring the politics of Third Way policy transfer', *Political Geography*, 20, 427–460.

Peck, J. and Theodore, N. (2015), *Fast Policy: Experimental Statecraft at the Thresholds of Neoliberalism*, Minneapolis: University of Minnesota Press.

Peck, J. and Tickell, A. (1994), 'Searching for a new institutional fix: The *after*-Fordist crisis and the global–local disorder', in A. Amin (ed.) *Post-Fordism: A Reader*, Oxford: Blackwell, 280–315.

Peck, J. and Tickell, A. (2002), 'Neoliberalizing space', *Antipode*, 34, 380–404.

Pedersen, L., Weise, H., Jacobs, S. and White, M. (2000), 'Lone mothers poverty and employment', in D. Gallie and S. Paugam (eds) *Welfare Regimes and the Experience of Unemployment in Europe*, Oxford: Oxford University Press, 175–199.

Performance and Innovation Unit (2000), *Reaching Out: The Role of Central Government in Regional and Local Level*, London: Cabinet Office.

Performance and Innovation Unit (2001), *In Demand: Adult Skills for the 21st Century*, London: Cabinet Office.

Perraudin, F. (2016), 'Sheffield region's bid to absorb Chesterfield faces legal setback after ruling', *The Guardian*, 22 December, 16.

Phelps, N., Lovering, J. and Morgan, K. (1998), 'Tying the firm to the region or tying the region to the firm? Early observations on the case of LG in South Wales', *European Urban and Regional Studies*, 5, 119–137.

Philpott, J. (1999), *Behind the Buzzword: 'Employability'*, London: Employment Policy Institute.

Piattoni, S. and Polverari, L. (eds) (2016), *Handbook on Cohesion Policy in the EU*, Cheltenham, UK and Northampton, MA, USA: Edward Elgar Publishing.

Pickvance, C. and Preteceille, E. (eds) (1991), *State Restructuring and Local Power: A Comparative Perspective*, London: Pinter.

Pierce, J. Martin, D.G. and Murphy, J.T. (2011), 'Relational place-making: The networked politics of place', *Transactions of the Institute of British Geographers,* 36, 54–70.

Pike, A. (2000), 'Survey—England's Regional Development Agencies', *Financial Times*, 11 May, 15.

Pike, A., Rodríguez-Pose, A. and Tomaney, J. (2016a), 'Shifting horizons in local and regional development', *Regional Studies*, 51, 46–57.

Pike, A., Kempton, L., Marlow, D., O'Brien, P. and Tomaney, J. (2016b). *Decentralisation: Issues, Principles and Practice*, Newcastle: Centre for Urban and Regional Development Studies.

Pike, A., Coombes, A., O'Brien, P. and Tomaney, J. (2018), 'Austerity states, institutional dismantling and the governance of sub-national economic development: The demise of the regional development agencies in England', *Territory, Politics, Governance*, 6, 118–144.

Pike, A., Marlow, D., McCarthy, A., O'Brien, P. and Tomaney, J. (2015), 'Local institutions and local economic development: The Local Enterprise Partnerships in England, 2010–', *Cambridge Journal of Regions, Economy and Society*, 8, 185–204.

Pike, A., Rodríguez, A., and Tomaney, J., Torrisi, G. and Tselios, V. (2012), 'In search of the "economic dividend" of devolution: Spatial disparities, spatial economic policy, and decentralisation in the UK', *Environment and Planning C: Government and Policy*, 30, 10–28.

Ploug, N. (2002), *Impact Evaluation of the European Employment Strategy—Denmark Synthesis Report*, Copenhagen: The Danish National Institute of Social Research.

Polanyi, K. (1944), *The Great Transformation: The Political and Economic Origins of Our Time*, Boston: Beacon Press.

Porter, M. (2001), 'Regions and the new economics of competition', in A. Scott (ed.) *Global City-Regions: Trends, Theory, Policy*, Oxford: Oxford University Press, 139–157.

Porter, M. (2003), 'The economic performance of regions', *Regional Studies*, 37, 549–578.

Poulantzas, N. (1978), *State, Power, Socialism*, London: New Left Books.

Poulantzas, N. (1979), 'The political crisis and the crisis of the state', in J.W. Freiberg (ed) *Critical Sociology: European Perspectives*, London: Wiley, 357–393.

Pratt, A.C. (1991), 'Discourses of locality', *Environment and Planning A*, 23, 257–266.

Pratt, A.C. (2004), 'Andrew Sayer', in P. Hubbard, R. Kitchin and G. Valentine (eds) *Key Thinkers on Space and Place*, London: Sage, 245–250.

Prior, D. and Barnes, N. (2011), 'Subverting social policy on the front line: Agencies and resistance in the delivery of services', *Social Policy and Administration*, 45, 264–279.

Pugalis, L. and Townsend, A.R. (2012), 'Rebalancing England: Sub-national development (once again) at the crossroads', *Urban Research & Practice*, 5, 157–174.

Purcell, M. (2001), 'Metropolitan political reorganization as a politics of urban growth: The case of the San Fernando Valley succession', *Political Geography*, 20, 613–633.

Putnam, R. (1993), *Making Democracy Work*, Princeton: Princeton University Press.

Quilley, S. and Ward, K. (1999), 'Global "system" and local "personality", in urban and regional politics', *Space and Polity*, 3, 5–33.

Raco, M., Street, E. and Freire-Trigo, S. (2016), 'The new localism, anti-political development machines, and the role of planning consultants: Lessons from London's South Bank', *Territory, Politics, Governance*, 4, 216–240.

Rancière, J. (1999), *Dis-agreement: Politics and Philosophy*, Minneapolis: University of Minnesota Press.

Rancière, J. (2010), *Dissensus: On Politics and Aesthetics*, London: Continuum.

Redwood, J. (2014), 'We were unanimous at Chequers: England needs a settlement of its own', *The Daily Telegraph*, 23 September, 2.

Rees, G. and Lambert, J. (1985), *Cities in Crisis: The Political Economy of Urban Development in Post-War Britain*, London: Edward Arnold.

Regergingen [The Government] (2002), *Flere I Arbejde—Et Debat Oplaeg* [More in Work—A Discussion Document], Copenhagen: Ministry of Labour.

Regional Policy Commission (1996), *Renewing the Regions: Strategies for Regional Economic Development*, Sheffield: PAVIC Publications.

Rentoul, J. (1996), *Tony Blair*, London: Warner Books.

Rhodes, J. (2009), 'The political breakthrough of the BNP: The case of Burnley', *British Politics*, 4, 22–46.

Rhodes, R. (2007), 'Understanding governance: Ten years on', *Organization Studies*, 28, 1243–1264.

Richards, S. (1998), 'An Evangelical DIY salesman', *New Statesman* (Special Supplement—Sowing the Seeds of Devolution), 26 June, 4–5.

Ridley, N. (1988), *The Local Right: Enabling Not Providing*, London: Centre for Policy Studies.

Robinson, F. and Shaw, K. (1991), 'Urban regeneration and community involvement', *Local Economy*, 6, 61–73.

Robinson, F. and Shaw, K. (1994), 'Urban policy under the Conservatives: In search of the big idea?', *Local Economy*, 9, 224–235.

Robson, B. (1988), *Those Inner Cities: Reconciling the Social and Economic Aims of Urban Policy*, Oxford: Clarendon.

Robson, B., Peck, J. and Holden, A. (2000a), *Regional Agencies and Area-Based Regeneration*, Bristol: Policy Press.

Robson, B., Parkinson, M., Boddy, M. and Maclennan, D. (2000b), *The State of English Cities*, London: DETR.

Robson, B., Barr, B., Lymperopoulou, K., Rees, J. and Coombes, M. (2006), 'A framework for city-regions', *Working Paper 1: Mapping City-Regions*, London: ODPM.

Robson, B., Bradford, M., Deas, I., Hall, E., Harrison, E., Parkinson, M., Evans, R., Garside, P. and Harding, A. (1994), *Assessing the Impact of Urban Policy*, London: HMSO.

Robyns, D. (1983), 'The Midlands: Special supplement to *The Regionalist*', *The Regionalist*, 2, 20–23.

Rodgers, B. (1980), 'The West Midlands and Central Wales', in G. Manners, D. Keeble, B. Rodgers and K. Warren (eds) *Regional Development in Britain*, Chichester: Wiley, 201–253.

Rodríguez-Pose, A. (1996), 'Growth and institutional change: The influence of the Spanish regionalisation process on economic performance', *Environment and Planning C: Government and Policy*, 14, 71–87.

Rodríguez-Pose, A. (2018), 'The revenge of the places that don't matter (and what to do about it)', *Cambridge Journal of Regions, Economy and Society*, 11, 189–209.

Rogers, C. (2015), 'Localism and the (re)creation of capitalist space in the United Kingdom', *British Politics*, 10, 391–412.

Rosdahl, A. and Weise, H. (2000), 'When all must be active—workfare in Denmark', in I. Lødemel and H. Trickey (eds) *An Offer you Can't Refuse: Workfare in International Perspective*, Bristol: Policy Press, 159–180.

Rotherham MBC (2014), *Scrutiny Review Department of Work and Pensions (DWP) Sanctions and Conditionality Regime*, Rotherham: Rotherham MBC.

RSA (2014), *Unleashing Metro Growth: Final Recommendations of the City Growth Commission*, London: RSA.

RSA (2016a), *Inclusive Growth Commission: Prospectus of Inquiry*, London: RSA.

RSA (2016b), *Inclusive Growth in Sheffield*, Evidence Hearing 1 Writeup, 29 June, London: Royal Society of Arts.

RSA (2017), *Inclusive Growth Commission: Making Our Economy Work for Everyone*, London: RSA.

Russell, H. (2001), *Local Strategic Partnerships: Lessons from New Commitment to Regeneration*, Bristol: Policy Press.

Rutherford, T.D. (2006), 'Local representations in crisis: Governance, citizenship regimes, and UK TECs and Ontario local boards', *Environment and Planning D: Society and Space*, 24, 409–426.

Samers, M. (1998), 'Maghrebin immigration, France, and the political economy of the "spatial vent"', in A. Herod, G.O. Tuathail and S.M. Roberts (eds) *Unruly World: Globalization, Governance and Geography*, London: Routledge, 196–218.

Samuel, R. (1998), *Island Stories, Unravelling Britain: Theatres of Memory, Volume II*, London: Verso.

Sandford, M. (2002), 'The place for England in an asymmetrically devolved UK', *Regional Studies*, 36, 789–796.

Sandford, M. (2018), *Devolution to Local Government in England*, Briefing Paper, Number 07029, 4 May, London: House of Commons Library.

Sassen, S. (1994), *Cities in the World Economy*, New York: Pine Forge.

Savage, M. (2009), *Townscapes and Landscapes*, Mimeograph, York: Department of Sociology.

Savage, M. and Duncan, S. (1990), 'Space, scale and locality: A reply to Cooke and Ward', *Antipode*, 22, 67–72.

Savage, M., Barlow, J., Duncan, S. and Saunders, P. (1987), 'Locality research: The Sussex programme on economic restructuring, social change and the locality', *Quarterly Journal of Social Affairs*, 3, 27–51.

Sayer, A. (1985), 'Industry and space: A sympathetic critique of radical research', *Environment and Planning D: Society and Space*, 3, 3–29.

Sayer, A. (1991), 'Behind the locality debate: Deconstructing geography's dualisms', *Environment and Planning A*, 23, 283–308.

Sayer, A. (1992), *Method in Social Science: A Realist Approach*, Routledge: London.

Sayer, A. (2018), 'Ontology and the politics of space', in M. Werner, J. Peck, R. Lave and B. Christophers (eds) *Doreen Massey: Critical Dialogues*, Newcastle upon Tyne: Agenda Publishing, 103–112.

Scarman Report (1981), *The Brixton Disorders, 10–12 April 1981*, Cmnd 8427, London: HMSO.

Scharpf, F.W. (1997), 'Economic integration, democracy and the welfare state', *Journal of European Public Policy*, 4, 18–36.

Scheur, S. (1998), 'Denmark: A less regulated model', in A. Ferner and R. Hyman (eds) *Industrial Relations in the New Europe*, Oxford: Blackwell, 146–170.

Scott, A.J. (1988), *New Industrial Spaces: Flexible Production Organisation and Regional Development in North America and Western Europe*, London: Pion.

Scott, A.J. (1991a), 'Book Review: Philip Cooke (ed) *Localities: The Changing Face of Urban Britain*', *Antipode*, 23, 256–257.

Scott, A.J. (1991b), 'Globalization and the rise of city-regions', *European Planning Studies*, 9, 813–826.

Scott, A. (1998), *Regions and the World Economy*, Oxford: Oxford University Press.

Scott, A. (ed.) (2001), *Global City-Regions: Trends, Theory, Policy*, Oxford: Oxford University Press.

Scott, A. and Storper, M. (2003), 'Regions, globalization, development', *Regional Studies*, 37, 579–593.

SCR Vision (2017), *A Better Future Together: A Prospectus for Sheffield City Region*, Sheffield: SCR Vision/University of Sheffield.

Shaw, K. (1993), 'The development of a new urban corporatism: The politics of urban regeneration in the north east of England', *Regional Studies*, 27, 251–259.

Sheffield City Region (2006), *Sheffield City Regional Development Programme: A Submission to the Northern Way*, Sheffield: Sheffield City Council.

Sheffield City Region LEP (2013a), *Regional Growth Plan Update*, Sheffield: Sheffield City Region LEP.

Sheffield City Region LEP (2013b), *Sheffield Independent Economic Review*, Sheffield: Sheffield City Region LEP.

Sheffield City Region LEP (2014), *Sheffield City Region Growth Plan*, Sheffield: Sheffield City Region LEP.

Sheffield City Region LEP (2016), *Sheffield City Region European Structural and Investment Funds Strategy*, Sheffield: Sheffield City Region LEP.

Sheffield City Region LEP (2017), *Skills Shortages and Hard to Fill Vacancies*, Sheffield: Sheffield City Region LEP.

Sheffield Fairness Commission (2013), *Making Sheffield Fairer*, Sheffield: Sheffield City Council.

Sheffield First (2003), *Sheffield City Strategy 2002–2005*, Sheffield: Sheffield First Partnership.

Sheffield One (2005), *Annual Review 2004/2005*, Sheffield: Sheffield One.

Sheffield Work and Skills Board (2007), *Draft Terms of Reference*, Sheffield: Sheffield Work and Skills Board.

Sheffield Work and Skills Board (2008), *Skills Strategy for Sheffield Draft version 7*, Sheffield: Sheffield Work and Skills Board.

Siim, B. (1998), 'Vocabularies of citizenship and gender: Denmark', *Critical Social Policy*, 56, 375–396.

Simmonds, D. and Emmerich, M. (1996), *Regeneration Through Work: Creating Jobs in the Social Economy*, Manchester: CLES.

Sheppard, E. and Barnes, T.J. (1990), *The Capitalist Space Economy: Geographical Analysis After Ricardo, Marx and Sraffa*, London: Unwin Hyman.

Skelcher, C. and Davis, H. (1995), *Opening the Boardroom Door: Membership of Local Appointed Bodies*, London: LGC Communications.

Smith, B.C. (1965a), *Regionalism in England 1: Regional Institutions—A Guide*, London: The Action Society Trust.

Smith, B.C. (1965b), *Regionalism in England 2: Its Nature and Purpose 1905–1965*, London: The Action Society Trust.

Smith, N. (1987), 'Dangers of the empirical turn: Some comments on the CURS initiative', *Antipode*, 19, 59–68.

Smith, N. (1990), *Uneven Development: Nature, Capital and the Production of Space*, Oxford: Blackwell.

Smith, N. (2002), 'New globalism, new urbanism: Gentrification as global urban strategy', *Antipode*, 34, 427–450.

Snape, S. (2000), 'Three years on: Reviewing local government modernisation', *Local Governance*, 26, 119–126.

Solow, R.M. (1998), *Work and Welfare*, Princeton: Princeton University Press.

South Yorkshire Partnership/Alliance Sub-Regional Strategic Partnership (2005), *City Region Development Programme*, Newcastle: Northern Way.

SSAC (2002), *Fifteen Report: April 2001–March 2002*, London: Social Security Advisory Committee.

Stewart, M. (1994), 'Between Westminster and Whitehall: The realignment of urban policy in England', *Policy and Politics*, 22, 133–145.

Stobart, J. (2001), 'Regions, localities and industrialization: Evidence from the East Midlands circa 1780–1840', *Environment and Planning A*, 33, 1305–1325.

Stoker, G. (1991), *The Politics of Local Government*, London: Macmillan.

Stoker, G. (2002), *Local Government You Are the Weakest Link: Goodbye*, Mimeograph, Manchester: Department of Government, University of Manchester.

Storper, M. (1997), *The Regional World: Territorial Development in a Global Ecomomy*, New York: Guilford Press.

Storper, M. (2013), *Keys to the City: How Economics, Institutions, Social Interaction, and Politics Shape Development*, Princeton: Princeton University Press.

Storper, M. and Scott, A.J. (eds) (1992), *Pathways to Industrialization and Regional Development*, London: Routledge.

Storper, M. and Walker, R. (1989), *The Capitalist Imperative: Territory, Technology, and Industrial Growth*, Oxford: Blackwell.

Storper, M., Kemeny, T., Makarem, N.P. and Osman, T. (2015), *The Rise and Fall of Urban Economies: Lessons from San Francisco and Los Angeles*, Stanford: Stanford University Press.

Sullivan, H. and Skelcher, C. (2002), *Working Across Boundaries: Collaboration in Public Services*, London: Macmillan.

Sum, N.L. and Jessop, B. (2013), *Towards a Cultural Political Economy*, Cheltenham, UK and Northampton, MA, USA: Edward Elgar Publishing.

Sunley, P., Martin, R. and Nativel, C. (2006), *Putting Workfare in Place: Local Labour Markets and the New Deal*, Oxford: Blackwell.

SURF (2003), 'City thinking: Transformation in principles and practice', unpublished paper, Centre for Sustainable Urban and Regional Futures, University of Salford, Salford.

Swyngedouw, E. (2000), 'Authoritarian governance, power, and the politics of rescaling', *Environment and Planning D: Society and Space*, 18, 63–76.

Swyngedouw, E. (2005), 'Governance innovation and the citizen: The Janus face of governance-beyond-the-state', *Urban Studies*, 42, 1991–2006.

Swyngedouw, E. (2010), 'Post-democratic cities. For whom and for what?', paper presented at the *Regional Studies Association Annual Conference*, Pecs, Budapest, 26 May.

Swyngedouw, E. (2011), 'Interrogating post-democratization: Reclaiming egalitarian political spaces', *Political Geography*, 30, 370–380.

Swyngedouw, E. (2017), 'Unlocking the mind-trap: Politicising urban theory and practice', *Urban Studies*, 54, 55–61.

Swyngedouw, E., Moulaert, F. and Rodriguez, A. (2002), 'Neoliberal urbanization in Europe: Large-scale urban development projects and the new urban policy', *Antipode*, 34, 542–577.

Tappin, M. (2010), 'Governing Stoke-on-Trent: A study of system, economic and political failure', Presentation at Keele University, Keele, Staffordshire.

Taylor, I. (2000), 'Local government under New Labour: Enabling or enabled?', *Local Governance*, 26, 39–46.

Taylor, P. (1991), 'The English and their Englishness: A curiously mysterious, elusive and little understood people', *Scottish Geographical Magazine*, 107, 146–161.

Taylor, P. (1993), 'The meaning of the North: England's "foreign country" within', *Political Geography*, 12, 136–155.

Taylor-Gooby, P. (1996), 'Eurosclerosis in European welfare states: Regime theory and the dynamics of change', *Policy and Politics*, 24, 109–123.

*The Business* (1994), 'High-tech park to draw new firms', *The Business*, June, 1.

*The Regionalist* (1988), 'A new regionalist movement', *The Regionalist*, 12, 4–5.

Theodore, N. and Peck, J. (1999), 'Welfare-to-work: National problems, local solutions?', *Critical Social Policy*, 19, 485–510.

Theodore, N. and Peck, J. (2001), 'Searching for best practice in welfare-to-work: The means, the method and the message', *Policy and Politics*, 29, 81–94.

Thomas, T. (1999), *Chairman's Statement with the Launch of the Draft Regional Economic Strategy*, Warrington: NWDA.

Thompson, J.B. (2012), 'The metamorphosis of a crisis', in M. Castells, J. Caraca and G. Cardoso (eds) *Aftermath: The Cultures of the Economic Crisis*, Oxford: Oxford University Press, 59–81.

Tickell, A. (1998), 'Creative finance and the local state: The Hammersmith and Fulham swaps affair', *Political Geography*, 17, 865–887.

Tickell, A. and Peck, J. (1992), 'Accumulation, regulation and the geographies of post-Fordism: Missing links in regulationist research', *Progress in Human Geography*, 16, 190–218.

Tickell, A. and Peck, J. (1995), 'Social regulation after Fordism: Regulation theory, neo-liberalism and the global–local nexus', *Economy and Society*, 24, 357–386.

Tomaney, J. (1999), 'New Labour and the English Question', *The Political Quarterly*, 70, 74–82.

Tomaney, J. (2000), 'End of the empire state? New Labour and devolution in the United Kingdom', *International Journal of Urban and Regional Research*, 24, 675–688.

Tomaney, J. (2001), 'Reshaping the English regions', in A Trench (ed.), *The State of the Nations 2001: The Second Year of Devolution in the United Kingdom*, Exeter: Imprint Academic, 107–133.

Tomaney, J. (2002), 'New Labour and the evolution of regionalism in England', in J. Tomaney and J. Mawson (eds) *England: The State of the Regions*, Bristol: Policy Press, 25–44.

Tomaney, J. (2007), 'Keep a beat in the dark: Narratives of regional identity in Basil Bunting's Briggflatts', *Environment and Planning D: Society and Space*, 25, 355–375.

Tomaney, J. (2016), 'Limits to devolution: Localism, economics and post-democracy', *The Political Quarterly*, 87, 546–552.

Tomaney, J. and Hetherington, P. (2003), 'England arisen?', in R. Hazell (eds) *The State of the Nations 2003*, Exeter: Imprint Academic, 49–77.

Tomlinson, P.R. and Branston, J.R. (2017), 'Turning the tide: Prospects for an industrial renaissance in the North Staffordshire ceramics industrial district', *Cambridge Journal of Regions, Economy and Society*, 7, 489–507.

Torfing, J. (1999), 'Workfare with welfare: Recent reforms of the welfare state', *Journal of European Social Policy*, 9, 5–28.

Townsend, A. (2002), 'Integrating government spending at the regional level: Progress with the "Single Pot" in England', paper presented to the *European Urban and Regional Studies Conference, (Re)placing Europe: Economies, Territories and Identities*, Barcelona, Spain, July.

Townsend, A. and Champion, T. (2014), 'The impact of the recession on city regions: The British experience, 2008–2013', *Local Economy*, 29, 38–51.

Toynbee, P. and Walker, D. (2017), *Dismembered: How the Attack on the State Harms Us All*, London: Guardian Books.

Training Agency (1989), *Training and Enterprise Councils: A Prospectus for the 1990s*, Sheffield: Training Agency.

Turok, I. and Edge, N. (1999), *The Jobs Gap in Britain's Cities: Employment Loss and Labour Market Consequences*, Bristol: Policy Press.

Turok, I. and Webster, D. (1998), 'The New Deal: Jeopardized by the geography of unemployment', *Local Economy*, 12, 309–328.

Urban Task Force (1999), *Towards an Urban Renaissance: Final Report*, London: E. & F.N. Spon.

Urwin, D.W. (1982), 'Territorial structures and political development in the United Kingdom', in S. Rokkan and D.W. Urwin (eds) *The Politics of Territorial Identity*, London: Sage, 19–73.

Valler, D., Wood, A. and North, P. (2000), 'Local governance and local business interests: A critical review', *Progress in Human Geography*, 24, 409–428.

VCSE (2016), *Greater Manchester Voluntary, Community and Social Enterprise Devolution Reference Group*, Manchester: VCSE.

Vidal de La Blache (1918), *Principles of Human Geography*, New York: Holt and Company.

Wachsmuth, D. (2016), 'Competitive multi-city regionalism: Growth politics beyond the growth machine', *Regional Studies*, 51, 643–653.

Wacquant, L. (1999), 'How penal common sense comes to Europeans: Notes on the transatlantic diffusion of the neoliberal *doxa*', *European Societies*, 1, 319–352.

Wagstyl, S. (1996), 'Business link row prompts review', *Financial Times*, 20 December, 12.

Waite, D., Maclennan, D. and O'Sullivan, T. (2013), 'Emerging city policies: Devolution, deals and disorder', *Local Economy*, 28, 770–785.

Walker, R. (1995), 'Regulation and flexible specialization as theories of capitalist development: Challenges to Marx and Schumpeter', in H. Liggett and D.C. Perry (eds) *Spatial Practices: Critical Explorations in Social/Spatial Theory*, London: Sage, 167–209.

Walsh, D. (2017), 'City region on target to hit 70,000 new jobs', *Sheffield Telegraph*, 2 March, 61.

Ward, K. (1997), 'Coalitions in urban regeneration: A regime approach', *Environment and Planning A*, 29, 1493–1507.

Ward, K. (2000), 'State license, local settlements, and the politics of "branding" the city', *Environment and Planning C: Government and Policy*, 18, 285–300.

Ward, M. and S. Hardy (eds) (2013), *Where Next for Local Enterprise Partnerships*, London: Smith Institute.

Ward, S.V. (1988), *The Geography of Interwar Britain: The State and Uneven Development*, London: Routledge.

Warde, A. (1989), 'A recipe for a pudding: A comment on locality', *Antipode*, 21, 274–281.

Warren, M.P., Forrest, P.L., Hassard, J.S. and Cotton, J.W. (2000), 'Technological innovation antecedents in the UK ceramics industry', *International Journal of Production Economics*, 65, 85–98.

Waugh, P. (2001), 'Immigrant must show loyalty to nation, says report', *The Independent*, 12 December, 7.

Weaver, M. (2003), 'Maze of initiatives "like spaghetti"', *The Guardian*, 14 January, 17.

Webber, M. and Rigby, D. (1996), *The Golden Age Illusion: Rethinking Postwar Capitalism*, New York: Guilford Press.

Webster, D. (2015), *'BRIEFING: The DWP's JSA/ESA Sanctions Statistics Release', 11 Nov 2015 and Hardship Payments Ad Hoc Statistical Release, 18 Nov 2015*, Glasgow: Glasgow University.

Werlen, B. (1993), *Society, Action and Space: An Alternative Human Geography*, London: Routledge.

Wessex Regionalists/Wessex Society/Wessex Constitutional Convention (2002), *The Case for Wessex: A Joint Response to the White Paper on Regional Governance*, Weston: Wessex Regionalists.

Wharton, J. (2016), 'The story so far', in *New Statesman*, 'Powering on: The Northern Powerhouse, two years in', *New Statesman*, 19–25 February, 8–9.

While, A., Gibbs, D. and Jonas, A. (2013), 'The competition state, city-regions and the territorial politics of growth facilitation', *Environment Planning A*, 45, 2379–2398.

Whitehead, M. (2003a), '"In the shadow of hierarchy": Metagovernance, policy reform and urban regeneration in the West Midlands', *Area*, 35, 6–14.

Whitehead, M. (2003b), '(Re)analysing the sustainable city: Nature, urbanisation and the regulation of socio-environmental relations in the UK', *Urban Studies*, 40, 1183–1206.

Whitelock, D. (1952), *History of England 2: The Beginnings of English Society (the Anglo-Saxon Period)*, Harmondsworth: Penguin.

Wright, E.O. (1978), *Class, Crisis, and the State*, New York: Schocken Books.

Wighton, D. (1996), 'Wirral Business Link—£600,000 goes missing', *Financial Times*, 7 November, 12.

Wilks-Heeg, S. (1996), 'Urban experiments limited revisited: Urban policy comes full circle?', *Urban Studies*, 33, 1263–1279.

Willetts, D. (1994), *Civic Conservatism*, London: Social Market Foundation.

Williams, A., Cloke, P. and Thomas, S. (2012), 'Co-constituting neoliberalism: Faith-based organisations, co-option, and resistance in the UK', *Environment and Planning A*, 44, 1479–1501.

Wilson, S. (1995), *New Challenges for Work and Society: Can the Social Economy Provide an Answer?*, London: Franco-British Council.

Wolf, A. (2007), 'Round and round the houses: The Leitch Review of Skills', *Local Economy*, 22, 111–117.

Wood, L. and Hamilton-Fazey, I. (1995), 'Monster that might soon haunt Heseltine', *Financial Times*, 17 March, 8.

Wood, M. (2000), *In Search of England: Journeys into the English Past*, Harmondsworth: Penguin.

Woods, M. (2007), 'Engaging the global countryside: Globalization, hybridity and the reconstitution of rural place', *Progress in Human Geography*, 31, 485–507.

Wood, M. and Flinders, M. (2014), 'Rethinking depoliticisation: Beyond the governmental', *Policy and Politics*, 42, 151–170.

Work Foundation (2007), *Ideopolis: Knowledge City Region. Sheffield Case Study*, London: Work Foundation.

Wright, P. (1998), 'An encroachment too far', in A. Barnett and R. Scruton (eds) *Town and Country*, London: Jonathan Cape, 18–33.

Wright, S. (2012), 'Welfare-to-work, agency and personal responsibility', *Journal of Social Policy*, 41, 309–328.

Yaffe, D. (1973), 'The Marxian theory of crisis, capital and the state', *Economy and Society*, 2, 186–232.

Yorkshire Forward (2003), *Regional Economic Strategy 2003–2012*, Leeds: Yorkshire-Forward.

Yorkshire Forward (2005), *Why Yorkshire?*, Leeds: Yorkshire-Forward.

# Index